THE COAL TRAP

Between 2009 and 2019, West Virginian politicians aligned themselves with the interests of the coal industry to the substantial detriment of the citizens and economy of the state. Despite the undeniable low-carbon transformation that was occurring in the energy industry in the US during this period, state political leaders doubled down on coal. Rather than provide the leadership necessary to manage the transition of the state's economic drivers away from fossil fuels, they largely blamed the demise of the coal industry on the federal government. At every turn, the interests of the coal industry were placed above the economic and environmental health of West Virginians. James Van Nostrand tells the story of why West Virginia now faces overwhelming obstacles to competing in the economic marketplace of the twenty-first century. The book serves as a warning of how a fair energy transition can be derailed by political failure.

James M. Van Nostrand is the Charles M. Love, Jr. Endowed Professor of Law at West Virginia University College of Law and Director of its Center for Energy and Sustainable Development. He has forty years' experience in a variety of roles in the energy industry, including positions as a regulator, energy lawyer, and director of a New York-based environmental nongovernmental organization.

T0384621

The Coal Trap

HOW WEST VIRGINIA WAS LEFT BEHIND IN THE CLEAN ENERGY REVOLUTION

JAMES M. VAN NOSTRAND

West Virginia University College of Law

CAMBRIDGE
UNIVERSITY PRESS

CAMBRIDGE
UNIVERSITY PRESS

University Printing House, Cambridge CB2 8BS, United Kingdom

One Liberty Plaza, 20th Floor, New York, NY 10006, USA

477 Williamstown Road, Port Melbourne, VIC 3207, Australia

314–321, 3rd Floor, Plot 3, Splendor Forum, Jasola District Centre, New Delhi – 110025, India

103 Penang Road, #05–06/07, Visioncrest Commercial, Singapore 238467

Cambridge University Press is part of the University of Cambridge.

It furthers the University's mission by disseminating knowledge in the pursuit of education, learning, and research at the highest international levels of excellence.

www.cambridge.org
Information on this title: www.cambridge.org/9781108830584
DOI: 10.1017/9781108902403

First published 2022

A catalogue record for this publication is available from the British Library.

Library of Congress Cataloging-in-Publication Data
NAMES: Van Nostrand, James M., author.
TITLE: The coal trap : how West Virginia was left behind in the clean energy revolution / James M. Van Nostrand, University of West Virginia School of Law.
DESCRIPTION: Cambridge, United Kingdom ; New York, NY : Cambridge University Press, 2022. | Includes bibliographical references and index.
IDENTIFIERS: LCCN 2021059604 (print) | LCCN 2021059605 (ebook) | ISBN 9781108830584 (hardback) | ISBN 9781108902403 (ebook)
SUBJECTS: LCSH: Coal trade – West Virginia – History – 21st century, | Coal mines and mining – West Virginia – History – 21st century, | Energy policy – Environmental aspects – United States – History – 21st century,
CLASSIFICATION: LCC HD9547.W4 V36 2022 (print) | LCC HD9547.W4 (ebook) | DDC 338.2/ 72409754–dc23/eng/20220204
LC record available at https://lccn.loc.gov/2021059604
LC ebook record available at https://lccn.loc.gov/2021059605

ISBN 978-1-108-83058-4 Hardback
ISBN 978-1-108-82215-2 Paperback

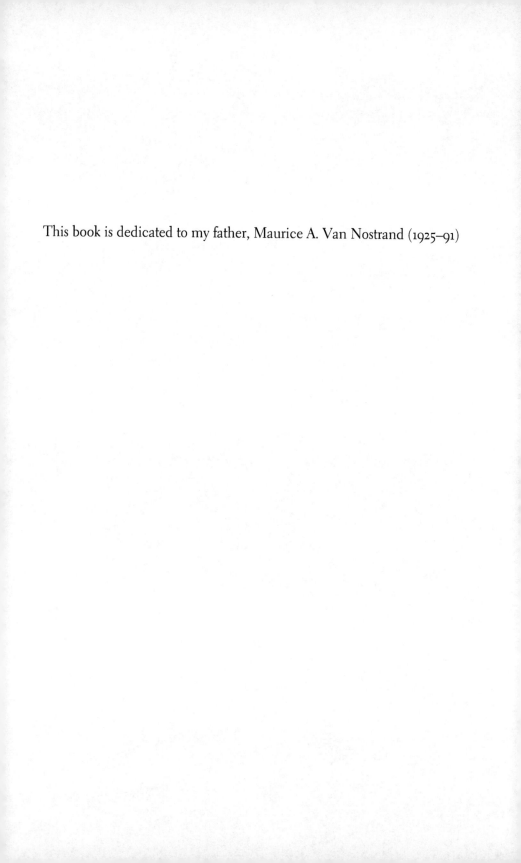

This book is dedicated to my father, Maurice A. Van Nostrand (1925–91)

Contents

Figures and Tables

Figures

Tables

Introduction: "The Lost Decade"

This book examines the impact of developments in the energy industry, and the associated political dynamics, in Central Appalachia – primarily West Virginia – over the ten years from 2009 to 2019, a period I refer to as "the lost decade." At the outset, it is worth answering the questions that are raised by the scope of this book: Why the energy industry? Why West Virginia? Why the years 2009 to 2019? And what does the "coal trap" mean? This introduction answers those questions, and provides a preview of what I will cover in the remainder of the book.

WHY THE ENERGY INDUSTRY?

It's what I know best. I grew up as the son of a utility regulator in Iowa; my father, Maurice ("Maury") Van Nostrand, was chairman of the Iowa Commerce Commission (now the Iowa Utilities Board), the agency charged with regulating the rates that energy utilities (electric and gas companies) can charge their retail customers. He had that job for over eight years, while I was in high school, college and law school (all within the state of Iowa). He was also known as the "energy czar" during that period, serving as a high profile and colorful energy advisor to a very popular fourteen-year governor, Robert D. Ray. That period included the nation's first "energy crisis" – the Arab oil embargo of 1973 – and my father toured the Hawkeye state touting the benefits of energy conservation and explaining why a fifty-five mile per hour speed limit used less gasoline than the seventy mile per hour limit that had existed prior to the energy crisis. He frequently carried around his utility bills during speeches across Iowa, bragging about his achievements in practicing energy efficiency and conservation in our family home on Willowmere Drive in Des Moines.

It seemed like the *Des Moines Register* was always calling Maury on a slow news day. He would give them some quotable comments for the next day's edition, ranging from the unknown costs of storing nuclear waste – he was sued by one of Iowa's major utilities for being biased against its proposal to build a nuclear plant – to the pressing need to price gasoline and other petroleum products to reflect their true costs so as to ensure that consumers received the correct price signals about the perceived scarcity of the resource. He had an amazing grasp of energy economics for a guy who never graduated from college, and he served Governor Ray and the state exceedingly well during a period of great transition in the energy industry.

My father stimulated my interest in politics and energy and, for better or worse, I also inherited from him my innate urge to speak out when I have something to say, regardless of the political consequences. The long-time *Des Moines Register* political columnist Jim Flansburg was spot-on when he wrote the following after my father's passing in October 1991: "He was capable of bad judgment and rash actions. But not deviousness. So his sense of honor and a solid intellect carried him out of holes his emotions had dug, holes where a dishonest man would have been buried and forgotten. Van Nostrand worshipped facts and didn't fear where they'd take him."[1]

I followed in my father's footsteps, more or less. After graduating from the law school at the University of Iowa, I spent five years learning the business of utility regulation at one of the best public utility commissions in the country, the New York Public Service Commission, including over a year as Assistant to the Chairman of that agency. I learned a great deal about thinking like a utility regulator. It is a difficult job; it requires balancing the interests of utility ratepayers – who want reliable utility service at reasonable rates – against the interests of utility shareholders – who want to earn a reasonable return on their investment in utility stock. The issues in a typical utility rate case are very complex, and require the regulators to exercise considerable judgment – the testimony from the competing experts is conflicting, and usually there is not one correct answer, but a range of reasonable outcomes.

From New York, I moved to the Pacific Northwest, where I changed sides, so to speak: rather than working for the regulators, I represented electric and gas companies in Washington and Oregon in rate cases before state commissions for over two decades, trying to convince regulators to strike the balance more on the side of utility shareholders than utility ratepayers. I was well-served in my career from my experience of thinking like a regulator; I had an appreciation for their difficult task, and a helpful perspective in crafting arguments that would resonate in convincing them, on behalf of my clients, of our view of what the "public interest" requires.

Over the course of my career in private practice, I had the good fortune to represent some great clients, including Puget Sound Energy in Washington, Northwest Natural Gas in Oregon, and PacifiCorp throughout its six-state service territory in the northwest and Rocky Mountain region. I also had the challenge of representing Berkshire Hathaway when it acquired PacifiCorp in 2005, and came to respect the management skills of that organization as one of the best utility

---

[1] James Flansburg, *The Last Frontiersman*, Des Moines Register, Oct. 12, 1991.

operators in the country. Unfortunately, part of the Berkshire Hathaway strategy for holding down utility rates was to move away from representation by the high-paid lawyers from the big-name law firms in the Pacific Northwest, so it was an opportune time for me to make a career switch. I had received national recognition from the Energy Bar Association as the State Regulatory Practitioner of the Year in 2007, so it seemed like I didn't have much more to accomplish in private law practice.

About the same time, the energy industry was also undergoing a transition. In April 2007, the US Supreme Court issued its opinion in *Massachusetts v. Environmental Protection Agency* (EPA) which concerned the authority of the EPA under the Clean Air Act to regulate "greenhouse gases" or carbon emissions (the heat-trapping gases that were alleged to be responsible for climate change and sea-level rise). Because the generation of electricity was the largest source of carbon emissions at the time, much more attention began to be focused on how electricity was generated, and on the role that utilities could play in achieving reductions of carbon emissions to minimize the impacts of climate change. As a result, energy law converged with environmental law: An energy lawyer needed to know about the environmental impacts of energy production, and an environmental lawyer needed to know enough about energy law to be able to represent energy clients. Law firms began to market their practices in "climate change law," as the impact of climate change cuts across many practice areas in large law firms (energy, environment, real estate, securities, and insurance, for example).

My transition away from private law practice in the Northwest took me to Pace University, one of the leading environmental law programs in the country, where I accepted an appointment as Executive Director of the Pace Energy Project (which I soon renamed as the Pace Energy & Climate Center), an environmental nongovernmental organization (NGO) operating primarily in New York but also throughout the Northeast. The Center advocated on "clean energy" issues in various New York administrative proceedings, including rate cases at the New York Public Service Commission, which was definitely within my comfort zone. While at Pace, I also took classes in the "climate change track" of its environmental law program, and received my LL.M. in environmental law from Pace (now the Elisabeth Haub School of Law at Pace University) in 2011, at the age of fifty-five.

In the interests of full disclosure, I had my "road to Damascus" experience with respect to climate change while at Pace. As a lifelong Republican, I was relatively hostile to Al Gore and his "Inconvenient Truth" when it came out in 2006. While I hadn't studied the issue closely, I was skeptical that human activity had anything to do with the climate trends that we began to see in the 2000s, and I really did not appreciate what all the fuss was about. I never bothered to learn what a "greenhouse gas" was, even though my partners at Perkins Coie began to talk about it quite a bit after *Massachusetts v. EPA*, given the business opportunities created by climate change in the practice of law.

At Pace, however, I was able to take classes from some outstanding professors in environmental law (Joe Siegel, a senior attorney from the EPA on the adjunct faculty at Pace, comes to mind, as does Alexandra Dapolito Dunn, formerly the Assistant Dean in the environmental program at Pace and, more recently, the Assistant Administrator for EPA's Office of Chemical Safety and Pollution Prevention during the Trump administration). I was also inspired by the climate activism of some of the "old lions" in the business like Dick Ottinger (the founder of the Pace Energy Project in 1987 following his retirement after fourteen years in Congress) and Nick Robinson, one of the most outstanding environmental law professors in the nation, with whom I had the pleasure of traveling to the Republic of Georgia for a ten-day trip in May 2011 to encourage Georgia's policymakers to participate in the global effort to address climate change. During that trip, I began to see Nick as an ambassador for planet Earth, and the breadth of his knowledge about, and the depth of his commitment to, the urgency of this issue provided me with a solid foundation as I prepared for the transition from the "blue state" environment of New York – where no one seriously debated the issue of climate change, or the role of human activity in contributing to it – to ground zero on the issue, the state of West Virginia.

WHY WEST VIRGINIA?

In July 2011, after receiving my LL.M. in environmental law from Pace, I accepted a tenure track position at West Virginia University (WVU) College of Law to teach energy and environmental law, and to establish and direct what became the Center for Energy and Sustainable Development. The Dean at WVU College of Law at the time, Joyce McConnell (who later went on to become Provost at WVU and then President of Colorado State University), had a vision about providing a counterbalance, of sorts, to the dominant role of the extractive industry in West Virginia, and the associated adverse environmental impacts on air and water quality. While the role of the Center was not to challenge the historical and ongoing reliance of the state on the extractive industry – primarily coal – the hope was that the Center could create a forum to facilitate conversations about the trade-offs between environmental protection and economic prosperity (a false dichotomy, I must admit) and offer a perspective favoring the minimization of environmental impacts while not jeopardizing the profitability of the extractive industries. The Center's first conference, in October 2011, which featured US Senator Joe Manchin as the keynote speaker, focused on "balancing preservation and profitability in the development of shale gas resources," as the various states in the Marcellus Shale play (West Virginia, Pennsylvania, Ohio, and New York) grappled with creating the environmental regulations necessary to address the issues presented by hydraulic fracturing and horizontal drilling, commonly referred to as "fracking."

Aside from purely personal reasons involving my career trajectory, West Virginia makes sense as the focus of this book because of the disproportionate impact of the regulation of carbon emissions on the coal industry and the skepticism that West Virginians had – and still have – regarding climate change and the contribution of human activity to it. Once the federal government began to focus on the role of carbon emissions in contributing to climate change, West Virginia, the second largest producer of coal in the nation (behind only Wyoming), would bear harsh consequences from any regulation of carbon emissions; coal was by far the largest contributor to carbon emissions in the electric industry, and the electric industry was the largest contributor to carbon emissions. Rather than being identified as an "energy" state, West Virginia had traditionally defined itself as a "coal" state. How would the policymakers in West Virginia respond to this threat? Would West Virginia be able to make the transition as coal's dominance as the primary fuel for generating electricity rapidly faded?

WHY THE DECADE FROM 2009 THROUGH 2019?

The year 2009 represents a logical starting point for several reasons. First, it marked the start of the eight-year term of Barack Obama as President. His election in 2008, followed by his inauguration in January 2009, was deeply opposed in West Virginia; Hillary Clinton defeated Obama by forty-one points in the May 2008 Democratic primary, followed by Obama's thirteen-point loss to John McCain in the general election. Upon President Obama's inauguration, the EPA moved quickly to begin to regulate carbon emissions under the Clean Air Act. Following the "roadmap" laid out by the US Supreme Court in *Massachusetts v. EPA* in 2007 – stating that the EPA has the authority to regulate greenhouse gas emissions as a "pollutant" under the Clean Air Act if it makes a finding that such carbon emissions "endanger" public health and welfare – in April 2009 the EPA promptly issued a proposed "endangerment" finding, which it formally adopted in December 2009.

The EPA thereafter quickly adopted a comprehensive scheme for regulating carbon emissions, ultimately leading to the adoption of the Clean Power Plan in August 2015, a highly controversial rule in West Virginia as it would have required reductions in carbon emissions from coal plants. Other significant EPA initiatives with impacts on coal plants followed, including the Mercury and Air Toxics Standard (MATS) rule,[2] adopted in February 2012; the MATS rule led to the closure of dozens of coal plants throughout the country, including several in West Virginia. Billboards through the state along Interstate 79 referred to "Obama's no-job zone," and the coal industry (and its political supporters) began referring to the Obama administration's "war on coal."

---

[2] National Emission Standards for Hazardous Air Pollutants from Coal and Oil-Fired Electric Utility Steam Generating Units and Standards of Performance for Fossil-Fuel-Fired Electric Utility, Industrial–Commercial Institutional, and Small Industrial Commercial–Institutional Steam Generating Units, 40 CFR Parts 60 and 63, 77 Fed. Reg. 9304, Feb. 16, 2012.

Second, apart from the initiatives of the EPA, in June 2009 the US Congress passed its own regulatory scheme for regulating carbon emissions, the American Clean Energy and Security Act (ACES), also known as the Waxman-Markey bill, named after its primary sponsors in the House of Representatives (Henry Waxman) and Senate (Edward Markey). ACES infamously called for a cap-and-trade program – carbon emissions would be reduced by 80 percent by 2050 through a complex market-based approach requiring carbon emitters to purchase allowances to cover their emissions; by reducing the number of allowances over time, the desired reduction in carbon emissions would be achieved. The measure ultimately went nowhere in the US Senate, and Joe Manchin, who was running for the US Senate in November 2010 in a special election to fill Robert Byrd's seat, received notoriety for filming a campaign commercial in which he used a rifle to shoot a copy of the cap-and-trade bill, thereby demonstrating his commitment to both gun rights and taking "dead aim" on things that are "bad for West Virginia."

Even with the demise of cap-and-trade legislation, however, it was clear that under the Obama administration, carbon emissions were going to be regulated one way or another, and this had clear implications for the coal industry and the West Virginia economy.

Third, in addition to these unfavorable developments on the environmental front, by 2009 the impact of larger market forces on the viability of the coal industry in Central Appalachia was becoming apparent. The biggest threat was the availability of natural gas from the Marcellus Shale play, which began to be extracted in massive quantities at relatively low cost as a result of fracking. Natural gas production in the Marcellus Shale play scaled up considerably between 2007 and 2010. The Pennsylvania Department of Environmental Protection, for example, reported that only 27 Marcellus Shale wells were drilled in that state in 2007, but by 2010 the number of wells drilled had increased fifty-fold, to 1,386. The impact on the electricity markets was rapid and significant, as it was much cheaper to generate electricity with natural gas than with coal.

Two factors contributed to the price disparity: the low cost of the fuel source itself (natural gas versus coal), and increased efficiency (i.e., how efficiently the plants turn the fuel source into electricity) of new natural gas plants versus the relatively inefficient coal plants in the region, many of which were over forty years old. As more of these new natural gas plants came online, the wholesale price of electricity in the region began to decline, and the older coal plants were simply "out of the money" in the highly competitive power markets. Utilities began to abandon plans to build new coal plants, and many existing coal plants were converted to use natural gas or closed. Later in the decade, coal was losing ground to renewable energy sources as well; utilities across the country were finding that it was cheaper to install wind farms or solar photovoltaic (PV) arrays than to continue operating existing coal plants, even if the renewable resources incurred the additional costs of being backed up by battery storage.

The year 2019 represents a logical ending point for "the lost decade"; the energy industry across the United States was transformed during this ten-year period. Coal ceased to be the primary means of generating electricity: while it had produced

48 percent of the nation's electricity in 2008, that figure had been reduced to 23 percent by 2019, and coal dropped behind natural gas (38 percent). By 2019, the Marcellus Shale region would prove to be the largest source of natural gas in the United States, producing nearly 40 percent of US supply. During the second quarter of 2019, even renewable energy surpassed coal as a source of electricity in the United States. The expected new generation additions in the United States in 2019 were dominated by renewable sources, both wind and solar, followed by natural gas, and no utility in the nation was considering new large coal plants. Nine states had gone so far as to adopt "clean energy" goals, with the objective of eliminating carbon-based sources (both coal and natural gas) from their generation mix by mid-century.

With respect to environmental regulations, candidate Donald Trump ran on a platform of ending the EPA's "war on coal" and bringing coal jobs back. The promised rollback was largely accomplished by 2019, through the efforts of Scott Pruitt (Trump's first EPA Administrator) and thereafter his successor, Andrew Wheeler. The Clean Power Plan was replaced with the ineffectual (and later found to be illegal) Affordable Clean Energy rule, and the EPA also began the process of rolling back the MATS rule, even though many of the coal plants shuttered as a result of MATS were unlikely to ever operate again. The promised renaissance of the coal industry never occurred; more coal plants were retired during the first two years of the Trump administration than during the first four years of the Obama administration. In 2019, US coal production had fallen to a forty-year low.

WHAT IS THE "COAL TRAP"?

As West Virginians, our birthright is coal. The ancient fossil is abundant here, and is as emblematic of our heritage and cultural identity as the black bear, the cardinal, and the rhododendron.

US Senator Robert Byrd[3]

It is likely that no state and industry are as closely identified with one another as West Virginia and coal.

Friends of Coal website, 2005[4]

The "coal trap" reflects the implications of West Virginia's close identity with the coal industry on potentially limiting its path forward. The Cambridge Dictionary

---

[3] Ken Ward, Jr., *New Commentary from Sen. Robert C. Byrd: Coal Industry Must Respect Miners, the Land and the People Who Live in the West Virginia Coalfields*, COAL TATTOO (May 5, 2010), http://blogs .wvgazettemail.com/coaltattoo/2010/05/05/new-commentary-from-sen-robert-c-byrd-coal-industry-must-respect-miners-the-land-and-the-people-who-live-in-the-west-virginia-coalfields/.

[4] Shannon Elizabeth Bell & Richard York, *Community Economic Identity: The Coal Industry and Ideology Construction in West Virginia*, 75 RURAL SOCIOLOGY 129 (2010).

defines "trap" as "a dangerous or unpleasant situation which you have got into and from which it is difficult or impossible to escape."[5] Does the coal industry have an inescapable grip on West Virginia that limits the state's future pathways? Can West Virginia continue to embrace and honor the heritage of the coal industry – and the distinct respect commanded by coal miners – and still move beyond that identity for the sake of the broader well-being of the average West Virginian?

The first element of the coal trap is understanding the legacy and heritage of coal in West Virginia. Upon my arrival in Morgantown in July 2011, I quickly learned about the profound connection between coal and West Virginia. Quite simply, the history of coal in the state is a source of great pride, and it is a measure of your patriotism, in a sense, to see how well your views align with the interests of the coal industry. Coal was first discovered by Peter Salley, in what is now Boone County, in 1742, more than a century before West Virginia became a state.[6] In the minds of many West Virginians, the United States achieved industrialization on the backs of the coal miners in the Mountain State; the large-scale Appalachian mining that started in the late 1800s fueled everything from iron and salt furnaces, to kilns and steam engines.[7] "[C]oal fueled the Industrial Revolution in the United States"[8] and, until the post-World War II era, "virtually all coal mined in the U.S. came from the Appalachian fields."[9] The great pride of West Virginians in the state's role in the industrialization of America is thus understandable.

Apart from the essential role that West Virginia coal played in the industrialization of America, the coal industry dominated the West Virginia economy for decades. West Virginia continues to be one of largest producing coal states in the country – a distant second to Wyoming. Coal mining in West Virginia began in 1745, and production was first recorded in 1863 when 444,648 short tons were reported. Production has varied dramatically, reaching peaks in 1924 (156.6 million tons), 1947 (173.7 million tons), 1990 (171.2 million tons), 1997 (181.9 million tons) and then beginning a steady decline during the twenty-first century, although as recently as 2008 West Virginia production was 165.8 million short tons.[10]

Coal employment figures tell an entirely different story, as the impact of mechanization (primarily the continuous mining machine, which was introduced in 1948) and modern strip-mining techniques – including mountaintop removal – allowed production levels to be maintained with about one-sixth the number of

---

5 Trap, CAMBRIDGE DICTIONARY, https://dictionary.cambridge.org/dictionary/english/trap.

6 Stuart McGehee, *A History of Coal in West Virginia*, FRIENDS OF COAL, https://www.friendsofcoal.org/education/a-history-of-coal-in-west-virginia.html.

7 Geoffrey L. Buckley, *History of Coal Mining in Appalachia*, in CONCISE ENCYCLOPEDIA OF THE HISTORY OF ENERGY 17 (Cutler J. Cleveland ed., 2009).

8 CRANDALL A. SHIFFETT, COAL TOWNS: LIFE, WORK AND CULTURE IN COMPANY TOWNS OF SOUTHERN APPALACHIA 1880–1960 27 (1995).

9 Buckley, *supra* note 7, at 18.

10 Calvin A. Kent, *Crisis in West Virginia's Coal Counties*, NACo (Oct. 17, 2016), https://www.naco.org/articles/crisis-west-virginia%E2%80%99s-coal-counties.

miners, as discussed further in Chapter 5. The year 1948 saw the greatest numbers of coal miners in West Virginia's history, at 125,669, and coal miners lived and worked in more than 500 company towns built to house them and their families.[11] By the end of "the lost decade," however, that figure had declined to fewer than 14,000,[12] and the decline in both coal production and coal prices decimated the coal industry and the coal-producing regions of the state in particular.[13]

In addition to the historical economic domination of the coal industry, there is the lure associated with the distinct respect commanded by coal miners in West Virginia. Former Senator Robert Byrd, the longest serving Senator in US history, tapped into this sentiment in his speech on the floor of the US Senate following the Sago and Aracoma mine disasters of 2006, which claimed the lives of fourteen miners:

> Our Nation's coal miners are vital to our national economy. During World War I, coal miners put in long, brutal hours to make sure that the Nation had coal to heat our homes, power our factories, and fuel our battleships. In World War II, American coal miners again provided the energy to replace the oil that was lost with the outbreak of that global conflict. During the oil boycott-induced energy crisis of the 1970s, our Nation once again called upon – yes, our Nation once again turned, yes, to the coal miners to bail the Nation out of trouble, and the coal miners did.[14]

Even Hillary Clinton, in her infamous statement from the 2016 presidential campaign about "put[ting] a lot of coal miners and coal companies out of business," quickly followed her gaffe with an acknowledgment of the critical role, historically, that coal miners had played in America's industrialization: "Those people labored in those mines for generations, losing their health, often losing their lives to turn on our lights and power our factories."[15]

At the same time, the broader implications of this heavy reliance on one industry throughout a state's history are problematic. Scholars have occasionally referred to a "coal trap" in the context of coal being the "fuel of choice" for developing nations – referred to by one author as "the lure of a dirty watt"[16] – because of its abundance throughout the world, its ease of transport and storage, and relatively low cost.[17] Coal was the "global workhorse of large-scale electricity" during the last two centuries,[18] and remains the biggest source of electricity worldwide today, largely due to its use

[11]   McGehee, *supra* note 6.
[12]   *Coal-Mining Employment in West Virginia from 2010 to 2019, by Mine Type*, STATISTICA, https://www .statista.com/statistics/215786/coal-mining-employment-in-west-virginia/#statisticContainer.
[13]   Kent, *supra* note 10, at 9.
[14]   CONG. REC., S1552, Feb. 5, 2007.
[15]   Eliza Relman, *Hillary Clinton: Here's the Misstep from the Campaign I Regret the Most*, INSIDER (Sept. 6, 2017), https://www.businessinsider.com/hillary-clinton-biggest-campaign-mistake-2017-9.
[16]   Omar S. Cheema, *Pakistan's Coal Trap*, DAWN (Feb. 4, 2018), https://www.dawn.com/news/1387151.
[17]   Will Wade, *Quick Take: Coal Power*, BLOOMBERG (May 7, 2019), https://www.bloomberg.com/quick take/confronting-coal.
[18]   Cheema, *supra* note 16.

by developing countries – notably India and China – to lift millions of people out of poverty.[19] In other words, coal is a "necessary evil for cheap electricity and competitive industrialization."[20] Over time, however, we have learned much more about the climate change impacts of continuing to burn coal to generate electricity and have become less accepting of the other environmental impacts associated with modern methods of coal extraction. Moreover, during "the lost decade," coal lost its economic advantage as natural gas became cheap and plentiful due to the shale gas revolution, and renewables began to provide a cost-competitive alternative to coal. Yet West Virginia seems unable to move past the "lure of the dirty watt," notwithstanding the availability of a cheaper and more sustainable path, much like the "coal trap" ascribed to developing nations.

Another potential trap arising from heavy reliance on one industry throughout a state's history is a phenomenon commonly identified as the "curse" of natural resources – the relatively poor economic performance of regions rich in natural resources, due largely to the failure to diversify to provide broader economic opportunities for their workers. While the natural resource curse is commonly applied at a national level – to countries with oil, mineral, or other natural resource wealth, for example – the analysis is equally applicable on a regional level. In fact, numerous scholars have referred to Central Appalachia as an "internal colony"[21] or an "internal periphery" that was created in the early nineteenth century by large corporations in America to provide cheap resources to fuel the rest of the country.[22] Others have written extensively about corporate ownership of the majority of the land and resources in West Virginia, the effect of which was to effectively block industries other than coal from entering the region so as to maintain this part of Appalachia as a "mono economy."[23]

The impact of the coal industry in "crowding out" the economic diversification that might otherwise have occurred is apparent from the economic devastation experienced by the leading coal producing counties in southern West Virginia: Those counties that have produced the most coal over their history today lead the state in levels of poverty. Boone County, for example, was featured in a December 2015 article in the *Wall Street Journal* as the county that had lost the greatest number of coal miners (2,700) in the country between 2011 and 2015; it was forced to close three of its ten elementary schools when coal severance tax revenues to the county declined from $5.5 million in 2010 to

[19] Wade, *supra* note 17.

[20] Cheema, *supra* note 16.

[21] Bell and York, *supra* note 4, at 119 (citing J. Gaventa, *Property, Coal, and Theft, in* COLONIALISM IN MODERN AMERICA: THE APPALACHIAN CASE 141–59 (H.M. Lewis, L. Johnson, & D. Askins, eds., 1978); and citing H.M. Lewis, & E.E. Knipe, *The Colonialism Model: The Appalachian Case, in id.* 9–31)).

[22] *Id.* (citing D.S. Walls *Internal Colony or Internal Periphery? A Critique of Current Models and an Alternative Formulation, in* COLONIALISM IN MODERN AMERICA: THE APPALACHIAN CASE 319–49 (H.M. Lewis, L. Johnson, & D. Askins, eds., 1978)).

[23] *Id.* (citing H.M. Lewis & E.E. Knipe, *The Colonialism Model: The Appalachian Case, in* COLONIALISM IN MODERN AMERICA: THE APPALACHIAN CASE 9–31 (H.M. Lewis, L. Johnson, & D. Askins, eds., 1978)).

$1.5 million in 2015. In order for teachers to receive their pay until the end of the 2015–16 school year, the legislature had to appropriate over $2 million as an emergency grant and, faced with a $6.9 million drop in revenue related to coal, the school district was also forced to cut teachers' and other employees' pay by an average of $4,000.[24] The experience was similar in Logan, McDowell, Mingo, and Wyoming counties. Statewide, the same *Wall Street Journal* article described the $250 million state budget deficit for the 2015–2016 fiscal year due to a $190 million drop in coal tax revenue. In other words, it became much harder to make the case during "the lost decade" that coal has been good for West Virginia.

In the face of the undeniable transformation occurring in the energy industry in the United States, however, political leaders in West Virginia were caught in the "coal trap" during "the lost decade" and chose to ignore the trends. Rather than address the realities of the inevitable and permanent decline in the fortunes of the coal industry – and provide the leadership necessary to manage the transition of the state's economic drivers away from coal – they largely blamed the demise of the coal industry on the Obama administration's alleged "war on coal," and created the narrative that the only thing ailing in the coal industry was excessive environmental regulation by the federal government and, in particular, the EPA. At every turn during "the lost decade," the interests of the coal industry were placed above the economic and environmental health of West Virginians, whether it took the form of regulatory approvals for utilities to invest in additional coal plants (rather than diversify into natural gas or renewables), or failing to ensure that utility ratepayers had access to energy efficiency programs to help them manage their energy costs, or repealing renewable energy incentives, or the abject failure to force coal operators to comply with environmental laws.

As a result, at the end of "the lost decade" West Virginia now faces overwhelming obstacles to competing in the economic marketplace of the twenty-first century. West Virginia's electricity prices grew faster during "the lost decade" than in any other state in the country, thanks to state regulators' approval of utility decisions to double down on an uneconomic, outmoded means of generating electricity. The state has difficulty attracting any large "new economy" employers, which are demanding low-cost, low-carbon electricity that West Virginia is incapable of providing with its expensive, 88 percent coal-fired electricity (as of 2020). Without any job growth, the state has been unable to stem a steady decline in population; according to the 2020 census, West Virginia lost a higher percentage of its residents (3.2 percent) than any other state in the nation, with about 59,000 fewer people in 2020 than in 2010, and it loses a congressional seat in 2022 as a result.[25] The state's taxpayers are burdened with the costs of remediating the environmental degradation

---

[24] Kris Maher and Dan Frosch, *Coal Downturn Hammers Budgets in West Virginia and Wyoming*, Wall Street Journal, Dec, 22, 2015, https://www.wsj.com/articles/coal-downturn-hammers-budgets-in-west-virginia-and-wyoming-1450822015.

[25] John Raby, *West Virginia Population Decline Is Largest in U.S.*, L.A. TIMES (May 22, 2011), https://www.latimes.com/world-nation/story/2021-05-22/west-virginia-population-downtick-is-largest-in-us.

resulting from decades of strip mining and mountaintop removal, due to the failure of state regulators to enforce environmental laws that would have required coal operators to reclaim mine lands and clean up polluted streams. And West Virginians now face the reality of the false narrative foisted on them by their political leaders during "the lost decade": The promised remedy for the ails of the coal industry – the repeal of the various elements of the Obama administration's "war on coal" – was largely accomplished during the first two years of the Trump administration, and yet the coal jobs did not, and are not, coming back. West Virginians were consistently deceived and sacrificed by their political leaders throughout "the lost decade," and it will take more than a few decades to recover.

To paraphrase the New York Times's review of Steven Stoll's excellent book, *Ramp Hollow: The Ordeal of Appalachia*, "[West Virginia] did not have to turn out this way; not at all."[26]

THE REST OF THE STORY

The first four chapters describe the forces behind the demise of the coal industry at the national level, including the impact of environmental regulations under Obama's EPA (Chapter 1), the shale gas revolution (Chapter 2), the rise of renewable energy (Chapter 3), and the trend toward decarbonization and decentralization in the electric utility industry (Chapter 4).

Chapters 5, 6, and 7 examine the responses of political leaders in West Virginia to the fundamental transformation that was underway in the energy industry. Chapter 5 describes the political evolution of West Virginia from a reliably "blue" state to a "red" state, including the impact of the "Friends of Coal" public relations effort and the subsequent narrative of a "war on coal." Chapter 6 takes a closer look at West Virginia's representatives in Congress, with particular attention to three of the four US Senators who represented West Virginia during "the lost decade." Chapter 7 – "Manchin in the Middle" – focuses on the fourth US Senator, Joe Manchin III, the politician who dominated the energy agenda in West Virginia throughout "the lost decade" and ultimately assumed an outsized influence on shaping national energy policies, beginning in January 2021 when the Democrats took control of the US Senate.

Chapters 8, 9, 10, and 11 consider the adverse impacts on West Virginians from the state continuing to cling to the coal industry even as market forces began to overwhelm the industry. Chapter 8 looks at the role of West Virginia Public Service Commission (PSC) and how its policies and decisions during "the lost decade" resulted in higher energy prices and unnecessary hardships on electricity ratepayers. Chapter 9 examines the impact of legislation adopted during "the lost

---

[26]   Dwight Garner, *The Story of Appalachia, with Plenty of Villains*, N.Y. Times (Nov. 20, 2017), https://www.nytimes.com/2017/11/20/books/review-ramp-hollow-ordeal-of-appalachia-steven-stoll.html.

decade" that was designed to benefit the coal industry at the expense of West Virginians. Chapter 10 focuses on the response of the electric utilities in the state as their coal plants ceased to be profitable, and the complicity of the PSC in response. Chapter 11 examines the failure of environmental regulators in West Virginia to force coal operators to bear the costs of cleaning up after themselves, and the extent to which the industry was able to exploit the bankruptcy process to shed environmental liabilities as well as postretirement obligations owed to coal miners.

Finally, Chapter 12 identifies several policies that should be given serious consideration as the state moves forward in the third decade of the twenty-first century. Thus far, West Virginia has missed out completely on the clean energy revolution that has been underway since the beginning of "the lost decade." But it is not too late to position the Mountain State to catch up, through strong leadership, political will, and deliberate strategies that embrace the clean energy technologies of the twenty-first century.

1

The Rise of Environmental Regulations under Obama's Environmental Protection Agency

In November 2008, when Barack Obama was elected as President of the United States, the focus of environmental policies turned to climate change and the reduction of greenhouse gases (GHGs), the heat-trapping pollutants that are produced by the burning of fossil fuels. Given coal's prominence as the source of nearly 80 percent of the GHGs in the electricity industry at the time, the focus on achieving GHG reductions necessarily had implications for the coal industry. Moreover, it was clear from some of the early initiatives at Obama's Environmental Protection Agency (EPA) that the administration had some hostility toward mountaintop removal in particular as a means of extracting coal. Other actions by the EPA had impacts on West Virginia – adoption of the Mercury and Air Toxics Standard (MATS) in late 2011, for example, resulted in the closure of several coal plants, as utilities determined that the cost of compliance was too great to justify additional investment in emission reduction measures. And late in Obama's second term, the EPA issued its rule regulating GHG emissions from power plants – the Clean Power Plan – which spurred even stronger opposition to the EPA in West Virginia and led to the rise of state Attorney General Patrick Morrisey as a leader of all the coal-dependent states across the country in challenging the rule in the courts. The story really begins near the end of the George W. Bush administration, however, with the decision of the US Supreme Court in *Massachusetts* v. *EPA* in April 2007.[1]

MASSACHUSETTS V. EPA AND THE REGULATION OF GHGS UNDER THE CLEAN AIR ACT

Massachusetts v. *EPA* was probably the most significant environmental law case of the first decade of the twenty-first century because of its impact on efforts in the United States to address climate change. The case involved a rather routine decision by the EPA in September 2003 to deny a request that had been submitted a few years earlier by a group of nineteen private organizations asking that the EPA regulate

[1] 549 U.S. 497 (2007).

tailpipe emissions from new motor vehicles as a means of addressing climate change.[2] In denying the request, the EPA claimed that the Clean Air Act did not grant it the authority to regulate GHG emissions.[3] The EPA further found that even if it had the authority, it would be "unwise" to exercise it given that the connection between increased concentrations of GHGs in the atmosphere and the observed increase in global surface temperatures "cannot be unequivocally established."[4] The EPA also reasoned that the "piecemeal" approach of using the Clean Air Act to regulate tailpipe emissions would interfere with a more comprehensive approach favored by the George W. Bush administration; that approach involved support for technological innovation, encouraging voluntary private sector reductions in GHG emissions, and further research on climate change, rather than the use of regulations.[5] Finally, the EPA noted that such unilateral actions by the United States might interfere with the President's ability to persuade key developing countries to reduce GHG emissions.[6]

The denial of the request was appealed by a group of states (led by Massachusetts), local governments, and environmental nongovernmental organizations (NGOs). In April 2007, the US Supreme Court issued its decision overturning the EPA's decision and granting relief to the petitioning parties. The 5 to 4 decision – a rare instance in which Chief Justice Roberts was on the losing side, and had to resort to writing a very strong dissent – was significant in four respects.

First, the Supreme Court was required to evaluate extensive scientific evidence offered by petitioners regarding the connection between GHG concentrations in the atmosphere and global warming, with a focus on sea-level rise in particular. This deep dive into climate science was necessary for the Court to find that petitioners had "standing" to bring the action. (Standing is legal jargon for "Do you have a dog in this fight?") Showing that standing exists requires, among other things, that petitioners suffer an "injury in fact" under Supreme Court precedent. The alleged injury upon which standing was based was the sea-level rise that could be expected to occur along the Massachusetts coastline. Citing the undisputed evidence offered by petitioners that global sea levels had risen somewhere between 10 and 20 centimeters over the twentieth century as a result of global warming, the Court found the rising seas "have already begun to swallow Massachusetts' coastal land" and the severity of that injury would only increase over the next century, giving Massachusetts the type of particularized injury that gave it the right to have its case heard in the courts.[7] Without five justices of the Supreme Court adopting the scientific evidence offered by petitioners, the case would have been dismissed.

[2] 68 Fed. Reg. 52922, EPA, *Control of Emissions from New Highway Vehicles and Engines*, Denial of Petition for Rulemaking, Sept. 8, 2003.
[3] *Id.* at 52925–29.
[4] *Id.* at 52930.
[5] *Id.* at 52931.
[6] *Id.*
[7] 549 U.S. at 521.

Second, the *Massachusetts* v. *EPA* decision slapped down the argument offered by the EPA that the relief sought by petitioners – regulation of tailpipe emissions on new motor vehicles – would not make any difference in addressing climate change, given the relatively small levels of emissions reductions that could potentially be achieved compared to the massive increases in emissions expected from developing nations such as China and India. This was a favorite argument of the Bush administration against regulation of GHG emissions – that it was useless to do so, and potentially put the US economy at a competitive disadvantage versus other nations that chose not to regulate GHGs, given the rate of growth of GHG emissions predicted from developing nations. In rejecting this excuse for not acting, the Court found that even a "small incremental step" is sufficient for obtaining judicial relief – accepting the Bush administration's premise "would doom most challenges to regulatory actions" given that agencies "do not generally solve massive problems in one fell regulatory swoop" – and, in any event, the emissions from US motor vehicles make a "meaningful contribution" to GHG concentrations and thus regulation would make a difference. According to the Court, "a reduction in domestic emissions would slow the pace of global emissions increases, no matter what happens elsewhere."[8]

Third, the Supreme Court determined that the EPA had clear authority under the Clean Air Act to regulate GHGs, given the broad definition of "pollutant." Whether the EPA should exercise that authority, in turn, would depend upon a finding by the EPA exercising its "judgment" that GHG emissions "may reasonably be anticipated to *endanger* public health or welfare," according to the specific language of the Clean Air Act.[9] According to the Court, it was impermissible (or, in legal terms, "arbitrary and capricious") for the EPA to simply decline to undertake the analysis necessary to inform its judgment.[10] On that basis, the Court sent the issue back to the EPA – or remanded the case – to give the EPA an opportunity to do its job and conduct the necessary analysis to inform a judgment on the issue.

Finally, the decision provided a road map for the EPA to proceed with regulation of GHG emissions, by requiring the agency to undertake this necessary analysis regarding the relationship between increased concentrations of GHGs in the atmosphere and climate change. In the parlance of the Clean Air Act, is there a basis for a finding that increased concentrations of GHGs in the atmosphere "may reasonably be anticipated to *endanger* public health or welfare"[11] and thus require a regulatory response by the EPA? Very soon after President Obama took office and Lisa Jackson became EPA Administrator, the EPA followed the Supreme Court's road map and issued a draft of the "endangerment finding" in April 2009, which was finalized in December 2009.[12] In its

---

[8]   *Id.* at 525.
[9]   Section 201(a)(1) of the Clean Air Act, 42 U.S.C. § 7521(a)(1).
[10] 549 U.S. at 463.
[11] Section 201(a)(1) of the Clean Air Act, 42 U.S.C. § 7521(a)(1).
[12] EPA, *Endangerment and Cause or Contribute Findings for Greenhouse Gases Under Section 202(a) of the Clean Air Act*, 74 Fed. Reg. 66496, Dec. 15, 2009.

endangerment finding, the EPA found that six greenhouse gases taken in combination endanger both the public health and the public welfare of current and future generations. According to its decision, the body of scientific evidence "compellingly supports" the finding.[13] In particular, the EPA cited major assessments by the US Global Climate Research Program (USGCRP), the United Nations Intergovernmental Panel on Climate Change (IPCC), and the National Research Council (NRC).[14] In reaching its endangerment finding, the EPA considered both observed and projected effects of GHGs in the atmosphere, their effect on climate, and the public health and welfare risks and impacts associated with such climate change.[15]

The endangerment finding triggered an aggressive agenda of GHG regulation by the EPA, including tailpipe emissions standards, GHG reporting requirements across a number of industries, and development of a program of GHG regulations from power plants that would later become the Clean Power Plan. Based on these initiatives, President Obama was able to take a leadership role in the months leading up to the climate summit in Paris in December 2015, formally known as the 21st Conference of the Parties (COP) under the United Nations Framework Convention on Climate Change, or UNFCCC. Between the fuel economy standards and the Clean Power Plan – the two primary prongs of Obama's "Climate Action Plan" – the United States promised a 26–28 percent reduction in GHG emissions by 2025 in its commitment, or "nationally determined contribution," under the Paris Agreement, and to use best efforts to achieve the 28 percent reduction.[16]

THE AMERICAN CLEAN ENERGY SECURITY ACT (ACES): CONGRESS ACTS TO REGULATE GHGs

As detailed in campaign speeches when he ran for President in 2008, Barack Obama promised a comprehensive "New Energy for America" plan that, among other things, included an economy-wide cap-and-trade program to reduce GHG emissions by 80 percent by 2050. He also declared that America's oil addiction is "one of the greatest challenges of our generation."[17] His early moves on climate change were encouraging. He appointed Carol Browner, the EPA head during the Clinton Administration and a close advisor of Al Gore, as a "climate czar," a high-level position in the White House, with authority over both the EPA and the Department of Energy. Because of the nature of the position, it did not require Senate confirmation. President Obama also appointed Steven Chu, a respected scientist with

---

[13] *Id.* at 66497.
[14] *Id.* at 66497, 66510–66516.
[15] *Id.* at 66536–66545.
[16] THE WHITE HOUSE, FACT SHEET: U.S. REPORTS ITS 2025 EMISSIONS TARGET TO THE UNFCCC (Mar. 31, 2015), https://obamawhitehouse.archives.gov/the-press-office/2015/03/31/fact-sheet-us-reports-its-2025-emissions-target-unfccc.
[17] Jeff Goodell, *As the World Burns*, ROLLING STONE (Jan. 7, 2010), www.rollingstone.com/politics/politics-news/as-the-world-burns-2-199797/.

a grasp of the urgency of the climate crisis, as Secretary of Energy. And, with Lisa Jackson heading up the EPA, the agency moved forward quickly to make the "endangerment finding" that would authorize the EPA to regulate greenhouse gases. Rather than relying on federal regulators and the EPA's existing authority under the Clean Air Act, however, the administration expressed a strong preference for Congressional action to enact comprehensive climate legislation to address carbon pollution. Former Senator Barbara Boxer (Democrat, California), who was then chair of the Senate Environment and Public Works Committee, summed it up this way: "If Congress does nothing, we will be watching EPA do our job."[18]

As it turned out, however, the Obama administration failed to take any leadership role on legislation to address climate change. The economic meltdown known as the "Great Recession" understandably had the administration's attention when it took office, and the response featured a $787 billion economic stimulus package and loans for the automakers in Detroit. "In the midst of the worst recession in a generation, climate change isn't what leaps to mind for the average voter," said Jason Grumet, Obama's top energy advisor during the campaign.[19] Health care became the top priority in the legislative agenda rather than global warming – it had a "populist feel to it," according to a campaign insider.[20]

Leaders in the House of Representatives, however, had already decided to push through a climate bill on their own, led by Representative Henry Waxman (Democrat, California), the chairman of the House Energy and Commerce Committee, and Edward Markey (Democrat, Massachusetts), chairman of the House Select Committee for Energy Independence and Global Warming. In June 2009, the US House of Representatives passed the American Clean Energy and Security (ACES) Act, also known as Waxman-Markey, which imposed a "cap-and-trade" program for GHG emissions that was geared toward achieving an 80 percent reduction in GHG emissions, from 1990 levels, by 2050. This level of GHG emissions reductions reflected the thinking of climate scientists at the time that in order to limit the temperature increase associated with GHG concentrations in the atmosphere to no more than 2 degrees Celsius – the objective adopted in the Kyoto Protocol of 1997 – the levels of GHG concentrations needed to be reduced to 350 parts per million by mid-twenty-first century. The 80 percent reduction required by ACES was designed to achieve that objective.

Under a cap-and-trade program, GHG emitters – such as coal-fired power plants – would be required to purchase allowances (pejoratively referred to as "licenses to pollute") corresponding to their level of GHG emissions during each reporting period. A coal plant emitting 10 million tons of CO_2 annually, for example, would

[18] Press Release, U.S. Senate Committee on Environment and Public Works, Boxer Delivers "Reality Check" on Global Warming Action (Mar. 19, 2009), www.epw.senate.gov/public/index.cfm/2009/3/post-20d52425-802a-23ad-4df6-771e1dffeeb6.

[19] Goodell, *supra* note 17.

[20] *Id.*

be required to secure allowances each year to cover that level of emissions. By reducing the number of allowances over time – that is, 80 percent fewer allowances would be issued in 2050 than in 2010 – the required GHG emissions reductions would be achieved. A cap-and-trade mechanism is referred to as a "market-based" approach to achieving emissions reductions as allowances could be freely traded among the emitters, enabling them to decide for themselves whether it is cheaper to cut emissions or buy allowances. As the number of allowances is reduced over time, the scarcity would result in higher prices for allowances, thereby sending a price signal that would encourage development of carbon-reduction technologies. The Acid Rain Program included as part of the Clean Air Act Amendments of 1990 – during the George H. W. Bush administration – was a successful cap-and-trade program that achieved a 50 percent reduction in sulfur dioxide emissions from power plants between 1990 and 2000 using a similar allowance-based approach, and at a cost far cheaper than anyone had anticipated.

In June 2009 ACES passed the US Congress by a vote of 219 to 212. Nancy Pelosi, then House of Representatives Speaker, was credited (or criticized, depending upon your point of view) for shepherding the measure through the process and securing enough votes to achieve passage in the House. Getting there, of course, required accommodation of dozens of special interests, whose influence was reflected in the allocation of allowances, which provided a form of financial assistance to sectors of the economy that were thought to be disproportionately affected by the regulation of GHG emissions (e.g., energy-intensive industries, merchant coal plants). Notwithstanding the unseemly "sausage-making" aspects of passing a major piece of legislation, ACES achieved its essential purpose of adopting a comprehensive program to regulate GHG emissions, and to achieve the reductions thought necessary to avoid the catastrophic impacts of temperature increases in excess of 2 degrees Celsius.

The West Virginia delegation, not surprisingly, was united in opposition to the measure. All three Congressmen – Shelley Moore Capito, Nick Rahall, and Alan Mollohan – voted against the measure. In a statement explaining her vote, Capito stated that "[t]his bill amounts to a national energy tax on consumers … [and] essentially pits states like West Virginia against states like California and Massachusetts."[21] She urged support for her "bipartisan plan" – the "Clean Coal-Derived Fuels for Energy Security Act of 2009" – that would "provide[ ] an opportunity to invest in renewable energy technology, invest in conservation and invest in clean coal – all without taxing consumers."[22] Nick Rahall, who was, at the time, Chairman of the House Natural Resources Committee, also voted against Waxman-Markey. Alan Mollohan "wait[ed] until

[21] Ken Ward, *Shelley Moore Capito, Denial and the Climate Change Bill*, COAL TATTOO (June 25, 2009), http://blogs.wvgazettemail.com/coaltattoo/2009/06/25/shelley-moore-capito-denial-and-the-climate-change-bill/.
[22] *Id.*

just about the last moment" to come out against the bill – his office issued a statement at 5:15 p.m. on the day before the vote[23] – and, according to one political observer, his delay in defending his district's interests cost him.[24] (He was subsequently defeated in the Democratic primary by Senator Mike Oliverio.)

The measure never gained traction in the Senate because, among other things, the White House did not have a plan for taking up the cause in the upper chamber. White House chief of staff Rahm Emanuel admitted when he called Markey to offer congratulations that "I didn't think you could do it."[25] The White House had turned its attention to health care reform and the ten months between June 2019 and the passage of the Affordable Care Act (ACA) in March 2010 were fully consumed with the debate over the depth and breadth of health care reform. By the time the ACA was passed, there was no appetite for addressing climate change. Even though the US Senate had passed cap-and-trade programs regulating GHG emissions three times before, sponsored by John McCain, Joe Lieberman, and Lindsay Graham, it had no chance in the US Senate in 2010. The bill considered in 2010 was sponsored by John Kerry (Democrat, Pennsylvania), Joe Lieberman (Democrat, Connecticut), and Lindsay Graham (Republican, South Carolina), and never gained enough support from Republicans in the Senate to earn the sixty-vote supermajority necessary for passage.

For West Virginia, Senator Byrd had expressed strong opposition to Waxman-Markey when it passed the House, but later sounded more open to a Senate climate bill.[26] As late as May 2010, both Senators Byrd and Rockefeller were listed as "on the fence" by *Environment & Energy Daily* in its tracking of the "Senate Climate Debate: The 60-Vote Climb."[27] Senator Rockefeller, for his part, expressed serious concerns about the House bill. In February 2010, he wrote a letter to EPA Administrator Lisa Jackson, along with other coal state senators, expressing opposition to the EPA taking administrative action to address climate change and in favor of these issues being "handled carefully and appropriately dealt with by the Congress."[28]

When Senator Byrd passed away on June 29, 2010, at age ninety-two, thirty-six-year -old Carte Goodwin was appointed to the seat and did not hesitate to express his view on climate legislation: "From what I've seen of the Waxman-Markey bill that passed the House of Representatives and other proposals pending in the Senate, they simply

[23] *Id.*
[24] Mark Ambinder, *A Democratic Congressman Is Defeated*, THE ATLANTIC (May 12, 2010), www
    .theatlantic.com/politics/archive/2010/05/a-democratic-congressman-is-defeated/56582.
[25] Ryan Lizza, *As the World Burns*, THE NEW YORKER (Oct. 3, 2010), www.newyorker.com/magazine/
    2010/10/11/as-the-world-burns.
[26] Jonathan Hiskes, *What Robert Byrd's Death Means for the Climate Bill*, GRIST (June 29, 2010), https://
    grist.org/article/2010-06-28-what-robert-byrds-death-means-for-the-climate-bill/.
[27] *Senate Climate Debate: The 60-Vote Climb*, ENVIRONMENT & ENERGY DAILY (May 12, 2010), https://
    grist.org/wp-content/uploads/2010/01/climate_debate_senate.pdf.
[28] Juliet Eilperin, *Coal-state Dems hit EPA on climate*, WASHINGTON POST (Feb. 19, 2010), http://views
    .washingtonpost.com/climate-change/post-carbon/2010/02/coal-state_dems_hit_epa_on_climate.html.

are not right for West Virginia."[29] Within months, cap-and-trade would be in the crosshairs of Joe Manchin's rifle in his infamous commercial leading to his election to the seat in November 2010.

THE WAR ON MOUNTAINTOP REMOVAL

Five months into President Obama's first term, his administration set its sights on mountaintop removal (MTR) mining, a method of surface mining often described as "strip mining on steroids"[30] that is commonly used to extract coal in the Appalachian region. As the name suggests, MTR involves using explosives to blast the tops of mountains off in order to extract the valuable coal buried underneath. As Earthjustice describes the process:

> Coal companies first raze an entire mountainside, ripping trees from the ground and clearing brush with huge tractors. This debris is then set ablaze as deep holes are dug for explosives. An explosive is poured into these holes and mountaintops are literally blown apart. Huge machines called draglines – some the size of an entire city block, able to scoop up to 100 tons in a single load – push rock and dirt into nearby streams and valleys, forever burying waterways. Coal companies use explosives to blast as much as 800 to 1,000 feet off the tops of mountains in order to reach thin coal seams buried deep below.[31]

Although Federal law requires that the rock and dirt be replaced to the approximate original contour (AOC) of the mountain,[32] "because rock taken from its natural state and broken up naturally 'swells,' perhaps by as much as 15 to 25%, the excess rock not returned to the mountain – the 'overburden' – remains in the valleys, creating 'valley fills'," which often bury intermittent and perennial streams and drainage areas that are near the mountaintop.[33] Between 2000 and 2008, federal and state authorities gave permission for 511 valley fills in West Virginia, according to the Government Accountability Office (GAO). The GAO estimated that, put back-to-back, it was the equivalent of filling a single valley at least 176 miles long.[34] The EPA estimates that over the past three

[29] Alex Kaplun, *New W.Va. Senator Signals Opposition to Cap and Trade*, N.Y. TIMES (July 16, 2010), https://archive.nytimes.com/www.nytimes.com/gwire/2010/07/16/16greenwire-new-wva-senator-sig nals-opposition-to-cap-and-28472.html.

[30] Peter Galuszka, *Strip Mining on Steroids*, BLOOMBERG (Nov. 17, 1997), www.bloomberg.com/news/ articles/1997-11-16/strip-mining-on-steroids.

[31] *What Is Mountaintop Removal Mining?*, EARTHJUSTICE, https://earthjustice.org/features/campaigns/ what-is-mountaintop-removal-mining.

[32] SMCRA, Sec. 515(b)3.

[33] Bragg v. West Virginia Coal Association, 248 F.3d 275, 286 (4th Cir. 2001).

[34] David A. Fahrenthold, *EPA Crackdown on Mountaintop Coal Mining Criticized as Contradictory*, WASHINGTON POST (Jan. 28, 2010), www.washingtonpost.com/wp-dyn/content/article/2010/01/27/ AR2010012704588.html.

decades, these valley fills are responsible for burying more than 2,000 miles of vital Appalachian headwater streams, and poisoning many more.[35]

The Obama administration's new direction on MTR was announced in June 2009 when three agencies with jurisdiction over MTR – the EPA, the Department of Interior, and the Army Corps of Engineers – executed a Memorandum of Understanding (MOU) in which they committed to use a coordinated approach among the three agencies to take "unprecedented steps to reduce the environmental impacts of mountaintop coal mining in the six Appalachian states of Kentucky, Ohio, Pennsylvania, Tennessee, Virginia, and West Virginia."[36] The MOU promised, among other things, that the agencies would take action to "[m]inimize the adverse environmental consequences of mountaintop coal mining," "tighten the regulation of mountaintop coal mining," and implement "stringent environmental reviews of permit applications under the Clean Water Act (CWA) and Surface Mining Control and Reclamation Act of 1977 (SMCRA)."[37] At the time, MTR accounted for about 10 percent of US coal production.[38]

That the EPA was going to get more involved in permitting MTR projects was not a good development for the future prospects of MTR. When the Federal Water Pollution Control Act was amended in 1972 to create what is known today as the Clean Water Act, the division of responsibilities between the EPA and the Army Corps of Engineers was more or less a "good cop, bad cop" compromise between the House of Representatives – which favored less stringent environmental regulation – and the Senate, which wanted stricter enforcement. In a compromise between the two chambers, the EPA was given authority to regulate discharges from point sources and to administer the National Pollution Discharge Elimination System (NPDES) program under Section 402 of the Clean Water Act, while the Corps would take the lead on issuing "dredge and fill" permits under Section 404 of the Act. The Corps was definitely the "good cop" as far as the coal industry was concerned, as it rarely acted to get in the way of an MTR project in issuing Section 404 dredge and fill permits. The "bad cop" had some tools under Section 404 as well; the EPA could veto permits issued by the Corps (although it rarely exercised that authority).

When the June 2009 MOU indicated that the EPA was going to play a more prominent role with respect to the MTR permitting process, it was a strong signal of

---

[35] Press Release, EPA, EPA Issues Comprehensive Guidance to Protect Appalachian Communities From Harmful Environmental Impacts of Mountaintop Mining (Apr. 1, 2010), https://archive.epa.gov /epapages/newsroom_archive/newsreleases/4145c96189a17239852576f8005867bd.html.

[36] Press Release, U.S. Department of Interior, Obama Administration Takes Unprecedented Steps to Reduce Environmental Impacts of Mountaintop Coal Mining, Announces Interagency Action Plan to Implement Reforms (Nov. 6, 2009), www.doi.gov/news/pressreleases/2009_06_11_releaseD.

[37] *Id.*

[38] Fahrenthold, *supra* note 33.

the bad things to come for the coal industry in West Virginia. The introductory language to the MOU also provided a pretty good clue where this was heading:

> The mountains of Appalachia possess unique biological diversity, forests, and freshwater streams that historically have sustained rich and vibrant American communities. These mountains also contain some of the nation's richest deposits of coal, which have been mined by generations of Americans to provide heat and electricity to millions in the U.S. and around the world. After generations of mining, however, the region's most readily available coal resources have diminished, and the remaining coal seams are less accessible to non-surface mining methods.
>
> In response, a surface mining technique commonly referred to as "mountaintop mining" has become increasingly prevalent in the Appalachian region. Although its scale and efficiency has enabled the mining of once-inaccessible coal seams, this mining practice often stresses the natural environment and impacts the health and welfare of surrounding human communities. Streams once used for swimming, fishing, and drinking water have been adversely impacted, and groundwater resources used for drinking water have been contaminated. Some forest lands that sustain water quality and habitat and contribute to the Appalachian way of life have been fragmented or lost. These negative impacts are likely to further increase as mines transition to less accessible coal resources within already affected watersheds and communities.[39]

During the first year of the Obama administration, the EPA scrutinized about 175 proposed MTR projects, and signed off on only 48.[40] Shortly after the issuance of the MOU, the Corps took action to suspend Nationwide Permit 21, a blanket authorization that provided a fast track approval process for the disposal of dredge and fill material from surface coal mining projects throughout the Appalachian region.[41] Without the blanket authorization provided by Nationwide Permit 21, MTR projects would be required to secure a Section 404 permit for each individual project.

Within three months of the MOU, the EPA set its sights on the poster child for MTR: the Spruce Mine project northeast of Blair in Logan County, referred to as the "mother of all mountaintop removal coal mines [inasmuch as it] would destroy thousands of acres of land, bury seven miles of streams and end a way of life for too many Appalachian families."[42] In 2007, the Bush administration had approved the project, which involved dynamiting the tops off mountains over 2,278 acres, with the

39 Memorandum of Understanding among the U.S. Department of the Army, U.S. Department of the Interior, and U.S. Environmental Protection Agency Implementing the Interagency Action Plan on Appalachian Surface Coal Mining, June 11, 2009.
40 Fahrenthold, *supra* note 33.
41 Department of the Army, Corps of Engineers, *Proposal to Modify and Suspend Nationwide Permit 21*, 75 FR 34311 (July 15, 2009); Suspension of Nationwide Permit 21, 75 FR 34711 (June 18, 2010).
42 John M. Broder, *E.P.A. Official Seeks to Block West Virginia Mine*, N.Y. TIMES (Oct. 15, 2010), https://www.nytimes.com/2010/10/16/science/earth/16westvirginia.html (quoting Sierra Club's executive director Michael Blune).

fill being disposed into the nearby valleys and streams (Seng Camp Creek, Pigeonroost Branch, Oldhouse Branch, and certain tributaries to those waters).[43] In September 2009, the EPA requested that the Corps use its discretionary authority to withdraw the permit it previously issued in 2007; the Corps promptly responded that it would not exercise that authority. The EPA thereafter commenced a formal process in January 2010 for withdrawing the authorization and, in its subsequent investigation, found that the project would bury more than seven miles of the Pigeonroost Branch and Oldhouse Branch streams under 110 million cubic yards of spoil, killing everything in them and sending downstream a flood of contaminants, toxic substances, and life-choking algae.

Based on these findings, in January 2011 the EPA used its "backstop" authority under Section 404(c) of the Clean Water Act to retroactively withdraw the permit issued by the Corps four years earlier during the Bush administration. The owner of Spruce Mine, Mingo Logan Coal Company, immediately filed suit to contest the action. Although Mingo Logan was successful in the trial court, in April 2013 the Fourth Circuit upheld the EPA's action, finding that because the EPA backstop authority had no temporal limit – it allowed the EPA to exercise its authority "whenever" the Administrator makes a determination that an "unacceptable adverse effect" will result – the permit could be withdrawn years after the Corps issued it.[44]

Contemporaneous with its investigation of the Spruce Mine impacts, in April 2010 the EPA also issued new water quality standards for surface coal mining in central Appalachia that effectively blocked MTR projects from dumping wastes in streams. The guidance adopted the first-ever numeric standard for "conductivity" – how well waters carry an electrical charge – which measures levels of salt, sulfides, and other pollutants in streams near surface coalmines. Under the new standards, mining companies would have to show that their project would not cause the pollutant concentrations to climb past roughly five times the normal level, a limit the agency said would protect 95 percent of aquatic life. In announcing the new standards, EPA Administrator Lisa Jackson said there were "no or very few valley fills that are going to meet this standard."[45]

Six months later, in the heat of a very close Senate race when Manchin – as Governor – was running against John Raese for the US Senate seat vacated upon the death of Robert Byrd, West Virginia announced it was suing the EPA over the water quality standards adopted in April. At a press conference one month before election day where he was joined by Bill Raney, President of the West Virginia Coal Association, Manchin claimed that the EPA's actions "usurped the authority of

[43]　*Id.*
[44]　Mingo Logan Coal Co. v. EPA, 714 F.3d 608 (D.C. Cir. 2013). According to the court, "Section 404 imposes no temporal limit on the Administrator's authority to withdraw the Corps's specification but instead expressly empowers him to prohibit, restrict or withdraw the specification 'whenever' he makes a determination that the statutory 'unacceptable adverse effect' will result." 714 F.3d at 613.
[45]　Press Release, EPA, *supra* note 34.

the state" and threatened "to end surface coal mining in West Virginia."[46] Recent polls in the race had shown Raese had pulled slightly ahead of Manchin through his relentless pounding of Manchin on coal issues and by tying him to President Obama, whose approval rating in the state was well below 40 percent.[47] The National Republican Senate Committee had begun running its own ad campaign, telling West Virginians that "a vote for Manchin is a vote for Obama." As described by *Mother Jones*, the race was coming down to nothing more than a "battle of who can love coal more," and Manchin was determined to win it.[48]

The following month, Manchin ended up defeating Raese in the general election by 53,000 votes. West Virginia's lawsuit against the EPA, meanwhile, was later combined with litigation commenced by the state of Kentucky and the National Mining Association, and was ultimately dismissed in 2014 in a decision of the DC Circuit Court of Appeals, with the opinion authored by then Judge Brett Kavanaugh.[49]

EPA ADOPTS THE MERCURY AND AIR TOXICS STANDARD (MATS) RULE

In December 2011, Obama's EPA adopted the Mercury and Air Toxics Standard (MATS) rule, which addressed the emissions of toxic air pollutants (mercury, arsenic, chromium, nickel, and acid gases) from electric power plants. This wasn't a new initiative by the Obama administration; rather, it was a matter of tying up loose ends on an issue first raised during the waning days of the Clinton administration and bungled during the George W. Bush administration. In December 2000, shortly before Christmas, Clinton's EPA made the finding that it was "appropriate and necessary" to regulate mercury from electric generating units as a "hazardous air pollutant," thus triggering EPA's obligation under the Clean Air Act to adopt standards to address mercury and related air toxics. Bush's EPA attempted to implement the requirement in March 2004 by adopting an ill-conceived market-based approach for regulating mercury emissions, the Clean Air Mercury Rule. This path was ultimately rejected by an appellate court in February 2008 in *New Jersey v. EPA.*[50] When Obama's EPA took charge of the issue, it was under pressure to develop and implement a rule that would satisfy a judicially imposed deadline for

---

[46] Patrick Reis, *W.Va. Sues Obama, EPA over Mining Coal Regulations*, N.Y. Times (Oct. 6, 2010), https://archive.nytimes.com/www.nytimes.com/gwire/2010/10/06/06greenwire-wva-sues-obama-epa-over-mining-coal-regulation-48964.html.

[47] *Id.*

[48] Kate Sheppard, *West Virginia Senate: The Battle of Who Can Love Coal More*, Mother Jones (Oct. 7, 2010), www.motherjones.com/politics/2010/10/west-virginia-senate-battle-who-can-love-coal-more.

[49] National Mining Association v. McCarthy, 758 F.3d 243 (D.C. Cir. 2014).

[50] New Jersey v. EPA, 517 F.3d 574 (2008).

regulating a pollutant that Clinton's EPA had found it "necessary and appropriate" to regulate nine years earlier.

The result was the MATS rule issued in December 2011, which was controversial in many respects. First, there was the issue of EPA's position on whether it was required to consider the compliance costs that industry would incur as a result of the EPA's decision to regulate mercury under its "appropriate and necessary" finding; these costs were estimated to be $9.6 billion. The EPA took the position that because of the hazardous nature of the pollutant, it was not required under the applicable provision of the Clean Air Act to take these compliance costs into account in reaching its decision to regulate the pollutant. While the EPA had performed a "regulatory impact analysis," which showed that the health benefits (in a range of $37 billion to $90 billion) exceeded the $9.6 billion compliance costs, it stood firm on its reading of the law that consideration of costs was not relevant when deciding whether or not to undertake the regulation of a hazardous air pollutant. This position was ultimately rejected by the US Supreme Court in a 5–4 decision in *Michigan* v. *EPA* in June 2015, in a memorable majority opinion written by the inimitable Justice Antonin S. Scalia. According to Justice Scalia, "[t]here are undoubtedly settings in which the phrase 'appropriate and necessary' does not encompass cost. But this is not one of them."[51]

A second controversy associated with MATS was the manner in which the EPA calculated the health benefits of the rule. The EPA's analysis showed that the regulation of mercury and other air toxics (arsenic, chromium, nickel, and acid gases, including hydrochloric acid and hydrofluoric acid) – the subject pollutant of the MATS rule – would produce benefits of only $4–$6 million annually, which was far exceeded by the $9.6 billion compliance costs. The EPA achieved its benefits calculation of $37–$90 billion by including "ancillary benefits," which reflect that the regulation of mercury under MATS would also result in the reduction of other pollutants emitted by electric generating plants, such as sulfur dioxide (SO_2) and fine particulate matter ($PM_{2.5}$). Opponents of the rule claimed that such an approach was "double counting" the health benefits, and thus the EPA's analysis failed to justify the stringency of the MATS rule, given that the compliance costs so vastly exceeded the benefits if properly limited to the scope of the pollutant directly regulated by the rule. (In its decision in *Michigan* v. *EPA*, the Supreme Court declined to comment on the appropriateness of the EPA's treatment of ancillary benefits in its analysis. On remand [when the issue was returned to the EPA for reconsideration following the Supreme Court decision], the EPA effectively reinstated the rule by reiterating its conclusion – this time after considering costs – that regulating mercury as a toxic pollutant is appropriate.) As it turned out, eight years later, during the Trump Administration, the EPA adopted a new methodology for calculating benefits associated with rules adopted under

---

[51] Michigan v. EPA, 576 U.S. 743 (2015).

the Clean Air Act, and eliminated the EPA's ability to use ancillary benefits in its calculations.[52]

Third, and of most importance to West Virginia, the MATS rule resulted in the closure of dozens of coal-fired generating plants across the country, including six of the sixteen coal plants that were operating in West Virginia at the beginning of the Obama administration. In order to achieve compliance with MATS, electric utilities would have been required to install additional emissions control equipment. (The need for this additional investment is the source of the $9.6 billion figure cited by the EPA in its regulatory impact analysis.) What this translates into for each utility is a plant-by-plant examination of whether this investment makes any economic sense. In other words, if the plant is only marginally profitable without the additional investment, then the additional expenditure may tip the scale in favor of prematurely retiring the unit rather than making the investment.

The economic analysis was made even more challenging by the impact of the massive quantities of natural gas that were beginning to be produced from the Marcellus Shale, as discussed in the next chapter. As a result of this cheap and plentiful natural gas, coupled with the construction of modern natural gas generating units that were able to convert gas into electricity very efficiently, wholesale electricity prices were rapidly falling in the PJM Interconnection (the wholesale electric market in the mid-Atlantic region). Only the newer and more efficient coal plants could pass the economic test that would justify the additional investment to allow continued operation once the MATS rule took effect.

Because the MATS rule, adopted in December 2011, allowed utilities three years to achieve compliance – and a fourth year was available, if necessary – the closure of coal-fired power plants across the United States was spread over the years 2012–15. As it turned out, the EPA's estimate of the impact of the MATS rule on coal plant closures was vastly underestimated, likely because of the double whammy of declining wholesale prices due to the impact of shale gas production on top of the estimated $9.6 billion in compliance costs that the utilities would be incurring to achieve compliance with MATS. The EPA had estimated that the MATS rule would result in the closure of about 4.7 gigawatts (GWs) of coal-fired generation (or about 0.5 percent of the nation's electricity generating capacity). The actual figure turned out to be more than four times higher. And the impact in West Virginia was devastating, with the loss of six of the state's operating coal-fired power plants, totaling almost 3 GW. Table 1.1 shows the MATS-related closures of coal-fired generating plants in West Virginia.

The initial compliance deadline under MATS was April 16, 2015. Between January 2015 and April 2016, about 87 GW of coal-fired plants across the United

[52] Coral Davenport, *New Trump Rule Aims to Limit Tough Clean Air Measures Under Biden*, N.Y TIMES (Dec. 20, 2020), https://www.nytimes.com/2020/12/09/climate/trump-pollution-regulations.html#:~:text=Agency%20economists%20will%20be%20required,directly%20governed%20by%20the%20regulation.

TABLE 1.1 *MATS-related closures of coal-fired generating plants in West Virginia*

Plant	Owner	Nameplate capacity (MW)	Location	Retirement date
Albright	FirstEnergy	278	Albright	September 2012
Rivesville	FirstEnergy	110	Rivesville	September 2012
Willow Island	FirstEnergy	213	Willow Island	September 2012
Philip Sporn	AEP	1,105	New Haven	May 2015
Kammer	AEP	713	Moundsville	May 2015
Kanawha River	AEP	439	Glasgow	May 2015
Total		**2,858**		

States installed pollution-control equipment, and nearly 20 GW of coal capacity was retired. About 26 percent of those retirements occurred in April 2015, meeting the MATS rule's initial compliance date. Another 142 GW of coal plants had applied for and received one-year extensions that allowed them to operate until April 2016 while finalizing compliance strategies.

The West Virginia delegation – with the exception of Senator Rockefeller – vehemently opposed the MATS rule throughout the process. All three members of the House of Representatives from West Virginia at the time – Shelley Moore Capito, David McKinley, and Nick Rahall – expressed opposition to the MATS rule when it was being promulgated by the EPA, and supported a resolution in February 2011 that would have denied any funds to the EPA to "implement, administer or enforce" a companion measure that imposed similar mercury and other toxic air pollution standards on cement plants.[53] In June 2012, on the Senate side, Senator Jim Inhofe (Republican, Oklahoma) sponsored a resolution of disapproval under the Congressional Review Act that would have invalidated the MATS rule. Letters supporting the resolution were sent by Democratic Governor Earl Tomblin of West Virginia, West Virginia Lieutenant Governor Jeffrey Kessler, and a group of bipartisan West Virginia legislators.[54]

Although the resolution failed 46–53 on a procedural vote, it gave Senator Manchin an opportunity to offer some remarks on behalf of "the little state of West Virginia that does the heavy lifting that helps this entire nation."[55] Expressing his support for the resolution as "an important step to rein in this out-of-control agency," he reiterated his determination "to stop the EPA's job-killing agenda." According to Senator Manchin's remarks, the EPA was "stepping way

[53] John Walke, *Meet the Members of Congress Who Sided with Corporate Polluters over Children and Your Health*, Grist (Feb. 25, 2011), https://grist.org/climate-policy/2011-02-24-meet-the-members-of-congress-that-sided-with-corporate-polluters/.

[54] Barry Cassell, *Resolution to Kill EPA's Utility MACT Rule Fails in Senate*, Transmission Hub (June 20, 2012), https://www.transmissionhub.com/articles/2012/06/resolution-to-kill-epas-utility-mact-rule-fails-in-senate.html.

[55] Cong. Rec., Senate, June 20, 2012, S4322.

beyond its boundaries, further than our Founding Fathers ever intended," the consequence of which is to put "an absolute burden on the backs of every American."[56]
Senator Rockefeller, for his part, broke ranks with all the other coal country lawmakers
and opposed the resolution. He explained his reasons for doing so in one of the
defining speeches of his long Senate career, as discussed further in Chapter 6.

Not surprisingly, political leaders across the spectrum in West Virginia, including
Governor Earl Ray Tomblin, celebrated the Supreme Court's decision in June 2015
in *Michigan* v. *EPA* to overturn the MATS rule. Many of the public statements
pointed out that the relief came too late to save many of the coal plants in West
Virginia that had already closed down as a result of the MATS rule. Congressman
McKinley admonished that "[s]tates and utilities considering complying with the
EPA's other economically destructive regulations should take notice of this
decision."[57] Shelley Moore Capito, who had by then been elected to the US
Senate, issued a statement that "[g]oing forward, states should not be forced to
bear the brunt of other costly EPA regulations before legal challenges are
complete."[58] Senator Manchin noted the then pending litigation challenging the
EPA's Clean Power Plan, and expressed hope that "in the coming weeks, the court
will also recognize that the EPA has again overreached with the Clean Power Plan in
order to prevent the loss of a million jobs, an increase in utility rates, and more
damage to our economy."[59] State Attorney General Patrick Morrisey said the
Supreme Court decision in *Michigan* v. *EPA* was a warning the EPA must heed,
referring to his anticipated challenge to the EPA's Clean Power Plan.[60]

As it turned out, eight months later, in February 2016, Morrisey – taking the lead
in an action brought by West Virginia and twenty-three other states – would use the
EPA loss in *Michigan* v. *EPA* as the linchpin for his argument to obtain a stay from
the US Supreme Court against implementation of the Clean Power Plan, the
ambitious rule from Obama's EPA regulating GHG emissions from coal-fired
power plants. In a decision that represented the first time the Supreme Court issued
a stay on regulations before an initial review by a federal appeals court, the court
ruled 5–4 that the Clean Power Plan could not move forward until all legal
challenges had been heard. The decision broke along "party lines," with the five

---

[56] *Id.* at S4323.
[57] Press Release, David B. McKinley P.E., *McKinley Statement on Supreme Court's Decision on EPA Power Plant Regulation* (June 29, 2015), https://mckinley.house.gov/news/documentsingle.aspx?DocumentID=381.
[58] Press Release, Shelley Moore Capito, *Capito Statement on Supreme Court MATS Ruling* (June 29, 2015), https://www.capito.senate.gov/news/press-releases/capito-statement-on-supreme-court-mats-ruling.
[59] Press Release, Joe Manchin, *Manchin Applauds Michigan v. EPA Ruling* (June 29, 2015), https://www.manchin.senate.gov/newsroom/press-releases/manchin-applauds-michigan-v-epa-ruling.
[60] Jeff Jenkins, *Supreme Court Strikes Down Pollution Rule; Coal Industry Applauds Action*, WV METRONEWS (June 29, 2015), https://wvmetronews.com/2015/06/29/supreme-court-strikes-down-pollution-rule-coal-industry-applauds-action/.

conservative-leaning justices voting for the stay and the liberal-leaning justices voting against it.[61]

Four days later, that thin philosophical majority ceased to exist with the death of Justice Antonin Scalia from a heart attack on a hunting trip at Cibolo Creek Ranch in remote west Texas. Given that the ruling was not accompanied by a written decision, it is not entirely clear why the court ruled as it did. On the heels of the *Michigan* v. *EPA* decision that overturned the MATS rule, which, by the time of the Court's opinion, had caused the closure of dozens of coal-fired power plants across the country, Morrisey and friends had a pretty compelling argument that the legality of Clean Air Act regulations needed to be established before they could be allowed to take effect.

EPA ADOPTS THE CLEAN POWER PLAN

The Clean Air Act is not a great tool for regulating GHG emissions. Carbon dioxide (CO_2), for example – the most common of the GHGs – is invisible and odorless, and does not directly lead to the sort of health impacts associated with most of the other pollutants regulated under the Clean Air Act, such as carbon monoxide, sulfur dioxide, and particulate matter. Moreover, regulating GHG emissions affects large sectors of the US economy and, arguably, a major policy decision to impose a regulatory scheme with such broad impacts should be directly addressed by Congress rather than through a technical extension of an existing law. Without Congressional action to address the issue, however – and it was clear by the end of 2010 that there would be no action on climate coming from Capitol Hill – the Clean Air Act was the only remaining tool available to President Obama to tackle climate change. He said as much in his State of the Union speech in 2013: "If Congress won't act soon to protect future generations, I will. I will direct my cabinet to come up with executive actions we can take, now and in the future, to reduce pollution, prepare our communities for the consequences of climate change, and speed the transition to more sustainable sources of energy."[62]

Shortly thereafter, in June 2013, President Obama released his Climate Action Plan. The Plan comprised two elements: reducing tailpipe emissions through fuel economy standards, and reducing GHG emissions from new and existing power plants using the EPA's authority to regulate air pollutants under the Clean Air Act. In September 2013, the EPA proposed new source performance standards for CO_2 pollution from *new* power plants under Section 111(b) of the Clean Air Act. In June 2014, the EPA proposed the Clean Power Plan to establish CO_2 emission

---

[61] Courtney Scobie, *Supreme Court Stays EPA's Clean Power Plan*, ABA (Feb. 17, 2016), https://www .americanbar.org/groups/litigation/committees/environmental-energy/practice/2016/021716-energy-supreme-court-stays-epas-clean-power-plan/.

[62] *Obama's 2013 State of the Union Address*, N.Y. TIMES (Feb. 12, 2013), https://www.nytimes.com/2013/ 02/13/us/politics/obamas-2013-state-of-the-union-address.html.

guidelines for *existing* power plants under Section 111(d). Both power plant rules were finalized in August 2015.

The Clean Power Plan was designed to produce a 32 percent reduction in CO_2 pollution from power plants in the United States by 2030, as compared with 2005 levels. On the transportation side, the EPA and the Department of Transportation proposed a new round of emissions and fuel efficiency standards in June 2015 for medium- and heavy-duty vehicles through model year 2025. The fuel economy standards, coupled with the Clean Power Plan, provided the foundation for the United States to quantify its commitment to the UNFCCC in preparation for the 21st annual Conference of the Parties to be held in Paris in December 2015. In its Nationally Determined Contribution (NDC), the United States committed to a goal of reducing GHG emissions by between 26 and 28 percent from 2005 levels by 2025.

Under the Clean Power Plan, the EPA established state-specific emission limits in the form of an emission rate (pounds of CO_2 per megawatt-hour of net electricity produced). The rule also translated this rate-based limit into a mass-based limit (in other words, total CO_2 emissions for the state, expressed in tons). The target established under the Clean Power Plan for West Virginia seemed, on its face, to be a heavy lift: It required a 37 percent reduction in the emissions rate – from 2,064 pounds per megawatt-hour in 2012 to 1,305 pounds per megawatt-hour in 2030 – and a 29 percent reduction under a mass-based standard – from 72,319 thousand short tons in 2012 to 51,325 thousand short tons by 2030 from existing sources.

Not surprisingly, the introduction of the Clean Power Plan generated considerable interest in coal country. The EPA convened two days of public hearings in Pittsburgh, which featured competing protest marches outside the federal building on Liberty Avenue. While environmental activists gathered wearing blue T-shirts with the phrase "climate action now," marchers supporting coal and union workers wore shirts or held signs with United Mine Workers Association logos, chanting "Hey, hey, EPA. Don't take our jobs away." In response, environmental supporters shouted back "No planet, no jobs."[63] The EPA also conducted hearings in Washington, DC, Atlanta, and Denver.

The Clean Power Plan stimulated an all-out assault on Obama's EPA by West Virginia's delegation, as well as by state leaders. Senators Capito and Manchin took the opportunity to introduce a Senate bill – the Affordable Reliable Energy Now Act, or ARENA – that would effectively halt the implementation of the Clean Power Plan. In introducing the legislation, Senator Capito said she was "proud to lead the fight against the Clean Power Plan's sweeping regulations" and to "fight back against

[63] Don Hopey, Stephanie Ritenbaugh, & Madeline Conway, *EPA Hearings on Controversial Carbon Emissions Regulations Continue in Pittsburgh*, PITTSBURGH POST-GAZETTE (Aug. 1, 2014), https://www.post-gazette.com/breaking/2014/07/31/Pro-and-con-voice-their-views-at-EPA-hearing-on-proposed-pollution-curbs/stories/201407310284.

the assault on coal."[64] She later sponsored a resolution of disapproval under the Congressional Review Act, which passed the Senate 52–46 on November 15, 2015, but was ultimately vetoed by President Obama; the measure had forty-eight cosponsors, including Senator Manchin.[65] During her speech on the Senate floor in favor of the resolution, Capito invoked a "war on coal" and called the Clean Power Plan "the most expensive environmental regulation that the EPA has ever proposed on our nation's power sector."[66]

Manchin cited the rule as an example of the "Administration's demonization of coal" and claimed that the EPA was attempting to "regulate coal into extinction." According to Manchin, "because of unattainable and unreasonable regulations, thousands of coal miners have been laid off in West Virginia alone, and more than 26 coal companies have filed for bankruptcy"[67] (apparently ignoring that the Clean Power Plan would not, under its own terms, become effective until five years later). Congressman Evan Jenkins – who would later run for the US Senate against Manchin but lose to Morrisey in the Republican primary – described the Clean Power Plan as the "continuation of this administration's anti-coal, anti-West Virginia policies," and claimed that "[i]f this administration had its way, no coal would be mined in West Virginia, no miners would be employed, and no coal would be used for generating electricity."[68] Representative David McKinley, for his part, tweeted a video from April 2015, in which he questioned whether current climate change was a result of natural cycles or influence by humans.

At the state level, Governor Tomblin described the Clean Power Plan as "unreasonable, unrealistic and ultimately unattainable for our state."[69] Attorney General Morrisey tweeted that "Pres. Obama is trying to convert EPA from an environmental regulator to a national, central energy planner. Fortunately, the law forbids it."[70] House of Representatives Speaker Tim Armstead described the Clean Power Plan as "the latest step in the Obama administration's pledge to bankrupt the coal industry," while Senate President Bill Cole – who would go on to lose to Jim Justice in the 2016 race for Governor, when Justice ran as a Democrat – vowed that "the Legislature

---

[64] *Senators Capito, Manchin Introduce Legislation to Roll Back EPA's Clean Power Plan*, Count On Coal (May 14, 2015), http://www.countoncoal.org/2015/05/senators-capito-manchin-introduce-legislation-to-roll-back-epas-clean-power-plan/.

[65] Chris Mooney, *Amid Record Global Temperatures, Senate Votes to Block Obama's Clean Power Plan*, Washington Post (Nov, 17, 2015), https://www.washingtonpost.com/news/energy-environment/wp/2015/11/17/amid-record-global-temperatures-congress-to-vote-to-stop-obamas-clean-power-plan/.

[66] *Id.*

[67] *Tomblin, Manchin Both Criticize Clean Power Ruling*, WV Metro News (Aug. 3, 2015), https://wvmetronews.com/2015/08/03/tomblin-manchin-both-criticize-clean-power-ruling/.

[68] Associated Press, *Reactions to Obama's new power plant regulations*, Herald- Dispatch (Aug. 4, 2015), https://www.herald-dispatch.com/news/recent_news/reactions-to-obamas-new-power-plant-regulations/article_7afe3913-75ce-564e-acb4-f6d7194e1f0d.html.

[69] *Id.*

[70] Patrick Morrisey (@MorriseyWV), Twitter (Aug. 3, 2015, 9:46 PM), https://twitter.com/MorriseyWV/status/628305928115367936?ref_src=twsrc%5Etfw.

absolutely will not approve any State Implementation Plan that will cause more harm, and bring more job losses, to our state's coal industry."[71] He cited the enactment of House Bill 2004, which he claimed would provide "an additional layer of protection against the relentless attacks on West Virginia's coal fields."[72]

While the emissions targets established for West Virginia by the EPA under the Clean Power Plan seemed to be ambitious – a 37 percent reduction in the emissions rate and a 29 percent reduction under a mass-based standard – the regulation did not, in fact, warrant the widespread "sky is falling" response from politicians throughout West Virginia. Two separate studies – the feasibility study by the DEP required under HB 2004[73] and an independent study conducted by the Center for Energy and Sustainable Development at West Virginia University College of Law, and Downstream Strategies, an environmental consulting firm in Morgantown[74] – identified compliance strategies that demonstrated how West Virginia could achieve the required emissions reductions in a relatively painless manner that would actually produce positive results for the state in terms of job creation in the emerging clean energy sector.

To its credit, the Clean Power Plan afforded the states considerable flexibility in charting a path to achieve compliance. It featured three "building blocks" that could be employed by states in their implementation plans. The first block – and the least controversial – was achieving emissions reductions at coal plants through increasing their efficiency, by investing in equipment that would lower their heat rate (and thereby reduce the waste associated with converting coal to electricity). This was

---

[71] Jeremiah Shelor, *State officials React as Obama Announces Finalized EPA CO2 Rule*, EXPONENT-TELEGRAM (Aug. 3, 2015), https://www.wvnews.com/theet/news/local/state-officials-react-as-obama-announces-finalized-epa-co2-rule/article_8of710a9-9955-5615-9c5e-a5fbc014d6cf.html.

[72] Dave Mistrich & Ashton Marra, *West Virginia Officials Respond to Final Rule of Clean Power Plan*, WV PUBLIC BROADCASTING (Aug. 3, 2015), https://www.wvpublic.org/news/2015-08-03/west-virginia-officials-respond-to-final-rule-of-clean-power-plan. In 2015, the state legislature had passed House Bill 2004 in which the legislature seized a leading role in defining how West Virginia would comply with the Clean Power Plan – rather than leaving it in the hands of the state's air pollution agency, the Department of Environmental Protection (DEP) – and, in a classic move of cutting off the nose to spite the face, expressly prohibited the DEP from exercising the flexibility that states were given under the Clean Power Plan to achieve compliance. The measure also required the DEP to submit a study to the legislature reporting on whether a state plan implementing the Clean Power Plan would be feasible. Finally, HB 2004 prohibited the DEP from filing such a plan with the EPA without the express consent of the majority of both houses of the legislature, thereby interjecting the legislature directly within the previously uncontroversial process of "cooperative federalism" under which state environmental agencies routinely work with the EPA to administer the Clean Air Act and the Clean Water Act.

[73] West Virginia Department of Environmental Protection, *Feasibility Report for a State Plan Under EPA's Clean Air Act Section 111(d) Rule Regulating Carbon Dioxide Emissions from Existing Fossil Fuel-Fired Electric Generating Units* (Apr. 20, 2016), https://dep.wv.gov/pio/Documents/WVDEP%20Feasbility%20Report%204%2020%202016.pdf.

[74] James M. Van Nostrand, Evan Hansen & Joseph James, *Expanding Economic Opportunities for West Virginia under the Clean Power Plan*, WVU COLLEGE OF LAW CENTER FOR ENERGY AND SUSTAINABLE DEVELOPMENT (July 2016), https://energy.law.wvu.edu/files/d/585cffce-0aea-4535-84d0-7344591cfbb8/cpp-phase-ii-final.pdf.

referred to as an "inside-the-fence" measure, inasmuch as the action would be taken at individual coal plants, at the source of the emissions. The other two building blocks, in contrast, were "outside-the-fence" measures and required utilities to reduce their CO_2 emissions by displacing coal-fired generation with natural gas-fired generation (building block #2) or renewable sources (building block #3). These second and third building blocks were referred to as "generation shifting" because the reductions would occur through shifting the source of power generation from higher-emission power plants to less polluting sources of energy. These "outside-the-fence" measures – arguably putting the EPA in the role of dictating resource portfolio decisions by electric utilities (or, as Morrisey described it, "convert[ing] EPA from an environmental regulator to a national, central energy planner")[75] – engendered strong legal opposition from the coal industry and coal-dependent states.

There is no question that the Obama administration's interpretation of a previously obscure provision of the Clean Air Act – Section 111(d) – was an aggressive one: essentially that, in determining the "best system of emissions reduction" (BSER) under the Clean Air Act, the EPA could implicitly dictate the decarbonization of electric utilities' resource portfolios through the substitution of natural gas and renewable sources for coal. (As it would turn out, however, the Obama administration's interpretation would ultimately be upheld several years later, in the DC Circuit Court's decision invalidating the Trump administration's successor regulation, the Affordable Clean Energy rule.)[76]

At the same time, the process of determining a strategy for achieving compliance with the Clean Power Plan stimulated a productive analysis in West Virginia. It required, for example, the energy regulator (the Public Service Commission, PSC) to coordinate with the environmental regulator (the DEP) in that whatever resource acquisition strategy was pursued in accordance with the state's implementation plan would need to be approved by the PSC, inasmuch as any compliance costs incurred by utilities would need to be recovered in rates through electric rate cases at the PSC. Any driver for diversifying the state's energy portfolio away from coal was a good thing for ratepayers, inasmuch as the "doubling down on coal" by the state's utilities during the preceding years was driving up utility rates.

That the driver was coming from the federal government, of course, and "Obama's job-killing EPA" in particular, was wildly unpopular. In any event, federal policies were stimulating the sort of discussions about the state's energy future that state leaders were too cowardly to initiate. Rather than leading serious conversations about the inevitable energy transition that was underway and the actions that West Virginia could take to position itself for the economy of the future, the contest in

---

[75] Morrisey, *supra* note 70.
[76] American Lung Association v. EPA, 985 F.3d 914 (D.C. Cir. 2021).

West Virginia was about who was the strongest advocate for the coal industry and who could demonstrate the strongest anti-EPA credentials.

In this contest, one politician probably rode it harder than anyone else: Patrick Morrisey, the Attorney General. Morrisey is a New Jersey native who moved to Harpers Ferry in 2006 and, four days after he received his license to practice law in West Virginia in 2012, he announced his candidacy to unseat Democrat Darrell McGraw, a twenty-year incumbent.[77] In a major upset, he ended up defeating McGraw by 16,000 votes in November 2012, becoming the first Republican Attorney General since 1933. Although he had never argued in a courtroom before (as far as anyone knew), Morrisey took office two months later as "the people's lawyer," charged with protecting West Virginians.

Morrisey would ultimately lead the charge of the coal-dependent states against the Clean Power Plan. This was just the sort of high-profile litigation that would allow him to shed the "carpetbagger from New Jersey" tag and earn his stripes among the coal miners and their supporters in West Virginia. Upon his election, Morrisey had elevated the talent level of the personnel in his office to pursue appellate litigation, including hiring two appellate lawyers with Supreme Court experience and Federalist Society credentials: Elbert Lin, a Yale Law graduate who had clerked for Justice Clarence Thomas,[78] and Misha Tseytlin, a Georgetown law graduate who had clerked for Justice Kennedy on the US Supreme Court and was a frequent speaker for the Federalist Society.[79] Lin, as Solicitor General for four-and-a-half years, led the efforts of the Attorney General's office in challenging the Clean Power Plan.[80] Tseytlin, served as general counsel to Morrisey, and would later play a prominent role in the oral argument at the D.C. Circuit Court of Appeals in West Virginia's challenge to the Clean Power Plan.[81] In addition to hiring highly credentialed lawyers, Morrisey seemed to have his eye on using the office to position himself for the next step in his political career. In September 2015, as the litigation regarding the Clean Power Plan was heating up, Morrisey hired a veteran political strategist, Lance James Henderson, as deputy chief of staff (even though Henderson had never practiced law) at a salary of $99,500, to be paid out of Morrisey's consumer protection fund. Henderson's previous experience? In 2014, he worked

[77] Eric Eyre, Death in Mud Lick: A Coal Country Fight against the Drug Companies that Delivered the Opioid Epidemic, 64 (2020).

[78] *Lin Starts Job as Solicitor General*, Wheeling Intelligencer (June 25, 2013), https://www.theintelligencer.net/news/community/2013/06/lin-starts-job-as-solicitor-general/.

[79] Jessica Karmasek, *General Counsel for W.Va. AG to Serve as Wisconsin's First Solicitor General*, Legal Newsline (Oct. 14, 2015), https://legalnewsline.com/stories/510642910-general-counsel-for-w-va-ag-to-serve-as-wisconsin-s-first-solicitor-general.

[80] Eric Eyre, *WV AG Morrisey's Solicitor General Lin to Resign*, Charleston Gazette-Mail (Aug. 17, 2017), https://www.wvgazettemail.com/news/politics/wv-ag-morrisey-s-solicitor-general-lin-to-resign/article_f4cd7af8-be56-516e-9d3c-1bf6107f588f.html.

[81] Maxine Joselow, *Lawyer who fought Clean Power Plan on ACE 'battle royal,'* Greenwire, June 14, 2019, https://www.eenews.net/articles/lawyer-who-fought-clean-power-plan-on-ace-battle-royal/.

for Maine Governor Paul LePage's reelection campaign, and for the previous twenty-five years was a consultant to politicians on field operations and building voter databases. Eric Eyre of the *Gazette-Mail* first reported the hire in October 2015 and, when newspapers and television and radio stations across the state picked up the article, Henderson resigned two days later.[82]

Morrisey was so eager to challenge the Clean Power Plan in court that he, along with Bob Murray of Murray Energy, sued the EPA just for issuing a *proposed* rule, long before the EPA finalized the Clean Power Plan in August 2015. Writing for a three-judge panel at the US Circuit Court of Appeals for the District of Columbia, then Circuit Court Judge Brett Kavanaugh said that legal challenges to the EPA rule were premature because the rule had not yet been finalized. According to Kavanaugh's opinion:

> Petitioners are champing at the bit to challenge EPA's anticipated rule restricting carbon dioxide emissions from existing power plants. But EPA has not yet issued a final rule. It has only issued a proposed rule. Petitioners nonetheless ask the court to jump into the fray now. They want us to do something that they candidly acknowledge we have never done before: review the legality of a proposed rule.[83]

Morrisey (and the eleven other states that joined the suit) and Murray Energy would have to wait until EPA finalized the rule – which occurred two months later, in early August 2015 – before challenging it in court.

Notwithstanding this ignominious start, Morrisey proved to be quite adept in organizing the Attorneys General from the coal-dependent states (and other Republican Attorneys General), ultimately including twenty-four states in his later challenge to the Clean Power Plan, *West Virginia* v. *EPA*, which was filed shortly after the rule was published in October 2015. According to Morrisey's statement at the time, "The Clean Power Plan is one of the most far-reaching energy regulations in this nation's history. I have a responsibility to protect the lives of millions of working families, the elderly and the poor, from such illegal and unconscionable federal government actions."[84]

Morrisey's legal challenge focused on four main issues:

(1) the EPA's attempt to regulate "outside-the-fence" activities of utilities (i.e., requiring them to reduce coal-fired generation in favor of natural gas-fired and renewable resources), which arguably was beyond its statutory authority to regulate individual sources under the Clean Air Act;

---

[82] Eric Eyre, *Political Strategist Hired by Attorney General as Deputy Chief of Staff Resigns*, CHARLESTON GAZETTE-MAIL (Oct. 21, 2015), https://www.wvgazettemail.com/news/politics/political-strategist-hired-by-attorney-general-as-deputy-chief-of-staff-resigns/article_ff963232-aefe-580b-906d-c2dd9f0347d1.html.

[83] *In re Murray Energy Corporation*, U.S. Circuit Court of Appeals for District of Columbia, Case No. 14–1112, June 9, 2015.

[84] Associated Press, *States, Industry Groups Sue to Block Obama's "Clean Power" Plan*, NBC NEWS (Oct. 23, 2015), https://www.nbcnews.com/business/energy/states-industry-groups-sue-block-obamas-clean-power-plan-n450216.

(2) a technical conflict between the House-passed version of the 1990 Clean Air Act Amendments and the Senate version, which arguably precluded EPA from regulating CO_2 from power plants under Section 111(d) of the Clean Air Act because the agency was already regulating hazardous air emissions from power plants under Section 112 of that law;

(3) constitutional issues based on the claim that the EPA was meddling in state regulatory programs and thereby violating principles of federalism;

(4) procedural issues under the Administrative Procedure Act inasmuch as the final rule adopted by the EPA in August 2015 was materially different from the proposed rule issued in June 2014, thereby requiring the EPA to solicit and analyze an additional round of comments before issuing a final rule.

Apart from all the political rhetoric lobbed against the Clean Power Plan by Morrisey, the legal case against it seemed, on its face, to be fairly strong. As part of his legal strategy, Morrisey filed a request with the DC Circuit Court of Appeals to issue a stay of the Plan's implementation (in other words, suspend EPA actions to begin implementing the rule), which was denied by the Court on January 16, 2016. What happened next was quite unexpected: the issuance of a stay by the US Supreme Court three weeks later, on February 9, 2016, to keep the Clean Power Plan on hold through review at the DC Circuit and through review at the Supreme Court (if it was appealed and accepted), the first time in history that the Supreme Court ever stayed a rule before any court ruled on the merits. One of the elements in obtaining a stay is "likelihood of success on the merits,"[85] so this ruling was a warning sign to the EPA that its Clean Power Plan might not be on solid legal footing. As described earlier, it is also worth noting that Justice Scalia – who provided the fifth and deciding vote in granting the stay – had authored the decision in *Michigan* v. *EPA* several months earlier to invalidate the EPA's MATS rule, which was unfortunately too late to prevent 20 GW of coal-fired generation from shutting down as the MATS rule took effect.

On September 27, 2016, the US Court of Appeals for the DC Circuit, sitting *en banc* with ten judges participating, heard oral argument in *West Virginia* v. *EPA*. The argument lasted seven hours and examined the constitutional, statutory, and procedural arguments described above regarding the validity of the Clean Power Plan.[86] Elbert Lin, as West Virginia's Solicitor General, took the lead in arguing the case on behalf of West Virginia and the other twenty-four states. We'll never know how the court would have ruled, however, because Donald J. Trump was elected President six weeks later and the Clean Power Plan was effectively dead. In his Executive Order on Promoting Energy Independence and Economic Growth

---

[85] Winter v. Nat. Res. Def. Council, Inc., 555 U.S. 7 (2008).

[86] Jonathan Adler, *The en Banc D.C. Circuit Meets the Clean Power Plan*, WASH. POST (Sept. 28, 2016), https://www.washingtonpost.com/news/volokh-conspiracy/wp/2016/09/28/the-en-banc-d-c-circuit-meets-the-clean-power-plan/.

issued on March 28, 2017, Trump directed the EPA to review and "if appropriate . . . publish for notice and comment proposed rules suspending, revising, or rescinding" the Clean Power Plan. That same day, the EPA asked the DC Circuit to halt deliberations while it reviewed the rule, and the court never issued an opinion regarding the legality of the Clean Power Plan.

The Trump EPA thereafter embarked on a rulemaking process to repeal the Clean Power Plan, and held hearings on the repeal proposal at the state capitol building in Charleston on November 28 and 29, 2017. More than 200 people showed up for the first of two days of testimony, and Morrisey opened the hearing as the first speaker. Another witness of note was Murray Energy CEO Bob Murray, the owner of West Virginia's largest coal producer, a staunch industry advocate and a major supporter of Trump. He referred to the Clean Power Plan as part of a "regulatory rampage" by the Obama administration, and said he was grateful the country "finally has a president who has vowed to protect coal jobs." About twenty-five Murray Energy employees, wearing their work clothes and miner caps, stood and greeted Murray when he entered the room just prior to the hearing. "God bless President Trump and you coal miners," Murray said, "I love you fellas."[87]

In August 2018, the Trump administration released its proposed replacement of the Clean Power Plan, the Affordable Clean Energy rule, or ACE. While the rule technically continued to regulate CO_2 emissions from coal plants, it ceased to regulate activity "outside the fence" (or generation-shifting strategies) and limited the scope of the rule to "inside-the-fence" measures. In fact, the EPA took the position that it felt itself statutorily compelled to repeal the Clean Power Plan because, in its view, "the plain meaning" of Section 111(d) of the Clean Air Act "unambiguously" limits the best system of emission reduction to only those measures "that can be put into operation at a building, structure, facility, or installation," and thus the EPA lacked the statutory authority to require the generation-shifting strategies of the second and third building blocks of the Clean Power Plan. The EPA's proposed system under ACE relied solely on heat-rate improvement technologies and practices that could be applied at and to existing coal-fired power plants, and it offered a list of candidate technologies for power plant efficiency measures that states could use when developing their individual implementation plans. In contrast to the 32 percent reduction in CO_2 emissions projected to be achieved under the Clean Power Plan, the ACE rule would achieve reductions of less than 1 percent from baseline emission projections by 2035.

The ACE rule was published in the Federal Register on July 8, 2019, and faced challenges in the DC Circuit Court of Appeals from two public health organizations (American Lung Association and American Public Health Association), twenty-two

---

[87] Ken Ward, Jr., *EPA Greenhouse Gas Rule Hearing in WV Draws Supporters, Opponents*, CHARLESTON GAZETTE-MAIL (Nov. 28, 2017), https://www.wvgazettemail.com/news/epa-greenhouse-gas-rule-hearing-in-wv-draws-supporters-opponents/article_5463c2ad-abb6-5e12-b265-7d95f699a34f.html.

states, seven cities, and ten environmental organizations. Following over nine hours of oral argument in October 2020, the DC Circuit issued its ruling on January 21, 2021 striking down the ACE rule and remanding it to the agency.[88] Of relevance to the Clean Power Plan, the decision firmly rejected the arguments made by Morrisey in *West Virginia v. EPA* regarding the EPA's authority under the Clean Air Act. Put simply, the EPA was plainly wrong when it repealed the Clean Power Plan based on its flawed reading of Section 111(d) as not authorizing the generation-shifting strategies contemplated by building blocks #2 and #3 of the Clean Power Plan. In addition to criticizing "EPA's tortured series of misreadings" of Section 111(d), the court cited the record before it, which showed that "generation shifting to prioritize use of the cleanest sources of power is one of the most cost-effective means of reducing emissions that plants have already adopted and that have been demonstrated to work, and that generation shifting is capable of achieving far more emission reduction than controls physically confined to the source."[89] The EPA's interpretation of the statute would thus "require the Agency to turn its back on major elements of the systems that the power sector is actually and successfully using to efficiently and cost-effectively achieve the greatest emission reductions."[90] The court acknowledged that while "[p]olicy priorities may change from one administration to the next, [ ] statutory text changes only when it is amended."[91]

The court also rejected arguments made by the coal industry (and also argued by Morrisey in *West Virginia* v. *EPA*) based on the inconsistency between House of Representative and Senate amendments when they adopted the 1990 Amendments to Section 112 of the Clean Air Act. According to the court's opinion: "At bottom, when confronted with two competing and duly enacted statutory provisions, a court's job is not to pick a winner and a loser. The judicial duty is to read statutory text as a harmonized whole, not to foment irreconcilability."[92] Finally, the constitutional arguments against the Clean Power Plan raised by Morrisey were rejected as well, in a ruling that the federalism doctrine does not support the EPA's "cramped reading" of Section 111(d). According to the court, "[i]nterstate air pollution is not an area of traditional state regulation," nor do "federalism concerns . . . bar the United States government from addressing areas of federal concern just because its actions have incidental effects on areas of state power."[93]

Long before the appellate court's firm rejection of his arguments, however, Morrisey was able to ride his advocacy for the coal industry to win the Republican nomination for the US Senate in 2018 – beating Congressman Evan Jenkins and former Massey CEO Don Blankenship in the Republican Party primary. Prior to the

---

[88] American Lung Association v. EPA, D.C. Circuit Court of Appeals, Case No. 19–1140, issued Jan. 19, 2021, slip opinion at 129.

[89] *Id.* at 47.

[90] *Id.*

[91] *Id.* at 59.

[92] *Id.* at 129.

[93] *Id.* at 93.

general election, he picked up the support from President Trump in a couple of tweets prior to Trump's appearance in Charleston for a Morrisey rally in August 2018:

> Big Rally tonight in West Virginia. Patrick Morrisey is running a GREAT race for U.S. Senate. I have done so much for West Virginia, against all odds, and having Patrick, a real fighter, by my side, would make things so much easier. See you later. CLEAN COAL!!!! Donald J. Trump (@realDonaldTrump) August 21, 2018

> Will be going to the Great State of West Virginia on Tuesday Night to campaign & do a Rally Speech for a hardworking and spectacular person, A.G. Patrick Morrisey, who is running for the U.S. Senate. Patrick has great Energy & Stamina – I need his VOTE to MAGA. Total Endorsement!
> Donald J. Trump (@realDonaldTrump) August 21, 2018[94]

Morrisey also picked up the endorsement of the West Virginia Coal Association whose president, Bill Raney, described him as a "tireless advocate" for the state's coal industry; the Coal Association had supported Manchin in his previous US Senate race in 2012.

However, Morrisey was rejected by West Virginia voters in his bid for federal office, losing by 19,000 votes to Joe Manchin in the general election. Two years later, it appeared that his arguments against the Clean Power Plan fared no better when the appellate courts finally had a chance to address them.

Morrisey may have the last laugh, however. Following the DC Circuit's adverse decision in the *American Lung Association* case in January 2021 he took the seemingly quixotic step three months later to lead the coal states in seeking review of the decision by the US Supreme Court. The thinking among legal pundits was that there was no way the Supreme Court would agree to hear the case. After all, a newly elected Democratic President, Joe Biden, had no interest in defending the Trump administration's weak Affordable Clean Energy rule.[95] Nor did the Biden administration have any interest in resurrecting the Obama administration's Clean Power Plan, even though the DC Circuit in *American Lung Association* had confirmed that the EPA's legal analysis underlying the Clean Power Plan was correct; the Biden administration had its sights set on more robust targets for GHG reductions than articulated in the Clean Power Plan and was charting a different approach.[96] In legal parlance, there was no "case or controversy" that would justify the Supreme Court making a ruling on the scope of the EPA's authority to regulate GHG emissions

94   *Trump Touts Coal, Morrisey Ahead of Charleston Rally*, WV Metro News (Aug. 21, 2018), https://wvmetronews.com/2018/08/21/trump-expected-to-tout-coal-morrisey-at-charleston-rally/.

95   Jonathan H. Adler, *Could the Supreme Court Revive the Trump Administration's ACE Rule?*, Reason (Oct. 7, 2021), https://reason.com/volokh/2021/10/07/could-the-supreme-court-revive-the-trump-administrations-ace-rule/.

96   Jonathan H. Adler, *Supreme Court Agrees to Hear Case Challenging EPA Authority to Regulate Greenhouse Gases (Updated)*, Reason (Oct. 29, 2021), https://reason.com/volokh/2021/10/29/supreme-court-agrees-to-hear-case-challenging-epa-authority-to-regulate-greenhouse-gases/.

under the Clean Air Act, and the Supreme Court is not in the business of issuing "advisory opinions."

But larger issues were at play at the Supreme Court. First, Brett Kavanaugh had been "promoted" from the DC Circuit Court of Appeals to be an Associate Justice on the US Supreme Court. Prior to his elevation, then Judge Kavanaugh had been very active in the questioning of EPA lawyers who defended the Clean Power Plan in the September 2016 oral arguments at the DC Circuit Court of Appeals. He was clearly hostile to EPA's position that a relatively obscure provision in the Clean Air Act – Section 111(d) – could be used as the basis for comprehensive regulation of GHG emissions in the electric utility industry, as contemplated by the Clean Power Plan.[97] Rather, given the "vast economic or political significance" of GHG regulation, the scope of the regulation was a "major question" that required express statutory authority from Congress. The "major questions" doctrine represents an exception to the broad deference that is virtually always granted to agencies in judicial review of agency action. Under *"Chevron"* deference – based on the 1984 Supreme Court decision in *Chevron* v. *NRDC*[98] – administrative agencies are granted considerable deference in their interpretation of statutes. So long as the agency's interpretation is a "reasonable" one, a reviewing court will generally defer to the agency's expertise and not substitute its judgment for that of the agency. This approach is justified in part by a "gap-filling" function assigned to the agency whereby Congress does not delve into the details in enacting the statute, but rather leaves it up to the agency, exercising its specialized expertise, to interpret and apply it.

The Clean Power Plan would survive judicial review under *Chevron* deference, and the DC Circuit Court of Appeals said as much in its decision in *American Lung Association* when it discussed the EPA's authority under the Clean Air Act in the context of the Affordable Clean Energy rule. Under the "major questions" doctrine, however, a reviewing court cannot be expected to defer to the agency's interpretation of its authority under a particular statute, and the court takes a much closer look to see if Congress expressly authorized such a wide-ranging exercise of administrative action. With Morrisey's petition for *certiorari* in *West Virginia* v. *EPA* to seek Supreme Court review of the DC Circuit decision in *American Lung Association*, Kavanaugh had an opportunity to impose his view on a larger stage that the EPA's authority to regulate GHG emissions was much narrower than claimed by the agency.

Second, Kavanaugh had allies on the Supreme Court, with Justices Neil Gorsuch, Samuel Alito, and Clarence Thomas having expressed strong reservations in the past about the amount of deference accorded to administrative agencies under *Chevron*, and a perceived need to reign in the "regulatory state" by limiting agency authority to enact sweeping regulations in the absence of a clear showing of

---

[97] Pamela King, *Should Kavanaugh Bow Out of Blockbuster SCOTUS Climate Case?* GREENWIRE (Feb. 2, 2022), https://www.eenews.net/articles/should-kavanaugh-bow-out-of-blockbuster-scotus-climate-case/.

[98] *Chevron U.S.A.Inc. v. Natural Resources Defense Council, Inc.*, 467 U.S. 837 (1984).

Congressional intent authorizing it.[99] In an indication that the Supreme Court may use *West Virginia* v. *EPA* as the vehicle for curtailing the EPA's authority to regulate GHG emissions, on October 29, 2021 the Supreme Court surprisingly granted Morrisey's petition for *certiorari* and agreed to hear the case, with oral argument scheduled for February 28, 2022. It is noteworthy that the "major questions" doctrine was used to strike down the Biden administration's use of a regulation promulgated by the Occupational Safety and Health Administration (OSHA) to impose a vaccine mandate for much of the country's workforce in a 6-3 decision by the Supreme Court.[100]

So the stars may be aligned for Morrisey to prevail at the Supreme Court in what would be seen as a major victory for the coal industry in rolling back the authority of the EPA to broadly regulate GHG emissions under the Clean Air Act. In reality, however, such an outcome would have virtually no impact on the prospects for the coal industry going forward. In fact, the EPA could be completely stripped of its authority to regulate GHGs under the Clean Air Act – which would require reversal of *Massachusetts* v. *EPA*, and that is unlikely – and it would not result in any electric utility in the United States building another coal plant. As explained in Chapters 2 and 3, coal ceases to be a cost-effective means of generating electricity, and EPA regulation of GHG emissions has very little to do with it. So a win in this case would do nothing more than cruelly raise the hopes of coal miners in West Virginia – fueled by Morrisey's self-congratulatory press releases as he lays the foundation to run for the US Senate or Governor in 2024. Once again, it won't make any difference, much like the election of Donald Trump as president and the rollback of environmental of EPA regulations during the Trump administration did nothing to "bring the coal jobs back." But reality will get lost in the propaganda machine of the West Virginia Coal Association and the public affairs section of the West Virginia Attorney General's office.

---

[99] David M. Driesen, *Major Questions and Juristocracy*, Regulatory Review (Jan. 31, 2022), https://www.theregreview.org/2022/01/31/driesen-major-questions-juristocracy/.

[100] *National Federation of Independent Business v. Department of Labor, Occupational Safety & Health Administration*, 595 U.S. – (2022), Nos. 21A244 and 21A247 (Jan. 13, 2022).

2

The Shale Gas Revolution

Beginning in 2007, shale gas development began to expand in a big way in West Virginia, due to advancements in hydraulic fracturing and horizontal drilling. As it turned out, parts of West Virginia are located atop what is now the nation's largest shale gas play, the Marcellus. Shale gas development has often been referred to as a "game changer" in the domestic energy industry, particularly as making natural gas the fuel of choice for generating electricity at baseload power plants (i.e., generating plants that are the cheapest and generally run around the clock). Within six years, natural gas would surpass coal as the leading source of fuel for electricity generation, due to its lower cost and the high efficiency of new natural gas fired combined cycle combustion turbines, especially compared with the economics of the region's aging fleet of coal plants, many of which were over forty years old. In the later years of "the lost decade," renewable sources of electricity – both wind and solar – would also contribute to the demise of coal in the region, as utilities across the country uniformly declined to consider breaking ground on new coal plants and, in fact, began to retire existing ones in favor of cheaper, cleaner renewable sources. Continuing down the coal path simply could not be justified as a matter of economics, even without considering the adverse environmental impacts associated with virtually every stage of the extraction, processing, and combustion of coal to generate electricity.

The technological breakthrough known as "fracking" had huge implications for the coal industry in West Virginia, and these implications were quite apparent by the start of "the lost decade." In fact, shale gas development was probably the largest single force leading to the demise of the coal industry, as utilities began converting some of their coal plants to burn natural gas, or retiring them entirely. Moreover, cheap and plentiful natural gas and the efficiency of natural gas generating units began to drive down prices in wholesale electricity markets, pushing coal plants "out of the money." As coal plants proved to be an uncompetitive means of generating electricity, West Virginia's two major utilities (FirstEnergy and AEP) would quickly take action to exit from the competitive generation business entirely and foist their money-losing coal plants on the backs of West Virginia ratepayers, as discussed in Chapter 10. Instead of acknowledging the overwhelming market forces that began to take aim at the coal industry, however, political leaders in West Virginia continued their narrative of the "war on coal" and Obama's job-killing Environmental Protection Agency (EPA) as the source of the woes in the coal industry.

After briefly describing fracking technology, this chapter will examine what was known at the start of "the lost decade" about the likely impact of the shale gas revolution on the coal industry in West Virginia. Why look at what was known at the start of "the lost decade"? In the esoteric world of utility regulation, there is a concept of "prudence" which precludes a utility from recovering through retail rates expenses that were imprudently incurred. In making this prudence determination, utility regulators evaluate the wisdom of utility decisions based on what utility management knew or should have known at the time they made their decisions. Utility actions – particularly resource acquisitions, such as undertaking to build a nuclear plant in the 1980s that ended up being woefully behind schedule and over budget, potentially resulting in its cancellation – are often challenged as being imprudent, with the potential consequence that the utility will be precluded from recovering the costs in rates, and thus the losses are borne by shareholders. In applying this standard, utility regulators are admonished to avoid decisions based on "20/20 hindsight" – in other words, to avoid holding utility management responsible for things that might have turned out badly but were not apparent at the time. In a similar vein, is it fair to hold political leaders in West Virginia accountable at the outset of "the lost decade" for failing to anticipate the impact that the shale gas revolution would have on the coal industry? As described in this chapter, there was overwhelming evidence at the time about the extent to which the shale revolution was going to be a "game changer" – in a bad way for coal – in the energy industry.

WHAT IS THIS THING CALLED "FRACKING"?

The idea of "fracking" – using explosives to extract more oil or natural gas from wells – dates back to the 1860s, when Colonel Edward A. L. Roberts took his experience from the Civil War's Battle of Fredericksburg and designed an "exploding torpedo" that could be lowered into an oil well and detonated to shatter surrounding rock.[1] This was followed by pumping water into the well, which would stimulate additional oil flows, in some cases by as much as 1,200 percent. Fracking was thus established as a means of increasing a well's productive potential. This evolved into "hydraulic" fracturing in the 1940s when explosives were replaced with high-pressure blasts of liquids.

In the early years of the twenty-first century, two key developments spurred the widespread use of fracking and produced the "shale revolution." One was the use of

---

[1]   B.A. Wells & K.L. Wells, *Shooters – A "Fracking" History*, American Oil & Gas Historical Society (Sept. 25, 2021), https://www.aoghs.org/technology/hydraulic-fracturing/.

industry-developed slickwater mixtures used as fracking fluid, which commonly consists of about 97 percent water, chemical additives, and proppants (or small, solid particles of sand used to keep the fractures in the rock formation open after the pressure from injection subsides). The second innovation was the use of horizontal drilling, which increases the production of each well by enabling more of the rock formation that contains the oil and gas to be traversed. Once a long vertical well is drilled about a mile or more into the earth, drilling then gradually turns horizontal and extends as far as thousands of feet. (The depth of the vertical wells varies across the various shale plays around the United States; within the Marcellus shale, the depth is typically 5,000 to 8,000 feet before the drilling turns from vertical to horizontal.) After the well is drilled, steel pipes called casings are inserted into it, and the space between the rock and the casing is fully or partially filled with cement. Small holes are made in the casing with a perforating gun, or the well is constructed with pre-perforated pipe. Fracking fluid is then pumped in at a pressure high enough to create new fractures or open existing ones in the surrounding rock.

It takes massive amounts of water to frack a well – anywhere between 1.5 million and 16 million gallons, according to the United States Geological Survey (USGS), depending on the type of well and rock formation. Within the Marcellus shale play, it typically takes about 5 million gallons of water to frack a well. Water used for hydraulic fracturing is typically fresh water taken from groundwater and surface water resources.

Once the factures are created in the rock, the oil or gas will flow to the surface for gathering, processing, and transportation. The contaminated wastewater also flows back to the surface, and is stored in nearby pits and tanks and subsequently recycled or disposed of in underground wells. This wastewater consists of a potentially hazardous mixture of flowback (used fracking fluid), produced water (naturally occurring water that is released with the oil and gas), and any number of other naturally occurring contaminants ranging from heavy metals, salts, and toxic hydro-carbons like benzene, to radioactive materials such as uranium.

FRACKING SCALES UP IN THE MARCELLUS

The shale revolution was entirely unanticipated at the turn of the twenty-first century. In the 2004 edition of the US Energy Information Administration's *Annual Energy Outlook*, for example, the forecast for the nation's natural gas industry did not look promising. Sustained high prices in the early half of the decade prompted the agency to change its long-term forecast for the industry, predicting slower growth for domestic production and much stronger reliance on higher-priced, remote resources in Alaska and Canada's Mackenzie Delta to meet US demand.[2] Several liquefied natural gas (LNG) facilities were in various stages of obtaining licenses and permits, and they

---

[2] ENERGY INFORMATION ADMINISTRATION, ANNUAL ENERGY OUTLOOK 2004 (Jan. 2004), https://www.nrc.gov/docs/ML0931/ML093160831.pdf.

were all designed to *import* natural gas from foreign sources, to supplement the declining US supply of natural gas. (Within ten years, most of those applications for LNG facilities would literally reverse course, to become *export* facilities.) In the entire 278-page *Annual Energy Outlook 2004* there is no reference to Marcellus.

In October 2004, the first productive Marcellus well – the Renz 1 well – was drilled by Range Resources in western Pennsylvania, using the sand-light, gel-light, fracking fluid mixture that had been shown to be successful in completing wells in the Barnett shale play near Fort Worth, Texas beginning in the late 1990s.[3] Drilling activity in both West Virginia and Pennsylvania ramped up quickly over the next five years. While West Virginia had issued only a few dozen total horizontal well permits as of 2006, by the end of 2007 the figure stood at 181 wells, with another 297 drilled in 2008 and 411 in 2009. By the end of 2019, the figure would stand at over 5,000, according to West Virginia's Department of Environmental Protection (DEP).[4]

At the start of "the lost decade," both West Virginia and the region were all abuzz about the impact the Marcellus Shale play could have on the economic prospects for the region. In November 2011, Senator Joe Manchin took the opportunity to convene his first ever field hearing of the Senate Energy and Natural Resources Committee in East Charleston, describing it as "an opportunity for West Virginia to demonstrate our unique position of strength in the energy industry, as we are literally sitting on top of the tremendous potential of the Marcellus Shale," and giving the state "a great opportunity to do two critical things at once: create jobs both now and into the future, and advance our goal of achieving energy independence within this generation."[5] His opening remarks at the hearing, where he referred to the Marcellus Shale as "truly a game-changer for our great state," cited a report by the National Energy Technology Laboratory which projected that developing shale gas in West Virginia would result in 17,000 additional jobs, $870 million generated from state and local taxes, and $1.3 billion in direct payments to households through royalties and industry payroll. And there was the prospect of developing the downstream petrochemical industry, where just one cracker plant – to convert ethane into ethylene, the feedstock for the chemical industry – would create 2,300 direct jobs and $1.5 to $2 billion in direct investment.[6] Then Congresswoman Shelley Moore

---

[3] *Range Resources Responds to Magnum Hunter's Marcellus Claim*, Hart Energy, (June 13, 2014), https://www.hartenergy.com/opinions/range-resources-responds-magnum-hunters-marcellus-claim -120526.

[4] Al Shaw & Kate Mishkin , *A Guide to Every Permitted Natural Gas Well in West Virginia*, Charleston Gazette-Mail (Mar. 6, 2019), https://projects.propublica.org/graphics/wva-well-pads.

[5] Press Release, Manchin Senate, Spotlight on Marcellus: Manchin to Bring Senate Energy Committee to Charleston to Highlight Tremendous Potential of Marcellus Shale (Nov. 9, 2011), https://www .manchin.senate.gov/newsroom/press-releases/spotlight-on-marcellus-manchin-to-bring-senate- energy-committee-to-charleston-to-highlight-tremendous-potential-of-marcellus-shale.

[6] Press Release, Manchin Senate, Manchin Chairs Senate Energy Committee Field Hearing on Marcellus Shale's Job Creation Potential (Nov. 14, 2011), https://www.manchin.senate.gov/news room/press-releases/manchin-chairs-senate-energy-committee-field-hearing-on-marcellus-shales-job- creation-potential.

Capito also testified at the hearing, and acknowledged the potential impact of the Marcellus on energy markets; it had "pushed the price of natural gas down allowing for lower electrical prices and heating costs." According to Capito, "[T]his plentiful supply makes West Virginia a very much more attractive place for non-energy businesses to locate due to the availability of fuel to power their operations."[7] (However, as discussed in the section below, West Virginia Utilities Take a Pass on Gas, the electric utilities in West Virginia failed to take advantage of the plentiful natural gas resource and the lower electricity prices did not materialize.)

Dr. Tom Witt of the West Virginia University (WVU) Bureau of Business and Economic Research also testified at the hearing and presented a Bureau report, *The Economic Impact of the Marcellus Shale Play in 2009*. This found that the employment impact of Marcellus Shale development for 2010 was between 7,600 and 8,500 additional jobs and predicted that, by 2015, the number of additional jobs would be between 6,600 and 19,600 with potential employee compensation impacts of up to $890 million.[8]

The American Petroleum Institute (API), for its part, released a report in July 2010 projecting the effects of three different development scenarios – low, medium, and high – on jobs, incomes, tax revenues, and other indicators of economic progress in the region. The "high development" scenario hypothesized daily production from Marcellus wells of 18.4 billion cubic feet by the year 2020. For West Virginia, the API report predicted the addition of 44,000 new jobs by the end of the decade.[9] One state legislator, noting that the job creation figure was greater than West Virginia's total number of unemployed, happily proclaimed, "We'll have more jobs than people!"[10]

As it turned out, the projections were way off target, in both directions. First, the Marcellus Shale play (and the nearby Utica Shale, slightly deeper in the ground and located just to the west, primarily in Ohio) turned out to be much more productive than anyone predicted. Between 2008 and 2019, Appalachia's Marcellus and Utica gas fields moved from producing a negligible portion of the nation's natural gas to nearly 40 percent. As compared to the "high development" scenario in the API study, which predicted daily production from Marcellus wells of 18.4 billion cubic feet

[7] Senate Energy and Natural Resources Committee, S. HRG. 112–223: *Hearing to Examine Marcellus Shale Gas Development and Production in West Virginia, East Charleston, WV*, Nov. 14, 2011.

[8] Amy Higginbotham, Adam Pellillo, Tami Gurley-Calvez, & Tom S. Witt, The Economic Impact of the Natural Gas Industry and the Marcellus Shale Development in West Virginia in 2009, WVU Bureau of Business and Economic Research (Dec. 2010), https://researchrepository.wvu.edu/cgi/viewcontent.cgi?article=1087&context=bureau_be#:~:text=The%20development%20of%20the%20Marcellus,wage%20level%20for%20the%20industry.&text=In%202009%20the%20oil%20and,over%20%20%2424551.9%20million%20in%20wages.

[9] Timothy Considine, The Economic Impacts of the Marcellus Shale: Implications for New York, Pennsylvania, and West Virginia, American Petroleum Institute (July 14, 2010), https://www.api.org/~/media/Files/News/2011/API%20Economic%20Impacts%20Marcellus%20Shale.pdf.

[10] Sean O'Leary, The Natural Gas Fracking Boom and Appalachia's Lost Economic Decade 5 Ohio River Valley Institute (Feb. 12, 2021), https://ohiorivervalleyinstitute.org/wp-content/uploads/2021/02/Frackalachia-Report-update-2_12_01.pdf.

(bcf) by the year 2020, the actual production of Marcellus gas wells in Pennsylvania and West Virginia in 2019 was 25 bcf/day – fully 35 percent more than the "high development" scenario – while Utica field wells in Ohio, which were not considered in the API study, were producing an additional 6 bcf/day.[11]

On the downside, the anticipated jobs and economic growth, as well as the hoped-for buildout of the petrochemical industry in Appalachia, never materialized, as discussed in the section The Failed Promises of Natural Gas. But the extraction of massive amounts of natural gas from the Marcellus and Utica Shale plays would bring the coal industry in the region to its knees before the end of "the lost decade," mostly due to the ruthlessly competitive markets for electricity, as discussed next.

THE RISE OF NATURAL GAS, AND THE FALL IN WHOLESALE ELECTRICITY PRICES

The impact on electricity markets of cheap and plentiful natural gas from the Marcellus was almost immediate. The North American Electric Reliability Corporation (NERC) – the nation's electric reliability organization – reported in October 2010 that power producers added about 11 gigawatts (GWs) of natural gas-fired generation during 2010 – the largest single-fuel increase in the electricity market. In 2011, NERC further predicted that natural gas would replace coal as electric utilities' fuel of choice during times of peak power demand. According to NERC's report, natural gas consumption was already at an all-time high, due to access to shale gas and the lower capital costs for building gas-fired power plants. NERC suggested that these factors, coupled with the need to meet climate change goals and anticipated EPA regulations, would drive a transition from coal to gas plants over the coming decade.[12] At about the same time, the Federal Energy Regulatory Commission (FERC) issued its winter energy market assessment report, which reported that natural gas market prices would be reduced 30 to 50 percent during the upcoming winter; that would translate into wholesale electricity prices dropping more than 20 percent in most regions of the United States. While a drop in wholesale prices of that magnitude was attributable in part to a short-term factor (predictions of a mild winter), the report also cited lower futures prices for gas – in other words, information from the gas markets about where prices were headed – which was a harbinger of things to come in the wholesale electricity markets.

At this point, it is worth discussing how electricity prices are determined in the wholesale markets. For the last twenty-five years, FERC has been adopting policies to promote competition in the generation of electricity. The most significant move was the issuance of Order No. 888 in April 1996, which essentially required the

---

[11] *Id.*
[12] Katherine Ling, *Gas to Supplant Coal at Times of Peak-Power Demand – Report*, E&E News PM (Oct. 21, 2010), https://www.eenews.net/eenewspm/stories/1059941323/search?keyword=wholesale+electricity+prices+shale+gas.

owners of electric transmission lines to provide "open access" to utilities and other power producers seeking to use their transmission lines to "wheel" electricity. The effect of this order was to create competition in the generating markets; power plant operators would have access to more buyers in a region, and utilities and other large users would have access to more sellers, thereby creating a fairly competitive or liquid market for electricity. The next major development was FERC's issuance of Order No. 2000 in December 1999, which encouraged the development of regional transmission organizations, or RTOs. These entities – also referred to as independent system operators, or ISOs – would assume responsibility for maintaining and operating the electric grid within various geographic regions across the country, and for providing a platform for buyers and sellers to engage in transactions in electricity.

In the region in which West Virginia is located, the wholesale power market is operated by PJM Interconnection, Incorporated (PJM), which is based in Valley Forge, Pennsylvania, and serves all or parts of thirteen states and the District of Columbia. The clearing price for electricity at PJM (and in other wholesale markets located throughout the United States) is determined through an auction process in which generation resources submit an offer based on the price at which they can supply a specific number of megawatt-hours of electricity. If a resource submits a successful bid and is therefore selected, or dispatched, to contribute its generation to meet demand, it is said to "clear" the market. The cheapest resource will "clear" the market first, and operators at PJM will continue to dispatch resources according to the relative ranking of their bid prices until demand is met. When supply matches demand, the market is "cleared," and the price of the last resource to offer in (plus other market operation charges) becomes the wholesale price of power, or the "market-clearing price."

As a result of FERC's actions to open the generation of electricity to competition, entities other than traditional electric utilities began building power plants and offering their output into the competitive wholesale markets. The best example of this in West Virginia is the 700 megawatt (MW) coal plant operated by Longview Power, which is located just north of Morgantown. At the time it commenced operating, in September 2011, it was the most efficient and cleanest coal plant in the United States. Longview is referred to as a "merchant" plant; unlike the power plants operated by traditional electric utilities where the output is sold to "captive" retail customers at rates regulated by state regulators (in West Virginia, the Public Service Commission), a merchant plant is a "price taker": It makes money only if it is able to compete successfully in the competitive wholesale markets. So whether or not a merchant generating plant makes money depends on whether the bid that it submits to PJM – which, in turn, is based on the costs it incurs to generate the power – "clears the market." Merchant plants that are "in the money" will receive the market clearing price for the electricity they deliver to the market, regardless of the level of their submitted bid. Merchant plants that submit a bid in excess of the market clearing price are simply not dispatched at the time – they are "out of the money" – and will fail to capture any revenue to cover their costs. If this situation persists, the plants will ultimately close, as they are uneconomic and cannot compete with other power suppliers that are able to generate power more cheaply.

Given the ruthlessly competitive structure of the power market operated by PJM, the impact of cheap and plentiful gas in the region from the Marcellus and Utica shale plays was to produce swift and large reductions in the wholesale price of electricity. As new, efficient natural gas-fired generating plants – fueled with very low-cost shale gas – began to come online, the auction process operated by PJM took care of the rest. In 2012, low natural gas prices drove coal-fired generation on the PJM electricity market to a record low; the load-weighted average energy price across PJM dropped to $35 per megawatt hour (MWh) in 2012, a ten-year low. Generation from natural gas units increased by 39 percent in 2012, while coal generation fell. Future prices at the time suggested that market energy prices would remain in the area of $40/MWh through 2019. As it turned out, those forecasts were fairly accurate through 2018 – $39.43/MWh for the first nine months. Prices dropped another 30 percent to $27.60/MWh in 2019, however, which was lower than in the corresponding period of any year since PJM's energy market was created in 1999. Since 2017, the nameplate capacity of gas-fired units has exceeded the nameplate capacity of coal and nuclear units in PJM, but 2019 represented the first time that the energy output – which reflects how often the plants are actually running – of gas-fired plants exceeded the energy output of coal and nuclear plants. According to PJM, natural gas-fired units made up almost 70 percent of the units "at the margin" (those units close to the market-clearing price), or nearly double the 37 percent share held by natural gas plants in 2015.[13]

The inability of coal-fired generation to compete in the wholesale markets presented a problem to the Trump administration, given President Trump's promise during his 2016 campaign stops in West Virginia to "bring the coal jobs back." Almost immediately upon taking office, Trump put pressure on Energy Secretary Rick Perry to do something to prop up the coal sector. Secretary Perry was armed with an "action plan" memo that had been prepared by Murray Energy, and which Bob Murray personally delivered to Perry just weeks after Trump took office. One of the strategies suggested in the memo for undermining the role of natural gas was to talk about "resilience," and the fact that coal plants, with their on-site inventory of coal, were much more resilient than natural gas-fired plants, the supply to which – transported by pipelines – could easily be interrupted by extreme weather events or terrorist activity. According to this argument, too much reliance on natural gas and renewable energy would leave the grid vulnerable to breakdowns and blackouts. The claim was that the design of the pricing structure in the competitive wholesale

[13]   Jared Anderson, *PJM Power Prices Lowest Since Energy Market Created, Market Challenges Persist: Monitor*, S&P GLOBAL PLATTS (Nov. 14, 2019), https://www.spglobal.com/platts/en/market-insights /latest-news/electric-power/111419-pjm-power-prices-lowest-since-energy-market-created-market-challenges-persist-monitor.

markets was failing to capture these resilience benefits of coal (and nuclear plants as well, although these were an incidental beneficiary of the Murray theory).

In September 2017, armed with the analysis from the Murray Energy memo, the Department of Energy (DOE) filed a petition for a rulemaking at FERC pursuant to its authority under an obscure section of the Federal Power Act (Section 201(b)) that would require regional wholesale market operators to implement pricing reforms to capture the resilience benefits of generating resources that had a ninety-day supply of fuel on site, a requirement that could be met by coal and nuclear, but not natural gas. (The ninety-day supply requirement provided an additional benefit for the coal industry inasmuch as that was more coal than was customary for power plant operators to maintain on site.) In a unanimous 5–0 ruling in January 2018, FERC rejected the proposal; at the time, three members of FERC – including its Chairman, Kevin McIntyre – were Trump appointees, a stinging rebuke for Perry and the Trump Administration, but a reminder that an independent agency (FERC) is not bound to adopt the policy proposals of an executive branch agency (DOE).[14]

At the end of the day, the impact of shale gas on the demise of the coal industry was undeniable and easily proven. A study by the Columbia Center on Global Energy Policy in April 2017, for example, analyzed the reasons for the collapse of the coal industry between 2011 and 2016. According to the study, domestic natural gas production grew by 37 percent between 2007 and 2016, which resulted in significantly lower prices for natural gas burned in power plants; in 2008, the average US power plant paid $10 per thousand cubic feet (tcf) for delivered natural gas, versus $3 in 2016, a decline of 71 percent. The study observed that the competitiveness of natural gas compared to coal improved dramatically, particularly in the East and Midwest. (The average delivered cost of coal decreased by only 8 percent during the same period.) Taking all the dynamics in the electricity markets into account, the study concluded that the drop in natural gas prices was responsible for nearly half of the decline in US domestic coal consumption between 2011 and 2017. Other contributing factors were lower than expected demand for electricity (26 percent) and growth in renewable energy (18 percent). Environmental regulations, which had the effect of accelerating coal power plant retirements, came in a very distant fourth at 3.5 percent.[15] The relatively minor role of environmental regulations in the demise of the coal industry was, of course, completely contrary to the narrative of Obama's "war on coal" that proved to be so popular with West Virginia politicians during "the lost decade."

[14] Gavin Blade, *FERC Rejects DOE NOPR, Kicking Resilience Issue to Grid Operators*, UTILITY DIVE (Jan. 8, 2018), https://www.utilitydive.com/news/ferc-rejects-doe-nopr-kicking-resilience-issue-to-grid-operators/514334/.

[15] Trevor Houser, Jason Bordoff, & Peter Marsters, CAN COAL MAKE A COMEBACK? COLUMBIA SIPA CENTER ON GLOBAL ENERGY POLICY (Apr. 2017), https://energypolicy.columbia.edu/sites/default/files/Center%20on%20Global%20Energy%20Policy%20Can%20Coal%20Make%20a%20Comeback%20April%202017.pdf.

WEST VIRGINIA UTILITIES TAKE A PASS ON GAS

While electric utilities across the country were taking advantage of the newly discovered cheap and plentiful natural gas and beginning to transition away from coal to natural gas to generate electricity – a subject we will explore more thoroughly in Chapter 4 – the shale gas revolution was largely ignored by West Virginia's electric utilities. FirstEnergy, and its Mon Power and Potomac Edison subsidiaries, generated nearly 100 percent of their electricity with coal plants throughout "the lost decade," and pretty much continue to do so today. In fact, as we will explore in Chapter 10, FirstEnergy not only ignored the shale gas revolution that was going on throughout the region, but "doubled down" on coal during this period by procuring additional coal-fired generation through the transfer of the Harrison coal plant to its West Virginia regulated operations in 2012 and a failed attempt to repeat the trick in the case of the Pleasants Station plant in 2018.

American Electric Power (AEP), and its Appalachian Power and Wheeling Power subsidiaries, did somewhat better. In May 2015, AEP closed down its three-unit, 705 MW coal-fired Clinch River plant in Carbo, Russell County, Virginia in order to convert it to a two-unit, 484 MW gas-fired plant. Both units began natural gas-fired operations in 2016.[16] But neither Appalachian Power nor Wheeling Power broke ground on any new natural gas-fired generation throughout "the lost decade." Rather, AEP followed FirstEnergy's lead and also doubled down on coal, by transferring its Amos and Mitchell plants from its competitive subsidiary to Appalachian Power (2013) and Wheeling Power (2014), respectively, as discussed further in Chapter 10.

In continuing down this coal-dependent path, both FirstEnergy and AEP departed radically from most other electric utilities in the United States during "the lost decade," which moved aggressively to get out of coal in favor of what was clearly becoming the least-cost means of generating electricity – baseload natural gas-fired generation, in the form of "combined-cycle combustion turbines." In contrast to the traditional "simple-cycle" combustion turbine which was commonly used as a "peaking unit" to meet occasional high periods of power demand, a combined-cycle power plant uses both a gas and a steam turbine together to produce up to 50 percent more electricity from the same fuel, by routing the waste heat from the gas turbine to the nearby steam turbine and thereby generating extra power.[17] While the combined-cycle units have a slightly higher upfront capital cost than simple-cycle turbines, their improved operating efficiency more than makes up for these higher costs over the life of the plant.

[16]   Dave Waitkus, *Clinch River Plant Receives New Life as a Natural Gas Plant*, AEP RETIREES AND ALUMNI (June 18, 2015), https://aepretirees.com/2015/06/18/clinch-river-plant-receives-new-life-as-a-natural-gas-plant/.
[17]   GE GAS POWER, *Combined Cycle Power Plant: How It Works*, https://www.ge.com/gas-power/resources/education/combined-cycle-power-plants.

These combined-cycle gas units became the baseload resource of choice during "the lost decade." According to the Energy Information Administration (EIA), between 2015 and 2019, about 40 GW of coal-fired capacity was retired in the United States, largely replaced by 30 MW net capacity of combined-cycle gas units (with the remaining capacity filled by output from new wind and solar generators).[18] By the end of 2018, the amount of generating capacity from combined-cycle natural gas plants (264 GW) surpassed coal-fired plants (243 GW) as the technology with the most electricity generating capacity in the United States, accounting for about half of all US natural gas-fired generating capacity at that time.

The significant transition to natural gas also stimulated the development of improved technology for natural gas turbines, which around the middle of the decade resulted in "advanced design" natural gas-fired combined-cycle units, referred to as ANGCC units. The latest generation of these larger natural gas-fired turbines was first installed in 2015 and incorporated into the design of 45 percent of the combined-cycle units installed in 2017.[19] According to EIA, of the new US natural gas capacity added between 2016 and mid-2019, 31 percent used ANGCC technology. This ramping up led to efficiency gains and economies of scale, thereby reducing capital construction costs. These additional cost savings were reflected almost immediately in competitive wholesale markets. According to an April 2018 report from PJM, the cost per unit of ANGCC installed capacity at PJM's next capacity auction was expected to be 25–30 percent lower compared with older, conventional natural gas-fired combined-cycle units.[20] In other words, this improved technology would result in even lower costs for generating electricity with natural gas, further threatening the future of the coal industry in the mid-Atlantic region. None of these lower costs were captured for West Virginia ratepayers, however, with FirstEnergy and AEP continuing to depend on decades-old coal-fired generating plants.

Several factors come into play to explain this course of action. First, replacing coal with natural gas would have been politically unpopular in West Virginia. For the reasons discussed in the Introduction, it is almost unpatriotic among West Virginians to turn away from coal. More importantly, policymakers in West Virginia – from the Governor, to members of the legislature, to the commissioners on the Public Service Commission (PSC) – would have looked very unfavorably upon such an act of disloyalty to the coal industry and its miners, who depend upon the continued operation of West Virginia's coal plants for their livelihood.

[18] *U.S. Natural Gas-Fired Combined-Cycle Capacity Surpasses Coal-Fired Capacity*, ENERGY INFORMATION ADMINISTRATION (Apr. 10, 2019), https://www.eia.gov/todayinenergy/detail.php?id=39012.
[19] *More New Natural Gas Combined-Cycle Power Plants Are Using Advanced Designs*, ENERGY INFORMATION ADMINISTRATION (June 19, 2019), https://www.eia.gov/todayinenergy/detail.php?id=39912.
[20] PJM Interconnection, Inc., *PJM Cost of New Entry, Combustion Turbines and Combined-Cycle Plants with June 1, 2022 Online Date* (Apr. 19, 2018), https://www.pjm.com/~/media/committees-groups/committees/mic/20180425-special/20180425-pjm-2018-cost-of-new-entry-study.ashx.

Second, prior to 2015, there was no rigorous long-term planning process where electric utilities were required to demonstrate that they were on the "least-cost path" in terms of acquiring and deploying a portfolio of resources that produced the lowest rates for utility customers over time. As we will explore further in Chapter 8, the process of "integrated resource planning" was not required in West Virginia until 2015 and, until then, electric utilities never really had to "show their work" to demonstrate that they were acting in ratepayers' best interests when they acquired and operated generating resources. So there was no logical platform for anyone to explore why all the other utilities in the United States were turning quickly to natural gas, while West Virginia utilities continued to burn coal. Nor was there any calculation of the extra costs that ratepayers were paying due to continued reliance on coal to the exclusion of less expensive means of generating electricity. (As we will discuss further in Chapter 8, even the integrated resource plans that were developed in 2015 were not all that rigorous, but at least the foundation of the necessary analysis was beginning to be laid.)

Third, West Virginia traditionally identified itself as a "coal" state, not an "energy" state. So even though most of the state was sitting on top of the largest shale gas "play" in the country that, by the end of the decade, would be producing 40 percent of the nation's natural gas supply, West Virginia was not about to abandon its coal heritage in favor of natural gas, regardless of the cost advantages that could have flowed from it in the form of lower electricity rates. Part of this can be explained by the reluctance of the natural gas industry to challenge Big Coal head on. Rather, both industries tended to coexist during most of "the lost decade," as joint extractors of West Virginia's abundance of energy resources, without the need to consider the electricity market as a zero-sum game. For example, in early 2011, Chris Hamilton of the West Virginia Coal Association denied that the coal industry was threatened by this competition, and suggested that the natural gas industry would be "an ally in contending with all the permitting and regulatory issues confronted by our state's energy industries."[21] But, as it turned out, it was a zero-sum game and, by the end of "the lost decade," coal would come in a distant third nationwide as the fuel of choice for generating electricity.

Fourth, is the failure of the West Virginia PSC throughout "the lost decade" to perform its essential function of protecting ratepayers from the increasing rates that resulted from imprudent resource acquisition decisions by utilities. As discussed further in Chapter 8, even in the absence of a formal integrated resource planning process, it was apparent throughout most of "the lost decade" that West Virginia was missing out on the economic benefits of the shale gas revolution that was underway throughout the United States. Electricity prices were either declining or holding steady across the country, as cheap and plentiful natural gas supplies resulted in the

---

[21]   Taylor Kuykendall, *Will Natural Gas Replace Coal?* Charleston Gazette-Mail (Jan. 2, 2011), https://www.wvgazettemail.com/will-natural-gas-replace-coal/article_869b59c1-ed66-5c22-8d8e-9915e949d891.html.

displacement of more expensive coal-fired generation and drove down prices in the competitive wholesale electricity markets. In contrast, West Virginia's prices rose at five times the national average between 2008 and 2020.[22] No one at FirstEnergy or AEP was "sharpening their pencils" to make resource acquisition decisions that would lower rates for electric ratepayers in West Virginia. There was no reason to do so – the PSC was certainly not requiring it.

In the absence of any action by West Virginia's investor-owned utilities to take advantage of the opportunities presented by cheap and plentiful natural gas in the region, it was up to independent power producers to fill the gap. And they did. Or at least they tried. Energy Solutions Consortium LLC (ESC), an energy project developer based in Buffalo, New York, proposed to build three natural gas-fired generating plants in West Virginia – at Moundsville (Marshall County) and in Brooke and Harrison Counties – at a total cost of about $2.1 billion, and would sell their output directly into PJM. Headed by Andrew "Drew" Dorn IV as President and Andrew "Andy" Dorn Jr. as Comanaging Director, ESC saw an opportunity to make money by generating electricity at a lower price than the region's aging coal fleet, and they had incentives to do so: By being able to generate electricity at a price that was below PJM's "market clearing price," they had the chance to make a handsome profit. If not, their investors would bear the losses. (The situation is different, of course, in the case of AEP and FirstEnergy, which were assured of recovering their costs from their captive ratepayers.)

The Dorns successfully secured approval from the PSC for the Moundsville plant in February 2015. (In order to build an electric generating plant in West Virginia, the developer must obtain a certificate of convenience and necessity [CCN] from the PSC.) The proposed 549 MW combined-cycle combustion turbine was to be built in Marshall County on a 37-acre brownfield site south of Moundsville where the Allied Chemical Plant had previously operated. Backers of Moundsville Power said the project would be a significant boost for the area, providing 500 jobs annually during a three-year construction period and 30 permanent jobs once it was operational. Supporters also said the project was a way for residents to capture more economic gains from West Virginia's booming natural gas industry.[23] Upon completion, the plant would use $105 million of natural gas and ethane, sourced annually from West

---

[22] According to the Energy Information Administration, electricity prices increased in West Virginia at an average annual rate of 3.77% between 2008 and 2020, while the national figure was only 0.70%. Electricity prices in West Virginia increased faster during this period than in any other state in the nation. For 2020, see Energy Information Administration, *State Electricity Profiles*, https://www.eia .gov/electricity/state/. For 2008, see Energy Information Administration, *State Electricity Profiles* 2008 (Mar. 2010), https://www.eia.gov/electricity/state/archive/sep2008.pdf.

[23] Ken Ward Jr., *WV's Largest Coal Operator Fighting Back Against Growing Natural Gas Industry*, CHARLESTON GAZETTE-MAIL (Sept. 28, 2018), https://www.wvgazettemail.com/news/wv_troubled_tran sition/wvs-largest-coal-operator-fighting-back-against-growing-natural-gas-industry/article_24ddbb89-d5f1-57dd-9f9a-49521b20fa3d.html.

Virginia producers and processors, and was expected to be the largest user of natural gas in the state. The project was originally scheduled to be operational in 2018.

The project was derailed, however, when Murray Energy, West Virginia's largest coal producer at the time, bankrolled a public interest organization, the Ohio Valley Jobs Alliance (OVJA), to intervene in the PSC proceedings and challenge the project. The issue raised by OVJA in the PSC related to tax breaks being awarded to the developers by local governments, known as payments in lieu of taxes, or PILOTs. Although the PSC generally rejected those concerns, it did provide PSC Chairman Mike Albert with an opportunity during the hearing to question the OVJA witness about who was paying the costs associated with their intervention; the witness ultimately admitted that "Murray Energy's paying for the legal work. But Murray Energy does not give me any money."[24] The PSC granted the necessary approvals for all three of the natural gas plants proposed by ESC.

But OVJA also created mischief in permitting proceedings before the West Virginia DEP. The basis for their challenge? Greenhouse gas (GHG) emissions, of course – even though Bob Murray famously referred to global warming as a "hoax," and had urged the Trump administration to reverse the endangerment finding that authorized the EPA to regulate GHG emissions. In an October 2017 interview on *PBS* Newshour, Murray stated his position "that the endangerment finding needs to be repealed, that carbon dioxide is not a pollutant."[25] No matter that in challenging permits on the grounds of a plant's GHG emissions Murray Energy's sham intervenors were citing the same kinds of government regulations that Bob Murray had railed against. In testimony before the West Virginia DEP related to the Moundsville project, the OVJA witness cited a concern about GHG emissions, but answered "no" when questioned about a concern regarding global warming. In their decision denying OVJA's appeal, DEP Air Quality Board members later wrote in their order that they were "somewhat concerned by the OVJA's apparent lack of knowledge about the contents of its appeal, lack of cognizable purpose related to the environment, and overall express intent to stop the construction of the plant solely to benefit another industry."[26]

When OVJA failed to block the Moundsville project at DEP, it appealed the decision to Kanawha County Circuit Court. The case languished before Judge Joanna Tabit for fifteen months and only after West Virginia Commerce Secretary Woody Thrasher prodded Tabit for a decision did she issue an opinion in November 2017 rejecting the OVJA appeal. In her order, she noted that "OVJA has, through its officers, admitted that it has taken this appeal solely to try to protect

[24] Ken Ward Jr., *"Jobs Alliance," Funded by Trump Backer, Tries to Block Gas Plants That Would Bring Jobs to West Virginia*, ProPublica (Sept. 28, 2018), https://www.propublica.org/article/jobs-alliance-tries-to-block-gas-plants.

[25] PBS NewsHour (@NewsHour) Twitter (Oct. 10, 2017), https://twitter.com/newshour/status/917886340867301376.

[26] West Virginia Air Quality Board, *Ohio Valley Jobs Alliance v. Durham*, Case No.15-01-AQB, Final Order, July 18, 2016, at 2, http://www.wvaqb.org/finalorders/15-01-aqb%20-%20final%20order.pdf.

the coal industry, not to protect human health or the environment," and that the right to mine coal "is not a substantial right in the context of this proceeding."[27] (Later, legislators passed a bill so that any future cases would bypass county courts and go directly to the West Virginia Supreme Court.) But it was too late for the Moundsville Project, which lost its place in the queue at PJM to be interconnected to the grid and, as a consequence, lost its financing. At this point in time, it is not clear whether the project will move forward. If it does, the Dorns will not develop it; the project is now controlled by Quantum Utility Generation, a private developer tied to private equity firm Quantum Energy Partners.[28]

In the case of the Harrison County project, on September 24, 2018, the DEP Air Quality Board found that OVJA lacked a legitimate interest in the outcome of the case to warrant its participation inasmuch as it "failed to offer sufficient threshold evidence" to support its objections to emissions limits and air-quality modeling for the project. According to the Board, "The OVJA, as an organization, has no demonstrated interest in protecting the health of the citizenry or the environment of Harrison County."[29] When OVJA appealed the decision to the courts, Drew Dorn of ESC issued a scathing press release complaining about the "frivolous lawsuits" funded by Murray Energy, and noted the potential consequences on the West Virginia economy – in the form of higher electricity prices that would discourage industry from making large investments in manufacturing plants – if the tactics proved to be successful. Dorn claimed that the state had slipped twenty places in the ranking of states with low-cost electricity, and that "every state with cheaper electricity uses more natural gas than West Virginia." According to the release, Murray Energy was "trying to achieve through the courts what it could not through the marketplace."[30] The following month, the Affiliated Construction Trades Foundation, a coalition of construction unions that support gas plants and whose members would build them, purchased half-page newspaper ads across the state to complain that Murray Energy was supporting a "shadowy front group holding West Virginia jobs hostage!" and decrying the potential loss of $2.1 billion in investment in West Virginia.[31] The Harrison project has been delayed beyond 2020, and ESC had

[27] *Ohio Valley Jobs Alliance v. Durham*, Circuit Court of Kanawha County, West Virginia, Civic Action 16-AA-67, Findings of Fact, Conclusions of Law and Final Order, issued Nov. 15, 2017, at 5, https://www.documentcloud.org/documents/4781897-Moundsville-Air-Permit-Circuit-Court-Order.html.

[28] Darren Sweeney, *W.Va. Regulators Approve Construction of 830-MW Gas Plant*, S&P GLOBAL MARKET INTELLIGENCE (Feb. 20, 2018), https://www.spglobal.com/marketintelligence/en/news-insights/trending/suc9nmcimcw4vl-tjnuxew2.

[29] West Virginia Air Quality Board, *Ohio Valley Jobs Alliance v. Durham*, Appeal No. 18-01-AQB, Findings of Fact, Conclusions of Law and Order, issued Sept. 24, 2018, at 20, https://www.documentcloud.org/documents/4945516-2018-09-24-AQB-Harrison-Ruling.html.

[30] Press Release, Harrison County Power, Frivolous Lawsuits Funded by Murray Energy Endangering Thousands of Jobs in West Virginia and Adding to Electricity Costs (July 9, 2018), https://www.documentcloud.org/documents/4940961-2018-07-19-Gas-Plant-Press-Release-About-Murray.html.

[31] CHARLESTON GAZETTE-MAIL, August 26, 2018, at 3A, https://www.documentcloud.org/documents/4940963-2018-08-26-Murray-Ad-in-CGM.html.

to secure an extension of an option from Harrison County to enable the later construction start date; its future is highly uncertain as of the date of this book's publication.[32]

The Brooke County project, for its part, got in the crosshairs of Governor Jim Justice, who challenged a $5.6 million loan guarantee for the project from the West Virginia Economic Development Authority. The Authority was scheduled to vote on the approval of the loan guarantee at its August 20, 2020 board meeting, until the topic was removed from the agenda without explanation.[33] At his daily COVID-19 press briefing on August 26, Governor Justice was asked about the project and he offered several disparaging – and apparently untrue, according to the Dorns – remarks in passing about the plant, questioning the need for it, the risk associated with the loan guarantee request, where the gas would come from, and how many jobs the plant would create. And he also raised the issue of why the state would need another gas plant if it would result in the closure of a coal plant:

> I am as pro-gas as I can possibly be, with a good smart business head. Now let's just also think about this. Do we need additional generation in this state? If we close another plant for the betterment of this plant, are we going to have to – are our ratepayers going to have to pay for years because the plant wasn't paid off or whatever it may be that goes through all the gyrations with AEP or whatever it may be?[34]

The gas industry trade press claimed that the Governor was "trash talking" the Brooke County plant. "His remarks are transparent. He supports coal and doesn't want any kind of competition between natural gas-fired electric generation and coal-fired generation."[35] Justice clarified his remarks a few days later and indicated that he was simply asking the Economic Development Authority to "take another look at the project," and would leave the decision about the loan guarantee in the board's hands.[36] His position on the project had been made clear, however. According to the Brooke County Commissioners, it was apparent that the state Economic

[32] JoAnn Snoderly, *Harrison County (West Virginia) Commission to Consider Extension of Agreement with Developer of Proposed Natural Gas-Fired Power Plant*, EXPONENT TELEGRAM (Dec. 7, 2020), https://www.wvnews.com/theet/news/harrison-county-west-virginia-commission-to-consider-extension-of-agreement-with-developer-of-proposed-natural/article_b85a1e57-6e52-5868-9e4f-35b7ea46e017.html.

[33] Joe Severino, *Questions About the Brooke County Power Project Were Answered Long Ago. So What's the Holdup?* CHARLESTON GAZETTE-MAIL (Sept. 5, 2020), https://www.wvgazettemail.com/news/energy_and_environment/questions-about-the-brooke-county-power-project-were-answered-long-ago-so-whats-the-holdup/article_1f0be1a1-a360-5312-9075-bc81b6ec344c.html.

[34] Governor Jim Justice, *Gov. Justice Holds Press Briefing on COVID-19 Response*, YOUTUBE (Aug. 26, 2020), https://www.youtube.com/watch?v=7VH0C4ATIho#action=share.

[35] *WV Gov. Jim Justice Trash-Talks Brooke County Gas-Fired Power*, MARCELLUS DRILLING NEWS (Aug. 27, 2020), https://marcellusdrilling.com/2020/08/wv-gov-jim-justice-trash-talks-brooke-county-gas-fired-power/.

[36] Steven Allen Adams, *Justice: Plant Decision Is in EDA's Hands*, THE INTER-MOUNTAIN (Sept. 2, 2020), https://www.theintermountain.com/news/local-news/2020/09/justice-plant-decision-is-in-edas-hands/.

Development Authority board and Governor Justice were "swayed by interests that see the plant as a threat to the coal industry."[37]

When the Economic Development Authority board acted on the loan guarantee proposal at a September 9, 2020 special meeting, it imposed conditions on financing that tracked the comments made by Justice at his August 26 press briefing: requiring that West Virginia sourced natural gas be used in the plant; that 75 percent of the construction and permanent workforce at the plant be from West Virginia; and that documentation be provided to demonstrate 100 percent funding for the project by July 1, 2021.[38] In October 2020, ESC pulled the plug on the Brooke County project, with Drew Dorn citing "the combination of alleged coal industry interference and market conditions" which created difficulty in securing enough investment.[39]

The Governor's expressed opposition to the Brooke County project – which would have produced a $440.5 million positive economic impact for the region and created 1,164 direct, indirect, and induced jobs[40] – was in sharp contrast to his personal involvement in driving a $12.5 million tax bailout for the Pleasants Station plant, as discussed in Chapter 9, including calling a special session of the legislature to approve the bailout. Perhaps it is because the Pleasants Station plant is a coal plant. And the Brooke County project would have been a natural gas-fired plant. Perhaps the Governor is not as "pro-gas as [he] can possibly be."

THE FAILED PROMISES OF NATURAL GAS: RESOURCE CURSE REVISITED

As it turned out, while the fracking boom and the associated rise of natural gas-fired generation was the leading cause of the demise of the coal industry in Appalachia, it was a failure in terms of delivering on the promised economic benefits to West Virginia. This aspect is not the primary concern of this chapter, which focuses on the impact of fracking on the energy markets, and the false claims of West Virginia leaders who ignored those impacts in favor of the much more popular narrative regarding the "war on coal" and the role of the EPA in contributing to the demise of the coal industry. But the false promise of the fracking boom illustrates another

[37] Warren Scott, *Brooke County Power Plant project May Be in Jeopardy*, WEIRTON DAILY TIMES (Aug. 26, 2020), https://www.weirtondailytimes.com/news/local-news/2020/08/brooke-county-power-plant-project-may-be-in-jeopardy/.
[38] Steven Allen Adams, *West Virginia Economic Development Authority OKs Direct Loan for Brooke County Power plant*, WEIRTON DAILY TIMES (Sept. 23, 2020), https://www.weirtondailytimes.com/news/local-news/2020/09/west-virginia-economic-development-authority-oks-direct-loan-for-brooke-county-power-plant/?fbclid=IwAR2PtfCK3DoFCTLNTm9obbfjjdf–lyzPOdRDV5REWv5cwTn1Bvn93VLOZLU;WVEDA.
[39] *Brooke County's Gas-Fired Power Plant's Future Uncertain; Property Deadline Extension in Harrison County for Similar Plant Expires at End of 2020*, WV NEWS (Oct. 11, 2020), https://www.wvnews.com/news/wvnews/brooke-countys-gas-fired-power-plants-future-uncertain-property-deadline-extension-in-harrison-county-for/article_e94586e2-84a7-530f-93f4-ce7af504e300.html.
[40] ESC BROOKE COUNTY POWER LLC, http://www.brookecountypower.com/#overview.

example of political leaders promoting the supposed economic benefits of yet another resource extraction industry in West Virginia and exemplifying, once again, the resource curse – discussed in the Introduction – that continues to afflict the Mountain State.

As late as August 2019, at the West Virginia Chamber of Commerce's annual meeting, Governor Justice was touting the economic benefits that the natural gas industry was bringing to the state. In announcing the creation of his "Downstream Jobs Task Force," he claimed he was "think[ing] big" regarding prospects for the jobs that would be created by the "downstream" processes that would be created from natural gas.[41] According to Justice, processing plants, chemical manufacturing facilities, and other downstream operations were on the way, and would produce $36 billion in capital investment as well as creating 100,000 new jobs from the decade-old boom in natural gas drilling. But none of the natural gas-related projects that were promised for the state during "the lost decade" have materialized.

First, there was the $4 billion ethane cracker plant in Wood County promised by former Governor Earl Ray Tomblin as a "game changer" in 2013, which was "reevaluated" by the developers in 2015 and later abandoned in 2019 before ever breaking ground.[42] Then, in 2017, there was the promised investment of $83.7 billion by the China Energy Investment Corporation, over twenty years, to assist in building new facilities in three areas: natural gas-burning power plants, steam crackers that turn gas into ethylene, and an underground reservoir that would store the excess energy until it could be processed or traded. This investment was announced with great fanfare by the Justice administration and then Commerce Secretary Woody Thrasher, with a signing ceremony in the Great Hall of the People as part of President Trump's unveiling of business deals with China totaling over $250 billion. A detailed list of projects or an accompanying timeline was, however, never released and the Memorandum of Understanding outlining the deal was never made public.[43] Even Joe Manchin was left scratching his head on this one:

> You can imagine that kind of carrot being swung out there. It's tremendous for a small state. Our budget is only $4 billion a year and they're going to invest $83 billion. What would be their interest? We cannot find out one iota of what

[41] Kate Mishkin, *State DEP Chief Picked to Lead New Petrochemical Manufacturing Task Force*, CHARLESTON GAZETTE-MAIL (Aug. 28, 2019), https://www.wvgazettemail.com/news/energy_and_environment/state-dep-chief-picked-to-lead-new-petrochemical-manufacturing-task-force/article_123edd58-63ed-5c42-8c3c-ca52b37d5680.html.

[42] Brad McElhinny, *"Game-Changer" Cracker Plant in Wood County Is Off, but Another Developer Could Step Up*, WV METRO NEWS (July 23, 2019), https://wvmetronews.com/2019/07/23/game-changer-cracker-plant-in-wood-county-is-off-but-may-fall-to-someone-else/.

[43] Kayla Tausche, *West Virginia Is Still Waiting on a Game-Changing $84 Billion Investment from China That Was Promised in 2017*, CNBC (June 21, 2019), https://www.cnbc.com/2019/06/20/west-virginia-still-waiting-on-84-billion-investment-from-china.html.

the [Memorandum of Understanding] is. I have asked them directly and cannot get a direct answer about their investments.[44]

Finally, there was the Appalachian Storage and Trading Hub, a massive $10 billion multistate underground storage facility for natural gas byproducts that started getting support in Washington in 2016 and had the support of Manchin and, later, the Trump administration. Proponents of the project said that it would provide a sizable and stable storehouse for ethane and other so-called gas liquids that in turn would result in the expansion of a chemical production corridor that is emerging along the upper Ohio River and would help bring thousands of jobs to the region.[45] With Manchin's assistance, developers tried to secure a $1.9 billion loan guarantee for the project; the source was a loans program at the Department of Energy that is geared toward achieving reductions in GHG emissions – an objective that seems to be at odds with expansion of natural gas extraction to support a vast petrochemical complex. The project is likely dead under President Biden, who has expressed a strong commitment to address climate change and reduce GHG emissions.

Another casualty of the failed plans for a petrochemical buildout in Appalachia is a multibillion dollar cracker plant in Belmont County, Ohio which was planned by Thailand-based PTT Global Chemical of America (and supported by $70 million from JobsOhio, the state's economic development arm, to develop the site), and is unlikely to move forward.[46] The current state of the buildout of the petrochemical industry in Appalachia is best summed up by Ted Boettner, senior researcher with the Ohio River Valley Institute: Rather than the "industrial phoenix, rivaling the Gulf Coast" that was promised to West Virginians, so far they've gotten "a small facility with a payroll close to that of an Applebee's or an Olive Garden."[47]

Even the surge in economic activity in the counties directly affected by the fracking boom has not produced economic benefits for West Virginians. A February 2021 study by Sean O'Leary of the Ohio River Valley Institute, *The Natural Gas Fracking Boom and Appalachia's Lost Economic Decade*, examined the twenty-two industrial and rural counties in Ohio, Pennsylvania, and West Virginia that comprise the Appalachian natural gas region for the years 2008–19. These counties – referred to in the report as "Frackalachian" counties – are responsible

44 Taylor Stuck, *Manchin Dubious of China Energy Investment Deal with WV*, Charleston Gazette-Mail (July 21, 2019), https://www.wvgazettemail.com/news/politics/manchin-dubious-of-china-energy-investment-deal-with-wv/article_4d9548c5-915c-5545-9c7e-55b7f92db586.html.

45 Keith Schneider, *West Virginia Bets Big on Plastics, and on Backing of Trump Administration*, ProPublica (July 31, 2019), https://www.propublica.org/article/appalachian-storage-and-trading-hub-ethane-west-virginia-plastics-backing-of-trump-administration.

46 Beth Burger, *Petrochemical Hub Along Ohio River in Belmont County Faces Indefinite Delay*, Columbus Dispatch (Feb. 4, 2021), https://www.dispatch.com/story/business/2021/02/04/petrochemical-hub-faces-indefinite-delay-market-forces-dont-support-buildout-in-appalachia/4386072001/.

47 Ken Ward, *West Virginians Were Promised an Economic Revival. It Hasn't Happened Yet*, Mountain State Spotlight (Oct. 29, 2020), https://mountainstatespotlight.org/2020/10/29/west-virginians-were-promised-an-economic-revival-it-hasnt-happened-yet/.

for over 90 percent of all the gas produced in Appalachia, while representing just 10 percent of the land area of the three states and less than 4 percent of the population. The study found that while the rate of economic growth (as measured by gross domestic product) in these counties was more than triple that of the nation overall, measures of *local* economic prosperity not only failed to keep pace with the increased share of output, but actually declined. As compared with the 10 percent increase in the number of jobs nationally between 2008 and 2019, job growth was less than 4 percent in Ohio, Pennsylvania, and West Virginia. And the story was even worse for the Frackalachian counties, with combined job growth of only 1.6 percent. As described in the report, "[i]t is a case of economic growth without prosperity, the defining characteristic of the resource curse."[48]

For West Virginia, the study focused on the counties of Doddridge, Harrison, Marshall, Ohio, Ritchie, Tyler, and Wetzel. Between 2008 and 2019, jobs in these counties grew by 4 percent, which, while well below the national average of 10 percent, was much better than the 2.9 percent drop in the number of jobs statewide in West Virginia. But the Frackalachian counties in West Virginia lost more of their population – a decline of 10,000 people (5.2 percent) – than the overall population decline in West Virginia (2.6 percent). Doddridge was the only West Virginia Frackalachian county to not experience population loss.

The Ohio River Valley Institute report concludes

> there is little in the numbers to support the contention that the Appalachian natural gas boom has been or can be an engine for economic prosperity. If high production volumes were capable of creating jobs and prosperity, it would have happened. And there is a great deal which suggests that, in some cases, the industry may have the opposite effect.[49]

One of the reasons cited in the report is the failure to attract the massive job expansion that would have resulted from regional growth of downstream industries, including petrochemical and plastics manufacturing, which, as described earlier in this chapter, has largely failed to materialize.

---

[48]   O'Leary, *supra* note 10, at 4.
[49]   *Id.* at 16.

3

The Rise of Renewable Energy

While the impact of the shale gas revolution was the biggest driver of the decline of the coal industry in West Virginia, the increasing cost competitiveness of renewable generating sources – primarily solar photovoltaic (PV) and wind – also played a role, albeit a much smaller one, in West Virginia than on the national stage. The April 2017 study by the Columbia Center on Global Energy Policy[1] found that growth in renewable energy across the United States was responsible for about 18 percent of the decline in domestic coal production between 2011 and 2017, a distant third to the role of natural gas (49 percent) and lower than expected demand for electricity (26 percent). By the end of "the lost decade," however, the impact of renewable energy on the decline in coal-fired generation nationwide was much greater, as utilities conducting competitive solicitations for new resources uniformly found that building *new* wind or solar generation was cheaper than continuing to run *existing* coal plants.

Wind and solar generation benefited from technological innovations throughout "the lost decade" that resulted in improved efficiencies of these renewable resources – as measured by increasing capacity factors – as well as reductions in upfront capital costs, as measured in dollars per megawatt (MW) of installed capacity. In contrast, no similar breakthroughs were achieved in the decades-old technology of burning coal to generate electricity. Rather than spending money on research and development – the sort of investment that produced innovations such as horizontal drilling for natural gas and technological advancements in the design, manufacture, and installation of wind and solar resources – the coal industry pretty much decided to spend its "energy" in the political arena, complaining about the "war on coal" allegedly being waged by the Obama administration and its environmental regulations. As a result, by the end of "the lost decade," the war was virtually over and, as confirmed by the Columbia study, the impact of the rise of renewables was about five times greater than the role of environmental regulations – 18 percent versus 3.5 percent – in contributing to the demise of the coal industry.

[1] *See supra* note 15 (Ch. 2).

As in the case of the shale gas revolution discussed in the previous chapter, West Virginia largely missed out on the benefits being created in the "clean energy" sector comprising wind, solar, and energy efficiency. Many utilities across the country began to revisit their commitment to coal-fired generation early in "the lost decade," based on favorable trends in the costs of renewable energy and the perceived risks associated with continuing to burn coal as the developed nations in the world began to focus on climate change. In West Virginia, however, there was very little growth in renewable energy during "the lost decade," for reasons that are discussed in Chapters 4, 8, and 9. First, at the beginning of "the lost decade," West Virginia, unlike the vast majority of states, had no policies that promoted the development of renewable energy resources, such as a renewable portfolio standard requiring utilities to procure a prescribed percentage of their electricity supply from renewable sources. Nor did the Public Service Commission (PSC) require electric utilities operating in West Virginia to implement a rigorous integrated resource planning process that would have revealed the increasing cost competitiveness of wind, solar, and energy efficiency versus continued reliance on decades-old, inefficient coal-fired plants. The complete absence of state policies promoting the development of renewable resources largely persists today.

Because of this lack of growth in renewable energy in West Virginia, this factor played a very minor role in the decline of the coal industry in the state during "the lost decade." Rather, it represents a lost opportunity for West Virginia to have participated in the massive growth of the clean energy economy during this period. Nearly all the surrounding states adopted policies promoting the development of renewable energy resources, and were able to capture jobs and associated economic activity. It also represents a lost opportunity for West Virginians to have benefited from a diverse electricity generating portfolio that could have kept electric bills from spiraling out of control at a pace that turned out to be five times greater than the national average.[2] And, in the case of distributed solar in particular, West Virginians would have benefited from the ability to generate their own electricity – and thereby have some hedge against spiraling electricity costs – through creative financing mechanisms for rooftop solar such as those adopted in the surrounding states.

THE STATE OF PLAY AT THE START OF "THE LOST DECADE"

Even though there were no policies in place to encourage renewable energy development within West Virginia, at the start of "the lost decade" several large

---

[2] Electricity prices increased in West Virginia at an average annual rate of 3.77% between 2008 and 2020, while the national figure was only 0.70%. *See supra* note 22 (Ch. 2).

wind projects had been built in the state, taking advantage of the high mountain ridges with good wind resource potential in Barbour, Randolph, Greenbrier, Tucker, Grant, and Mineral counties. As of 2010, there were six large wind projects operating in West Virginia totaling 583 MW, ranging from the Pinnacle Wind Farm in Mineral County (55 MW) to the Mount Storm project in Grant County (264 MW).[3] In addition to wind farms, West Virginia was also home to what was at the time the world's largest lithium-ion battery farm – a 32 MW integrated battery-based energy storage system at the AES Laurel Mountain project, a 97.6 MW wind farm that stretches across 12.5 miles of the western ridge of the Allegheny Mountains in the Belington area. (The use of battery storage technology helps to optimize the value of the renewable energy generated, by helping to address the variability in the power output of renewable energy facilities.) Other renewable energy resources in West Virginia at the time included ten hydro projects totaling 462 MW, the largest of which were the Summersville Dam on the Gauley River (80 MW) and the Hawks Nest Dam on the New River (69 MW). There were no "utility-scale" solar facilities (i.e., 1 MW or larger) in West Virginia. The only solar arrays consisted of small customer-sited rooftop solar projects with an aggregate capacity of less than 1 MW (specifically 637.32 kW), the largest of which was the Appalachian Offroad Motorcycle Company in Cross Lanes (a suburb of Charleston) (36 kW). Collectively, renewable energy resources represented less than 5 percent of the state's electricity supply at the start of "the lost decade."

In the absence of any incentives to build renewable energy projects within West Virginia, developers had to rely on the incentives offered by surrounding and other states within the PJM wholesale market. A state with a renewable portfolio standard (RPS) will typically provide its utilities three options for complying with the obligation to procure a prescribed percentage of its electricity supply from renewable resources. The utility can: (1) own the renewable energy resource, (2) purchase the output of a renewable energy resource owned by a third party, or (3) purchase renewable energy certificates, or RECs, which reflect the renewable attributes of a renewable energy project. Essentially the output from a renewable energy project is unbundled into two components: the electrons, or electricity produced by the project, and the RECs, which represent the additional value associated with their use for complying with a state's RPS. There is a separate market for these RECs within the PJM wholesale market that provides value for the developers of renewable energy projects in West Virginia. The fact that the adjacent states of Ohio, Pennsylvania, and Maryland have an RPS therefore allowed West Virginia to be a "free rider" to some extent – it could benefit from the renewable energy development within its borders, while ratepayers in the surrounding states bear any additional costs associated with the renewable nature of the project. The operation of

---

[3]   West Virginia Public Service Commission, *Report to the West Virginia Legislature Joint Committee on Government and Finance, Initial Results of Alternative and Renewable Energy Planning Assessment* (June 2012).

the REC market, and the ability of utilities to use renewable energy projects in West Virginia to satisfy their RPS-related obligations in the states in which they operate, explain how West Virginia was able to attract several hundred MWs of wind power within its borders.

Meanwhile, in other parts of the mid-Atlantic region as well as other regions of the United States, the transition to renewables was already underway at the start of "the lost decade." Between 2001 and 2010, the market share for wind and the utility-scale solar market had grown slowly but steadily to 2.4 percent nationwide.[4] Within PJM, wind generation increased almost 1,300 percent between 2005 and 2010, while solar increased from less than 100 MWh in 2005 to more than 81,000 MWh in 2010, a 3,000-percent increase. As a result of the increased contributions of renewable energy – as well as the beginning of the replacement of coal-fired generation with natural gas – the amount of carbon dioxide (CO_2) emissions per megawatt-hour (MWh) of generation in the PJM region declined by 12 percent between 2005 and 2010.[5]

In February 2009, the *New York Times* cited a "growing outlook" that favored clean energy, and reported that utilities' plans for eighty-three new coal plants in the United States had either been voluntarily withdrawn or denied permits by state regulators over the preceding two-and-a-half years. Duke Energy, which at the time generated 71 percent of its electricity from coal, announced plans to buy the entire output of a large solar farm in North Carolina and was planning to install solar panels on rooftops at hundreds of customer sites. At about the same time, Duke Energy's first purchase from a wind farm started flowing to customers in Indiana. In Colorado, Xcel Energy, which at the time generated about half of its electricity from coal, erected 274 wind turbines on the gusty plains of northeastern Colorado and produced more of its power from wind, almost 3,000 MW, than any other utility.[6] In the southwest, some of the largest electric utilities announced plans to shift away from coal-fired power generation and toward an increased reliance on renewables and energy efficiency. Arizona Public Service, Arizona's largest utility with 1.1 million customers, released a five-year plan in 2009 that included no new coal-fired plants; instead, it planned to fulfill virtually all of its demand growth with wind and solar projects and increased energy efficiency. NV Energy, which serves 2.4 million customers in Nevada and northeastern California, also began to move away from coal, and announced in February 2009 that it was postponing the

4   Dennis Wamsted & Seth Feaster, *IEEFA US: The coal-to-renewables transition takes off*, INSTITUTE FOR ENERGY ECONOMICS AND FINANCIAL ANALYSIS (May 5, 2021), https://ieefa.org/ieefa-u-s-the-coal-to-renew ables-transition-takes-off/?utm_source=rss&utm_medium=rss&utm_campaign=ieefa-u-s-the-coal-to-renewables-transition-takes-off.

5   PJM Environmental Information Services, *First 5 Years of GATS' Data Show Renewables More Than Doubled in PJM*, PR NEWSWIRE (Apr. 22, 2010), https://www.prnewswire.com/news-releases/first-5-years-of-gats-data-show-renewables-more-than-doubled-in-pjm-91833389.html.

6   Melanie Warner, *Is America Ready to Quit Coal?*, N.Y. TIMES (Feb. 14, 2009), https://www .nytimes.com/2009/02/15/business/15coal.html.

development of a massive, 1,500 MW coal-fired power plant near Ely, in sparsely populated eastern Nevada. Its latest resource plan also indicated that all demand growth through 2012 would be met through renewable sources and energy efficiency.[7] Meanwhile, in the northeast, about 17,000 MW of planned renewable energy projects were planned for the early part of the decade, including biomass, geothermal, hydroelectric, solar, and wind resources, driven largely by ambitious renewable energy requirements set by many states.[8]

A TRANSFORMATIONAL DECADE FOR RENEWABLE ENERGY

"The lost decade" was truly transformational for renewable energy, as solar PV prices dropped by 89 percent and the cost of wind declined by 72 percent between 2009 and 2019.[9] A good way to compare the relative economics of renewables versus coal and natural gas is to examine the levelized cost of electricity, or LCOE,[10] which reflects the cost of building the power plant itself – the upfront capital costs – as well as the ongoing costs for fuel and operating the plant over its lifetime. The LCOE thus captures the zero fuel costs for wind and solar resources, which over the lifetime of a plant will achieve savings versus coal and natural gas that more than offset the higher upfront capital costs associated with renewable resources. Or, put another way, the LCOE is the minimum level of revenue that a power plant needs to recover from selling its output to enable it to break even over its lifetime. In 2009, solar and wind didn't stand a chance against a coal plant: wind was 22 percent, and solar 223 percent more expensive than coal.[11] Between 2009 and 2019, however, the LCOE for coal declined by only 2 percent, from $111 per MWh to $109 per MWh, while solar PV's LCOE declined from $359 per MWh to $40 per MWh and onshore wind's LCOE declined from $125 per MWh to $41 per MWh. In other words, the cost advantage of coal over wind and solar flipped during "the lost decade": the cost of operating an *existing* coal plant is now much higher than building and operating a *new* wind or solar facility.

Meanwhile, the LCOE for a natural gas-fired combined-cycle unit – the electric utility's new baseload generator of choice during this period, as discussed in Chapter 2 – declined by 32 percent, from $83 per MWh to $56 per MWh. That decline was primarily due to lower cost natural gas, as a result of the shale gas revolution (as described in Chapter 2), rather than a significant breakthrough in

---

[7] John Collins Rudolph, *Big Utilities Pull Back on Coal Plant Plans*, N.Y. Times (Sept. 29, 2009), https://green.blogs.nytimes.com/2009/09/29/big-utilities-pull-back-on-coal-plant-plans/.

[8] Sindya Bhanoo, *Snapshot: Northeast Clean Energy Projects*, N.Y. Times (Oct. 29, 2009), https://green.blogs.nytimes.com/2009/10/29/snapshot-northeast-clean-energy-projects/?searchResultPosition=154.

[9] Max Roser, *Why Did Renewables Become So Cheap So Fast?*, Our World in Data (Dec. 1, 2020), https://ourworldindata.org/cheap-renewables-growth.

[10] *Levelized Cost of Energy and Levelized Cost of Storage 2019*, Lazard (Nov. 7, 2019), https://www.lazard.com/perspective/lcoe2019.

[11] Roser, *supra* note 9.

natural gas-turbine technology. In the case of solar, however, the decline was attributable to a dramatic reduction in the cost of solar modules, which declined by a staggering 99.6 percent, from $106 per watt to $0.38 per watt, during "the lost decade." This was primarily due to the "learning rate" of solar PV modules – the relationship between experience with the technology, as measured by the cumulative installed capacity of that technology, and its price. In the case of solar, as the amount of installed capacity increased exponentially, the price of solar modules declined exponentially, thereby producing a learning effect of 20.2 percent from 2009 to 2019. Stated differently, with each doubling of installed cumulative capacity, the price of solar modules declined by 20.2 percent.

No similar technological breakthrough occurred in the case of coal, of course, given that there is little room for achieving much improvement in the efficiency of coal-fired power plants. Typically, plants have efficiencies of around 33 percent, while the most efficient ones today – such as the Longview Power facility north of Morgantown – reach 47 percent. Moreover, the price of electricity from a coal plant is determined not only by the technology but, to a significant extent, by the cost of the fuel itself. The cost of the coal that a power plant burns comprises about 40 percent of total costs, which results in an impenetrable lower bound below which the cost of electricity cannot fall, even if the price of constructing the power plant declines.

As a result of this transformation, the market share for wind and utility-scale solar increased to more than 11 percent in 2020. The market share of coal, on the other hand, fell to less than 20 percent nationwide, as it was undercut first by gas generation that benefited from falling prices due to fracking and more recently by a "relentless" buildout of lower-cost renewables. As a result, a 2021 report by the Institute for Energy Economics and Financial Analysis (IEEFA) concluded that in 2020 the share of power from coal slumped to what may have been the lowest level since the dawn of the electric age in the United States, 140 years ago.[12] IEEFA noted the "record-setting" levels of renewable energy and battery storage added to the grid in 2020 – nearly 14 gigawatts (GW) of utility-scale solar, 5 GW of rooftop solar, 16.9 GW of wind, and 1 GW of battery storage – a preview of the "massive green energy buildout" that it expects between 2021 and 2030. IEEFA cited projections of additional capacity of 324 GW of solar, 34.7 GW of wind, and 30 GW of battery storage installations by 2030, the combination of which is likely to result in retirement of 75.5 GW of coal capacity over the same period (nearly double the 37.4 GW of coal retirement by 2030 that had been announced in March 2020).

By the end of 2020, 31 percent of the coal-fired generation capacity that existed at its peak in 2011 had been retired. That percentage is expected to grow to 55 percent by 2030. Even before their retirement, the remaining coal plants are gradually being operated less, in the face of lower cost generation from natural gas and renewables;

---

[12] Wamsted & Feaster, *supra* note 4.

the average annual capacity factor (which compares the output of a plant if it were operating all the time versus its actual annual output, given frequent "down times" when it is not cost competitive to dispatch it) of installed coal plants fell from 62.8 percent in 2011 to 40.2 percent in 2020. A good example is the four-unit, 3,440 MW Scherer station in Georgia, which is the largest coal-fired power plant in the United States. In 2020, Scherer had a capacity factor of only 18.6 percent, or less than half of the 40 percent capacity factor the plant had in 2019. Based on planned retirements and an expectation that remaining plants will be operated less often, IEEFA concludes that coal's share of the US generation sector will likely fall to as low as 10 percent by 2025.[13]

The story is not much better for the "other" fossil fuel in West Virginia, natural gas. Of further concern to West Virginia policymakers hoping to continue to ride the fracking boom is IEEFA's conclusion that the "gas bridge" – the notion that natural gas provides the "bridge" between coal as the primary source of electricity generation and a future reliance on renewables – is now "closed."[14] According to IEEFA's analysis, due to improvements in wind and solar technology over the past decade and the resulting price declines in the LCOE for these electricity sources, these two generation resources are now the least-cost option across much of the United States. In other words, the slight price advantage that natural gas-fired generation previously held over renewables has vanished in most parts of the country, allowing utilities to transition directly from coal to renewables. The sharp rise during the last decade in the use of combined-cycle combustion turbines – the baseload power plant of choice during "the lost decade," as discussed in Chapter 2, has reached a "plateau," according to IEEFA." The environmental benefits of using natural gas versus coal – natural gas has about one half of the greenhouse gas (GHG) emissions as coal when used to generate electricity – have become largely irrelevant in the face of growing evidence of methane emissions throughout the gas production, distribution, and consumption chain, and this has contributed to the closing of the natural gas "bridge." (In terms of "global warming potential," which measures the impact of a GHG in terms of its heat-trapping characteristics, methane is over thirty times more potent than CO_2.)[15]

Even natural gas peaking plants (typically simple-cycle combustion turbines), which are occasionally dispatched by utilities to meet peak demands on their system,

[13] Press release, IEEFA U.S., Energy Transition to Renewables Likely to Accelerate over Next Two to Three Years (Mar. 31, 2021), https://ieefa.org/ieefa-u-s-energy-transition-to-renewables-likely-to-acceler ate-over-next-two-to-three-years/#:~:text=March%2031%2C%202021%20(IEEFA),U.S.%20Power%20Sec tor%20Outlook%202021.&text=The%20increase%20in%20renewables%20is%20happening%20largely%2 0at%20the%20expense%20of%20coal.

[14] Dennis Wamsted, Seth Feaster, & David Schlissel, *U.S. Power Sector Outlook 2021: Rapid Transition Continues to Reshape Country's Electricity Generation*, INSTITUTE FOR ENERGY ECONOMICS AND FINANCIAL ANALYSIS (Mar. 2021),http://ieefa.org/wp-content/uploads/2021/03/US-Power-Sector-Outlook_March-2021.pdf.

[15] *Understanding Global Warming Potentials*, ENVIRONMENTAL PROTECTION AGENCY, https://www .epa.gov/ghgemissions/understanding-global-warming-potentials.

TABLE 3.1 *Potential cost by resource per MWh post-2023–4*

Resource	Cost per MWh
Near-firm[1] wind	$20–30
Near-firm solar	$30–40
Natural gas	$30–40
Existing coal	$35–50
Existing nuclear	$35–50

Source: Presentation by NextEra (2020), a large renewable developer, to its investors. *See supra* note 14, at 11.
[1] The term "near-firm" refers to NextEra's ability to pair battery storage with renewables to extend the period for which the energy supply is firm, or reliable.

can be replaced by grid-scale battery storage. Using four-hour duration lithium batteries gives utilities the ability to store wind and solar generation when it is not needed and to use it during periods of peak demand or, as described by one utility executive, the ability to provide "solar after sunset."[16] The cost effectiveness of wind and solar coupled with battery storage is illustrated in Table 3.1.

During a January earnings call to discuss NextEra's 2020 results, CEO Jim Robo confirmed the impact of renewables plus storage on the prospects for the future of coal-fired generation: "There is not a regulated coal plant in this country that is economic today – full period and stop – when it's dispatched on any basis, not a single one, OK."[17]

Chris Beam, the president of Appalachian Power, made a similar point to lawmakers in West Virginia when he testified during the 2021 legislative session regarding a bill that would have required coal plants not only to remain open in West Virginia, but to continue burning coal at 2019 levels. In explaining to lawmakers the rationale behind closing coal plants, Beam said "[i]t's an economics decision. These units are no longer economical. You cannot and should not force onto the customer an uneconomical solution."[18] Appalachian Power's parent company, American Electric Power (AEP) is one of the utilities that is accelerating its transition to renewables in light of the rapid transformation that is underway in the industry. In late 2020, AEP announced plans to add roughly 8 GW of new renewable energy capacity to its eleven-state system by 2030. During its first quarter 2021 earnings call, AEP went even further and "literally doubled down" on renewable energy, announcing plans to build 16,595 MW of new renewables capacity by 2030,

[16] Press release, IEEFA U.S., *supra* note 13.
[17] *Id.* at 11.
[18] Lucas Mansfield, *W.Va. Lawmakers Remain Desperate to Prop Up the Dying Coal Industry. Residents Are Paying the Cost with Higher Electric Bills*, MOUNTAINS STATE SPOTLIGHT (Mar. 11, 2021), https://mountainstatespotlight.org/2021/03/11/west-virginia-lawmakers-remain-desperate-to-prop-up-the-dying-coal-industry-residents-are-paying-the-cost-with-higher-electric-bills/.

with 10 GW of that total being online by 2025. This new strategy would result in the retirement of another 4,979 MW of coal-fired capacity by 2028, with an additional 595 MW slated for 2030.[19]

The dismal prospect for coal's future was confirmed in a report, *Coal Cost Crossover*, issued in May 2021 by Energy Innovation, a clean energy think tank. The report found that 80 percent of coal plants in America are either already slated to retire by 2025, or are currently uneconomic compared to wind and solar.[20] The report calculated the estimated lifetime cost of building and running new wind and solar facilities (or LCOE, as discussed above) based on publicly available data from the National Renewable Energy Laboratory (NREL), and compared these figures with the going-forward cost of operating existing coal plants, based on information from the Energy Information Administration (EIA). The analysis was performed for specified geographic regions – based on 134 "balancing areas" in the case of solar and 356 "resource supply regions" in the case of wind – which enabled the comparison to be presented on a plant-by-plant basis. In other words, based on the particular wind and solar conditions for a geographic area, and the specific operating costs for each coal plant, the report was able to show whether it made sense for a coal plant to continue operating versus being shut down in favor of wind or solar. Bear in mind, this is *new* wind and solar (which is reflected in the LCOE figures) versus continuing to operate *existing* coal plants. The *Coal Cost Crossover* report included the data necessary to analyze the prospects for nine coal plants in West Virginia, as shown in Table 3.2.

TABLE 3.2 *LCOE of West Virginia coal plants versus wind, solar*

Plant	Owner	Coal cost (per MWh)	Savings with wind	Savings with solar
Mitchell	AEP	$45.78	34%	16%
Amos	AEP	38.89	–	–
Mountaineer	AEP	26.99	–	–
Ft. Martin	FirstEnergy	34.89	8%	–
Harrison	FirstEnergy	27.35	–	–
Grant Town	Amer Bitum Power	35.04	36%	–
Pleasants Station	FirstEnergy	34.57	14%	–
Longview	Genpower LLC	30.78	1%	–
Mount Storm	Dominion	66.98	65%	43%

Source: See supra note 21.

[19] Wamstad & Feaster, *supra* note 4.
[20] Eric Gimon, Amanda Myers, & Mike O'Boyle, *Coal Cost Crossover 2.0*, Energy Innovation (May 2021), https://energyinnovation.org/wp-content/uploads/2021/05/Coal-Cost-Crossover-2.0-1.pdf.

The LCOE calculations show that the economics for new wind in West Virginia are fairly strong – for the "resource supply region" covering most of the state, the LCOE is $22.29 per MWh – which helps explain why many of the coal plants appear uneconomic when compared to wind. On the other hand, solar appears to be relatively more expensive in the state – the figures for the various "balancing areas" range from $36.85 to $39.39 per MWh – which helps explain the relative advantage of existing coal plants over new solar facilities.

For many of the reasons described earlier in this chapter – including the continuing improvement in the cost effectiveness of wind, solar, and battery storage technology – the economic case for coal-fired generation will continue to deteriorate. As noted in the *Coal Cost Crossover* report, the cost of renewables fell even faster over the past two years than NREL had forecast in its 2018 Annual Technology Baseline (ATB). This same analysis performed in 2019, based on the 2018 ATB, suggested that 62 percent of coal capacity was uneconomic versus wind or solar (as compared with 72 percent in the 2021 report), which demonstrates how the declining cost of renewables – and the lack of any corresponding technological break-through for coal – changes the analysis for the worse for coal. In addition, the extension of the federal investment tax credit for small and large solar systems at 26 percent through 2022, 22 percent for 2023, and 10 percent indefinitely thereafter for larger systems improves the economics for solar, while wind qualifies for a production tax credit ($15 per MWh for 2021). Finally, as capacity factors for existing coal plants continue to decline, the efficiency of the plants' operation suffers and the fixed operational and ongoing capital maintenance costs are spread over fewer hours, further burdening the cost figures for coal.

THE ELUSIVE TRANSITION IN WEST VIRGINIA

As described in the preceding section, in early 2021 AEP proclaimed that it was transforming from what AEP's CEO Nick Atkins described as "the largest coal-fired utility to one of the largest regulated renewable companies in the U.S."[21] This transformation apparently does not extend to West Virginia, however. AEP has announced no plans to retire its three large coal-fired plants in the state – the single unit, 1,299 MW Mountaineer station, the three-unit, 2,900 MW John Amos plant, and the two-unit, 1,560 MW Mitchell station. In fact, rather than seriously consider-ing the retirement of these units, in October 2021 AEP secured approval from the West Virginia PSC to spend $448.3 million in additional ratepayer dollars in order to keep the plants open through 2040.[22] (These are the compliance costs that AEP will

[21] *CEO Nick Akins on Q1 2021 Results - Earnings Call Transcript*, Seeking Alpha (April 22, 2021), https:// seekingalpha.com/article/4420741-american-electric-power-company-inc-aep-ceo-nick-akins-on-q1 -2021-results-earnings-call.

[22] West Virginia PSC, Case No. 20–1040-E-CN, *Appalachian Power Company and Wheeling Power Company Application for the Issuance of a Certificate of Public Convenience and Necessity for the*

incur to comply with newly adopted Environmental Protection Agency [EPA] regulations governing the disposal of coal combustion residuals (CCRs) and effluent limitation guidelines (ELGs) at all three plants.) Without the additional investment to comply with the CCR and ELG requirements, the plants would be unable to continue operating after 2028.

In the case of the Mitchell plant, AEP's own numbers in the filing showed that ratepayers would be better off by $27 million per year by not making the additional investment at Mitchell, and instead replacing the plant, after 2028, with other generating resources in the region with available capacity. This concession by AEP was hardly surprising; in fact, it was supported by the analysis in the *Coal Cost Crossover* report, which showed that replacing Mitchell with wind would be 34 percent cheaper for ratepayers. Rather than admit that it was unable to make the case for Mitchell's continued operation after 2028, however, AEP simply punted the decision to the PSC, claiming that the latter was obligated to consider a "broad range of other interests" in addition to the economic analysis submitted by AEP.[23] This course of action would "preserve maximum flexibility for regulators," according to Appalachian Power president Chris Beam's testimony in the case. In other words, AEP declined to take a position that protected ratepayers' interests, and instead decided to leave it up to the PSC to determine whether it made sense to keep the plant open after 2028. That was a safe bet for AEP, knowing that the PSC, consistent with its rulings throughout "the lost decade" that put the interests of the coal industry ahead of West Virginia's electric ratepayers (discussed further in Chapters 8 and 10), would likely approve the expenditures. And AEP's gamble paid off when the PSC issued its decision in October 2021 approving the waste of additional ratepayer dollars on uneconomical coal plants (this decision is discussed further in Chapter 10).

With respect to the purported "rise in renewables," AEP's ruse illustrates that the policy it claimed to be pursuing at the corporate level in Columbus – AEP's transformation "from the largest coal-fired utility to one of the largest regulated renewable companies in the U.S." – simply did not extend to West Virginia. It was obvious to AEP that regardless of whether keeping coal plants open made economic sense for ratepayers, the West Virginia PSC would approve it, so there was no sense in putting any shareholder dollars at risk by pursuing a transition to renewables in the Mountain State.

In contrast to the fast-paced transition from coal to renewables that was apparent at a national level, there was very little movement toward renewable energy in West Virginia during "the lost decade." Through 2020, West Virginia had added about another 160 MW of wind generation, including the expansion of the Beech Ridge Project in Greenbrier County, which grew from its original 100 MW in 2010 by another 56 MW when Beech Ridge II became operational in April 2020. West

---

Internal Modifications at Coal-Fired Generating Plants Necessary to Comply with Federal Environmental Regulations.

[23] *Id.* at 8 (testimony of Chris Beam).

Virginia's total installed wind capacity of 742 MW – representing about 2.2 percent of its electricity supply – placed West Virginia at number twenty-six in the United States. (Texas is ranked number one in installed wind capacity, with over 25,000 MW, while Iowa is ranked number one with respect to the percentage of its energy generated with wind, at 37 percent.)

The new decade, however, looks somewhat more promising for renewable energy development in West Virginia. In 2020, the state legislature passed two measures that improved the prospects for development of utility-scale solar projects in the state. First, SB 578 adjusted the capacity rate that is used for the purposes of assessing state business and occupation taxes – setting it at 8 percent of the nameplate capacity – which brought the tax rate more in line with the actual generating capacity of solar units, thereby removing what was formerly a punitive calculation. Second, SB 583, a bill promoted by Speaker Roger Hanshaw in the West Virginia House of Delegates, established a streamlined process for electric utilities and independent power producers to develop utility-scale solar projects by waiving many of the requirements that would otherwise apply in the normal certificate of convenience and necessity (CCN) process for generating units, and imposing an expedited time limit for the PSC to process such applications. SB 583 also provided financial incentives for the regulated electric utilities to build or purchase utility-scale solar projects through expedited rate recovery of their investment and expenses related to such projects, including a legislative finding that such projects were presumed to be in the public interest, thereby removing some of the regulatory risk associated with utility projects.

Apart from the positive development in the legislature, new renewable energy projects are at various stages of development in West Virginia. In January 2021, Clearway Energy announced that it was breaking ground on a $200 million project in Mineral and Grant Counties, the 115 MW Black Rock Wind project. The output from the project will be purchased by Toyota and AEP Energy. (As discussed in Chapter 4, Toyota, which has had a manufacturing facility in West Virginia since 2012, is committed to generating or purchasing 100 percent of its electricity from renewable sources. AEP Energy, for its part, is a competitive retail energy supplier owned by AEP, offering a renewable energy option to its subscribing customers.) In announcing the Black Rock project, West Virginia Governor Jim Justice claimed that he was "a complete believer [that] West Virginia has to become a diversified state." At the same time, he wanted to assure workers in the state's traditional fossil fuel industries that while "we absolutely want to embrace the all-encompassing thing … we absolutely do not run off and leave our coal mine jobs, our natural gas jobs, or oil jobs. We do not run off and leave them in any way."[24] After watching the Governor's speech, Michelle Lewis of *Electrek* observed that Justice "can't bring himself to tell them the hard, scary truth." According to Lewis, West Virginia is

---

[24] Michelle Lewis, *Coal-Dependent West Virginia Gets a $200 Million Wind Farm*, ELECTREK (Jan. 26, 2021), https://electrek.co/2021/01/26/coal-dependent-west-virginia-200-million-wind-farm/.

"dependent on a rapidly disappearing fuel" and "[t]hose folks who work in coal in West Virginia need a Plan B."[25]

On the solar side, while there was still no utility-scale solar project operating in West Virginia as of the end of 2020, at the time of writing three new projects are at various stages of development. In April 2020, the PSC issued a siting certificate to Longview Renewable Power LLC for its proposed 70 MW solar facility, 20 MW of which will be located in Monongalia County – adjacent to the existing Longview coal-fired plant – with another 50 MW across the border in Pennsylvania. Six months later, the PSC granted a siting certificate for a $90 million 90 MW project in Raleigh County being developed by Dakota Renewable Energy LLC, an alternative energy developer with a track record of installing more than 3,300 MW of alternative energy projects representing capital investment of over $4.1 billion. Finally, in November 2020, Wild Hill Solar LLC, an indirect subsidiary of EDF Renewables, Incorporated, filed a solar siting certificate application with the PSC for a 92.5 MW facility to be built in Jefferson County.

The next chapter examines some of these developments from a slightly different perspective. The rise of renewables contributed to a reshaping of the electric utility industry that occurred throughout "the lost decade," as utilities both "decarbonized" – by reducing the carbon intensity of their generating portfolio through increased use of renewables (as well as natural gas) – and "decentralized" – by moving away from the traditional utility business model featuring large, centralized generating plants (coal-fired in West Virginia, of course) in favor of smaller, generating resources dispersed throughout a utility's service territory that increase the resilience of the grid. Unfortunately, in the case of both the shale gas revolution and the rise of renewables, it was a development that largely bypassed West Virginia.

---

[25] *Id.*

4

The "Ds" of Today's Electric Utility Industry: Decarbonization and Decentralization

Throughout "the lost decade," two trends dominated the landscape of the electric utility industry in the United States: decarbonization, or a dramatic reduction in the "carbon footprint" of the typical electric utility, and decentralization, the movement away from the historic, large, centralized generating station model toward greater reliance on smaller, dispersed generating resources – rooftop solar, for example – throughout a utility's service territory. For the most part, these trends were driven by economics or market forces rather than specific government policies.

With respect to decarbonization, as discussed in Chapter 2, the displacement of coal-fired generation with natural gas-fired combustion turbines throughout "the lost decade" – largely as a result of cheap, plentiful "fracked" gas and improvements in combined-cycle combustion turbine technology – produced significant reductions in greenhouse gas (GHG) emissions from the electric utility industry. Natural gas is twice as clean as coal in terms of carbon emissions when combusted to generate electricity.[1] The rise of renewables described in Chapter 3, due in large part to the dramatic cost reductions achieved in the solar and wind industries, resulted in additional decarbonization, as many utilities moved directly from coal to renewables, completely bypassing the natural gas "bridge." Due to this decarbonization trend, the electricity sector ceased to be the largest source of GHG emissions in the United States as of the end of "the lost decade," as it fell behind GHG emissions from the transportation sector for the first time in history.

Apart from economics, however, there were other drivers of decarbonization, and these are discussed in this chapter. One was the demand of large, corporate utility customers for renewable energy, to meet robust corporate sustainability goals. Another was action by states to move from the typical renewable portfolio standard to a "clean energy" or "zero-carbon" standard, which required utilities to pursue a path that would get them to zero carbon by a specified date, usually 2045 or 2050. Later in "the lost decade," many electric utilities were

---

[1] *Natural Gas: At a Glance*, CENTER FOR CLIMATE AND ENERGY SOLUTIONS, https://www.c2es.org/content/natural-gas/.

getting on the zero-carbon bandwagon, and announcing their own commitments to get to zero carbon.

Decentralization was also driven in large part by economics, as the declining cost of rooftop solar made it a very attractive option for utility customers across all classes (residential, commercial, and industrial) to reduce their energy costs by generating their own power. The 99.6 percent reduction in the cost of solar modules between 2009 and 2019, as described in Chapter 3, translated into dramatic reductions in the installed cost of rooftop solar that jumpstarted the distributed (as distinguished from utility-scale) solar industry in the United States. There were other drivers as well that will be discussed in this chapter. One of these was state policies promoting the deployment of distributed generation (DG) resources, such as net metering laws that were widely adopted across the country and required utilities to purchase the output from rooftop solar at prices corresponding to the utility's retail rate. Another driver was a desire to improve the resilience of the utility grid in the face of extreme weather events caused by climate change. Increased deployment of DG resources reduces reliance on a system that has proven to be vulnerable to extreme weather events, whether as a result of downed transmission lines or flooded substations. Simply put, generating power closer to where it is used results in a more resilient grid. Another driver was that solar installers themselves were able to help achieve decentralization by offering creative financing options, in the form of power purchase agreements, that would relieve the typical homeowner of the massive upfront costs of rooftop solar by spreading those costs over the lifetime of the solar panels.

Finally, decentralization is driven to some extent by states moving to address what is perceived as a fundamental change in the utility business model. Utility regulators began to take note of the inherent deficiency in a regulatory model that depended upon utilities selling more kilowatt hours (KWhs), in the face of customers generating more of their energy through rooftop solar and using less energy due to scaled-up utility energy efficiency programs. In many states, utilities began to move from a model of one-way power flows from large, centralized generation stations to a new role as operators of the distribution system platform, where they were expected to manage two-way flows of both power and communications.

Where was West Virginia as these decarbonization and decentralization trends played out across the United States during "the lost decade? "Largely absent. On the decarbonization front, West Virginia's electricity supply at the end of "the lost decade" was still 88 percent coal-fired as of 2020. Although there had been some substitution of natural gas into the mix with Appalachian Power's conversion of the three-unit Clinch River coal plant – located in Virginia – to two natural gas-fired units, West Virginia largely missed out on both the shale gas revolution and the rise of renewables, as discussed in Chapters 2 and 3. With respect to decentralization, West Virginia's net metering program, approved by the legislature in 2009, remained in place but had to survive a couple of challenges at the legislature – including a temporary repeal of the net metering statute (later restored) when the legislature repealed a companion provision, the Alternative and Renewable Energy Portfolio Standard, in January 2015 – that needlessly created some uncertainty in the market. As a result, rooftop solar remains a very small part of West Virginia's energy portfolio. One positive development was the passage of a bill in the 2021 legislative session that allows power purchase agreements for rooftop solar, which could stimulate some additional development in the coming years.

GETTING THE CARBON OUT OF THE ELECTRICITY SUPPLY

The Job Creators Demanding Renewable Energy

A major driver in the decarbonization of the electric utility industry is the demand of large customers for access to renewable energy, to help meet robust corporate sustainability objectives. Due to the magnitude of their energy needs – and the corresponding bargaining power that comes with it – large companies are playing a major role in pushing electric utilities to acquire more renewable energy. As of 2017, for example, 48 percent of Fortune 500 and 63 percent of Fortune 100 companies had promised to cut their GHG emissions and to increase their use of renewable energy or improve their energy efficiency.[2]

These commitments have become even firmer in recent years. A good example of the strong demand from businesses for renewable energy is the RE100 Initiative, which comprises dozens of major companies that have committed to procure 100 percent of their electricity requirements from renewable sources. Sixty-five new companies joined the RE100 in 2020, bringing the number of members to 285.[3] RE100 members include businesses like Anheuser-Busch, General Motors, Kellogg's, Trane, and PNC Bank. Of particular interest to West Virginia, members of the RE100 with operations in the Mountain State include Walmart (West Virginia's second largest employer), Procter & Gamble, Target, and General Mills. Looking beyond the RE100 initiative, other major employers in West Virginia with significant renewable energy procurement efforts include Kroger's, the state's fifth largest employer, with a commitment to achieving a 30 percent reduction in GHG emissions by 2030,[4] and Lowe's, the sixth largest employer, which has a commitment to reducing its carbon emissions by 40 percent by 2030.[5] Other

2   Robert Walton, *Report: Almost Half of Fortune 500 Companies Have Climate, Energy Goals*, Utility Dive (Apr. 28, 2017), https://www.utilitydive.com/news/report-almost-half-of-fortune-500-companies-have-climate-energy-goals/441535/.
3   *Corporate Clean Energy Buying Grew 18% in 2020, Despite Mountain of Adversity*, Bloomberg NEF (Jan. 26, 2021) https://about.bnef.com/blog/corporate-clean-energy-buying-grew-18-in-2020-despite-mountain-of-adversity/.
4   *Kroger Targets 30% Emissions Reduction*, Smart Energy Decisions (Aug. 18, 2020), https://www.smartenergydecisions.com/energy-management/2020/08/18/kroger-targets-30-emissions-reduction.
5   Mike Hendrix, *Wind Farm Takes Lowe's Sustainability Commitment to New Heights*, Lowe's (June 24, 2020), https://corporate.lowes.com/newsroom/stories/fresh-thinking/wind-farm-takes-lowes-sustainability-commitment-new-heights.

employers with a significant presence in West Virginia include Amazon, AT&T, PepsiCo, Toyota, and UPS. Amazon was the leading buyer of clean energy in 2020; it announced thirty-five separate clean energy acquisitions in 2020 that totaled 5.1 GW. Amazon has purchased over 7.5 GW of clean energy (as of 2021), placing it ahead of Google (6.6 GW) and Facebook (5.9 GW) as the world's largest clean energy buyer.[6]

Why are corporations demanding renewable energy? In 2016, the consulting arm of PwC carried out a survey of companies headquartered in the United States to determine their motivation for actively pursuing additional purchases of renewable energy. According to the survey results, the drivers were a desire to meet sustainability goals and to reduce GHG emissions (cited by 85 percent of respondents), to generate an attractive return on investment (76 percent), and to limit exposure to energy price variability (59 percent).[7] The cost certainty element is clearly an important consideration – while no one knows what coal or natural gas fuel prices will be in 2030, sunshine and wind will continue to be free, and that predictability is important to the chief financial officers (CFOs) of large corporations.

The need to meet these corporate demands for renewable energy has changed the narrative, to some extent, in West Virginia. This is not some sort of government mandate imposed on the states from Congress or bureaucrats in Washington, DC, or an environmental regulation enacted by "Obama's job-killing EPA." Rather, the pressure is being exerted by some of the state's largest employers (or potential employers) that are demanding access to renewable energy as a condition for locating or expanding in the state. West Virginia's economic development officials are on the front lines of these conversations. In February 2020, Commerce Secretary Ed Gaunch relayed to state legislators that when a company is considering an investment in West Virginia "[i]nvariably ... the first or second question in terms of criteria [is]: Where does your state stand in terms of renewable energy?" Because of the current lack of renewable energy in West Virginia, "[f]rankly, we don't ever make the cut," Secretary Gaunch explained.[8] This unfortunate situation was reiterated to legislators by Mike Graney, Executive Director of the West Virginia Development Office, who said: "Not having, frankly, the solar box checked is a problem, and we've heard that from a lot of different companies."[9]

Utilities in West Virginia – including American Electric Power (AEP, the parent company of Appalachian Power and Wheeling Power) – are starting to recognize

[6]   Bloomberg NEF, *supra* note 3.

[7]   PwC, Corporate Renewable Energy Procurement Survey Insights (Apr. 2016), https://www.pwc
      .com/us/en/sustainability-services/publications/assets/pwc-corporate-renewable-energy-procurement-sur
      vey-insights.pdf.

[8]   Brittany Patterson, *Sparks Fly in W.Va. Legislative Energy Committees over Utility Solar Bill*, W.V.
      Pub. Broadcasting (Feb. 4, 2020), https://www.wvpublic.org/news/2020-02-04/sparks-fly-in-w-va-
      legislative-energy-committees-over-utility-solar-bill.

[9]   Phil Kabler, *Solar Energy Bill Advances in Senate, with Pro-Coal Provision Added*, Charleston
      Gazette-Mail (Feb. 13, 2020), https://www.wvgazettemail.com/news/legislative_session/solar-
      energy-bill-advances-in-senate-with-pro-coal-provision-added/article_9500a115-7cdb-5161-82c5-
      b586cfb444cb.html.

this widespread demand for renewable energy from their customers. According to AEP, "What we have learned is that a strong majority of customers, especially large commercial and industrial customers, want clean energy."[10] Ken Silverstein of *Forbes* has observed that policymakers in West Virginia are beginning to respond favorably to testimony from economic developers who say that prospective companies are demanding more access to renewable energy.[11]

The issue is whether the necessary sense of urgency exists. With its electricity supply still 88 percent coal-fired as of 2020, West Virginia will have a difficult job attracting employers that are trying to achieve compliance with corporate clean energy goals. Until the grid is decarbonized sufficiently to compete with surrounding states, large employers in West Virginia will need to be creative in figuring out how to access renewable energy. One approach that was recently used in West Virginia for Toyota's purchase of one-half of the output of the Black Rock wind project (discussed in Chapter 3) is a "sleeved" power purchase agreement, where a buyer of renewable energy can contract with an offsite project through its utility. The utility essentially shops for the project, takes the power and then passes the cost on to the individual customer, thereby creating a pathway for the renewable energy transaction.[12] The problem with such targeted approaches, of course, is that it does not achieve decarbonization of the grid for everyone, but is limited to corporations with the resources and sophistication to craft such innovative arrangements. As noted in the PwC survey, corporations want renewable energy because it is an investment that provides good returns, and its zero fuel costs provide long-term certainty and stability. What's good for corporate buyers is also good for the average retail ratepayer, and West Virginia policymakers need to adopt policies that procure renewable energy for *all* utility customers, not just the Amazons and Toyotas of the world.

The Movement toward Clean or Zero-Carbon Energy Standards

Another noteworthy development during "the lost decade" is the trend of states to move beyond the renewable portfolio standards that were so popular during the 2000s to "clean energy standards." A clean energy standard typically refers to a technology-neutral portfolio standard that requires that a certain percentage of utility sales be met through "clean" zero- or low-carbon resources. The difference

[10] WEST VIRGINIA'S ENERGY FUTURE, WVU COLLEGE OF LAW CENTER FOR ENERGY AND SUSTAINABLE DEVELOPMENT 10 (Dec. 2020), https://energy.law.wvu.edu/files/d/b1ff1183-e9ae-4ad0-93bf-aa3afa1da785/wv-s-energy-future-wvu-col-cesd-final.pdf.

[11] Ken Silverstein, *The Dam Has Broken and West Virginia Has Awoken to Solar Power*, FORBES (May 16, 2021), https://www.forbes.com/sites/kensilverstein/2021/05/16/the-dam-has-broken-and-west-virginia-is-waking-up-to-solar-power/?sh=443a004e6d76.

[12] Julia Pyper, *Large Corporations Are Driving America's Renewable Energy Boom. And They're Just Getting Started*, GREENTECH MEDIA (Jan. 10, 2017), https://www.greentechmedia.com/articles/read/large-corporations-are-driving-americas-renewable-energy-boom.

between a renewable energy standard and a zero-carbon or clean energy standard is the inclusion of zero-carbon resources that are not renewable, such as nuclear generation, and fossil fuel-fired resources (coal and natural gas) that are equipped with carbon capture and sequestration (CCS) technology.[13] Clean energy standards drive the decarbonization of the electricity supply by specifying a percentage of supply that must be met with zero-carbon resources, and typically include an "end date" such as 2045 or 2050 under the standards recently enacted by states. Eligible technologies are awarded credits – according to the number of megawatt hours (MWhs) of zero-carbon generation – that can be traded, which provides an efficient, market-based solution to meeting a standard.

The trend toward clean energy standards was led by the usual "blue" states of New York, California, and Massachusetts, but, by the end of 2020, fifteen states had taken legislative or executive action to adopt 100 percent clean or renewable energy targets. Of particular relevance to West Virginia is the action of its neighboring state, Virginia, in adopting the Clean Economy Act in April 2020 which, among other things, requires Dominion Energy Virginia and AEP to produce their electricity from 100 percent renewable sources by 2045 and 2050, respectively. To replace Virginia's existing coal- and natural gas-fired generation, the Clean Economy Act calls for the development of 5,200 megawatts (MW) of offshore wind, 16,100 MW of solar, and 2,700 MW of energy storage.[14] Virginia's action potentially has significant implications for West Virginia given that Appalachian Power – the operating subsidiary of AEP – operates in both states and has traditionally allocated the cost of running its multistate system between the two jurisdictions. As noted in *West Virginia's Energy Future*, a recent report by the Center for Energy and Sustainable Development,

> [w]hile Virginia builds out its renewable energy economy over the next decade, coal plants in West Virginia will likely continue to provide power to the grid in Virginia …[but] [o]nce Virginia has adequately built out its renewable energy economy, the coal-fired power plants in West Virginia likely will no longer be able to compete on price with the new renewable resources in Virginia.[15]

On the issue of statewide electricity standards, West Virginia moved decisively in the opposite direction in 2015, when the legislature repealed the Alternative and Renewable Energy Portfolio Standard in its first major action of the legislative

---

[13] With CCS technology, carbon emissions are captured at source, and then transported and sequestered in an underground geologic formation that prevents the carbon from being released into the atmosphere. While CCS technology has not been proven to be technologically feasible on a commercial scale in the United States, its inclusion in a clean energy standard would help drive the development of the technology.

[14] The Virginia Clean Economy Act was passed as House Bill 1526 and Senate Bill 851. *See* Press Release, Governor Ralph S. Northam, Governor Northam Signs Clean Energy Legislation (Apr. 12, 2020), https://www.governor.virginia.gov/newsroom/all-releases/2020/april/headline-856056-en.html.

[15] WEST VIRGINIA'S ENERGY FUTURE, *supra* note 10.

session. The measure had been in effect in West Virginia since 2009, when Joe Manchin was Governor. This repeal is discussed in greater detail in Chapter 9. Given how far away West Virginia is from zero carbon in its electricity supply, it would be very surprising if there was any movement toward adoption of a clean energy standard.

The Utilities Getting on Board the "Zero Carbon" Train (so Long as the Destination Is Twenty-Five Years Away)

It is, perhaps, because they are being driven by state clean energy standards or informal pressure from regulators or environmental organizations that utilities throughout the United States are adopting zero-carbon goals, or deadlines for their generating portfolio to consist entirely of zero-carbon resources. A survey of power sector participants carried out by Deloitte found that in embarking on the decarbonization path, utilities identified two leading drivers: consumer support for reducing emissions, and new business models and "value-creation opportunities."[16] Other factors cited by utilities were significant new pressure from investors and customers to embrace decarbonization, and the rapidly changing economics that favored clean energy.[17] Regardless of the motivation, the role of utilities in achieving decarbonization is an important one: The US electric grid relies on carbon-emitting fossil fuels for 60.3 percent of its generation.[18]

Electric utilities seem, at first glance, to be rising to the challenge: According to the Utility Carbon Reduction Tracker reported by the Smart Electric Power Alliance, seventy-three electric utilities across the United States (serving 71 percent of customer accounts nationally) have publicly stated carbon- or emission-reduction goals. In the case of fifty-one utilities, the goals call for carbon-free or net-zero emissions by 2050.[19] Notably, both AEP and FirstEnergy – the two major utilities operating in West Virginia – are included in the list of utilities with zero-carbon goals. In February 2021, AEP announced a goal to achieve net-zero carbon emissions by 2050, with an interim target to cut emissions by 80 percent from 2000 levels by 2030.[20] This

---

[16]   Stanley Porter et al., *Utility Decarbonization Strategies, Renew, Reshape and Refuel to Zero*, 2020 (Sept. 21, 2020),https://www2.deloitte.com/us/en/insights/industry/power-and-utilities/utility-decarbonization-strategies.html.

[17]   David Pomerantz & Matt Kasper, *Many U.S. Electric Utilities Plan Slow Decarbonization over Next Decade, Out of Sync with Biden Plan*, ENERGY AND POLICY INSTITUTE (Dec. 1, 2020), https://www.energyandpolicy.org/utilities-carbon-goal-biden-climate-plan/#:~:text=Many%20U.S.%20electric%20utilities%20plan,of%20sync%20with%20Biden%20plan&text=In%202019%20and%202020%2C%20most,net%2Dzero%E2%80%9D%20by%202050.

[18]   *FAQ: What Is U.S. Electricity Generation by Energy Source?*, ENERGY INFORMATION ADMINISTRATION (Feb. 27, 2020), https://www.eia.gov/tools/faqs/faq.php?id=427&t=3.

[19]   *Utility Carbon Reduction Tracker*, SMART ELECTRIC POWER ALLIANCE https://sepapower.org/utility-transformation-challenge/utility-carbon-reduction-tracker/.

[20]   Press Release, American Electric Power, AEP Releases Climate Scenario Analysis (Mar. 22, 2021), https://www.aep.com/news/releases/read/6051#:~:text=AEP%20Releases%20Climate%20Scenario%20Analysis&text=In%20February%2C%20AEP%20announced%20a,from%202000%20levels%20by%202030.

followed the announcement by FirstEnergy in November 2020 that it was pledging to achieve carbon neutrality by 2050, with an interim goal of a 30 percent reduction in GHGs within the utility's direct operational control by 2030, based on 2019 levels.[21]

Unfortunately, most of the utilities stepping up to the "zero-carbon" pledge – including AEP and FirstEnergy – are "end-loading" their carbon reduction strategies so that they occur primarily after 2030. Their failure to take dramatic action now to reduce emissions to any significant degree prior to 2030 will result in millions of additional tons of carbon in the atmosphere that will persist for hundreds of years and continue to contribute to climate change. This is of particular concern in the case of AEP, the fourth-largest emitter of GHG emissions across the entire United States in 2019. According to an analysis by the Energy and Policy Institute, most of the nation's largest utilities plan to decarbonize at a "sluggish pace" over the next decade, and "have not yet aligned their actual business plans with their decarbonization pathways, as they continue sinking money into new gas plants and forestalling the retirement of largely uneconomic coal plants."[22] By way of illustration, achieving a 100 percent reduction in GHG emissions in the power sector by 2035 – as incorporated in the climate goals enunciated by President Biden – would require a 6.25 percent reduction annually between 2019 and 2035.

Compared with that 6.25 percent annual rate, AEP is projecting to reduce its carbon emissions by only 1.36 percent annually between 2020 and 2030. FirstEnergy is moving at a slightly faster pace; it is projecting to reduce its carbon emissions by 2.73 percent annually between 2020 and 2030. As a related point, neither AEP nor FirstEnergy has made any commitment regarding the timing of closure of any coal plants, a fact noted in the Energy and Policy Institute report. In fact, in AEP's case, we know from its West Virginia Public Service Commission (PSC) filing for recovery of compliance costs related to the Environmental Protection Agency's (EPA) effluent limitation guidelines (ELGs) and coal combustion residuals (CCRs) that it plans to keep its Mitchell, Amos, and Mountaineer plants open through 2040, as discussed in Chapters 8 and 10.

A second issue is that many of the utilities are engaging in accounting "gimmickry" in their strategy to achieve net-zero carbon by 2050 by using carbon offsets. The simple fact is that most utilities taking the "zero-carbon" pledge are not actually committing to provide carbon-free electricity to their customers by 2050. Phrasing the commitment as "net-zero carbon" is the key: utilities using the term "net" in their commitment will continue to have carbon emissions in their electricity portfolio after 2050, but will use carbon offsets to address the remaining emissions.[23] The Energy and Policy Institute report cites Duke Energy's plan as an example; the utility plans to

[21] *FirstEnergy Pledges to Achieve Carbon Neutrality by 2050*, FIRSTENERGY (Nov. 9, 2020), https://www .firstenergycorp.com/newsroom/news_articles/firstenergy-pledges-to-achieve-carbon-neutrality-by -2050.html.

[22] Pomerantz & Kasper, *supra* note 17.

[23] On this point, AEP states its goal as "net-zero carbon," while FirstEnergy refers to "carbon neutrality" in stating its goal, which is simply another way of saying that any remaining carbon emissions after 2050 will be addressed through offsets, thereby achieving "neutrality."

source up to 23 percent of its generating capacity from fossil gas in 2050, and it would need to offset this through tree planting or other "modified agricultural practices."[24] And Southern Company has stated it may count any avoided emissions caused by the electrification of other sectors, like transportation, toward its net-zero goal.[25]

A third issue in the case of both FirstEnergy and AEP is their sophistry in carefully stating their goals in a manner that cleverly exaggerates their commitment. FirstEnergy's carbon commitments, for example, cover only the emissions associated with the power plants it owns, and excludes a large portion of the emissions associated with the electricity that FirstEnergy sells to customers. (Note that FirstEnergy's interim goal for a 30 percent reduction in GHG emissions by 2030, as stated above, refers to emissions "within the company's direct operational control.") In 2018, for example, 38 percent of the emissions associated with FirstEnergy's electricity sales came from power that it purchased. Another misleading element of FirstEnergy's record is that it shows a reduction in emissions of nearly one-third between 2018 and 2019. That "achievement," however, was attributable to the bankruptcy of FirstEnergy Solutions (the FirstEnergy subsidiary that owned its merchant coal plants), which emerged as a separate company called Energy Harbor; the emissions reductions never occurred, as the coal plants remain in operation.

AEP also does not appear to count purchased power as covered by its emissions reduction goals or, at best, is not clear about this accounting. Moreover, AEP manages to avoid acknowledging responsibility for the emissions from two coal-fired power plants (Clifty Creek in Indiana, and Kyger Creek in Ohio, both built in the 1950s) that are owned by the Ohio Valley Electric Corporation (OVEC) and its wholly owned subsidiary, Indiana-Kentucky Electric Corporation (IKEC). While OVEC is owned by a consortium of utilities, AEP, with its 43.47 percent ownership stake, holds the largest equity stake, and has considerable influence over whether these plants continue to operate or retire. According to the Energy and Policy Institute report, AEP ignored the emissions from these plants entirely in its 2019 emissions report to investors and categorized them under "purchased power" in 2020, thereby excluding them from the company's emissions reduction goals.[26]

SMALLER IS BETTER, AND MORE RESILIENT

Net Metering for All

Net metering is a billing mechanism that credits the owners of distributed generation (DG) resources – typically rooftop solar panels – for the electricity they add to the grid. When the customer consumes more energy than the solar panels produce, the utility provides the difference, and the meter runs forward to measure the number of KWhs of

[24] Pomerantz & Kasper, *supra* note 17.
[25] *Id.*
[26] *Id.*

electricity sold to the customer. On the other hand, when the customer's solar panels produce more energy than the customer consumes – such as during daytime hours – the customer is delivering energy (or "net exports") to the utility, and the meter runs backwards. This is the "net" part of net metering – the amount of energy the customer produces is netted against the amount of energy the customer consumes. This billing process results in the customer being paid for all the energy it produces behind the meter, including the energy it delivers (or exports) to the utility. Generally, the level of compensation paid for electricity delivered to the grid is tied to the retail rate of the utility. In the case of Mon Power, for example, the residential rate is currently 8.8 cents per kWh, so Mon Power would be required to any pay 8.8 cents per KWh for any net "exports" made by a customer's generating resource over the course of a month.

Net metering began to be offered in the United States in the 1980s to enable small solar and wind installations to provide electricity to the grid whenever available, and allow use of that electricity whenever it was needed. Currently forty states plus the District of Columbia have net metering in place. In West Virginia, the PSC adopted net metering rules in 2010 after the legislature adopted the Alternative and Renewable Energy Portfolio Standard in 2009 (discussed in Chapter 9). The net metering scheme in place in West Virginia is fairly typical of those adopted in other states. For example, it includes a "cap" which places a limit on the utility's obligation to purchase the output of customer-sited generation; that figure is currently 3 percent of the utility's aggregate load. This cap recognizes that net metering is somewhat costly to the utility, inasmuch as it is paying the retail rate for electricity purchases (8.8 cents per KWh in the case of Mon Power) when, in the absence of net metering, it would purchase its electricity supply in the wholesale markets at a price less than half that, based on the prevailing energy prices in the PJM wholesale market. These higher costs of purchases through net metering are passed on to ratepayers as a "cost of service" in the rate-setting process, so the effect of the cap is to limit the cost exposure of a program that is somewhat generous for those customers fortunate enough to own solar panels.

Another feature included in West Virginia's net metering scheme that is common to other states' programs is a limit on the size of customer-sited generation: 25 kW for residential customers, 50 kW for commercial customers, and 2 MW for industrial customers. These limits recognize that customer-sited generation must generally be sized according to the customer's load (rather than for purposes of producing electricity for export to the grid). The typical size of a residential solar system is 6 kW.

Returning to the issue of whether net metering programs are too generous for customer generators, several states have taken action to reduce the level of compensation as the cost of rooftop solar has declined. When net metering programs began, the notion of setting the compensation at the retail rate was an elegant solution, as it greatly simplified the program. A customer-generator with occasional net exports to the grid would benefit from simply having the meter "run backwards," thus being compensated at the retail rate without much hassle or complication. At the same time, net metering programs raise some questions of equity, as the upfront costs of solar installations – around $12,000 for a typical 6 kW array – put such systems out of reach of the average utility customer. And if the utility is paying wealthy customers the retail rate for net exports to the grid when it would otherwise pay a much lower price for its power supply, that forces costs up for everyone – including nonparticipants in the program who can't afford solar.

The issue of "cross-subsidization" or "cost-shifting" has become a hot topic in the industry in recent years: that nonparticipating customers should not be forced to subsidize customers that have the financial wherewithal to own solar panels. The issue took on greater urgency as the cost of solar panels declined, as the perception was that compensating customer-owned solar panels at the retail rate was paying far more than necessary. Those states that have revisited their net metering programs, to minimize or eliminate the cross-subsidization, have generally tried to adjust the compensation to reflect the actual value of the contributions of net exports to the grid, which is generally much lower than the retail rate (depending upon the retail rate in the various states). (These are commonly referred to as "value-of-solar" tariffs.) Some states have gone so far as to set the compensation at the utility's "avoided cost," which is generally the rate prevailing in the regional wholesale power market. As noted, in the case of Mon Power, that figure would be less than half of the 8.8 cents per KWh retail rate for residential customers.

The electric utilities in West Virginia caught the "cross-subsidization" fever in 2015, and were able to convince the legislature to pass a bill (HB 2201) directing the PSC to study the issue and make sure that no such cross-subsidization was going on in the Mountain State. In May 2015 the PSC appointed a task force to consider the issue, and it filed its report with the PSC five months later, in September 2015.[27] The task force recommended that "cross-subsidization" be defined narrowly to include only the direct costs incurred by utilities to interconnect customer-generators, and found that interconnection fees needed to be adjusted to ensure that utilities recovered the direct costs of interconnection from customer-generators. The task force found no basis for finding that the broader "cost shifts" alleged by the utilities was occurring.[28] At the time of the task force report, there were only about 500 net metered customers in West Virginia with a total output of slightly over 3 MW. In light of this miniscule level of penetration of net metering in the state, several task force members argued that the utilities' claims about cross-subsidization were theoretical, and did not even justify the costs of further study of the issue. In any event, the PSC sat on the report for more than three years, finally issuing an order

[27] West Virginia PSC, Case No. 15–0682-E-GI, *Net Metering Task Force Final Report,* Sept. 30, 2015.
[28] AEP, for example, had proposed a "buy all/sell all" arrangement whereby the utility would pay only its avoided costs (i.e., wholesale prices) for *any* generation produced on the customer's side of the meter, even if the output was used to offset the customer's load and not exported to the grid, which would have reduced compensation for customer-sited generation by over 50%.

acting on the report in September 2018 that largely adopted the recommendations of the task force.[29]

The Resilience Benefits of DG Resources

Extreme weather events, which are occurring with increasing frequency as a result of climate change, threaten the reliability and resilience of the nation's electricity grid. Increased flooding due to intense rainfall, hurricane damage fueled in part by a warmer atmosphere and warmer, higher seas, as well as widespread wildfires caused by extended drought conditions constitute potential hazards for utility infrastructure and delivery of essential electricity services. As a possible adaptation strategy, increased deployment of DG resources can improve the resilience of the electric system in the face of the increasing frequency of extreme weather events by avoiding some of the systemic vulnerabilities of a centralized large grid.

The experience of Hurricane Sandy (ultimately downgraded to "Superstorm" Sandy by the time it hit the coasts of New York and New Jersey in late October 2012) provides a case study of the resilience benefits of DG resources and the lessons that can be learned as utilities plan for increasingly frequent extreme weather events in the future. Superstorm Sandy was the deadliest and most destructive hurricane of the 2012 Atlantic hurricane season, resulting in 286 deaths and $68 billion in damages. The storm's diameter extended almost 1,000 miles, and produced a storm surge of fourteen feet at the Battery in lower Manhattan, at least three feet higher than prior reported storm tides. Approximately 8.5 million utility customers along the eastern United States lost power during Sandy. Apart from the sheer magnitude of the disaster in terms of fatalities and destruction, Superstorm Sandy provided a "wake up call" for energy providers, and electric utilities in particular, on the need to adopt a different set of long-term planning tools to improve the resilience of the electric system to cope with the anticipated extreme weather events of the future.

One such tool is an expanded role for DG resources and microgrids. If the electrical grid is impaired, DG resources can be configured to "island" from the grid, thereby ensuring an uninterrupted supply of power to utility customers within a "microgrid." That was the experience from Superstorm Sandy, where the use of microgrids and DG resources enabled power to be provided to pockets of consumers in the face of widespread outages of central power plants and associated transmission and distribution (T&D) systems. While extended power outages affected the region for days, many commercial and industrial facilities and educational institutions in the area (including Princeton University's campus in New Jersey and New York University's campus in lower Manhattan) were able to continue operating uninterrupted, due to on-site DG resources, primarily cogeneration or combined heat and

[29] West Virginia PSC, Case No. 15–0682-E-GI, *Commission Order*, Sept. 8, 2018.

power (CHP) facilities. New York University's Washington Square Campus, for example, was served during Superstorm Sandy by a 14.4 MW combined-cycle CHP system installed in 2010; the electricity supplied twenty-two campus buildings, while the steam was used to produce hot water to meet 100 percent of the space heating, space cooling, and hot water needs of thirty-seven campus buildings. Several hospitals equipped with on-site DG resources, as well as a housing complex in the Bronx, were also able to function normally during Superstorm Sandy and its aftermath. Critical facilities such as data centers and manufacturing facilities were also able to remain operational.[30]

The resilience benefit of DG resources was confirmed in a report prepared pursuant to the Energy Policy Act of 2005, which required the Department of Energy (DOE), in consultation with the Federal Energy Regulatory Commission (FERC), to conduct a study of the benefits of DG resources. The DOE study identified the potential role of DG resources in improving resilience, "through its reliance on larger numbers of smaller and more geographically dispersed power plants, rather than large, central station power plants and bulk-power transmission facilities."[31] While acknowledging that the greater number of smaller-scale power plants in a DG-based system would increase the number of targets vulnerable in an attack, the study remarked that this also "reduce[s] the number of customers who might potentially be affected." The study also noted the reduced vulnerability when utility customers are able to "island" themselves in microgrid arrangements, which are particularly important in the case of "critical infrastructure facilities such as fire and safety buildings, telecommunications systems, hospitals, and natural gas and oil delivery stations." The DOE study described DG as a "viable means" for "improving the resilience of electrical infrastructure," and cited "actual cases in which DG continued to provide power to critical facilities during times of large-scale power disruptions and outages." According to the conclusions of the DOE study, "[a] resilient grid can avert many types of losses, be they economic, material, or information, or losses of human life, health, safety, and communications."[32]

The DOE study also identified further advantages of deploying DG resources on a wide scale, including improved power quality (making sure that the voltage, frequency, and waveform of a power supply system conform to established specifications); providing ancillary services to the grid (which help grid operators maintain a reliable electricity system by maintaining the proper flow and direction of electricity and addressing imbalances between supply and demand); and using DG

---

[30] James M. Van Nostrand, *Keeping the Lights on During Superstorm Sandy: Climate Change Adaptation and the Resiliency Benefits of Distributed Generation*, 23 N.Y.U. Envtl. L.J. 92 (2015); James M. Van Nostrand, *Quantifying the Resilience Value of Distributed Energy Resources*, 35 J. Land Use & Envtl. L. 15 (2019).

[31] U.S. Department of Energy, The Potential Benefits of Distributed Generation and Rate-Related Issues that May Impede their Expansion (2007), https://www.ferc.gov/sites/default/files/2020-04/1817_study_sep_07.pdf.

[32] *Id.* at 7–12.

resources to shave peak loads. Other possible benefits of DG resources noted in the DOE study include avoiding investments in generating plants and T&D infrastructure, reducing land use effects and the costs of right-of-way acquisition, and increasing the security of the grid against acts of terrorism.

Power to the People: The Use of Power Purchase Agreements (PPAs)

The dramatic reduction in the cost of solar modules, as discussed in Chapter 3, translated into much lower costs for a typical residential solar installation, which decreased from over $8 per watt in 2009 to under $3 per watt in 2019, a decline of more than 60 percent in ten years. The significant upfront costs for a typical residential solar array, however, still represent a major barrier to widespread deployment of solar. For a 10 kW solar array – a common size for large homes or small offices, with an average cost of around $2.96 per watt (in 2020) – the upfront cost is about $29,600. Federal tax credits can help reduce those costs; through 2022, a 26 percent tax credit is available – basically, a 26 cents reduction to federal tax liability for every dollar spent on a solar array. For a $29,600 10 kW solar array, that would represent an almost $7,700 reduction in federal income tax liability. These tax credits are being phased down, however; the figure for 2023 is 22 percent, and this ultimately drops to 10 percent in 2024 for commercial and utility-scale solar and 0 percent for residential solar. Depending upon the price of electricity, the payback period – the period of time over which the solar panels "pay for themselves" through savings on energy bills – can range anywhere from 5–15 years. But even reduced to less than $22,000, that is a substantial outlay for most homeowners or small business owners.

That's where power purchase agreements (PPAs) come into play. A PPA is a long-term contract with an energy developer that enables a property owner to avoid the large up-front investment of purchasing and owning their own solar array. The energy developer will install, own, and maintain the solar panels on a residence or business, and the electricity generated by the facility is sold to the property owner using a long-term, fixed-rate contract, usually at a price below that charged by the customer's electric utility provider. In addition to reducing or eliminating the initial capital costs, PPAs allow a solar developer to take advantage of tax credits and pass those savings along to the property owner, making solar energy more affordable and reducing energy costs. This is particularly important for nonprofit entities (e.g., churches) and government organizations because they don't pay income taxes, and thus don't have an income tax liability to offset through the use of tax credits. For these customers, the tax credits associated with solar arrays installed on their property would be "left on the table," so to speak. Through the use of PPAs, the solar developer can take advantage of the tax credits associated with solar arrays installed on churches or schools, and those savings are passed on to the property owner through more favorable terms in the PPA.

The PSC Making PPAs Unavailable in West Virginia

As of 2020, third-party solar PPAs were permitted in at least twenty-eight states, including the adjacent states of Virginia, Maryland, Pennsylvania, and Ohio. But prior to a new statute being enacted in 2021, PPAs were not allowed in West Virginia due to a restrictive interpretation of the public service law by the West Virginia PSC. The legal analysis went this way. A solar panel generates electricity, and is thus an electric generating facility. The output of an electric generating facility can be provided to the owner without any regulatory implications. In the event that the output is provided to someone other than the owner – such as when a solar developer, through a PPA, owns a solar array and the output is provided to the property owner – then the solar developer becomes a "utility," as it is now providing electricity to a third party (i.e., someone other than the owner). As a utility, the solar developer would be subject to rate regulation by the PSC. In other words, the rates that the solar developer collects for electricity supplied to the property owner would be set by the PSC. The developer would be subject to regulatory oversight in other respects as well, just as is the case with larger electric utilities.

The PSC did not necessarily have to interpret the laws in a manner that produced this outcome; its position is based on an overly strict interpretation of the statutory scheme that really should not trigger rate regulation. Unlike the traditional utility, which holds itself out as offering a service to all, and exercises monopoly power with respect to the provision of an essential service (electricity), a solar developer has no monopoly power and the customer class is limited to one. As has been done in many states with a similar statutory structure, the PSC could simply have issued a declaratory ruling indicating that its interpretation of the statute would not extend the definition of a "utility" to an owner of a solar array where the output is delivered only to the property owner. The PSC has the discretion to interpret the statute in this manner, and that interpretation would likely have been upheld in the event anyone – likely a utility – challenged it, given the considerable deference that reviewing courts afford utility commissions in the specialized, complex realm of utility regulation. The West Virginia PSC, of course, declined to make such a ruling; it apparently sees its role as protecting the revenue stream – and profits – of the utilities it regulates rather than interpreting the laws in a manner that serves ratepayers by enabling them to access solar power more easily through the use of PPAs.

A Simple Solution but a Difficult Path

A grassroots organization, West Virginians for Energy Freedom, offered a rather simple piece of legislation to tackle this issue. The bill, introduced in the 2019, 2020, and 2021 legislative sessions, would have clarified the applicable sections of the public service law (the set of statutes administered by the PSC) to make it clear that a third-party owner of a solar array does not become a utility by virtue of ownership of the array and sale of the output solely to the property owner. That is all there is to it, and utility customers throughout West Virginia would be able to take advantage of PPAs to increase their ability to access solar power. In its case to legislators to gain support for the bill, West Virginians for Energy Freedom produced an analysis showing that even a restricted PPA pilot program likely would have led to 13 MW of clean energy project deployment (or almost double the state's 8 MW of solar installations as of 2019).[33]

Assuming half of this capacity was installed on commercial buildings and half on residential buildings, nearly 400 solar project development and installation jobs could be supported. How were such estimates calculated? The West Virginians For Energy Freedom report considered the experience of the neighboring state of Virginia, where, in 2013, Dominion Energy implemented a pilot project allowing solar PPAs. Over the following five years, Virginia added 1,900 new solar jobs – rising from fewer than 2,000 jobs in 2015 to 3,900 jobs in 2018 – and nearly the full 50 MW limit under the pilot program was fully subscribed as of December 2019. Apart from the experience in Virginia, three other states surrounding West Virginia – Maryland, Ohio, and Pennsylvania – allowed PPAs, resulting in the solar jobs and megawatts of solar generating capacity shown in Table 4.1.

Notwithstanding the effective grassroots campaign by West Virginians for Energy Freedom, their PPA bill never made it out of a legislative committee in either the House of Delegates or the Senate during the 2019 and 2020 legislative sessions, and it met a similar fate during the 2021 legislative session. Then, House leadership mysteriously became engaged on the issue, albeit not on behalf of the PPA bill offered by West Virginians for Energy Freedom. On the last day before "crossover day" – the fiftieth day of the regular session and the last day for most bills to be passed in the house of origin – Delegate Moore Capito (Republican, Kanawha County), chair of

TABLE 4.1 *Solar generating capacity and solar jobs*

State	MW of solar	Solar jobs
Maryland	1,042	4,515
Ohio	202	7,162
Pennsylvania	420	4,219
Virginia	731	3,890

Note: The jobs classified as "solar jobs" include installation, sales and distribution, project development, and operations and maintenance.

---

[33] West Virginians for Energy Freedom, *Power Purchase Agreements: A No-Nonsense Way to Energize Economic Growth in West Virginia* (Jan. 2020), https://static1.squarespace.com/static/582874babe bafb7de36e23c4/t/5e14e6ca141f9b6e39274ef0/1578428114758/2020+WV+PPA+report_final.pdf.

the House Judiciary Committee, and Speaker Roger Hanshaw (Republican, Clay County) rolled out HB 3310, which contained the essential provisions of the Energy Freedom bill (i.e., simply excluding the owners of solar arrays under PPAs from PSC jurisdiction). The utilities had an opportunity to weigh in on the proposal before its introduction, and added the same size limitations as contained in the net metering rules (25 kW cap for residential, 50 kW for commercial, and 2 MW for industrial) and also made sure that the aggregate cap of 3 percent of a utility's load applicable to net metered installations would apply to any PPA-financed installations as well. With the strong support of Delegate Capito and Speaker Hanshaw in the House, and the capable stewardship by Senate Judiciary Committee chair Charles Trump (Republican, Morgan County) on the Senate side of things, HB 3310 sailed through both houses just prior to the close of the legislative session. All in all, it took just two weeks from introduction on March 26 to passage by both houses on April 9. Governor Jim Justice, not wanting to be associated with any form of electricity generation not involving coal, let the bill take effect without his signature.

Delegate Capito is the son of US Senator Shelley Moore Capito and the grandson of former West Virginia Governor Arch Moore. It is fair to say that the Capitos comprise one of the political dynasties in West Virginia. Moore Capito was first elected to the House in 2016, and was quickly named as vice chair of the House Judiciary Committee (in 2018) before becoming chair in 2020. In announcing Capito's appointment as chair, Speaker Hanshaw remarked that as vice chair, Capito "played a vital role in our work to ensure West Virginia has a fair legal climate that attracts job creators."[34] While his motivations in taking the lead on passage of the PPA bill are unclear – it is unusual for a Republican in the West Virginia legislature to take a position contrary to the once-powerful coal industry or to the interests of the influential electric utilities – the legislature seems to be getting the message that "job creators" (the major employers with corporate renewable energy goals, as discussed in the Section The Job Creators Demanding Renewable Energy) are demanding access to renewable energy if they locate or expand in West Virginia. As noted in Chapter 3, Speaker Hanshaw was instrumental in the passage of SB 583 during the 2020 legislative session, and this provided incentives for the development of utility-scale solar in West Virginia. Ken Silverstein, a native West Virginian who writes for *Forbes*, observed that with the passage of SB 583 in 2020 and HB 3310 in 2021, "[t]he coal industry's tight grip on West Virginia is loosening" and "the dam has broken" to give way to solar energy in West Virginia.[35]

---

[34] Brad McElhinny, *Moore Capito Is Named W.Va. House Judiciary Chairman, One of a Few Committee Changes*, METRONEWS (Dec. 14, 2020), https://wvmetronews.com/2020/12/14/moore-capito-is-named-w-va-house-judiciary-chairman-one-of-a-few-committee-changes/.

[35] Silverstein, *supra* note 11.

The Fundamental Change in the Utility Business Model

The traditional "cost-of-service" model of utility regulation is based on the historical structure of the electric utility industry in the United States. Producing and delivering electricity to retail customers is very capital intensive, given the cost of large, centralized generating plants and the extensive T&D systems necessary to move the electricity from often remote locations where power plants are sited to the cities where customers are located. In order to minimize the risk and enable the raising of sufficient capital to create vast power systems, a structure based on the "regulatory compact" came into play in the early twentieth century. Under this compact, utilities were granted exclusive service territories – in other words, protected from competitors in the regions in which they were granted exclusivity – and, in return, had an "obligation to serve" any customer within their service territories seeking an electrical service. This arrangement is the quid pro quo of utility ratemaking: A utility has a defined service territory that it is obligated to serve, and it is protected against competition from other utilities in serving that territory, which helps it determine the amount of electricity it must generate or procure to serve its retail load. The final element of the regulatory compact is that the utility is entitled to earn a reasonable return on the assets it devotes to public service. In other words, the utility will make investments in generating plants, transmission lines, substations, and distribution lines that produce a "rate base" upon which the utility will earn a return, defined as the profit level necessary to attract capital on reasonable terms and allow the utility to maintain its financial integrity.

In setting rates to generate that reasonable return, the historical practice has been to use a "cost-of-service" model, which looks at the actual costs incurred by the utility in rendering retail service, and then calculates a rate per kWh that will produce sufficient revenues to recover those costs as well as generate the necessary level of profit. This system works reasonably well under the traditional utility system, with large, centralized generating plants and a one-way flow of energy from the utility's generating resources over the utility's T&D system to retail customers. It breaks down, however, as the penetration of DG resources increases, and as customers take advantage of technology to reduce their energy usage through energy-saving appliances, more aggressive building codes, and demand response programs that allow customers greater control over the timing and amount of electricity usage (generally referred to as "demand-side management" programs). Rates can no longer be set on the basis of an assumed continuing level of electrons being delivered to retail customers when those sales are declining due to customers generating their own electricity with DG resources or reducing their usage by taking advantage of demand-side management programs. In response, many states are exploring changes to the traditional cost-of-service regulatory model to move toward a system that better reflects the impact of new technologies, allows utilities to take advantage of the growing service economy, and sets rates based on metrics other than selling more electricity.

A good example is the "Reforming the Energy Vision" (REV) proceeding in New York, which commenced in April 2014 following a Con Edison decision involving the utility's response to Superstorm Sandy.[36] In examining "where the lights stayed on" during and in the aftermath of Superstorm Sandy, the New York Public Service Commission (NYPSC) began to move to a new regulatory paradigm that would accommodate, and in fact encourage, utilities to move toward a decentralized model that would achieve a more resilient grid in the face of increasing extreme weather events. This decentralized model would also require a new regulatory approach given that the traditional cost-of-service model – based on compensating utilities primarily for their sales of electrons – was not well-suited to the electric utility industry of the future.

The initial order in the REV proceeding referred to the utilities' role as operating the "distribution system platform" rather than building power plants and selling electricity.[37] As distribution platform operator, the utilities' role would be to manage the integration of DG resources owned by customers and other third parties, and to help customers meet their energy service needs, which were defined more broadly to include demand-side management programs (energy efficiency, conservation, and demand response) that would help them manage their energy costs. Utilities were also encouraged to explore "non-wires alternatives" rather than investing in additional T&D infrastructure. In other words, rather than building more transmission lines, substations, and distribution lines – the "wires" solution – in order to serve a growing load, the focus was on *reducing* the load placed on the grid by generating electricity closer to the loads – through promoting the deployment of DG resources – or by reducing the load on circuits that would require upgrades through targeted deployment of energy efficiency programs. Under the traditional cost-of-service model, utilities are rewarded for making additional investments in T&D infrastructure by increasing the assets in their rate base upon which they get to earn a return. The "non-wires alternative" was not in the utilities' economic interest, so the NYPSC developed an innovative "share the savings" approach that would allow the utility to share in the savings created from proceeding down the non-wires path versus just building more infrastructure.

Other aspects of New York's REV focused on compensating utilities for actions that were in the customers' interests or the broader public interest, rather than sales of electrons. New metrics were based on how well the utility performed in integrating DG resources, achieving systemwide GHG reductions, and reducing overall load placed on the grid. Another aspect of the new utility business model is a more broad-based distribution planning process, so that the utility does not retain the

---

[36] New York Public Service Commission, Case 14-M-0101, Proceeding on Motion of the Commission in Regard to Reforming the Energy Vision, *Order Instituting Proceeding* (issued Apr. 25, 2014).

[37] *Id.*

inherent advantage of being the only entity with the information regarding "pressure points" on the utility's network where DG resources or targeted energy efficiency programs are particularly valuable. The notion is that third parties should have the opportunity to compete with incumbent utilities to offer energy services that help meet customers' energy needs – whether DG resources or demand-side management programs – as that competitive model will help reduce the costs of serving customers. But the distribution planning process must be more stakeholder-based to allow a broader sharing of information that would make this new market for energy services work.

This exploration of the new utility business model, and the regulatory approaches necessary to accommodate it, is not limited to New York. Another state taking a leading role is Hawaii, which has traditionally suffered from very high electricity rates due to the need to import the fuel oil used to generate electricity. Because of these high electricity prices, customer ownership of solar PV arrays coupled with battery storage systems became cheaper than buying from the utility years ago, requiring action by Hawaii regulators to deal with the rapidly deteriorating utility business model. California, Massachusetts, Minnesota, and Colorado are some of the other states that are exploring new utility regulatory models and innovative distribution planning processes that focus on integration of DG resources to the exclusion of simply building more T&D infrastructure and selling more electricity.[38]

Unfortunately for the ratepayers in West Virginia, the Mountain State is largely observing these developments from the sidelines. The business model is still very much focused on utilities building and operating large, centralized generating stations – preferably coal-fired – and utilities continue to be compensated on the basis of selling more electricity, which is contrary to the interests of ratepayers. There is very little penetration of DG resources in West Virginia – only about 1,100 DG resources totaling 14.6 MW, as of 2020, throughout the state. Nor is there any involvement by utilities in offering energy efficiency programs that would help customers manage their energy costs (as discussed further in Chapter 8). It's all about selling more electricity, which translates into the coal plants operating more in a futile effort to maintain coal production. One of the more basic ratemaking innovations over the past two decades has been "revenue decoupling," which simply removes the linkage between sales and profits. The mechanism is a recognition that it is contrary to utilities' economic interests to promote energy efficiency, as selling less of their product will lead to a decline in profits under the traditional cost-of-service ratemaking model. Revenue decoupling simply holds the utility harmless from the impact on profits of a decline in sales due to energy efficiency programs. As of March 2019, twenty-four states plus the District of Columbia have decoupling in place;[39] West Virginia is not included in that group.

Rather than discouraging traditional investment in T&D infrastructure, the West Virginia legislature has taken action in recent years to encourage *more* investment in the distribution infrastructure of natural gas utilities. As discussed in Chapter 8, natural gas distribution companies operating in West Virginia have strong incentives to put more pipe in the ground as they get expedited rate recovery of that additional investment. As a result, while the cost of the natural gas commodity has declined in recent years due to the shale gas revolution, customers' overall bills continue to rise because the gas distribution companies have invested massive amounts of money in additional pipes and distribution mains in response to the enactment of an industry-proposed statute in 2015. Who was the lobbyist for the West Virginia Oil and Gas Association and chief proponent of the bill when it was enacted in 2015? Charlotte Lane, current chairman of the West Virginia PSC.[40] But more on that in Chapter 8. For the purposes of this discussion, however, it is fair to say that the goal of the PSC does not seem to be exploring a new regulatory paradigm that would put the interests of ratepayers first.

---

[39]   *Decoupling Policies*, CENTER FOR CLIMATE AND ENERGY SOLUTIONS (March 2019), https://www.c2es.org /document/decoupling-policies/.

[40]   Lucas Mansfield & Ken Ward Jr., *Natural Gas Is Getting Cheaper. Thousands Are Paying More to Heat Their Homes Anyway*, MOUNTAIN STATE SPOTLIGHT (Apr. 17, 2021), https://mountainstatespotlight .org/2021/04/17/natural-gas-getting-cheaper-thousands-paying-more-anyway/.

5

From "Friends of Coal" to the "War on Coal": How West Virginia Went from Blue to Red

Between 1996 – the first year that Joe Manchin ran for statewide office in West Virginia – and 2020, West Virginia changed from a reliably "blue" state, with Democratic registrations outnumbering Republican by 2 to 1, to a state captured by the Republican nominee in every presidential election beginning in 2000, capped by Donald Trump's 42- and 39-point margins in 2016 and 2020, respectively. As noted by *Politico*, "few spots in America have shifted politically faster and more decisively than this state, swinging from nearly entirely blue to almost totally red over the last 20 years."[1] In February 2021, party registrations in West Virginia actually edged in favor of Republicans for the first time.[2]

A few distinct but interrelated threads help explain this extraordinary turn in political fortunes for the Democratic Party in West Virginia, and they are largely grounded in the dominant role of the coal industry in the state, and the appropriation for political purposes of the state's strong identification with coal. A major contributing factor that played out through the end of the twentieth century was the decline in the influence of the United Mine Workers of America (UMWA) as a political force, due largely to the sheer decline in the number of miners (as a result of mechanization) as well as the success of coal operators in engaging in union-busting tactics. Opportunistically filling the vacuum was "Friends of Coal," an organization formed in 2002 to redefine the image of the coal industry – a misdirection, as it were – to draw attention away from the seemingly ruinous combination of the industry's declining economic contribution and increasing environmental devastation as the industry moved from underground mines to blowing off the tops of mountains. The comprehensive Friends of Coal public relations campaign throughout the first decade of the twenty-first century – described in the section "Friends of Coal": The Brainwashing of a Generation – laid the foundation for what would become the "war on coal" following the election in 2008

---

[1] Michael Kruse, *How the Most Endangered Democrat in America Survived*, POLITICO (Nov. 6, 2018), https://www.politico.com/magazine/story/2018/11/06/manchin-win-west-virginia-senate-2018-elections-midterms-222226/.

[2] John Raby, *Registered Republicans Outnumber Democrats in West Virginia*, AP (Feb. 11, 2021), https://apnews.com/article/voter-registration-west-virginia-political-parties-3acf5f5082fa975c7a09222f87265b04.

of an unpopular (at least in West Virginia) president, Barack Obama, and his unwanted environmental initiatives to address climate change, end mountaintop removal, and regulate greenhouse gas (GHG) emissions from coal plants.

Throughout the eight years of the Obama administration, political leaders in West Virginia, regardless of party affiliation, blamed the decline of the coal industry on Obama's "job-killing" Environmental Protection Agency (EPA). Of course, this narrative conveniently relieved them of the responsibility of leading the state through an inevitable and necessary transition away from coal, for the cause of the problem was external, not intrinsic. Even when the evidence became clear during Obama's second term that forces much stronger than the impact of EPA regulations were driving the demise of coal, politicians continued to lay blame almost exclusively upon the EPA, and created an expectation that, upon a rollback of GHG regulations, the coal industry would recover. Following the election of Donald J. Trump in November 2016, with 68 percent of the vote in West Virginia, the rollback of EPA regulations in fact occurred – including the repeal of Obama's Clean Power Plan that regulated GHG emissions from power plants; however, this had minimal impact on coal production and employment in West Virginia.

THE DECLINE OF THE UNITED MINE WORKERS

At the height of its industry dominance in the 1940s, the UMWA had nearly 500,000 members and UMWA mines accounted for 90 percent of domestic coal production.[3] Employment numbers in West Virginia told a similar story: 1948 saw the greatest numbers of coal miners in West Virginia's history, at 125,669.[4] As a result of mechanization – 1948 was the year that the continuous mining machine was introduced, which revolutionized the extraction of coal in underground mines[5] – the number of coal miners would never approach those figures again, either nationally or in West Virginia. Over the following fifteen years, employment nationally plunged to 141,646 by 1963.[6] And in West Virginia, the number of miners fell to 44,854 in 1963, a decline of over 64 percent.[7] With the use of the continuous mining machine, coal production per man-day increased from 5.57 tons in 1945 to 10.05 tons in 1957.[8]

Apart from a slight surge in the number of coal miners between 1973 and 1978, as a result of the nation's first energy crisis triggered by the Organization of the Petroleum Exporting Countries (OPEC) (more than 17,000 new miners were placed

---

[3] Patrick C. McGinley, *From Pick and Shovel to Mountaintop Removal: Environmental Injustice in the Appalachian Coalfields*, 34 ENVTL. L. 21, 31 (2004).

[4] *Coal Facts 2019, Coal Production and Employment 1900–2018*, WEST VIRGINIA COAL ASSOCIATION (Nov. 22, 2019), https://www.wvcoal.com/resources/coal-facts/5176-coal-facts-2019.

[5] Sylvia Ryerson, *Precarious Politics: Friends of Coal, the UMWA, and the Affective Terrain of Energy Identification*, 72 AMERICAN QUARTERLY 719, 724 (Sept. 2020), https://muse.jhu.edu/article/765830.

[6] *Id.*

[7] *Coal Facts 2019, supra* note 4.

[8] Stephen W. Brown & Otis K. Rice, *West Virginia: A History* 280 (2d ed. 1993).

on payrolls in West Virginia during this five-year period),[9] the number of coal miners has steadily declined since the peak in 1948. In the decade after 1978, the number of miners declined by over 50 percent, to fewer than 29,000 jobs in 1987. By 1999, there were fewer miners in the state than there were nurses or telephone solicitors, and Walmart had more employees in West Virginia than any coal company. (Coal industry apologists would still insist that "five thousand people working at Walmarts in this state don't equal 400 coal jobs.")[10] The number of coal miners in West Virginia ultimately fell below 12,000 in 2017, before increasing slightly to 13,887 by the end of "the lost decade" in 2019.[11]

Production levels tell a different story, however. The 1970s brought a drastic increase in aboveground "surface mining" or "strip mining" operations, which made extraction cheaper and faster through the use of enormous machinery that required little labor. By the 1990s, strip mining had evolved into the highly controversial practice of mountaintop removal (MTR) mining in which companies use explosives to blow off mountaintops to access the coal seams below, dumping the "overburden" into adjacent valleys and streams, as discussed in Chapter 1. Despite the environmental destruction caused by blasting mountaintops and filling streambeds, MTR could produce 2.5 times more coal per worker than underground mines.[12]

With the expanded use of strip mining and MTR, coal production in West Virginia reached nearly 182 million tons in 1997, a total that was greater than the 168 million tons that was mined almost fifty years earlier, when the number of miners employed in West Virginia was at its peak.[13] (These numbers, of course, tell a story that is completely different to what coal operators would say about the cause of job losses in the coal industry – that this was due to environmental regulations. With the expanded use of mechanization and MTR, more coal was produced in West Virginia in 1997 *with one–seventh the number of miners* that were employed at the height of the "pre-mechanization" years in 1948.) As coal began to be displaced by natural gas to generate electricity, production fell to below 85 million tons in 2016 before recovering slightly in 2017 and 2018.[14] As Ronald Eller writes, "During the last two decades of the twentieth century, the number of coal mining jobs throughout all of Appalachia declined by 70 percent, falling from 159,000 to 46,000 … the disappearance of jobs in the 1980s and 1990s was permanent."[15]

[9] McGinley, *supra* note 3, at 43.
[10] Testimony of Patrick C. McGinley Before the United States House of Representatives, Committee on Natural Resources, Subcommittee on Energy and Mineral Resources Hearing on "Coal Miner Employment and Domestic Energy Act," Nov. 18, 2011, at 5 (citing Professor John Alexander Williams), https://republicans-naturalresources.house.gov/uploadedfiles/mcginleytestimony11 .18.11.pdf.
[11] *Coal Facts 2019*, *supra* note 4.
[12] *Coal*, NATIONAL GEOGRAPHIC ENCYCLOPEDIA, https://www.nationalgeographic.org/encyclopedia/coal/.
[13] *Coal Facts 2019*, *supra* note 4.
[14] *Id.*
[15] R.D. ELLER, MINERS, MILLHANDS, AND MOUNTAINEERS: INDUSTRIALIZATION OF THE APPALACHIAN SOUTH, 1880–1930 (1982).

Apart from the loss of jobs due to mechanization and MTR, the UMWA also suffered from the union-busting activities of coal operators. Beginning in the 1980s, first Massey Coal under Don Blankenship and then Pittston Coal worked to systematically weaken the UMWA by breaking union contracts and opening nonunion mines.[16] In the case of Massey Energy, Don Blankenship touted his infamous twenty-seven-page "Massey Doctrine," which outlined strategies for effectively breaking the control of unions.[17] Massey opened its first fully nonunion facility in 1981; by 2002, just 200 of its 4,500 employees had UMWA cards.[18] Smaller coal companies followed the lead of the larger operators, and by the end of the 1980s, nonunion mines were common. Of the 257 active underground coal mines in Central Appalachia and Northern Appalachia in 2014, only 16 were union mines.[19] As of the end of 2016, there were fewer than 8,000 UMWA members still mining coal.[20]

Ultimately, whether as a result of the decline in required labor due to mechanization and MTR, or the success of coal operators' union-busting initiatives, by the 1990s the UMWA ceased to be a political force in the region. This would prove to have political implications for West Virginia's transitioning from a reliably "blue" state to a "red" one, beginning with the 2000 presidential election. And the decline in the influence of the UMWA left a vacuum in political influence that the Friends of Coal quickly filled.

"FRIENDS OF COAL": THE BRAINWASHING OF A GENERATION

In a moment of acute uncertainty and painful transition, and in the void left open by the UMWA's decline, [Friends of Coal] provided a new affective map for communities to collectively experience and process the emotions of loss, anger, pride, and connectedness, and to maintain a sense of control in a rapidly changing landscape.[21]

In the early 2000s the coal industry in West Virginia needed a new strategy to address what was described as a "crisis of legitimacy" in Appalachia: "[i]t was enacting a radically more destructive form of mining on a massive scale while providing far fewer jobs."[22] The expanded use of MTR and other forms of strip mining allowed the industry to maintain coal production – which was at about the same levels at the beginning of the twenty-first century as it was in the late 1940s – while employing far fewer miners. With the advent of the continuous mining machine,

---

[16] Ryerson, *supra* note 5, at 725.
[17] Tim Murphy, *The Epic Rise and Fall of America's Most Notorious Coal Baron*, MOTHER JONES (Sept. 30, 2015), https://www.motherjones.com/politics/2015/09/blankenship-trial-king-coal-west-virginia/.
[18] *Id.*
[19] Taylor Kuykendall & Hira Fawad, *Latest Numbers Suggest Unionized Coal Mines Safer, More Productive Than Nonunion Operations*, SNL (Mar. 30, 2015), https://www.snl.com/interactiveX/Article.aspx?cdid=A-31867608-11563&FreeAccess=1.
[20] Dylan Brown, *Mining Union Faces "Life-and-Death" Test*, GREENWIRE (Apr. 11, 2017), https://www.eenews.net/stories/1060052929.
[21] Ryerson, *supra* note 5, at 723.
[22] *Id.* at 726.

the longwall mining machine, and MTR mining, a vast coal-mining workforce was no longer needed. The cost to the environment of these newer extractive techniques was far higher, of course, and scientific evidence was beginning to mount regarding the health impacts on communities living near MTR sites, such as abnormally high rates of cancer, brain tumors, and other serious health issues. Sylvia Ryerson, who spent five years working as a radio producer, describes the image of life in the Appalachian coalfields for which the coal industry needed a public relations answer: "hemorrhaging population loss, the accompanying loss of social and public infrastructure, the loss of the environment itself (destroyed mountaintops, streambeds, and ecosystems) and community health, a looming loss of purpose, of futurity."[23]

Another issue of pressing concern in the early 2000s was the fallout from a series of fatal accidents involving coal trucks carrying over twice the legal weight limit. In 2002, Delegate Mike Caputo (Democrat, Marion County) introduced a bill in the West Virginia House of Delegates to increase enforcement of truck weight limits.[24] In response, legislators supporting the coal industry quickly introduced "retaliatory" legislation that would raise maximum legal weight limits for coal trucks from 80,000 pounds to 132,000 pounds (with a 5 percent variance).[25] Although neither bill passed, it led to a key strategic planning meeting of board members and officers of the West Virginia Coal Association during the summer of 2002 to discuss ways they could improve public relations.[26]

The outcome of that meeting was the birth of "Friends of Coal," which was to be a "volunteer" organization "dedicated to informing and educating West Virginia citizens about the coal industry and its vital role in the state's future."[27] A more accurate statement of its mission was "to reverse the perception that coal mining has declined in importance in West Virginia and the country"[28] and to "remove 'impediments' to coal mining."[29] West Virginia Coal Association president Bill Raney explained at the time that:

> For many years ... we have claimed that coal represents many more West Virginians beyond the thousands directly employed by the industry. Friends of Coal clearly indicates that this is the case ... With Friends of Coal, we are making an effort to count, organize and mobilize these people. It's time to clearly demonstrate to public officials, to media representatives and to the general public, just how many lives are touched in a positive way by the coal industry.[30]

---

[23] *Id.* at 730.
[24] Shannon Elizabeth Bell & Richard York, *Community Economic Identity: The Coal Industry and Ideology Construction in West Virginia*, 75 RURAL SOCIOLOGY 111, 126 (2010).
[25] *Id.* (citing Paul Nyden, *Heaviest Trucks Carrying Coal; Most Stopped Trucks above Limit Sought by Industry, Group Says*, CHARLESTON GAZETTE, Feb. 25, 2002).
[26] *Id.*
[27] *Id.* (citing Friends of Coal, *Who We Are*, https://www.friendsofcoal.org/about-foc/who-we-are.html).
[28] *Id.* at 127 (citing Friends of Coal, COAL LEADER (Mar. 2003), http://www.coalleader.com/).
[29] *Id.* (citing *Nehlen to Pitch for Coal Group; Ex-WVU Coach Calls Industry "Vital" to State's Future*, CHARLESTON DAILY MAIL, Dec. 13, 2002).
[30] *Id.* at 126 (citing Shanghai Zoom Intelligence Co., Ltd.).

It is notable that while Friends of Coal claims that it is a "grassroots" organization, its funding comes from member companies of the West Virginia Coal Association.[31]

The first item on Friends of Coal's agenda was to prepare for the 2003 legislative session, when the coal truck issue would likely be revisited. With that in mind, the West Virginia Coal Association contracted with the West Virginia-based firm Charles Ryan Associates "to provide public relations, advertising and internet services for Friends of Coal."[32] Shortly after the first "Friends of Coal" campaign was completed, the legislature passed Senate Bill 583, which raised the legal coal-truck weight limits.[33] According to Bill Reid, managing editor of *Coal Leader*, "[t]here is no doubt that Friends of Coal had a significant impact on the passage of the Coal Truck Bill."[34]

In 2003, on the heels of this victory, Friends of Coal "launched a full-scale campaign within West Virginia to reconnect the people of the state to an industry that can no longer truly be characterized as the 'lifeblood' of the economy."[35] In 2010, Shannon Elizabeth Bell and Richard York, sociologists at the University of Oregon, carried out an empirical analysis of this "massive public relations campaign" the underlying strategy of which, they said, was "to attempt to counter the coal industry's loss of citizens' employment loyalties by constructing an ideology of dependency and identity."[36] They found that the main strategy of the Friends of Coal campaign was to present coal mining as the defining feature of the state, which, they claimed, was nicely captured by this statement in 2005 from the Friends of Coal website: "It is likely that no state and industry are as closely identified with one another as West Virginia and coal."[37] According to Bell and York, Friends of Coal employed two primary strategies to equate the coal industry with the "identity" of West Virginia: (1) appropriating West Virginia cultural icons, and (2) creating a visible presence in the social landscape of West Virginia through stickers, yard signs, and sponsorships.[38]

Football Coaches, NASCAR, an Air Force General, and a Bass Fisherman

Don Nehlen, a popular, retired West Virginia University Mountaineers football coach (and, at that time, recent inductee into the College Football Hall of Fame) became the primary spokesperson for Friends of Coal, joined soon thereafter by retired Marshall University football coach Bobby Pruett. Nehlen is the all-time winningest football coach in WVU history, as was Pruett for Marshall at the time

---

[31]　*Id.* (citing G. Hohmann, Capitol Rallies to Reflect Divergent Opinions on Coal, CHARLESTON DAILY MAIL, Mar. 20, 2005).

[32]　*Id.*

[33]　*Id.*

[34]　*Id.* at 127.

[35]　*Id.* at 127–28.

[36]　*Id.* at 128.

[37]　*Id.* at 129.

[38]　*Id.*

(since surpassed by Doc Holliday). The point of selecting these icons, according to Bell and York, was to appropriate football and winning as part of Friends of Coal's identity. The connection between football and coal was strengthened when, with the encouragement of then Governor Joe Manchin, the Coal Association brought the WVU Mountaineers and Marshall University Thundering Herd teams together for seven years of football games, which became the "Friends of Coal Bowl." Prior to the first Friends of Coal Bowl game in 2006, the teams had met only five times in the previous ninety-five years. (The last Friends of Coal Bowl game was played in 2012, and WVU won all of them.) Friends of Coal also sponsored a Kentucky version of the event: the 2011 game between University of Kentucky and Louisville.

In addition to sponsoring the Friends of Coal Bowl, the connection with coal, winning, and football was promoted by two 30-second television commercials involving each team. According to Bell and York's description:

> The first commercial begins with a chorus singing, "When we go down deep through the dark today, we come up with the light for America." Next, the narrator announces, "Champions are born of hard work and determination, and just like the Thundering Herd, coal miners are a championship team. During this 2008 season, the Friends of Coal honor our coal miners and our Thundering Herd – all champions indeed." Then, the chorus concludes the commercial by singing, "Coal is West Virginia!" The second commercial is similarly worded, praising coal miners and the West Virginia University Mountaineers for both being "championship team[s]," making the Friends of Coal's message difficult to miss.[39]

In another effort to promote the "winner" message, Friends of Coal became the primary corporate sponsor for National Association for Stock Car Auto Racing (NASCAR) driver Derek Kiser, who drove a car with the "Friends of Coal" logo prominently placed across the hood. In 2009, Friends of Coal sponsored a longtime West Virginia sportsman, drag racer Greg Fowler, in International Hot Rod Association (IHRA) events throughout the Eastern United States.[40]

Bell and York also associate the "provider and defender" icon with the Friends of Coal campaign, through the use of retired Air Force General "Doc" Foglesong in Friends of Coal television commercials. As described by Bell and York:

> In the first of these commercials, called "American Hero," retired Air Force General "Doc" Foglesong narrates as images of (male) coal miners hard at work flash across the screen:
>
> Doc: You could say the West Virginia coal miners are modern-day pioneers. Men and women of courage, pride and adventure, who safely go where no one's been before and harvest the coal that powers our nation. ... In fact, if these miners didn't produce coal, our nation would be in trouble. More than half of the nation's

---

[39] *Id.* at 130.
[40] *Friends of Coal Team up with Fowler Racing,* Friends of Coal (July 29, 2009), https://www.friendsofcoal.org/171-friends-of-coal-team-up-with-fowler-racing.html.

electricity is generated by coal. West Virginia is the national leader in underground coal-mining production, and America needs that energy – today more than ever. So if you know a West Virginia coal miner, say "Thanks." Not that he or she is doing it for the thanks. They're doing it for their family and for our future. I'm retired Air Force General Doc Foglesong. Friends of Coal salute [sic] the pioneering spirit of the West Virginia coal miner. Why not join us and do the same?[41]

According to Bell and York, the image seeks to portray the West Virginia coal industry as "defender" of our country: "If these miners didn't produce coal, our nation would be in trouble." Another Friends of Coal commercial, "Tracking the Source," reinforces the defender theme: "Without West Virginia coal, our nation's economic status as a leader would be in jeopardy. It may seem like a daunting task to supply the nation with energy. But clean coal technology continues to gain momentum, helping us reduce our dependence on foreign oil and creating jobs for the men and women who proudly call themselves coal miners." In other words, "the coal industry is responsible for defending the United States from economic disaster and foreign conflict over oil."[42]

A third icon appropriated by Friends of Coal, Bell and York suggest, is that of the outdoorsman, and hunting and fishing in particular. In 2006, Friends of Coal retained professional bass fisherman Jeremy Starks as an official spokesperson and also became his primary corporate sponsor. Starks appeared in two 60-second Friends of Coal television commercials. The first featured football coaches Don Nehlen and Bobby Pruett fishing from Starks's 21-foot bass boat with "Friends of Coal" on its side, and talking about West Virginia's coal industry:

NEHLEN: Thousands of tons of coal are mined in this area.

STARKS: And scientific tests have shown

PRUETT: That the water is clean, clear, and a strong provider for wildlife. And the coal mining industry is proud of that.

NEHLEN: And of their role in making sure that it stays that way.

The second commercial showed Starks on a stream bank fishing with five children, and the scenes alternatively showing images of the coal mining process:

STARKS: Hi. I'm Jeremy Starks – a Friend of Coal and a pro fisherman who's concerned about the environment. . . . This clear stream is proof that sustaining water quality is a big part of the reclamation process. Scientific tests have shown that this water quality is better now than it's ever been. And this is after 22 million tons of coal have been mined in nearby land. Our need for energy is greater than ever. And with responsible practices in place, we can safely mine coal while restoring our land for future generations.

---

[41] Bell & York, *supra* note 24, at 131.
[42] *Id.* at 132.

This ad not only provides assurances that coal extraction and a clean environment can coexist but, incredibly, it suggests that coal mining actually improves water quality. Bell and York sum up Friends of Coal's appropriation of cultural icons as follows:

> Through appropriating some of the most potent cultural icons of the region, such as football, the military, race-car driving, the accomplished outdoorsman, and the work-ing-class provider, the Friends of Coal has attempted to amplify the connection between West Virginia and coal so that this industry appears to be more than a provider of jobs; it embodies all of the characteristics of the archetypal West Virginian.[43]

Logos (Everywhere!), Sponsorships, and Curriculum for the Classroom

The second strategy employed by Friends of Coal to strengthen the connection between West Virginia and the coal industry was to create a presence virtually everywhere, through its images and logos being displayed throughout the state, extensive sponsorship of events, and development of a curriculum that could be used in public schools, primarily in the southern coalfields. Friends of Coal aggressively distributed its stickers, hats, buttons, and yard signs throughout West Virginia, and these were designed to create "visible proof that there are Friends of Coal all over West Virginia."[44] Beginning in 2009 – after Friends of Coal ran a campaign in the West Virginia legislature to have a special "Friends of Coal" license plate authorized by the state – the Division of Motor Vehicles offered one featuring the logo on a black background and the motto "Coal Keeps the Light On!" printed across the bottom. The cost? Only $76.50 per year.[45] Kentucky and Virginia followed suit, and it quickly became the most popular specialty plate in the region, with tens of thousands sold since 2009.[46] One of the most popular T-shirt and sticker slogans of the Friends of Coal campaign became "Coal Mining: Our Future" which, according to Ryerson, was effective because it:

> [P]laces mining on a historical continuum, existing in time rather than behind the times, honoring the sacrifices of one's ancestors while building toward a more promising future. In refusing to be defined as obsolete, "Coal Mining Our Future" reaffirms coal's proper place on the linear timescale of American Progress, defined by the growth of American industry fueled by American energy.[47]

In addition to the Friends of Coal Bowl, one of the very high-profile sponsorships for the organization was the Friends of Coal Auto Fair (FOCAF), the first of which was held in 2004, quickly becoming one of West Virginia's largest annual car shows. The fourteenth annual FOCAF in West Virginia took place in 2018, and the attractions

[43]   *Id.* at 134.
[44]   *Id.* at 135.
[45]   *Special Plate, General Interest: Friends of Coal,* WEST VIRGINIA DMV, https://transportation.wv.gov /DMV/Vehicle-Services/License-Plates/Special-Plates/Pages/Special-Plate.aspx?p=75.
[46]   Ryerson, *supra* note 5, at 734.
[47]   *Id.* at 730.

"brought nearly 4,000 people into the two-day event" and "raised $70,903.62 for Hospice of Southern West Virginia and the Humane Society of Raleigh County."[48] As portrayed in the film *Overburden* – a section of which follows the story of Betty Harrah, a pro-coal activist from southern West Virginia as she visits the FOCAF – the weekend schedule was like "that of any other car show: a cruise, a burnout competition, music, and more," seemingly without coal being anywhere on the schedule. Yet "coal was everywhere": tents "where tables are laden with FOC stickers, T-shirts, bumper stickers, pens, and more, all being given away for free."[49] By 2021, however, the FOCAF had ceased to exist, and became the Friends of Charity Auto Fair; it is still held at the Raleigh County Memorial Airport in Beckley.[50]

Summing up the Friends of Coal strategy on sponsorships, Bell and York describe it this way:

> Friends of Coal's massive campaign to have its name attached to everything from soccer fields to auto fairs to the capital city's Fourth of July celebration to volleyball games to theater performances is a clear attempt to broaden its base of support to those individuals who may not care about football or fishing and who may not come from a working-class background. Through appearing to sponsor everything and anything, the Friends of Coal gives the impression that the coal industry is still acting as the backbone of the state, regardless of whether it provides many jobs or contributes significantly to public services. Thus, these diverse sponsorships serve to perpetuate an ideology of dependency: Without the coal industry, West Virginians would not only be without jobs, they would also be without sporting events, soccer fields, cultural events, and community centers.[51]

The curriculum for schools is offered by the Coal Education Development and Resources (CEDAR) program operated by Friends of Coal. Its motto is "Securing Coal's Future Today, by Educating our Leaders of Tomorrow."[52] CEDAR's mission is to "facilitate the increase of knowledge and understanding of the many benefits the coal industry provides in daily lives."[53] It accomplishes this "by providing financial resources and coal education materials to implement its study in the school curriculum."[54] Bell and York cite the CEDAR program as an example of "manipulative socialization," which is directed not at changing the values of the working class, but perpetuating the values that keep the working class from interpreting "the reality it actually experiences." In other words, "the coal industry actively works to maintain and amplify its status as the state's economic identity in order to prevent the working class from recognizing the coal industry's role in the economic and

---

[48] *Id.* at 728.

[49] *Id.*

[50] Friends of Charity Auto Fair, https://www.wvautofair.com/.

[51] Bell & York, *supra* note 24, at 135.

[52] Friends of Coal, Education, Cedar West Virginia, http://www.cedarswv.com/index.php/educate.html.

[53] *Id.*

[54] *Id.*

environmental degradation of coalfield communities."[55] And, of course, school systems have a crucial role in the manipulative socialization of children. CEDAR was created to provide curriculum resources and financial incentives to educators in six of the leading coal-producing counties in West Virginia – Mingo, Logan, Boone, McDowell, Wyoming, and Wayne – counties on the front line of the economic and environmental degradation caused by the coal industry.

CEDAR has many resources for educators to assist in this "manipulative socialization" process. First, there are the classroom teaching materials. CEDAR offers an extensive online video library for grades K–12 including such titles as "America's Fuel" (which "demonstrates the importance of coal to the American economy and overall quality of life"), "Coal People: A Century of Pride," "Common Ground: Modern Mining and You," "Balancing the Needs – Coal and the Environment," "Clean Coal Technologies," "Building a Future on Reclaimed Land," and "Coal Today" ("a modern story about the new technologies and the people who produce coal and generate the power that is the foundation of our nation's economy"). Lesson plans can also be downloaded, including recipes for "cookie bar coal" (which "observe[s] the effect of heat and pressure on materials representing those involved in the formation of coal") and "marshmallow moosh" (which "investigate[s] the effect of weight on compression"). Booklets, newspapers ("The Energist"), and posters are also available, free of charge. And CEDAR can, upon request, provide guest speakers for the classroom on such issues as reclamation, underground mining, trucking, and engineering.

Second, teachers in these six coal-producing counties are offered grant money to create and implement classroom study units on coal using CEDAR materials. The unit must be designed "to teach students about the importance of coal in their daily lives," and should include "critical thinking and decision-making about coal, including the role of coal in the nation's energy future, in the economics of West Virginia and the nation, the historical and cultural aspects of coal production, and the challenges and possibilities relating to production and using coal while protecting the environment." Cash prizes are awarded to teachers for the top three units at three grade levels (K–4), (5–8), and (9–12).

Third, each school is encouraged to organize a coal fair at the school, designed to give each student the opportunity to enter a project on coal in one of the following seven categories: science, math, English literature, art, music, technology–multimedia, or social studies. The winners of the local coal fairs are invited to enter their projects in a regional coal fair, where sixty-three winners in each of the seven categories (first through third place) in three different age groups receive cash prizes. Nine overall age group winners also receive cash prizes. To reward educators for their role in organizing a coal fair, CEDAR offers a "Coal Fair Coordinator's Program" providing cash prizes to the top three coordinators "for excellence in performing their duties."

[55] Bell & York, *supra* note 24, at 136.

Finally, the CEDAR Program offers ten $1,000 scholarships to students from the six participating coalfield counties to be used at one of the Southern West Virginia Community and Technical College campuses. As part of the application process, students must submit an essay of at least 100 words "telling why you feel the coal industry is important to West Virginia."

Bell and York sum up the CEDAR curriculum program in southern West Virginia counties as follows: "By engaging students and teachers in coal-education units, encouraging participation in coal fairs, and offering college scholarships, the coal industry is working to ensure that the future citizenry of southern West Virginia is socialized to believe that coal is indispensable to the life, culture, and economic future of their communities and state."[56]

Filling the Vacuum Left by the UMWA

The rise of Friends of Coal coincided with the demise of the UMWA, but with a cruel twist for the miners: the Friends of Coal campaign "appropriated and repurposed union culture through narratives of producerism to bind the interests of workers to the interests of coal companies."[57] Or, in other words, "workers and communities reidentif[ied] with corporate interests as their own."[58] Ryerson cites three particular "cultural artifacts" – the Friends of Coal license plate, miners' work clothes, and a popular Friends of Coal sticker depicting an underground miner – as effective tools used by Friends of Coal to appropriate union culture and turn it on its head into support for the coal companies.

Miners often wore their work clothes – commonly referred to as their "stripes" because of their reflective orange safety stripes – to pro-coal protests and rallies. Miners in their stripes "command[ed] a distinct respect in the region,"[59] and were used quite effectively in the EPA hearings regarding the Clean Power Plan in July 2014, when thousands of miners protested in front of the federal building in Pittsburgh where the public hearing was convened.[60] The same scene was repeated in November 2017 when the Trump EPA convened public hearings in Charleston to take public comments on rolling back the Clean Power Plan, and hundreds of Murray Energy miners in their uniforms showed up to show their support for Bob Murray's testimony in favor of the repeal.[61]

---

[56] Bell & York, *supra* note 24, at 138.
[57] Ryerson, *supra* note 5, at 724.
[58] *Id.* at 721.
[59] *Id.* at 734
[60] Don Hopey, Stephanie Ritenbaugh, & Madeline Conway, *EPA Hearings on Controversial Carbon Emissions Regulations Continue in Pittsburgh*, PITTSBURGH POST-GAZETTE (Aug. 1, 2014), https://www .post-gazette.com/breaking/2014/07/31/Pro-and-con-voice-their-views-at-EPA-hearing-on-proposed-pollu tion-curbs/stories/201407310284.
[61] Brady Dennis, *In the Heart of Coal Country, EPA Gets an Earful About Clean Power Plan's Fate*, WASH. POST (Nov. 28, 2017), https://www.washingtonpost.com/news/energy-environment/wp/2017/11/ 28/in-the-heart-of-coal-country-epa-gets-an-earful-about-clean-power-plans-fate/.

The third cultural artifact cited by Ryerson – a "dominant image in the extensive visual landscape of pro-coal stickers and bumper stickers" – is of an underground miner crawling on his hands and knees. In its various iterations, the image is captioned with numerous pro-coal slogans including "Coal Keeps the Lights On," "Like Father Like Son," "I've Got Friends in Low Places," "In Memory of My Dad," "Coalminer's Wife," "It's a Family Tradition," and sexually provocative slogans such as "Coal Miners Do It in the Dark" and "Coal Miners Go Deeper." These three cultural objects show how the Friends of Coal campaign was able to use race, gender, and sexual orientation in its "affective appeals" to appropriate UMWA culture: "Each object enacts tropes of masculinity and sexual power: license plates for big trucks, safety stripes for dangerous and physical (masculine) labor, and an image accompanied with slogans that define the coal mining subject as a white heterosexual man."[62]

Ryerson describes how Friends of Coal was able to go beyond the role historically played by the UMWA to strengthen the identity between the organization and support for coal communities:

> Where the UMWA once played a central role in community life outside the mines in addition to inside them, [Friends of Coal] events created new spaces for people to come together in the act of building, celebrating, and belonging to community. In raising funds for hospice [sic] and the humane society, coal becomes a benevolent community contributor. Attending [Friends of Coal] events thus becomes an act of participating in this benevolence. Furthermore, in permeating the visual landscape with [Friends of Coal] iconography, displayed on everything from billboards to soccer fields to NASCAR sponsorships to personal clothing, the [Friends of Coal] logo appropriated the once-dominant iconography of UMWA stickers, hats, and T-shirts. Publicly displaying [Friends of Coal] affiliation marks one's solidarity and allegiance to their community, and to all mining communities: to a culture bonded through shared risk and incredible sacrifice.[63]

While at some level, one can admire the genius of the Friends of Coal campaign to reframe the narrative by refocusing attention away from the declining number of mining jobs and the increasing environmental devastation inflicted upon coal communities through modern surface mining techniques, the appropriation of UMWA culture to create support for coal operators was particularly appalling. The gap between what was good for the coal *operators* versus what was good for coal *miners* was widening drastically throughout this period. What were the first liabilities that coal operators sought to shed in their frequent abuses of the bankruptcy process to "reorganize" their operations? The pension and healthcare benefits of the retired coal miners, as described in Chapter 11. And then there were the various proposals by the West Virginia Coal Association in the West Virginia legislature to roll back safety protection for miners – as described in Chapter 9 – to shave a few dollars off their

[62] Ryerson, *supra* note 5, at 735.
[63] *Id.* at 729.

operating expenses in a futile effort to cope with the overwhelming market forces that were crushing the economics of coal-fired electric generation.

On top of that, there were repeated failures by the coal operators to protect the safety of miners, leading, among other things, to the death of twenty-nine of the thirty-one miners at the Massey-owned Upper Big Branch mine in April 2010, caused by a coal dust explosion that was "entirely preventable" had ventilation regulations been followed.[64] There was also the abject failure of coal operators to protect miners from black lung disease that could have been prevented if they had simply followed the protocols required by federal black lung statutes and implemented Mine Safety and Health Administration regulations, as corroborated by autopsies showing that seventeen of the twenty-nine miners who died at Upper Big Branch had signs of black lung disease that likely would have killed them had the mine explosion not done so earlier.[65] Furthermore, there were ongoing efforts by coal operators to deny miners the black lung benefits to which they were entitled through endless litigation using unethical litigation tactics.[66]

In light of this abysmal track record of coal operators failing to protect their "most precious resource"[67] – the miners – it was particularly reprehensible that the Friends of Coal campaign effectively appropriated the highly valued image of the Appalachian coal miner to redefine coal miners as synonymous with the coal industry. Nothing could be further from the truth. But the campaign laid the groundwork for enlisting these same valued coal miners as effective soldiers in the "war on coal" that commenced in 2009 with the election of Barack Obama as president.

DECLARATION OF THE "WAR ON COAL"

As described in Chapter 1, the EPA adopted several policies under President Barack Obama that were seen as hostile to the coal industry. There was the June 2009 agreement among the Army Corps of Engineers, the Interior Department, and the EPA that took aim at mountaintop removal in Appalachia. Shortly thereafter, in December 2009, the EPA issued its "endangerment finding," which authorized it to begin regulating GHG emissions and ultimately led to EPA's adoption of the Clean Power Plan in August 2015. Probably the most devastating action for the coal industry in Appalachia was EPA's issuance, in December 2011, of the Mercury and Air Toxics Standard (MATS) rule. This resulted in several coal plants shuttering in West Virginia when the additional investment necessary to achieve compliance did not

---

[64]   *Id.*

[65]   Chris Hamby, *Persistent Black Lung, Old Scourge of Coal, Found in Autopsies of Most Massey Miners,* CENTER FOR PUBLIC INTEGRITY (May 19, 2011), https://publicintegrity.org/environment/persistent-black -lung-old-scourge-of-coal-found-in-autopsies-of-most-massey-miners/.

[66]   Chris Hamby, *Coal Industry's Go-To Law Firm Withheld Evidence of Black Lung, at Expense of Sick Miners,* CENTER FOR PUBLIC INTEGRITY (Oct. 29, 2013), https://publicintegrity.org/environment/coal- industrys-go-to-law-firm-withheld-evidence-of-black-lung-at-expense-of-sick-miners/.

[67]   UNITED MINE WORKERS OF AMERICA, https://umwa.org/about/history/.

prove to be cost-effective as coal began to lose the battle with cheaper and cleaner natural gas-fired generation.

To many in the coal industry, however, Obama tipped his hand in a January 2008 interview with the *San Francisco Chronicle* editorial board during his first campaign for president, when he showed his support for a cap-and-trade program to regulate GHG emissions:

> So if somebody wants to build a coal-fired power plant, they can. It's just that it will bankrupt them because they're going to be charged a huge sum for all that greenhouse gas that's being emitted . . . [U]nder my plan of a cap-and-trade system, electricity rates would necessarily skyrocket. Regardless of what I say about whether coal is good or bad, because I'm capping greenhouse gases, coal-powered plants . . . would have to retrofit their operations. That'll cost money; they will pass that money on to consumers.[68]

Four years later, Republican nominee Mitt Romney would describe Obama's 2008 statement about bankrupting the coal industry as the "one promise he's kept,"[69] and he regularly referred to Obama's policies as a "war on coal" during the 2012 presidential campaign.[70]

The "war on coal" was born much before the 2012 presidential election, however. As described by Sylvia Ryerson, the "war on coal" began in 2009, almost immediately after Obama's election, and was quickly embraced – and to some degree weaponized – by Friends of Coal:

> Observing the "War" on Coal next to the "Friends" of Coal demonstrates the necessary expansiveness of this affective map. While industry-sponsored car shows, sporting events, and school curriculum incorporated primarily positive emotions, the War on Coal incorporated the opposite: anger, blame, resentment, and fear. The War on Coal began in 2009, after President Barack Obama's election. It targeted specific enemies – the EPA, President Obama, environmentalists – and cast miners as the real American Heroes, under attack from irrational extremists and an overreaching federal government. Where UMWA miners gained critical information, analysis, and ideally protection in union meeting halls, at conventions, and on picket line protests, by the 2000s, these spaces were largely gone. Absent a union counternarrative and support, in an education system inundated with pro-coal curriculum, pro-coal rallies, under the banner of the War on Coal, offered a clear explanation, solution, and protection.[71]

During President Obama's first year in office, the coal industry rallied in opposition to the proposed cap-and-trade regulation described in Obama's *Chronicle* interview. Friends of Coal funded a spin-off organization, the Federation for American Coal,

[68] Erica Martinson, *Uttered in 2008, Still Haunting Obama*, POLITICO (Apr. 5, 2012), https://www .politico.com/story/2012/04/uttered-in-2008-still-haunting-obama-in-2012-074892#ixzz300lEoxDY.

[69] *Id.*

[70] Seema Mehta, *Romney Accuses Obama of "Waging a War on Coal*," L.A. TIMES (Aug. 14, 2012), https:// www.latimes.com/politics/la-xpm-2012-aug-14-la-pn-romney-accuses-obama-of-waging-a-war-on-coal -20120814-story.html.

[71] Ryerson, *supra* note 5, at 731.

Energy and Security (FACES), which launched a FACES of Coal campaign in 2009.[72] The campaign depicted Central Appalachia as the battlefield in Obama's "war on coal," and billboards featuring the slogan "The Obama Administration's No Job Zone" began to appear throughout the region.[73] A popular sticker on pickup trucks showed a cartoon figure of a coal miner peeing on the name "Obama."[74]

The industry also began to sponsor huge pro-coal rallies across the region. The largest was a 2009 Labor Day rally hosted by Massey Energy held on the site of the former Holden 22 mountaintop mine site near Logan.[75] The event was billed as the "Friends of America" rally, featuring Ted Nugent as emcee, who condemned the Obama administration "for its assault on the American way of life." Sean Hannity of Fox News, Hank Williams Jr., John Rich (formerly of Big and Rich), and Lord Christopher Monckton, a vocal critic of climate and global warming science and former science adviser to Margaret Thatcher, also appeared at the rally, as did Massey's Don Blankenship, who wore an American flag hat and an American flag shirt for the occasion.[76] Friends of Coal reported that 100,000 people attended the event. Bill Raney, president of the West Virginia Coal Association, described the rally as a "great gathering of the real America," and remarked that the coal miners in attendance were "scared for their future with the public policies in Washington being driven by selfish personal agendas."[77]

The "war on coal" was a prominent issue in the 2010 elections in West Virginia. One of the more controversial races featured the challenge to seventeen-term Democratic incumbent Congressman Nick Rahall by Spike Maynard, a well-known former state supreme court judge who switched his party registration to Republican to run against Rahall. In announcing his candidacy, Maynard claimed that "West Virginians deserve a congressman who will fight to end this war on coal instead of standing by idly as thousands of local jobs are threatened." He said his message was a simple one: "If you vote for Spike Maynard, you're voting for your job and to mine coal. If you're against me, you're voting against your job and against mining coal."[78] In response, Rahall compared the "war on coal" to a terrorist attack at a candidate debate with Maynard, and claimed that coal "has always been under attack" and defending the coal industry is "kind of like fighting terrorist attacks – when an attack doesn't occur, then you never knew the threat was there to begin with."[79] (Rahall would win

[72] *Id.*
[73] *Id.*
[74] *Id.*
[75] *Friends of America Festival Brings 100,000 to Mountaintop Mine Site*, Friends of Coal (Sept. 9, 2009), https://www.friendsofcoal.org/news/183-friends-of-america-festival-brings-100000-to-mountaintop-mine-site.html.
[76] Murphy, *supra* note 17.
[77] Friends of Coal, *supra* note 75.
[78] Jonathan Martin, *GOP Mines Coal-Country Anxieties*, Politico (Feb. 15, 2010), https://www.politico.com/story/2010/02/gop-mines-coal-country-anxieties-032955.
[79] Ry Rivard, *Maynard, Rahall Wage "War on Coal,"* Charleston Gazette-Mail (Sept. 20, 2010), https://www.wvgazettemail.com/news/maynard-rahall-wage-war-on-coal/article_f25596c0-3242-5f7a-bb53-a7aa262f8db1.html.

reelection in both 2010 and 2012 before losing to Republican Evan Jenkins in 2014; Jenkins was a former Democratic state senator who became a Republican in 2013 before challenging Rahall.)

In its coverage of the Congressional races in West Virginia and Kentucky in 2010, *Politico* observed that:

> Republicans believe there are three words so powerful that they might reshape the political order in an economically beleaguered corner of the country: War on coal. With Democrats holding total control of the federal government and a cap-and-trade bill still looming, the GOP [Grand Old Party, the Republican Party] is fanning widespread coal country fears that the national Democratic Party is hostile to the coal mining industry, if not outright committed to its demise.[80]

In 2010, then Governor Joe Manchin ran in a special election to fill the seat of the late Robert Byrd, and while he did not use the term "war on coal" at the time, he complained about the Obama administration's "attempts to destroy our coal industry and way of life in West Virginia."[81] He made that statement in October 2010 – just a month before the election – in announcing the lawsuit filed by West Virginia against the EPA to overturn new federal rules on mountaintop removal mining. From 2013, the "war on coal" would become a regular part of Manchin's vocabulary.[82]

State officials got into the act during the 2012 election season, and "war on coal" messaging was, on occasion, paid for by taxpayers. In May 2012, for example, the public relations firm behind the FACES of Coal campaign organized – at taxpayer expense – a three-city tour (Charleston, Wheeling, and Beckley) of the "Coal Forum" group headlined by Governor Earl Ray Tomblin. The tour featured some of the themes of the FACES of Coal campaign. Tomblin referred to "Obama's no jobs zone" – including verbal attacks on the EPA, which, he said, "has waged an outright war on everyone who works so hard to keep the lights on in our country." Vowing never to "back down," Tomblin promised to "do everything possible to protect our coal industry."[83] Another theme developed by the industry for the 2012 campaign was the so-called train wreck situation created by the combination of the various EPA regulatory measures – a cross-state pollution rule, mandated reductions in toxic air releases, and a limit on GHG emissions.[84] One commentator, who analyzed public relations campaign "framing" of the issues, found that "many

[80] Martin, *supra* note 78.
[81] Patrick Reis, *W.Va. Sues Obama, EPA over Mining Coal Regulations*, N.Y. TIMES (Oct. 6, 2010), https://archive.nytimes.com/www.nytimes.com/gwire/2010/10/06/06greenwire-wva-sues-obama-epa-over-mining-coal-regulation-48964.html.
[82] *See* Press Release, Senator Manchin, Manchin Slams Obama's War on Coal and Economy (June 25, 2013), https://www.manchin.senate.gov/newsroom/press-releases/manchin-slams-obamas-war-on-coal-and-economy.
[83] Ken Ward Jr., *W.Va. Leaders Vow Continued Fight Against EPA's "War on Coal,"* CHARLESTON GAZETTE-MAIL (May 24, 2012), https://www.wvgazettemail.com/news/special_reports/w-va-leaders-vow-continued-fight-against-epa-s-war/article_6d13ce64-3d14-5b6b-8341-44166aa8eb5e.html.
[84] *Id.*

environmental debates – clean coal, climate change, cap and trade, etc. – those against legislation or action to combat CO_2 emissions or change our energy sources in any way, use the threats to capitalism, the American way of life, and our economy to counter any positive/progressive action."[85]

Commenting on the 2012 election cycle, veteran environmental reporter Ken Ward of the *Charleston Gazette-Mail* observed that: "From the presidential race to heated battles for statewide and local legislative offices, talk of Obama's 'war on coal' still sucks all the oxygen out of every room and dominates most campaign ads. No one wants to consider anything else, and they most certainly don't want to hear talk about what might come next."[86]

Following the 2012 elections, the "war on coal" label was a popular term used by Republican lawmakers during the 113th United States Congress. According to the Congressional Record, the term was used 100 times in both the House of Representatives and the Senate between 2013 and 2014. Based on a sample of fifty congressional floor speeches and committee meetings during 2013 and 2014, Senator Mitch McConnell (Republican, Kentucky) used the term more frequently than any other member of Congress. Congresswoman Shelley Moore Capito – who would go on to be elected to the US Senate in November 2014 – came in at number four in the rankings, with three references to the "war on coal" in her remarks in committee meetings and on the House floor.[87]

WEST VIRGINIA QUICKLY GOES FROM RELIABLY BLUE TO BRIGHT RED

On the heels of Trump's overwhelming victories in West Virginia in the last two presidential elections – he carried the state 68 percent to 26 percent versus Hillary Clinton in 2016 and 69 percent to 30 percent versus Joe Biden in 2020 – it is difficult to grasp that when Joe Manchin first sought statewide office in 1996, registered Democrats outnumbered registered Republicans by a 2–1 margin. The Democrats had unbroken control of both state legislative bodies from 1933 until 2014. Prior to Jim Justice's reelection as a Republican Governor in 2020 – he was a Democrat when he was first elected in 2016 – West Virginia had elected only two Republicans as governor since the New Deal – Arch Moore (in 1968 and 1984) and Cecil Underwood (in 1956 and 1996).

At the presidential level, West Virginia was one of only ten states (and the only "southern" state, as defined by the US Census) to vote for Michael Dukakis in the Republican landslide of 1988; it was one of only six states to support Jimmy Carter over Ronald Reagan in 1980; and it supported Bill Clinton by large margins in both

[85] Matthew C. Nisbet, *Analyzing the Framing Battle over Coal as an Energy Source*, BIG THINK (Apr. 25, 2011), https://bigthink.com/age-of-engagement/analyzing-the-framing-battle-over-coal-as-an-energy-source.
[86] Ward Jr., *supra* note 83.
[87] *War on Coal Debate*, Ballotpedia, https://ballotpedia.org/War_on_coal_debate.

1992 (by 13 points) and 1996 (by almost 15 points). Since 2000, however, West Virginia has voted consistently for the Republican candidate for president, by growing margins. In February 2021, the reversal of fortunes of the state's political parties became complete – Republican registrations outnumbered Democratic registrations for the first time in state history.[88]

Several factors contributed to this turn of events, including the decline in the influence of the UMWA in West Virginia in the last two decades of the twentieth century – as discussed in the section The Decline of the United Mine Workers – which meant a loss of the formerly strong union get-out-the-vote efforts for Democrats. Another significant event was the presidential election of 2000, which featured an environmental candidate – Al Gore – as the Democratic nominee. As Clinton's vice president, Gore had negotiated the Kyoto Protocol in 1997 with the message that the world needed to start addressing climate change. Although Clinton signed the agreement on behalf of the United States in November 1998, the US Senate passed a resolution – cosponsored by Democratic Senator Robert Byrd – by a 95–0 vote that prohibited the United States from ratifying the treaty. The 2000 election pitted a "climate change activist" against a popular Texas governor, George W. Bush, who was proud of the business-friendly environment he had fostered in the Lone Star State.

The coal lobby responded by throwing its support behind Bush in a big way. According to Bill Raney, president of the West Virginia Coal Association, "we all felt threatened by" Gore. The 2000 election was on the heels of a controversial ruling in early 1999 by US District Court Judge Charles Haden to block Arch Coal's proposed expansion of its mountaintop removal project in Logan County. That was followed by a more sweeping order issued by Judge Haden in October 1999 severely limiting mine-related damage to streams, which typically are buried when adjacent peaks are blasted. When the coal industry appealed the decision to the Fourth Circuit Court of Appeals, the Clinton–Gore administration filed a plaintiff-friendly brief, arguing that federal courts had jurisdiction in the matter. Then, when Democratic Senator Robert Byrd of West Virginia tried to overturn the Haden order legislatively, the administration successfully opposed him. According to John McCutcheon, Bush's West Virginia campaign director, "[t]he mountaintop-removal controversy played significantly in the electoral events of 2000. For many people, this foreshadowed what would happen to the entire state"[89] (if Al Gore won).

As described by the *Wall Street Journal*, Raney was "the middleman in an unlikely triumvirate" that convinced Bush he had a chance to win West Virginia. The effort was led by James H. "Buck" Harless, "the union-battling patriarch of West Virginia's coal industry"; Charles "Dick" Kimbler, an unemployed miners' union official who blamed Clinton–Gore environmental policies for killing his job, joined the team. Kimbler's job was "to neutralize the Democrats' advantage with union voters." Harless had traveled to

[88] Raby, *supra* note 2.
[89] Tom Hamburger, *A Coal-Fired Crusade Helped Bring Crucial Victory to Candidate Bush*, WALL St. J. (June 13, 2001), https://www.wsj.com/articles/SB992378085878375783.

Texas in April 1999 to meet with Bush and played an instrumental role in urging the Bush campaign not to cede West Virginia to Al Gore. After his introduction to Bush, Harless stated that "[i]t was obvious then that he wasn't going to be like Gore and stop coal." The Bush team signed Harless up as a "pioneer" – charged with raising $100,000 – and, by August 1999, West Virginians had contributed $200,000 to Bush. That figure would ultimately grow to $275,000, five times the amount raised by Gore. Coal interests nationwide donated $3.8 million to the 2000 election, tripling their 1996 contributions; about 88 percent went to Republicans.[90] As for the union votes, the UMWA endorsed Gore, but Kimbler, a lifelong Democrat, refused to go along with this claiming that "Al Gore was an extreme environmentalist, and if he won, he'd shut down the whole state." As it turned out, Raney would end up driving Kimbler around the state in 2000 to join him in making pro-Bush pitches to miners and executives.

The result was West Virginia flipping narrowly to red (52 percent to 46 percent), and George W. Bush became the first Republican to carry the state since Reagan in 1984, and only the fourth time a Republican had carried the state since 1932. Bush, who also carried Kentucky and Gore's home state of Tennessee, apparently referred to his win in 2000 as a "coal-fired victory." He carried the state again in 2004, this time by 13 points. As further evidence that the tide was turning for Republicans, West Virginia was one of only five states – the others were Arkansas, Louisiana, Oklahoma, and Tennessee – where Republican nominee John McCain won by a larger margin in 2008 than George W. Bush in 2004.

McCain was also helped, of course, by Obama's remarks during the *San Francisco Chronicle* interview, which were seized upon by Republican vice-presidential candidate Sarah Palin shortly before election day in 2008; she claimed that Obama's plans for dealing with climate change would "bankrupt the coal industry."[91] Obama was never popular in West Virginia; he lost the Democratic primary to Hillary Clinton by 41 points in 2008, even though her campaign was all but over by the time of the May 13 primary. According to a report in the *New York Times*, "racial considerations emerged as an unusually salient factor"; 2 in 10 white West Virginia voters said that race was an important factor in their vote, and more than 8 in 10 of them backed Mrs. Clinton.[92]

Largely because of the environmental policies described in Chapter 1, Obama would become so unpopular in West Virginia during his first term that Keith Judd, a felon serving a seventeen-and-a-half-year prison sentence for extortion at the Federal Correctional Institution in Texarkana, Texas, received 41 percent of the vote in West Virginia's 2012 Democratic primary, 72,000 votes to Obama's 106,000.[93] Due to Obama's

[90] *Id.*

[91] Ken Ward Jr., *The Myth of the War on Coal*, THE NATION (Oct. 10, 2012), https://www.thenation.com /article/archive/myth-war-coal/.

[92] Patrick Healy, *Clinton Beats Obama Handily in West Virginia*, N.Y. TIMES, May 14, 2008), https:// www.nytimes.com/2008/05/14/us/politics/14dems.html?_r=1&pagewanted=all.

[93] Rachel Weiner, *Why Felon Keith Judd Did So Well Against Obama in West Virginia*, WASH. POST (May 9, 2012), https://www.washingtonpost.com/blogs/the-fix/post/why-felon-keith-judd-did-so-well-against-obama-in-west-virginia/2012/05/09/gIQA7GwtCU_blog.html.

disapproval ratings in West Virginia and in the face of their own reelection challenges that November, the three leading Democrats – Governor Earl Ray Tomblin, Senator Joe Manchin, and Congressman Nick Rahall – all declined to attend the Democratic National Convention in Charlotte where Obama was renominated in 2012.[94]

In the general election in 2012, the coal industry rallied around Mitt Romney to "end Obama's war on coal."[95] Romney also contributed to the rhetoric when he popularized the phrase "makers and takers" in his infamous statement that "[m]y job is not to worry about those people" with respect to the 47 percent of Americans who were likely to vote for Barack Obama and constitute a "taker class" that pays little or nothing into the federal government but wanted to tax the productive classes for free health care, food, housing, and other government benefits.[96] In West Virginia, miners were recruited to identify as "makers," according to Sylvia Ryerson, even as coal jobs continued to disappear, which left "workers [with] nowhere to turn to affirm their producer [maker] identities except to the companies themselves."[97] Romney went on to win the state with 62 percent of the vote, and became the first Republican candidate for president in modern American history to win every county in the state.

Donald Trump's margin of victory in West Virginia in 2016 was so large that the state was referred to as "Trump Country," and journalists offered all sorts of explanations for the phenomenon. In terms of energy issues, however, coal again played a central role, and the explanation was fairly simple: Hillary Clinton was "going to put a lot of coal miners and coal companies out of business" while "Trump digs coal." Clinton's unfortunate comment – in what she later described as the biggest regret of her 2016 campaign[98] – occurred at a town hall meeting in Columbus, Ohio in March 2016 when she was explaining her plan for a transition from fossil fuel energy to renewables: "I'm the only candidate which [sic] has a policy about how to bring economic opportunity using clean renewable energy as the key into coal country. Because we're going to put a lot of coal miners and coal companies out of business."[99] Although she quickly added that she wanted to help coal miners and other fossil fuel workers – "we're going to make it clear that we don't want to forget those people [who] labored in those mines for generations, losing their health, often losing their lives to turn on our lights and power our factories"[100] – that explanation was just as quickly forgotten.

[94] Eric Eyre, *Manchin, Tomblin, Rahall to Skip DNC*, Charleston Gazette-Mail (June 18, 2012), https://www.wvgazettemail.com/news/politics/manchin-tomblin-rahall-to-skip-dnc/article_785d0d2f-0f40-5488-afb8-3872c9dc2508.html.

[95] Ryerson, *supra* note 5, at 736.

[96] Ezra Klein, *Romney's Theory of the "Taker Class," and Why It Matters*, Wash. Post (Sept. 17, 2012), https://www.washingtonpost.com/news/wonk/wp/2012/09/17/romneys-theory-of-the-taker-class-and-why-it-matters/.

[97] Ryerson, *supra* note 5, at 736.

[98] Eliza Relman, *Hillary Clinton: Here's the Misstep from the Campaign I Regret the Most*, Insider (Sept. 6, 2017), https://www.businessinsider.com/hillary-clinton-biggest-campaign-mistake-2017-9.

[99] *Id.*

[100] *Id.*

Meanwhile, Trump had been promising throughout the campaign to "end the war on coal" and to repeal Obama's Clean Power Plan, as this would put "thousands of miners back to work." In early May 2016, Trump drew a crowd of 10,000 to a rally in Charleston, West Virginia; he had received the endorsement of the West Virginia Coal Association shortly before the rally began and was joined on stage by Coal Association Vice President Chris Hamilton, who presented him with a miner's hard hat.[101] Trump famously put on the hard hat and mimed the act of shoveling coal. He pledged to the crowd that day, "Miners, get ready, because you're gonna be working your asses off, alright!?"[102] As described by Sylvia Ryerson, the contrast between the two candidates was striking: "While Trump embodied being a miner and declared that miners would make him proud, to thundering applause, Clinton promised 'those people' that she wouldn't forget about them – while already locating them as an afterthought."[103] Trump had effectively incorporated Friends of Coal rhetoric into his campaign[104] and the rest, as they say, was history. Trump's win in West Virginia with 68.5 percent of the vote was his largest share of the vote in any state in 2016.

A "takeaway" that Ryerson explored in her essay is how easily the Friends of Coal campaign could be "reappropriated, in this current conjuncture of unprecedented abandonment, into new political formations that offer the same modes of affective continuity with no material economic promises: the far right and white nationalism."[105] She describes the phenomenon as follows:

> The collapse of coal in Appalachia is requiring nothing less of miners and mining families than a transition from one world to another – toward a necessarily different world that remains uncertain and unknown. Without a political formation that recognizes and acknowledges the personal and communal magnitude of this shift, the present conjuncture of corporate abandonment remains dangerously vulnerable to being claimed and mobilized by the far right, under the white supremacist banner of "heritage."[106]

Joe Manchin has his own view of why West Virginians will no longer vote Democratic:

> I can tell you how West Virginia feels. We feel like returning Vietnam veterans. We've done every dirty job you've asked us to do. We never questioned. We did it and performed well. And now all of a sudden we're not good enough, we're not

[101]   Ashton Marra, *"Trump Digs Coal" at Charleston Rally*, West Virginia Public Broadcasting (May 5, 2016), https://www.wvpublic.org/news/2016-05-05/trump-digs-coal-at-charleston-rally.

[102]   Donald Trump, *Presidential Candidate Donald Trump Rally in Charleston, West Virginia*, C-Span (May 5, 2016), www.c-span.org/video/?409094-1/donald-trump-addresses-supporters-charleston-west-virginia.

[103]   Ryerson, *supra* note 5, at 737.

[104]   *Id.*

[105]   *Id.* at 741–42.

[106]   *Id.* at 743.

clean enough, we're not green enough and we're not smart enough. You want to know why they quit voting for Democrats, that's the reason.[107]

Trump's commandeering of West Virginia politics and his role as the self-proclaimed savior of the coal industry[108] was confirmed a few months later when coal baron Governor Jim Justice, elected as a Democrat in 2016, appeared alongside Trump at a rally in Huntington in August 2017 and announced his intention to switch his parties and become a Republican.[109] Justice told the crowd at the rally "I will tell you with lots of prayers and lots of thinking, today I will tell you as West Virginians that I can't help you anymore being a Democrat governor." He then wrapped his arms around Trump and said "This man is a good man. He's got a backbone, he's got real ideas. He cares about us in West Virginia." In response, Trump said "Having Big Jim as a Republican is such an honor. Fantastic man, Fantastic guy."[110]

As the democratic candidate for governor in 2016, Justice had picked up the endorsement of the UMWA.[111] In his reelection campaign in 2020 as a Republican, the UMWA endorsed his Democratic opponent, Ben Salango, while Justice received the endorsement of Bill Raney's West Virginia Coal Association. Justice won handily, with 65 percent of the vote to Salango's 31 percent, and carried all fifty-five counties in the process (although he underperformed Trump by just under 4 percent). Justice's reelection made him the first Republican to be elected governor of West Virginia since Cecil Underwood in 1996, and the first incumbent Republican governor to win reelection since Arch A. Moore Jr. in 1972.

---

[107] Associated Press, *Miners' Union and Sen. Manchin Back Shift from Coal in Exchange for Renewable Energy and Tech Jobs*, MARKETWATCH (Apr. 20, 2021), https://www.marketwatch.com/story/miners-union-and-sen-manchin-back-shift-from-coal-in-exchange-for-renewable-energy-and-tech-jobs-01618927591.

[108] Glenn Kessler, *Trump's Claim That He's "The One That Saved Coal" in WV is False*, WASH. POST (Dec. 29, 2017), https://www.wvgazettemail.com/news/politics/trumps-claim-that-hes-the-one-that-saved-coal-in-wv-is-false/article_030fc50c-493f-52ad-a18f-4fe29cf7454c.html.

[109] Michael D. Shear & Jonathan Martin, *In West Virginia, Trump Hails Conservatism and a New G.O.P. Governor*, N.Y. TIMES (Aug. 3, 2017), https://www.nytimes.com/2017/08/03/us/politics/west-virginia-governor-to-switch-from-democrat-to-republican-trump.html.

[110] *Id.*

[111] Brad McElhinny, *Justice Gets Endorsement from W.Va. Coal Association After Salango Gets UMW*, WV METRONEWS (Aug. 19, 2020), https://wvmetronews.com/2020/08/19/justice-gets-endorsement-from-w-va-coal-association-after-salango-gets-umw/.

6

"Leadership" from Washington, DC: The Congressional Delegation That Could Have but Didn't

Throughout "the lost decade," West Virginia's Congressional delegation largely joined in the "war on coal" rhetoric, and the narrative was one that both parties could enthusiastically join. Whether Republican or Democrat, the problem was the Obama administration's "job-killing EPA." Legislative efforts were directed at funding for "clean coal technology" – a mythical remedy – stripping the Environmental Protection Agency (EPA) of its regulatory authority to regulate greenhouse gas (GHG) emissions, and generally doing the bidding of the large coal companies.

The upper chamber, however, is worth a closer look. At the beginning of "the lost decade," West Virginia was represented in the US Senate by Robert C. Byrd and John Davison "Jay" Rockefeller IV, both of whom seemed to have a change of heart regarding their loyalty to the coal industry once they were in a position where they didn't have to face the voters again. In the last year of his five decades of representing West Virginia in the US Senate, Robert Byrd issued some strong statements about the way West Virginia was treated by the coal industry, and how things needed to change. Jay Rockefeller, for his part, gave a stirring speech on the floor of the Senate in June 2012 regarding the need for West Virginia to move forward beyond coal. It was late in the game at that point for Senator Rockefeller, however – who had served in the Senate since 1984 – and the speech was an obvious clue that he would not be seeking reelection in 2014.

Byrd's seat was later filled by Joe Manchin III – "Manchin in the middle," discussed in the next chapter – while Rockefeller was succeeded by Shelley Moore Capito. She was one of the strongest voices in the "war on coal" narrative and used her anti-EPA rhetoric to secure a promotion from the House of Representatives – where she had served for fourteen years – to the US Senate, where she has risen to great influence as Ranking Member of the Senate Public Works and Environment Committee. During the spring of 2021 she served as the point person negotiating with the White House on behalf of Senate Republicans regarding the size and shape of President Biden's proposed infrastructure package. So long as the US Senate remains at 50–50, and the Democrats retain control of the US House of

Representatives – either or both of which could change with the November 2022 midterm elections – West Virginia's two senators will have extraordinary influence that could potentially be used to improve the lives of average West Virginians. Whether that influence will be deployed to the benefit of average West Virginians, however, remains very much in doubt.

In the lower chamber, David McKinley, the Republican Congressman from Morgantown who was elected in 2010 and rode hard on the "war on coal" rhetoric, has moderated his views on energy and is starting to earn a name for himself as a bipartisan dealmaker himself. His middle ground path on clean energy legislation may be worth a serious look in the absence of any breakthrough on the Senate side of the Hill.

SENATOR ROBERT BYRD: "A VOICE OF PRINCIPLE AND REASON"

When Senator Robert C. Byrd died at age ninety-two in June 2010 after serving in the Senate longer than anyone in US history, President Barack Obama remarked that "America has lost a voice of principle and reason."[1] He went on to say that Senator Byrd "had the courage to stand firm in his principles, but also the courage to change over time,"[2] a reference to his evolving views on climate change and the coal industry.

Byrd was elected to the House of Representatives from West Virginia in 1952 and served there for six years before beginning a fifty-one-year career in the Senate in 1959. Much has been written about Senator Byrd, including the Senator's own autobiography in 2005, and there is little new information this book can add to the narrative. He is probably best known as being an "institution" in the Senate and for "know[ing] more about it than anyone living or dead," according to Bob Dole, the former senator from Kansas and Republican leader.[3] In fact, his legacy lives on through the "Byrd rule," which governs the budget reconciliation process and enables bills with spending or revenue impacts to be approved with only a simple majority in the Senate (rather than the sixty votes necessary to invoke cloture and end a filibuster).[4]

It is a curious development that the rule giving Senator Joe Manchin such influence in the 2021 Senate – as the most conservative Democrat in the 50–50 Senate his vote is indispensable to passage of any bill through the reconciliation process – was authored by the senator who held the very Senate seat that Joe Manchin now occupies. (When Byrd died in 2010, then Governor Manchin won a special election in November of that year to fill the position, which had been held by Carte Goodwin in the interim.) The Byrd rule came into being as an amendment

---

[1]   Adam Clymer, *Robert C. Byrd, a Pillar of the Senate, Dies at 92*, N.Y. TIMES (June 28, 2010), https:// www.nytimes.com/2010/06/29/us/politics/29byrd.html.

[2]   Ken Ward Jr., *Remembering Robert C. Byrd*, COAL TATTOO (June 28, 2010), http://blogs .wvgazettemail.com/coaltattoo/2010/06/28/remembering-sen-robert-c-byrd/.

[3]   Clymer, *supra* note 1.

[4]   *The Budget Reconciliation Process: The Senate's Byrd Rule*, CONGRESSIONAL REVIEW SERVICE (May 4, 2021), https://fas.org/sgp/crs/misc/RL30862.pdf.

offered by Senator Byrd to the Consolidated Omnibus Budget Reconciliation Act
(COBRA) of 1985 and was necessary, according to Senator Byrd, to "preserve the
deliberative process in the U.S. Senate" by excluding extraneous issues unrelated to
the budget process that should be debated using regular procedures.[5] The Byrd rule
was modified several times in subsequent years before being codified in 1990 under
the Congressional Budget Act of 1974.[6]

Senator Byrd's legacy in West Virginia owes primarily to his role as chairman of
the Senate Appropriations Committee from 1989 through 2009. At the time of his
appointment, Senator Byrd remarked: "I hope to become West Virginia's billion-
dollar industry. By the time this six-year term of mine is up, I will have added at least
a billion dollars. That's my goal for West Virginia."[7] In 1991, the Associated Press
examined the projects delivered by Senator Byrd to West Virginia and found that he
had already reached his goal, four years early. And Byrd was not the least bit
defensive about his ability to bring home the "pork" to West Virginia: "I lost no
opportunity to promote funding for programs and projects of benefit to the people
back home."[8] Notable projects in West Virginia attributable to Senator Byrd's
strategic role on the Appropriations Committee include the FBI Fingerprinting
Identification Center in Clarksburg, Internal Revenue Service offices in
Parkersburg, the Fish and Wildlife Training Center at Shepherdstown, a Bureau
of Alcohol, Tobacco and Firearms office in Martinsburg, a NASA research center in
Wheeling, the National White Collar Crime Center in Fairmont and Morgantown,
and the National Energy Technology Laboratory in Morgantown.[9] In addition,
there are dozens of projects throughout West Virginia bearing the Senator's name,
including the Robert C. Byrd Highway, two Robert C. Byrd federal buildings, the
Robert C. Byrd Freeway, the Robert C. Byrd Center for Hospitality and Tourism, the
Robert C. Byrd Drive, and the Robert C. Byrd Hardwood Technologies Center.[10]

Of more relevance to this book is Senator Byrd's record with respect to support of
the coal industry in West Virginia. He was an early and consistent supporter of coal
and mountaintop removal, as well as an opponent of measures to address climate
change. Among other things, he sponsored a 1997 Senate resolution (along with
Senator Chuck Hagel [Republican, Nebraska]) that essentially blocked US ratifica-
tion of the Kyoto Protocol to regulate GHG emissions (the resolution passed 95–0).
He was also highly critical of Judge Haden's 1999 ruling in *Bragg* v. *Robertson* to
limit mountaintop removal, a decision that was subsequently reversed by the Fourth
Circuit on constitutional grounds. Commenting on environmental protesters that
were showing up at his campaign events, Senator Byrd said: "These head-in-the-cloud

[5] *Id.*
[6] *Id.*
[7] Clymer, *supra* note 1.
[8] *Id.*
[9] Michael Barone, *Robert C. Byrd*, THE WEST VIRGINIA ENCYCLOPEDIA, https://www.wvencyclopedia.org
     /articles/756.
[10] Clymer, *supra* note 1.

individuals peddle dreams of an idyllic life among old-growth trees, but they seem ignorant of the fact that, without the mines, jobs will disappear, tables will go bare, schools will not have the revenue to teach our children, towns will not have the income to provide even basic services."[11] As Ken Ward of the *Charleston Gazette* observed, however, Senator Byrd's positions changed over time "as the urgency for action on climate change became more and more apparent, and as the science showing the harmful effects of mountaintop removal grew more clear."[12]

In mid-2009, Senator Byrd "sent his staff into the coalfields on a fact-finding mission," and issued his "findings" in a statement published that December admonishing the coal industry to "embrace the future." Among other things, it acknowledged some of the challenges facing the coal industry in West Virginia:

> The increased use of mountaintop removal mining means that fewer miners are needed to meet company production goals. Meanwhile the Central Appalachian coal seams that remain to be mined are becoming thinner and more costly to mine. Mountaintop removal mining, a declining national demand for energy, rising mining costs and erratic spot market prices all add up to fewer jobs in the coal fields. . . . The greatest threats to the future of coal do not come from possible constraints on mountaintop removal mining or other environmental regulations, but rather from rigid mindsets, depleting coal reserves, and the declining demand for coal as more power plants begin shifting to biomass and natural gas as a way to reduce emissions.[13]

Senator Byrd said, "the time has come to have an open and honest dialogue about coal's future in West Virginia" and that "the most important factor in maintaining coal-related jobs is demand for coal." He also took the opportunity to address climate change: "To be part of any solution, one must first acknowledge a problem. To deny the mounting science of climate change is to stick our heads in the sand and say 'deal me out.' West Virginia would be much smarter to stay at the table."[14] The statement concluded:

> Change has been a constant throughout the history of our coal industry. West Virginians can choose to anticipate change and adapt to it, or resist and be overrun by it. One thing is clear. The time has arrived for the people of the Mountain State to think long and hard about which course they want to choose.[15]

Politico observed that "Byrd's position represents a departure from his long record as a fierce defender of the coal interests and mountaintop removal."[16] It also noted that the

---

[11] Ken Ward, Jr., *Over the Years, Byrd Evolved on Coal Stance*, CHARLESTON GAZETTE-MAIL (June 28, 2010), https://www.wvgazettemail.com/news/special_reports/over-the-years-byrd-evolved-on-coal-stance/article_fcf59f9d-a0c3-5826-949d-f058e0f88c89.html.

[12] Ward Jr., *supra* note 2.

[13] Ken Ward Jr., *Sen. Byrd: "Coal Must Embrace the Future,"* COAL TATTOO (Dec. 3, 2009), http://blogs.wvgazettemail.com/coaltattoo/2009/12/03/sen-byrd-coal-must-embrace-the-future/.

[14] *Id.*

[15] *Id.*

[16] Alex Isenstadt, *Byrd's Coal Comments Rock W.Va.*, POLITICO (Dec. 18, 2009), https://www.politico.com/story/2009/12/byrds-coal-comments-rock-wva-030770.

situation was "clouded" by Byrd's advanced age, his limited public appearances, and his health issues – he had been in and out of the hospital several times during 2009.[17]

Seven months later, after twenty-nine miners lost their lives in the Upper Big Branch disaster, Senator Byrd issued another statement, titled "Our Greatest Resource," which, among other things, urged the coal industry to "respect the miner and his family" and scolded that "[a] single miner's life is certainly worth the expense and effort required to enhance safety."[18] On the broader issue of the impact of the coal industry in West Virginia, Senator Byrd stated:

> The industry of coal must also respect the land that yields the coal, as well as the people who live on the land. If the process of mining destroys nearby wells and foundations, if blasting and digging and relocating streams unearths harmful elements and releases them into the environment causing illness and death, that process should be halted and the resulting hazards to the community abated. The sovereignty of West Virginia must also be respected. The monolithic power of industry should never dominate our politics to the detriment of local communities. Our coal mining communities do not have to be marked by a lack of economic diversity and development that can potentially squelch the voice of the people. People living in coal communities deserve to have a free hand in managing their own local affairs and public policies without undue political pressure to submit to the desires of industry.
>
> The old chestnut that "coal is West Virginia's greatest natural resource" deserves revision. I believe that our people are West Virginia's most valuable resource. We must demand to be treated as such.[19]

One of Byrd's last Senate roll-call votes was against a resolution sponsored by Senator Lisa Murkowski (Republican, Alaska) that would have overturned EPA's endangerment finding that authorized the regulation of GHG emissions. In opposing the resolution, Senator Byrd stated:

> This in essence is like voting to assert that there is no climate change or global warming going on, and to dismiss scientific facts that already exist. As I have pointed out before, to deny the mounting science of climate change is to stick our heads in the sand and say "deal me out." West Virginia needs to stay at the table, as should all Senators who have concerns about our energy policy.[20]

Within a month, Senator Byrd would be dead.

---

[17]   *Id.*

[18]   *Byrd Pens Scorching Opinion Piece on Coal*, CHARLESTON GAZETTE-MAIL (May 5, 2010), https://www.wvgazettemail.com/news/byrd-pens-scorching-opinion-piece-on-coal/article_3a56582a-d3f4-5be7-8cb0-1be683e57584.html.

[19]   *Id.*

[20]   Ken Ward, Jr., *Sen. Byrd: A Vote for Murkowski Resolution Is a Vote "to Dismiss Scientific Facts" About Climate Change*, COAL TATTOO (June 10, 2010), http://blogs.wvgazettemail.com/coaltattoo/2010/06/10/sen-byrd-a-vote-for-murkowski-resolution-is-a-vote-to-dismiss-scientific-facts-about-climate-change/.

Commenting on Senator Byrd's life, Joe Lovett, a longtime opponent of mountaintop removal and the executive director and cofounder of an environmental public interest law firm, said: "To his credit, Senator Byrd evolved on many issues, and he was a person who thought about things for himself and made decisions about what he thought was best for the people of the country and our state, and he came to see things differently regarding the coal industry and its relationship to the state."[21]

SENATOR JAY ROCKEFELLER: "THE VOICE OF COMPASSIONATE GOVERNMENT"

Senator John Davison ("Jay") Rockefeller IV was the junior senator in West Virginia at the start of "the lost decade," having been elected to the US Senate in 1985 following two terms as governor of West Virginia. Upon the death of Senator Robert Byrd in June 2010 (with whom Rockefeller served in the Senate for twenty-five years), Rockefeller became the senior senator. Although he announced early in the election cycle for 2014 that he would not be seeking reelection for a sixth term (he made the announcement in January 2013), it was already apparent to most observers in June 2012, following his courageous speech about the coal industry in West Virginia on the floor of the US Senate, that reelection was not in his future. Since moving to Emmons, West Virginia in 1964 at the age of twenty-seven as a Volunteers for Service to America (VISTA) volunteer, the great-grandson of oil tycoon John D. Rockefeller and nephew of former Vice President Nelson Rockefeller had a tortured relationship with the coal industry.[22]

In his first run for governor in 1972 (following two years in the state House of Delegates and a term as Secretary of State, and after changing his party registration from Republican to Democrat in 1966), Rockefeller faced popular incumbent Republican Arch Moore. Rockefeller tried to cast himself as a reformer, and he opposed strip mining in the coal industry. He said at the time that "[w]e cannot have strip mining as an industry, and still hope to have my children, and more important, their children, have a place where they can happily live and work. And I think only an abolition of strip mining will make that possible."[23] In response, coal miners began showing up at Rockefeller's rallies and town hall meetings to heckle him, and the coal companies offered a cash bounty to anyone who pilfered his campaign signs.[24]

Moore's campaign, on the other hand, featured a "he's not one of us" theme that included television spots involving man-on-the-street interviews in which

[21] Ward Jr., *supra* note 11.
[22] Robin Toner, *Rockefeller's Assets*, N.Y. TIMES MAGAZINE (July 21, 1991), https://www.nytimes.com/1991/07/21/magazine/rockefeller-s-assets.html.
[23] *Jay: A Rockefeller's Journey*, WEST VIRGINIA PUBLIC BROADCASTING (June 21, 2015), https://www.pbs.org/video/jay-rockefellers-journey-jay-rockefellers-journey/.
[24] Jean Chemnick, *Jay Rockefeller – The Evolution of a Coal-State Senator*, N.Y. TIMES (Jan. 18, 2011), https://archive.nytimes.com/www.nytimes.com/gwire/2011/01/18/18greenwire-jay-rockefeller-the-evolution-of-a-coal-state-s-4772.html?pagewanted=all.

New Yorkers were asked how they would feel about a West Virginian as their governor; the response, according to one ad, was: "That makes as much sense to me as having the next Governor of West Virginia be a New Yorker."[25] In a state that then held a 2 to 1 Democratic majority, Rockefeller lost by 73,000 votes, a roughly 55–45 percent margin of victory for Moore, even though Rockefeller had outspent Moore by more than 2 to 1 ($1.5 million compared to Moore's $696,000). At the national level, the Democratic nominee for president, George McGovern, suffered a massive defeat to Richard Nixon, and lost West Virginia by a 64–36 percent margin; this was, no doubt, a drag on the Rockefeller campaign as well. Rockefeller believed his stand on strip mining influenced his poor showing in the coal counties in the southern part of the state, and contributed to the only loss of his forty-five-year political career.

In the interim, until the next statewide election, Rockefeller served as president of West Virginia Wesleyan College, a small, conservative, Methodist institution located in Buckhannon; he was the first president of the college to be neither an ordained minister, a Methodist, nor an educator with a Ph.D. While at Wesleyan, he spurred the construction of a multipurpose recreational center – and personally contributed $250,000 toward its cost – that still bears his name today. He resigned from Wesleyan in May 1975 in order to take another shot at being governor of West Virginia.

In his 1976 campaign, Rockefeller reversed his opposition to strip mining, citing better reclamation practices encouraged by the environmental community. He stated during the campaign: "I think there has been a change in the way the coal industry itself has reacted to some of the pressure that has been brought upon them by environmentalists."[26] Rockefeller also saw a prominent role for coal as a tool for addressing what was beginning to emerge as a national energy shortage, and he said that "the long-term future of coal is a strong one."[27] The state Supreme Court had ruled that Moore could not run for a third consecutive term, and former Governor Cecil Underwood became the Republican nominee. Rockefeller also began a practice of largely self-financing his campaign, spending $1.1 million of his own money to win the Democratic primary (out of the $1.7 million total raised by his campaign) and $2 million out of $2.7 million raised in the general election. He defeated Underwood by 240,000 votes, a 66–34 percent margin – the largest majority in state history at that time.

During his first term as governor, Rockefeller had to deal with heavy snowfalls across the state, acute fuel shortages, rampaging floods in four southern coal counties, and a 111-day coal strike. The first term also saw a construction accident at the Pleasants Power Station in April 1978, in which fifty-one workers died; Rockefeller described it as the worst nonmining industrial accident in the state's

[25] Toner, *supra* note 22.
[26] Jay: A Rockefeller's Journey, *supra* note 23.
[27] Id.

history.[28] Later in 1978, Rockefeller began to receive national attention when he was appointed by President Jimmy Carter to be chairman of the President's Commission on Coal. In this role, he insisted that coal – particularly Appalachian coal – should be given a higher standing in the national energy policy and he worked to expand coal markets in the United States and abroad.

The gubernatorial race of 1980 featured a rematch with Arch Moore. This time Rockefeller prevailed, defeating Moore by about 64,500 votes after outspending Moore by about 12 to 1 – $11.6 million ("enough to buy every man, woman and child in West Virginia a $6 dinner")[29] compared to just under $1 million for the Moore campaign. A popular bumper sticker for Moore declared, "Make Him Spend It All, Arch." During Rockefeller's second term as governor, the state plunged into a deep recession – unemployment increased to 21 percent in West Virginia, the highest in the nation – and coal mining jobs continued to decline. The collapsing state economy left no money in the state budget to pursue any new initiatives and instead Rockefeller was forced to preside over the shrinking of state programs. At the end of his eight years as governor, Rockefeller's approval rating was only 19 percent.

That did not stop him, however, from being elected to the US Senate in 1984, succeeding Jennings Randolph, who had represented West Virginia for just over twenty-six years. Rockefeller defeated Morgantown businessman John Raese – the same John Raese who nearly thirty years later ran against Joe Manchin twice, in 2010 and 2012 – by about 4 percentage points, 52 to 48. The Rockefeller campaign outspent Raese's by about 11 to 1 ($12 million to $1.1 million), with $10.2 million coming from Rockefeller's personal fortune. (As it turned out, Raese financed his own campaign too, to the tune of $441,000.)

According to a profile in the *New York Times Magazine* in 1991, Rockefeller spent his first term in the Senate "in careful, penitential devotion to West Virginia concerns, with almost no profile in national politics."[30] During his thirty years in the US Senate, Rockefeller chaired a number of committees, including Veterans Affairs, the Select Committee on Intelligence, and the Committee on Commerce, Science and Transportation. He achieved national prominence by chairing two blue-ribbon commissions, one on health care, and one on children. In 1990, the United States Bipartisan Commission on Comprehensive Health Care – often known as the Pepper Commission – produced a plan that would have provided universal health insurance and extensive new long-term nursing care benefits. In a report issued in June 1991, the National Commission on Children called for major new initiatives to combat poverty among the young, including a $1,000 income tax credit for each child in America.

---

[28] Iver Peterson, *51 Killed in Collapse of Scaffold at Power Plant in West Virginia*, N.Y. TIMES (Apr. 28, 1978), https://www.nytimes.com/1978/04/28/archives/51-killed-in-collapse-of-scaffold-at-power-plant-in-west-virginia.html.

[29] Toner, *supra* note 22.

[30] Id.

Rockefeller was most closely recognized as chair of the Finance Committee's subcommittee on health care, as a champion of health care coverage for all. He authored the Children's Health Insurance Program (CHIP) which, by 2015, provided health care to eight million children in low-income families.[31] Rockefeller would later say that his motivation to achieve universal health care coverage was largely driven by his experience of living in Emmons, West Virginia in 1964 and 1965.[32]

Rockefeller seriously considered running for President in 1991. On the heels of the US military victory in Operation Desert Storm, President George H. W. Bush was riding high in the polls, and the Democratic field was fairly wide open. As he campaigned for several months in some of the early voting states, Rockefeller often told this joke about himself: "The good news is I have 100 percent name identification in Iowa. The bad news is one-third of the people think I'm the banker who foreclosed on their farm, one-third think I run the oil company that raised the price of gasoline and one-third think I'm the guy who sold Manhattan to the Japanese."[33] The *New York Times Magazine* described Rockefeller on the campaign trail as having "the air of a patrician camp counselor or social worker, peering down, empathetically, from his 6-foot-6 1/2-inch height, trying to do good."[34] He ultimately decided against a run for president, saying, "I don't think my finest quality is being a CEO, I'm an advocate. I fight for things."[35]

In 1992, Rockefeller turned his attention to developing a strategy to save the United Mine Workers' (UMWA) union health and retirement funds, which were headed toward insolvency. His involvement led to enactment of the Coal Industry Retiree Health Benefit Act of 1992, commonly referred to as the Coal Act or the Rockefeller Coal Act.[36] For Rockefeller, it was a significant step toward shifting the Rockefeller legacy in the coal industry away from an event that occurred in Colorado in 1914, commonly referred to as the Ludlow Massacre. In response to a miner strike that was underway at a coal mine operated by the Rockefeller family, mine managers brought in Colorado national guardsmen. Shortly thereafter a fire broke out followed by a gun battle that resulted in twenty-four deaths, including eleven women and two children. According to Senator Rockefeller, it was a life-changing event – an "Epiphany" – for his grandfather, John D. Rockefeller Jr., who was responsible at the time for all Rockefeller family businesses. As Senator Rockefeller describes it, his grandfather was "rooted out" of his comfort zone by the event, and entered a life of public service. John D. Rockefeller Jr. thereafter expanded his philanthropic endeavors, focusing on the conservation of natural

---

[31]   *Jay: A Rockefeller's Journey, supra* note 23.
[32]   *Id.*
[33]   Toner, *supra* note 22.
[34]   *Id.*
[35]   *Jay: A Rockefeller's Journey, supra* note 23.
[36]   *Id.*

landscapes and the preservation of historic landmarks, and ultimately gave away over a half a billion dollars. Nearly seventy years later, Senator Rockefeller's work on the Coal Act was seen as a further measure of atonement for what was referred to as the "worst black mark on the Rockefeller family."[37] In 1995, the UMWA named him an honorary member, a distinction rarely bestowed on an elected official, because of his efforts on behalf of miners.[38]

Over a decade later, Rockefeller also authored the Mine Improvement and New Emergency Response (MINER) Act of 2006, which amended the Federal Mine Safety and Health Act of 1977 to provide greater protections for underground coal miners and improve emergency preparedness. It has been described as the most significant mine safety legislation in a generation. And, in his final year in office, he was instrumental in the adoption of a rule by the Mine Safety and Health Administration (MSHA) that reduced by one-half the concentration limits for respirable coal mine dust, to reduce the incidence of black lung disease. In 2014, he also worked with Senator Bob Casey (Democrat, Pennsylvania) to introduce legislation to ensure that miners receive fairer treatment when pursuing benefits claims, following an investigation by the Center for Public Integrity and *ABC News* that examined how doctors and lawyers, working at the behest of the coal industry, helped defeat the benefits claims of sick miners.[39]

In contrast to his consistent track record protecting the interests of coal miners, Rockefeller's record on environmental stewardship and his stance on EPA regulations affecting the coal industry was quite mixed. On climate change, Rockefeller was on the record for years believing that climate change is happening and that human activity is contributing to it. Consistent with that view, he voted for a cap-and-trade bill in 2003 sponsored by Senators John McCain (Republican, Arizona) and Joe Lieberman (Democrat, Connecticut); the bill received only forty-three votes and was defeated.[40] Six years later, however, when another piece of cap-and-trade legislation – the American Clean Energy Security Act, or Waxman-Markey – passed the US House of Representatives in 2009, Rockefeller, then chairman of the Senate Commerce, Science, and Transportation Committee, was one of six chairmen with partial jurisdiction over the Senate version of the bill, sponsored by John Kerry (Democrat, Pennsylvania), Lieberman, and Lindsey Graham (Republican, South Carolina). Although Rockefeller met with Senate negotiators six times in early 2010, he hung back and never committed to support the process, and his committee never held markups of the bill. One national environmentalist contrasted the role of Rockefeller – or the lack thereof – with the effectiveness of another coal-state

[37] *Id.*
[38] *About Senator John Davison (Jay) Rockefeller IV*, West Virginia and Regional History Center, West Virginia University, https://rockefeller.lib.wvu.edu/about.
[39] Frederic J. Frommer, *New Legislation Introduced for Black Lung Victims*, Claims Journal (Sept. 19, 2014), https://www.claimsjournal.com/news/national/2014/09/19/254981.htm.
[40] The Climate Stewardship Act of 2003, S. 139, H.R. 4067, was defeated in the U.S. Senate by a vote of 55 to 43.

Democrat, former Representative Rick Boucher of Virginia, who used his senior position on the House Energy and Commerce Committee to negotiate concessions for coal-fired electric utilities on allowance allocation and other issues, actions that allowed the bill to clear the committee and narrowly pass the House.[41]

In the absence of comprehensive energy and climate legislation, attention turned to the EPA's existing authority to regulate carbon emissions under the Clean Air Act, on the heels of its Endangerment Finding in December 2009. What was Rockefeller's response? On March 10, 2010, he introduced the "Stationary Source Regulations Delay Act," which would have put a two-year stay on the EPA's ability to take action under the Clean Air Act to impose permitting requirements for nonvehicle sources of carbon emissions (in other words, coal-fired power plants).[42] According to Rockefeller, the temporary moratorium on permitting requirements for power plants would give the coal industry time to make changes and give both industry and environmentalists a reason to compromise. The bill, described by one observer as "simply a subterfuge to allow skittish Democrats an opportunity to oppose the EPA without really opposing the EPA,"[43] was never passed by the Senate.

Rockefeller had another chance to oppose the EPA in early 2011, when it vetoed a permit that had been issued earlier by the Army Corps of Engineers for the Spruce No. 1 surface mine in Logan County, the largest single mountaintop removal permit in West Virginia's history. In response, Rockefeller issued a statement saying he was "deeply angered by the EPA's decision to revoke the Spruce Mine permit," and vowed to "continue to do everything in my power to stand up for our West Virginia miners and their jobs."[44]

The occasion for Senator Rockefeller's "last stand" against the coal industry, in June 2012, was a floor debate on a resolution of disapproval proposed by Senator James Inhofe (Republican, Oklahoma) that would have blocked the EPA's implementation of its proposed Mercury and Air Toxics Standards (MATS) rule. (As discussed in Chapter 1, this rule had significant consequences for the coal industry, and ultimately resulted in the closure of several coal-fired power plants in West Virginia.) In contrast to Senator Manchin's speech, in which Manchin reiterated his determination "to stop the EPA's job-killing agenda" by supporting the resolution as an "important step to rein in this out-of-control agency,"[45] Senator Rockefeller called Inhofe's proposal a "foolish" move that "wastes time and money that could have been invested in the future of coal."[46]

---

[41] Chemnick, *supra* note 24.

[42] S. 3072, introduced Mar. 4, 2010.

[43] Wayne T. Brough, *Rockefeller Is Wrong: Delay Is Denial*, THE HILL (Mar. 25, 2011), https://thehill.com /blogs/congress-blog/energy-a-environment/151887-rockefeller-is-wrong-delay-is-denial.

[44] Ken Ward, *Breaking News: EPA Vetoes Spruce Mine Permit*, COAL TATTOO (Jan. 13, 2011), http://blogs .wvgazettemail.com/coaltattoo/2011/01/13/breaking-news-epa-vetoes-spruce-mine-permit/.

[45] 158 CONG. REC. 94, S4,322 (June 12, 2012).

[46] *Id.* at S4,317.

He blasted "those who run the coal industry," saying they were denying "the inevitability of change in the energy industry" and "abrogating their responsibilities to lead," which would result in unfairly "leav[ing] coal miners in the dust."[47] Rockefeller claimed that the need for change "has been staring them in the face for decades" – "[t]hey have known about it," and "[t]hey have ignored it."[48]

Rockefeller identified three challenges facing the coal industry: (1) declining and increasingly expensive coal reserves in the Central Appalachian Basin given that the "cheap, easy coal seams are diminishing rapidly"; (2) the rise of natural gas, and the actions by electric utilities to switch to a fuel that is cheaper, cleaner, more efficient, and more plentiful; and (3) the inevitable shift to the reduction of carbon emissions. On this point, Senator Rockefeller stated:

> [T]he shift to a lower carbon economy is not going away. It is a disservice – a terrible disservice – to coal miners and their families to pretend it is, to tell them everything can be as it was. It can't be. That is over. Coal companies deny that we need to do anything to address climate change, despite the established scientific consensus and mounting national desire – including in West Virginia – for a cleaner, healthier environment.[49]

Rockefeller also made it clear that it was unfair to blame the EPA for the coal plants in West Virginia that would close because of the MATS rule, noting that the plants were no longer economical for electric utilities compared with low-emission natural gas plants. According to Rockefeller, "[e]very single coal plant slated for closure in West Virginia was already on the chopping block from their own corporate board's decision." While coal executives "pine for the past," the natural gas industry has instead "look[ed] to the future, investing in technology to reduce their environmental footprint." The Inhofe resolution, he said, "does nothing to look to the future of coal," but instead "moves us backward." Coal miners will be "the big losers," he added, "[u]nless this industry aggressively leans into the future."[50]

The resolution failed 53–46. Following the vote, Senate Environment and Public Works Chairwoman Barbara Boxer (Democrat, California), hailed Rockefeller's speech, saying: "I believe when the next historian writes a book about leadership, courage and integrity in the United States Senate, that this speech today will be featured in that book."[51] Six months later, Rockefeller announced he would not be seeking reelection.

---

[47] *Id.* at S4,316.
[48] *Id.*
[49] *Id.*
[50] *Id.* at S4,317.
[51] Manu Raju, *Rockefeller Bucks Coal State Allies*, POLITICO (June 20, 2012), https://www.politico.com /story/2012/06/rockefeller-bucks-coal-state-allies-on-inhofe-vote-077639.

SHELLEY MOORE CAPITO: THE MOORE DYNASTY CONTINUES

Shelley Moore Capito is the middle of three children born to Arch Moore, the former governor of West Virginia, and his wife Sadie Shelley Moore, known as Shelley. Much like her colleague in the US Senate, Joe Manchin, Capito is from a family with a long history in West Virginia politics. Her great grandfather was mayor of Moundsville – in the northern panhandle, where her father Arch was born – and a great uncle was minority leader in the state House of Delegates.[52] She grew up as the daughter of one of the most popular, colorful, and occasionally controversial politicians in West Virginia's history.

By the time Shelley Moore Capito was born in Glen Dale in 1953 (in the northern panhandle), her father was already serving his first term in the West Virginia House of Delegates. He would later serve six terms in the US House of Representatives from the first district (from 1957 to 1969), which was quite an accomplishment as a Republican in what was an overwhelmingly democratic state at the time. While her father was serving in Congress, Capito attended the Holton-Arms School, a private college-preparatory school in Bethesda, Maryland. She later graduated from Duke University and received a master's degree from the University of Virginia. A little-known fact about Capito is that she represented West Virginia as the 1972 Cherry Blossom Princess, joining her Senate colleague Lisa Murkowski (Republican, Alaska) as Cherry Blossom Princess alumnae.[53]

Moore was elected governor of West Virginia in 1968, and served two terms, easily winning reelection in 1972 by defeating Democratic nominee Jay Rockefeller, who was then Secretary of State. When the West Virginia Supreme Court of Appeals ruled that Moore was prohibited by the state constitution from running for a third term in 1976, he set his sights on the US Senate, where he waged an unsuccessful campaign in 1978 to unseat Democrat William Jennings Randolph, losing narrowly by fewer than 5,000 votes. He ran again for governor in 1980 in a rematch of the 1972 race against Jay Rockefeller, and this time lost by about 65,000 votes thanks in large part to Rockefeller outspending him by a 12 to 1 margin. Four years later, while Rockefeller was pursuing his successful bid for the US Senate, Moore was elected to an unprecedented third term as governor, when he comfortably defeated House Speaker Clyde See. He was unsuccessful in his bid for a fourth term in 1988; after narrowly defeating John Raese in the Republican primary, Moore was defeated in the general election by millionaire businessman Gaston Caperton in the worst campaign defeat of his political career, a 59–41 percent margin of victory for Caperton.

Moore has been described by historian John Morgan as a "strong and spectacular governor,"[54] while the *Washington Post* referred to him as a "charismatic

---

[52] *News and Noted*, DOORWAYS: HOLTON-ARMS SCHOOL MAGAZINE, Summer 2018, at 5.

[53] Kris Kitto, *Queens of the Cherry Blossoms*, THE HILL (Mar. 18, 2008), https://thehill.com/capital-living/24023-queens-of-the-cherry-blossoms.

[54] Phil Kabler, *3-Term West Virginia Gov. Arch Moore Dies*, CHARLESTON GAZETTE-MAIL (Jan. 7, 2015), https://www.wvgazettemail.com/news/politics/3-term-west-virginia-gov-arch-moore-dies/article_9e7d7d69-8d83-5cbc-8e50-75138fd73a18.html.

populist."[55] The *Gazette-Mail* cited Moore's "dynamic personality, including a near-photographic memory that assured he never forgot a name or face on the campaign trail, his unique oratory and a strong ego."[56] The controversial part of Moore's political career involved frequent allegations of corruption, beginning with allegations of federal tax evasion in 1969, and a 1975 indictment against him and the manager of his 1972 gubernatorial campaign – both of whom were acquitted – for allegedly extorting money from a savings and loan company. In 1990, twelve years after he left the governor's office, Moore signed a plea agreement in which he admitted wrongdoing during his 1984 campaign, during his third term as governor from 1985 to 1989, and during his 1988 reelection campaign. He also admitted efforts to thwart the grand jury's investigation by falsifying documents and trying to persuade witnesses to lie.[57] Moore later tried to rescind his guilty pleas; he ended up serving about three years of his prison sentence of five years and ten months, and was released in 1993. He died in Charleston in January 2015 at the age of ninety-one, one day after his daughter Shelley Moore Capito was sworn in as the first female US senator in West Virginia's history.

It seems altogether fitting that Moore would still be alive when his daughter ascended to the US Senate, particularly as she took the seat formerly held by Jay Rockefeller. Apart from the contentious and somewhat ugly gubernatorial campaigns between Moore and Rockefeller in both 1972 and 1980, Rockefeller was involved behind the scenes in thwarting Moore's 1984 Senate campaign to unseat William Jennings Randolph. It was common knowledge that Rockefeller was supportive of Randolph and his campaign, which would keep the seat in Democratic hands and make it easier for Rockefeller to succeed Randolph upon his presumed retirement six years later. An article in *Politico* embraced the rumor that Rockefeller went so far as to bankroll Randolph's campaign in 1978; in the *Charleston Gazette-Mail's* investigation of the rumor, however, it found "no evidence of that connection in campaign records on file at the archives."[58] Brad Crouser, a Charleston attorney who wrote *Arch*, a biography about the former governor, also expressed doubts about the veracity of the rumor.[59]

Capito's ascension to the US Senate in 2014 was the next logical step in what has been a remarkable political career. She first held elective office as a member of the West Virginia House of Delegates from Kanawha County from 1997 to 2001. When

---

[55] Adam Bernstein, *Arch Moore Jr., Charismatic W.Va. Governor Convicted of Corruption, Dies at 91*, WASHINGTON POST (Jan. 8, 2015), https://www.washingtonpost.com/politics/arch-moore-jr-charismatic-wva-governor-convicted-of-corruption-dies-at-91/2015/01/08/e5857798-974d-11e4-927a-4fa2638cd1b0_story.html.

[56] Kabler, *supra* note 54.

[57] *Ex-West Virginia Governor Admits Corruption Schemes*, N.Y. TIMES (Apr. 13, 1990), https://www.nytimes.com/1990/04/13/us/ex-west-virginia-governor-admits-corruption-schemes.html.

[58] Ashley B. Craig, *Heavy Hitters Faced Off in 1978 Senate Election*, CHARLESTON GAZETTE-MAIL (Nov. 3, 2014), https://www.wvgazettemail.com/news/politics/heavy-hitters-faced-off-in-1978-senate-election/article_c43be616-2112-5d03-8a71-56a5c926e974.html.

[59] *Id.*

Capito was elected to the first of seven terms in Congress in 2000, she had the distinction of being the first woman elected to Congress from West Virginia who was not the widow of a member of Congress. She was also the first Republican to represent West Virginia in Congress since 1983.

Capito announced her run for Rockefeller's Senate seat very early in the 2014 election cycle, within weeks of being reelected to her seventh term in Congress in 2012. It was only six months earlier, in June 2012, that Rockefeller had delivered his infamous "last stand" against the coal industry speech from the floor of the US Senate. At the time of her announcement, there was speculation that Rockefeller would not seek reelection, fueled largely by his taking an increasingly hard line on the coal industry. Capito had clearly distinguished her position from Rockefeller's with respect to support for the coal industry in an op-ed piece titled "100% Support for Coal," published in the *Charleston Gazette-Mail* about three months after Rockefeller's speech: "As a West Virginian, I am proud to stand up for the thousands of workers who help power America with home grown natural resources, and I won't stop until the president halts his War on Coal."[60] Six weeks after Capito's announcement, in mid-January 2013, Rockefeller would make it official, announcing that he would not be seeking reelection.[61]

When Capito was elected to the US Senate in November 2014, it was the first time a Republican had been elected to a statewide office in West Virginia since the 1980s. Her trajectory in West Virginia politics largely paralleled the state's rather rapid transition from a blue state to a red state, and she effectively tapped into the pro-coal, anti-EPA sentiment as well. As noted in *Politico*, the "war on coal" was a mantra for nearly all the candidates in the 2012 election cycle in West Virginia – "with the battle turning into a contest on who could hate EPA more." Capito easily won that contest in the Second District in 2012 when she won with nearly 70 percent of the vote. During her fourteen years in Congress, Capito cofounded the Congressional Coal Caucus. She was also the lead sponsor of 198 bills and amendments, "including bills to expand rural access to hospice care, make it easier for Medicaid to cover infant healthcare, establish an independent mine-safety board, delay regulations of the Dodd–Frank financial reform bill that applied to credit- and debit-card interchange fees, and to block energy and environmental regulations."[62]

Capito's US Senate campaign in 2014 continued the EPA bashing that had worked so well in 2012; her website claimed that "[Capito] is leading the effort to stop the Environmental Protection Agency's use of regulatory injunction and bureaucratic over-reach against the coal and natural gas industry," and went on to

[60] Shelley Moore Capito, *100% Support for Coal*, CHARLESTON GAZETTE-MAIL (Sept. 27, 2012), https://infoweb.newsbank.com/apps/news/document-view?p=NewsBank&t=pubname%3ACIZB%21Charleston%2BGazette%2B%2528WV%2529&sort=YMD_date.

[61] John Bresnahan, *Jay Rockefeller to Retire*, POLITICO (Jan. 11, 2013), https://www.politico.com/story/2013/01/jay-rockefeller-to-retire-086054.

[62] Chris Good, *Shelley Moore Capito: Everything You Need to Know*, ABC NEWS (July 19, 2016), https://abcnews.go.com/Politics/shelley-moore-capito/story?id=40278708.

denounce "an overbearing EPA that is set on crushing West Virginia's energy production."[63] She easily won the Senate race in 2014, defeating Secretary of State Natalie Tennant by a 62–34 percent margin. Early in her Senate career, she was known as a moderate Republican; Capito was a member of the centrist Republican Main Street Partnership, along with fellow Republican Senators Susan Collins (Maine), Mark Kirk (Illinois), and the late John McCain (Arizona).[64] She joined Democrat Heidi Heitkamp of North Dakota to sponsor a pro-coal measure under the Congressional Review Act that registered the Senate's disapproval of the Clean Power Plan's regulation of existing coal plants;[65] the resolution was vetoed by President Obama on December 1, 2015.[66] In early 2016, she cosponsored a bill with Senator Kirsten Gillibrand (Democrat, New York) to address opioid addiction, the Preventing Overprescribing for Pain Act, and coauthored an op-ed piece in the *Charleston Gazette-Mail* with Gillibrand to support the measure.[67]

Although her early support of Trump was lukewarm (once Trump had emerged during the 2016 presidential campaign as the likely Republican nominee, Capito was one of a few senators to meet with him on Capitol Hill in May 2016, where she expressed concern about the tone of his campaign),[68] her enthusiasm climbed after Trump's EPA started rolling back Obama's regulation of coal plants. In an August 2018 op-ed in *The Intelligencer/Wheeling News-Register*, Capito praised the Trump administration's Affordable Clean Energy Rule, stating, "[f]ortunately, under the leadership of President Trump, the EPA is ending the war on coal that was so devastating to our state."[69]

Capito handily won reelection in 2020 with 70 percent of the vote, defeating environmental activist Paula Jean Swearingen, who had previously run unsuccessfully for the US Senate (losing to Joe Manchin in the 2018 Democratic primary). As the ranking member on the Senate Environment and Public Works Committee, Capito emerged, along with Senator Joe Manchin, during the early months of the Biden administration, to give West Virginia far greater influence in shaping federal

[63] Erica Martinson, *Capito May Keep Coal in Conversation*, POLITICO (Nov. 27, 2012), https://www.politico.com/story/2012/11/capitos-senate-bid-keeps-coal-in-conversation-084244.
[64] Good, *supra* note 62.
[65] Press Release, Senator Shelley Moore Capito, Capito and Heitkamp to Introduce Resolution to Overturn Clean Power Plan Rules for Existing Power Sources (Oct. 23, 2015), https://www.capito.senate.gov/news/press-releases/capito-and-heitkamp-to-introduce-resolution-to-overturn-clean-power-plan-rules-for-existing-power-sources.
[66] Good, *supra* note 62.
[67] Sens. Shelley Moore Capito & Kirsten Gillibrand, *We Must Fight Back Against Opioid Addiction*, CHARLESTON GAZETTE-MAIL (March 24, 2016), https://www.wvgazettemail.com/opinion/sens-shelley-moore-capito-and-kirsten-gillibrand-we-must-fight-back-against-opioid-addiction/article_f7524f86-7072-5fd3-9c67-9df17532c395.html.
[68] Good, *supra* note 62; Bridget Bowman, *What This Woman Senator Plans to Tell Trump*, ROLL CALL (May 12, 2016), https://www.rollcall.com/2016/05/12/what-this-woman-senator-plans-to-tell-trump/.
[69] Shelley Moore Capito, *New Plan Levels Playing Field for W.Va. Coal*, THE INTELLIGENCER/WHEELING NEWS REGISTER (Aug. 16, 2018), https://www.theintelligencer.net/opinion/local-columns/2018/08/new-plan-levels-playing-field-for-w-va-coal/.

legislation and national energy policies than could be expected for a state with only 1.7 million people and five (soon to be four) electoral votes. The Moore/Capito dynasty lives on.

CONGRESSMAN DAVID MCKINLEY: TRYING TO FIND A MIDDLE GROUND ON COAL AND CLIMATE

Another West Virginia Congressman beginning to make a mark on energy issues is David McKinley (Republican, Wheeling). McKinley served in Congress throughout "the lost decade"; he was first elected to Congress in 2010 by narrowly beating State Senator Mike Oliverio, who had defeated longtime Democratic Congressman Alan Mollohan in the primary. McKinley rode the anti-Obama, "war on coal" theme pretty hard in winning in 2010. During the campaign, he stated "If you like me, you get pro-coal, pro-business. If you like my opponent, you get [House Speaker] Nancy Pelosi [Democrat, California] and her job-killing legislation. It's pretty clear."[70] McKinley previously served in the West Virginia House of Delegates, and was state Republican Party chair in the early 1990s. He unsuccessfully ran for governor in 1996, coming in third in a three-way Republican primary won by Cecil Underwood, who would go on to win the general election.

It's fair to say that McKinley's position has been pretty consistent on challenging climate science and, in particular, denying the impact of human activity on climate change. In a piece he wrote for the *Washington Times* in July 2013, he cited a column from a 1975 issue of *Newsweek* about a "cooling world" which predicted a coming global ice age. He noted that while those predictions were later "proven to be bogus because they were based on flawed scientific climate models ... climate alarmism is still alive and well. This time the doomsayers are predicting increasing temperatures and manmade global warming." According to McKinley's column: "President Obama's climate change plan depends on unreliable theories, much like those that previously forecast a cooling period. There are tens of thousands of scientists who disagree with the so-called consensus on manmade global warming."[71]Two months later, in September 2013, he picked up the same theme in challenging Secretary of Energy Ernest Moniz and EPA Administrator Gina McCarthy at a hearing on climate policy convened by the House of Representatives Subcommittee on Energy and Power. According to McKinley's remarks, "[o]ver 40 years, there's been almost no increase in

[70] Nick Sobczyk, *How a Pro-Coal Republican Became a Climate Deal-Maker*, E&E News (May 11, 2021), https://www.eenews.net/eedaily/2021/05/11/stories/1063732197?utm_campaign=edition&utm_mediu m=email&utm_source=eenews%3Aeedaily.

[71] David McKinley, *Basing Crucial Economic and Energy-Related Decisions on Flawed Scientific Climate Models, in Energy: The Road Ahead*, Special Report, Washington Times (July 24, 2013), at 10, http://media.washtimes.com/media/misc/2013/07/23/0724_energylo.pdf.

temperatures, very slight."[72] His statements drew an immediate response from Representative Henry Waxman, the ranking Democrat on the committee, who referred to McKinley's statements as "incredibly inaccurate and contrary to what everybody in the scientific community has said to us." Energy Secretary Ernest Moniz also criticized McKinley's remarks: "This decade is the warmest decade in recorded history. The issues in terms of risk of climate change are not based upon models ... the anthropogenic changes from CO_2 are clearly of a scale that has long been expected."[73]

The following year, McKinley sponsored an amendment approved by a Republican-controlled Congress that prohibited the Pentagon from using any of its budget to address climate change and specifically instructed the Department of Defense to ignore the latest scientific reports on the threats posed by global warming.[74] In a letter to the House before the amendment passed, Democratic Representatives Henry Waxman and Bobby Rush wrote that the "McKinley amendment" is "science denial at its worst and it fails our moral obligation to our children and grandchildren."[75] In 2016, McKinley clarified that he does not deny that climate change is occurring: "Look, I'll be the first person to tell you I believe in climate change. As an engineer, that would be absurd for me to say it's not occurring, when 150 years ago the oceans were 8 inches lower and the temperature was 1.4 degrees cooler. I understand that." His point is that the change in climate is not due to human activity; he claimed that "only 4% of the CO_2 emissions are anthropogenic."[76]

Regardless of his position on climate science, McKinley has been a consistent supporter of energy efficiency. In May 2013, for example, he introduced the Better Buildings Act of 2014, which would have amended federal law aimed at improving the energy efficiency of commercial office buildings by creating a program called "Tenant Star" similar to the existing Energy Star program.[77] In promoting the bill, McKinley said that "finding ways to use energy efficiently is common sense. We ought to be promoting efficiency as a way to save energy, money and create jobs."[78] He has also prominently worked with Representative Peter Welch (Democrat, Vermont) on energy efficiency legislation.[79]

---

[72] David Gutman, *Climate Change Comments Draw Ire for W.Va.'s McKinley*, CHARLESTON GAZETTE-MAIL (Sept. 13, 2013), https://www.wvgazettemail.com/news/politics/climate-change-comments-draw-ire-for-w-va-s-mckinley/article_13bc6ec3-b1b4-53b6-8de7-5ca75e675db6.html.

[73] *Id.*

[74] J.C. Sevcik, *House Bans Pentagon from Preparing for Climate Change*, UPI (May 23, 2014), https://www.upi.com/Top_News/US/2014/05/23/House-bans-Pentagon-from-preparing-for-climate-change/5391400882186/.

[75] *Id.*

[76] Geof Koss, *Senator Has Handy Response for Science Skeptics*, E&E DAILY (Apr. 22, 2016), https://www.eenews.net/stories/1060036074.

[77] HR 2126, https://www.cbo.gov/publication/45127.

[78] *House Committee Approves "Better Buildings Act,"* AMERICAN CHEMISTRY COUNCIL (January 30, 2014), https://blog.americanchemistry.com/2014/01/house-committee-approves-better-buildings-act.

[79] Sobczyk, *supra* note 70.

McKinley drew national attention as "a pro-coal Republican [who] became a climate deal-maker" when, at the end of the 2020 Congressional session, he and Kurt Schrader (Democrat, Oregon) introduced the Clean Energy Future through Innovation Act of 2020. According to McKinley, the act is designed "to keep coal and natural gas in the mix and try to clean it as much as we can."[80] The bill would inject millions of dollars into research on carbon capture and clean energy tax credits. Then, after ten years of research, it would implement a clean electricity standard that targets an 80 percent reduction in power-sector emissions by 2050. Upon implementation of the clean energy standard, the EPA would lose its authority to regulate GHG emissions. According to the Columbia Center on Global Energy Policy, the bill's "combination of innovation and standards reflects some of the two parties' priorities in Congress and represents a potential bipartisan compromise to move forward on climate change."[81]

Following the retirement of Illinois Representative John Shimkus, McKinley took over the top Republican spot on the Energy and Commerce Subcommittee on Environment and Climate Change. According to one energy industry observer, McKinley "could be a key energy and environmental deal-maker for Republicans in the tumultuous political years to come."[82] He has a reputation for working across the aisle; Georgetown University's Lugar Center ranked him the tenth most bipartisan member of the 116th Congress.[83] Notably, McKinley was one of only thirteen Republicans in Congress to support the $1.2 trillion bipartisan infrastructure bill that passed the House in November 2021,[84] and joined thirty-four other Republicans (along with all the House Democrats) to vote to create a commission to investigate the January 6, 2021 attack on the Capitol by supporters of President Trump.[85] (The legislation failed in the Senate, and the House proceeded with a bipartisan committee to investigate the incident.)

Since his narrow win over Oliverio in 2010, McKinley has been reelected with over 60 percent of the vote in subsequent elections. The picture is more complicated in 2022, however. As a result of declining population reflected in the 2020 census, West Virginia is losing a Congressional district. Under the redistricting boundaries drawn by the state legislature, McKinley will be facing fellow Republican Congressman Alex Mooney in the May 2022 primary. Mooney was first elected in 2014 after moving across the state border into West Virginia from Maryland, where

[80] *Id.*

[81] *Bipartisan Action on Climate Change*, COLUMBIA CLIMATE SCHOOL (Mar. 18, 2021), https://climate.columbia.edu/events/bipartisan-action-climate-change.

[82] Sobczyk, *supra* note 70.

[83] *Id.*

[84] Alex Thomas, *US House Passes Infrastructure Bill; Mckinley One of 13 Republicans Who Supported Legislation*, METRO NEWS (Nov. 6, 2021), https://wvmetronews.com/2021/11/06/us-house-passes-infrastructure-bill-mckinley-one-of-13-republicans-who-supported-legislation/.

[85] Timothy Cama, *Trump Backs Mooney over Mckinley in W.Va. House Primary*, E&E DAILY (Nov. 16, 2021), https://subscriber.politicopro.com/article/eenews/2021/11/16/trump-backs-mooney-over-mckinley-in-wva-house-primary-283252.

he had served in the state senate for twelve years and later as chair of the Maryland Republican party.[86] Mooney picked up the endorsement of former President Trump in the race, who noted that Mooney had voted against both the bipartisan infrastructure bill and the creation of a commission to investigate the January 6 attack on the US Capitol.[87] The primary race will be an interesting test of the value of Trump's endorsement of a relative newcomer to the state (Mooney) versus McKinley's decades-long track record of Republican party politics in West Virginia and his demonstrated willingness to work across party lines.

---

[86]   Abby Livingston, *West Virginia Newcomer Battles Carpetbagger Label*, ROLL CALL (July 10, 2014), https://rollcall.com/2014/07/10/west-virginia-newcomer-battles-carpetbagger-label/.

[87]   Timothy Cama, *3 House Races to Watch After Redistricting*, E&E DAILY (Dec, 14, 2021), https://www.eenews.net/articles/3-house-races-to-watch-after-redistricting/.

7

Manchin in the Middle

No politician dominates "the lost decade" in West Virginia more than Joe Manchin III, who, at the time of writing, is currently serving his second term in the US Senate. With the Democrats taking control of the Senate in January 2021, Manchin is now chairman of the Senate Energy and Natural Resources Committee, through which all energy-related legislation must pass, and thus has ascended to become the point person on energy and climate legislation.[1] Moreover, as the most conservative Democrat in the Senate, Manchin has outsized influence on the scope of virtually all elements of President Biden's spending agenda under the current Senate rules shaped by his predecessor, Robert C. Byrd.

Manchin has held office at the state and federal level almost continuously since 1982, when he was elected to the West Virginia House of Delegates at the age of thirty-five. After two terms in the House, he served ten years in the state Senate. Manchin unsuccessfully ran for governor in 1996; he was defeated in the Democratic primary, the only electoral loss of his career. He achieved statewide office for the first time when he was elected to a four-year term as Secretary of State in 2000, followed by nearly six years as governor. In his first election as governor in 2004, he won 63 percent of the vote – at the same time that West Virginia voted for Republican President George W. Bush by a 13-point margin – and was reelected with nearly 70 percent of the vote in 2008.

Following the death of Senator Byrd in 2010, Manchin won a special election to fill his seat by defeating businessman John Raese by a margin of 53–43 percent. Manchin began his service in the US Senate on November 15, 2010. He handily won reelection in 2012 in a rematch against Raese, and in doing so widened his margin of victory to 60–36 percent. He became West Virginia's senior US senator when fellow Democrat Jay Rockefeller retired in 2015. As the state became "redder" following Donald Trump's election as President in 2016 (described in Chapter 5), Senator Manchin narrowly won reelection in 2018, defeating Attorney General Patrick Morrisey by about 19,000 votes.

---

[1] James Bruggers, *The Senate's New Point Man on Climate Has Been the Democrats' Most Fossil Fuel-Friendly Senator*, INSIDE CLIMATE NEWS (Jan. 13, 2021), https://insideclimatenews.org/news/13012021/joe-manchin-west-virginia-senate-democrat-climate-legislation/.

Manchin comes from a family of Italian and Czechoslovakian immigrants who moved to West Virginia a century ago; much of his family, including several siblings, still live in West Virginia.[2] Manchin was born and raised in the small coal-mining town of Farmington. According to a *Time Magazine* profile written in 2014 by Pulitzer Prize-winning author and historian Jon Meacham, "[a] childhood spent in his grandparents' store tending to customers – listening to them, figuring out what they needed and how to get paid for it – prepared him for the folkways of state politics."[3] A star quarterback in high school, Manchin earned a scholarship to play football at West Virginia University (WVU) in Morgantown.[4] With approximately 445 people, Farmington today is about half the size it was when Manchin grew up.

Manchin has been described as part of a "minor West Virginian political dynasty."[5] His father and grandfather were mayors of Farmington. An uncle, Antonio James Manchin – known as "A. James" Manchin, or "Uncle Jimmy" – was elected to the West Virginia House of Delegates at the age of twenty-one, and later became the state's secretary of state and treasurer. "Uncle Jimmy" was widely credited with helping John F. Kennedy win the state's pivotal primary in 1960, a victory that propelled him to the Democratic nomination and the presidency.[6] A. James did not fare as well as JFK politically, however; in his stewardship of the West Virginia State Treasury, on the heels of a loss of $279 million from the state's consolidated investment fund due to mismanagement, he was impeached by the House of Delegates and resigned from office in July 1989, before the trial in the Senate was completed.[7]

THE HOUSEBOAT IN THE POTOMAC AND THE ART OF COMPROMISE

Since the Democrats won both Senate seats in Georgia in January 2021 and forged a 50–50 tie in the US Senate, Joe Manchin has been regarded as probably the second most powerful man in Washington, behind only President Biden. Under the "Byrd rule," described in Chapter 6, it would take all fifty Democratic senators – plus the vote of Vice President Kamala Harris – to pass any legislation through the reconciliation process. So for any legislation that might qualify for the reconciliation process –

2 Scott Goldsmith, *Almost Heaven: Joe Manchin in West Virginia & Washington, Scenes from the Life of a Red-State Democratic Senator*, POLITICO MAGAZINE (Mar./Apr. 2017), https://www.politico.com/magazine/gallery/2017/03/joe-manchin-photos-west-virginia-senator-washington-000715?slide=18.
3 Jon Meacham, *Joe Manchin: The Outlier*, TIME (Jun 19, 2014) https://time.com/2899492/joe-manchin-west-virginia-senator/.
4 *Id.*
5 Kenneth Surin, *Joe Manchin, the Good Ol' Corporate Boy from West Virginia*, COUNTERPUNCH (Oct. 10, 2018), https://www.counterpunch.org/2018/10/10/joe-manchin-the-good-ol-corporate-boy-from-west-virginia/.
6 Goldsmith, *supra* note 2.
7 Rob Cornelius, *29 Years Ago Yesterday, Joe Manchin's Uncle Had to Resign for Incompetence*, MEDIUM (July 10, 2018), https://medium.com/@robcwv/29-years-ago-yesterday-joe-manchins-uncle-had-to-resign-for-incompetence-14b1e6ad6129.

such as repealing the Trump tax cuts, or increasing the minimum wage, or adopting a clean energy standard that has fiscal impacts – the White House cannot lose a single Democratic vote. Manchin, along with Kyrsten Sinema (Republican, Arizona), is commonly identified as one of two senators on the margin, and Manchin enjoys additional attention as chair of the Senate Energy and Natural Resources Committee if the topic relates to energy. By expressing his opinion on White House proposals for possible elements of legislation that could be passed through reconciliation, Manchin has single-handedly killed suggestions that the corporate tax rate should be increased from 21 to 28 percent (he would support an increase to 25 percent),[8] or that the minimum wage should be increased to $15 - per hour (he could only go as high as $11 per hour).[9]

Similarly, it would take all fifty Democratic Senators to vote to revise the filibuster rule to move away from the sixty votes necessary to invoke cloture and pass legislation, requiring instead only a simple majority. (The filibuster rule has gradually eroded over the past twenty years to require a simple majority for Senate confirmation of cabinet secretaries, Supreme Court Justices, and other federal judges.) Manchin has consistently held out against any suggestion of revisiting the filibuster rule, insisting that bipartisanship requires that legislative proposals attract the necessary ten Republican votes to pass legislation. The door was firmly shut most recently in an op-ed piece in the *Charleston Gazette-Mail* on June 6, 2021, where Manchin stated: "I will not vote to weaken or eliminate the filibuster. For as long as I have the privilege of being your U.S. senator, I will fight to represent the people of West Virginia, to seek bipartisan compromise no matter how difficult and to develop the political bonds that end divisions and help unite the country we love."[10]

Being a champion of bipartisanship is not a new thing for Joe Manchin – he has played that role since becoming a member of the US Senate in November 2010. Jon Meacham's 2014 profile in *Time Magazine* observes that Manchin "believes his most productive hours as a lawmaker are spent not on the Senate floor or in the cloakroom or committee rooms but on the waters of the Potomac River aboard his houseboat."[11] Rather than buying or renting a place to stay in Washington, DC for the two or three nights per week when Congress is in session, Manchin stays aboard a large boat anchored in the Potomac in National Harbor, about eight miles south of the Capitol. Initially, the boat was the "Black Tie," a 2001 540 Sea Ray Sundancer of which Manchin

[8]   Erik Wasson & Steven T. Dennis, *Manchin Balks at Biden's Corporate Tax Increase, Favors 25% Rate,* BLOOMBERG (Apr. 5, 2021), https://www.bloomberg.com/news/articles/2021-04-05/manchin-balks-at-biden-s-corporate-tax-increase-favors-25-rate.

[9]   Jason Lemon, *Joe Manchin and Kyrsten Sinema Open to $11 Minimum Wage, but Other Dems Less Willing to Compromise,* NEWSWEEK (Mar. 24, 2021), https://www.newsweek.com/joe-manchin-kyrsten-sinema-open-11-minimum-wage-other-dems-less-willing-compromise-1578443.

[10] Joe Manchin, *Joe Manchin: Why I'm Voting Against the For the People Act,* CHARLESTON GAZETTE-MAIL (June 6, 2021), https://www.wvgazettemail.com/opinion/op_ed_commentaries/joe-manchin-why-im-voting-against-the-for-the-people-act/article_c7eb2551-a500-5f77-aa37-2e42d0af870f.html.

[11] Meacham, *supra* note 3.

was a "wee little small owner."[12] (A typical Sundancer features two bedrooms, a wet bar, a washer and dryer, an entertainment center and a 600-gallon gas tank.)[13] Meacham referred to Manchin's boat as "a kind of floating incubator of that tenderest of Washington flowers in the first decades of the 21st century: bipartisanship."[14]

Manchin later replaced the Black Tie with a 65-foot boat (also built in 2001) which he christened "Almost Heaven," named after John Denver's ode to West Virginia, *Country Roads*. In August 2018, the National Republican Senatorial Committee (NRSC) took aim at Manchin and his "$700,000 DC luxury yacht," claiming that "West Virginia Joe" had transformed himself into "Washington Joe."[15] FactCheck. org investigated the NSRC claim and, in response, Manchin's office produced a 2014 bill of sale showing the sale price to be only $220,000. And PolitiFact noted that while the boat's length technically qualifies it as a "yacht," given that Manchin lives there when he is in town, "it could be just as easily described as a houseboat."[16] It therefore scored the claim as "Half True."

The more relevant point, regardless of whether the vessel is characterized as a yacht or a houseboat, is Manchin's frequent use of it as a refuge for senators – both Republicans and Democrats – to be able to engage in candid discussions about the issues of the day over pizza and beer (and, apparently, the occasional moonshine from a glass jar). When asked about the size of the boat, Manchin replied "we can get 10 or more senators and have a good time. And you know what? We can go float out there and you can't find us."[17] And, he added, the "cheapest thing you can do is feed people."[18]

The Black Tie, for example, played a prominent role in Manchin's first high profile effort to reach across the aisle: In the wake of the mass shooting at Sandy Hook Elementary School in Newtown, Connecticut in December 2012, Manchin cosponsored a bill, along with Republican Senators Pat Toomey of Pennsylvania and Mark Kirk of Illinois, that would have expanded background checks for gun buyers to cover transactions at gun shows and internet sales. Kirk told reporters in Washington that members from both parties who were open to compromise often met on the Black Tie, which Kirk said was "much of the reason for much of the bipartisan cooperation around here."[19] Kirk told reporters that, "What happens on

---

[12] Ed O'Keefe, *Joe Manchin: "What We Did, We Did Right,"* Washington Post (Apr. 11, 2013), https://www.washingtonpost.com/news/post-politics/wp/2013/04/11/joe-manchin-what-we-did-we-did-right/.

[13] *Booze and a Boat Helped Forge Senate Gun Compromise, Sen. Mark Kirk Says*, DNAInfo (Apr. 11, 2013), https://www.dnainfo.com/chicago/20130411/chicago-citywide/booze-boat-helped-forge-senate-gun-compromise-sen-mark-kirk-says/.

[14] Meacham, *supra* note 3.

[15] Joseph Kennedy, Kenna Richards, & Douglas Soule, *Fact-Check: Does Joe Manchin Have a $700,000 Luxury Yacht?*, PolitiFact (Oct, 5, 2018), https://www.100daysinappalachia.com/2018/10/fact-check-does-joe-manchin-have-a-700000-luxury-yacht/.

[16] *Id.*

[17] O'Keefe, *supra* note 12.

[18] *Id.*

[19] *Booze and a Boat Helped Forge Senate Gun Compromise, supra* note 13.

the Black Tie stays on the Black Tie."[20] Although the bill ultimately failed, the effort "positioned Manchin as a man willing to take political risks back home for the greater good," according to Meacham.[21] It also prompted *The Washington Post* to publish a front-page piece that exposed the Black Tie as Manchin's secret weapon in promoting bipartisanship.[22]

Manchin has a well-earned reputation as the most conservative of all the Democrats in the US Senate. He voted against the Don't Ask, Don't Tell Repeal Act of 2010, as well as for removing federal funding from Planned Parenthood in 2015.[23] He has voted with Republicans on issues such as abortion and gun ownership; prior to cosponsoring the gun control legislation with Pat Toomey in 2013, Manchin enjoyed "A+" and "A" ratings with the National Rifle Association (NRA) (although that grade dropped to a "D" in 2018 and the NRA actually supported his opponent in the US Senate race, Patrick Morrisey).[24]

During the Trump administration, Manchin voted to confirm most of Trump's cabinet and judicial appointees, and was the only Democrat to vote to confirm Jeff Sessions for Attorney General and Brett Kavanaugh for the Supreme Court. He was infamously identified by *Roll Call* as the "Democrat who hugged the President" when he briefly embraced President Trump following his address to a joint session of Congress in March 2017.[25] Manchin's US Senate website proudly proclaimed that he was the Senator (Democrat or Republican) most likely to break away from the party, citing twenty-three votes in which he was the only Democrat to vote with the Republicans on issues such as immigration and border security and increasing domestic energy production.[26] According to his website, Senator Manchin voted with the Trump administration 74 percent of the time,[27] and claimed to "share many of the President's [Trump] priorities when it comes to promoting fair trade, repealing Obama-era regulations, and protecting our national security."[28]

[20] Ed O'Keefe & David Fahrenthold, *Sen. Joe Manchin Bridges Gun-Control Divide to Pave Way for Expanded Laws*, WASHINGTON POST (Apr, 10, 2013), https://www.washingtonpost.com/politics/sen-joe-manchin-bridges-gun-control-divide-to-pave-way-for-expanded-laws/2013/04/10/3353ef42-a1fd-11e2-be47-b44febada3a8_story.html.

[21] Meacham, *supra* note 3.

[22] O'Keefe & Fahrenthold, *supra* note 20.

[23] Surin, *supra* note 5.

[24] Jamie Green, *"Joe Manchin Has a 'D' Rating from the NRA,"* POLITIFACT (Sept. 28, 2018), https://www.politifact.com/factchecks/2018/sep/28/patrick-morrisey/does-joe-manchin-have-d-rating-national-rifle-asso/.

[25] Stephanie Aiken, *The Democrat Who Hugged the President*, ROLL CALL (Mar. 7, 2017), https://www.rollcall.com/2017/03/07/the-democrat-who-hugged-the-president/.

[26] Joe Manchin, About *Bipartisanship, Legislation*, https://www.manchin.senate.gov/about/bipartisanship/legislation?latest=148.

[27] Percentage based on the votes Congressional Quarterly reports as having an official administration position. The full list of votes included is available at https://www.manchin.senate.gov/about/bipartisanship/legislation?latest=148.

[28] Manchin, *supra* note 26.

THE "FOSSIL FUEL GUY" FROM WEST VIRGINIA

Manchin has long-standing ties to the coal industry. His grandfather went to work in the mines as an eleven-year-old.[29] His uncle died in the Farmington Mine disaster in November 1968, when an explosion occurred at the Consol No. 9 coal mine. At the time of the explosion, ninety-nine miners were inside, and only twenty-one were able to escape during the hours that followed; the remaining seventy-eight who were still trapped all perished, and the bodies of nineteen of the dead were never recovered. The cause of the explosion was never determined.[30]

Before his political career took him to statewide office, and later Washington, Manchin ran the family business, a coal brokerage firm known as Enersystems, Inc. On his financial disclosures for 2009 and 2010 filed with the US Senate, Manchin reported significant earnings from Enersystems – an operating income of $1,363,916 in the nineteen months before winning his Senate seat, which declined to $417,255 during the next reporting period but was still as high as $492,000 in 2020.[31] The *Washington Examiner* reported in 2018 that Manchin had made more than $5 million in profits since entering the Senate in 2010; it described Manchin as "the unfortunate poster child of Elizabeth Warren's anti-corruption effort." (In response to Senator Warren's announcement in August 2018 of new anti-corruption policies aimed at policing self-interested politicians and cleaning up Capitol Hill, the Republican National Senate Committee ran an ad targeting the income Manchin gained while "serving on subcommittees overseeing the family business.")[32]

When pressed upon entering the Senate in 2011 about his earnings from Enersystems, Manchin said the investment had "absolutely not" affected his policy decisions regarding the coal industry, pointing out that the investment has been in a blind trust "for a long time."[33] *Greenwire* confirmed from public records and media reports that Manchin handed day-to-day control of Enersystems to his son after being elected West Virginia secretary of state in 2000 and moved his company holdings into a blind trust between 2005 and 2010, while he served as governor. Following his election to the US Senate, his Enersystems holdings and other in-state assets were transferred to a new blind trust that conformed with federal rules. Manchin's most

---

[29] Goldsmith, *supra* note 2.

[30] Douglas Imbrogno, *Farmington No. 9: The West Virginia Disaster That Changed Coal Mining Forever*, WV PUBLIC BROADCASTING (Nov. 20, 2018), https://www.wvpublic.org/news/2018-11-20/farm ington-no-9-the-west-virginia-disaster-that-changed-coal-mining-forever.

[31] David Moore, *Manchin Profits from Coal Sales to Utility Lobbying Group Members*, SLUDGE (July 1, 2021), https://readsludge.com/2021/07/01/manchin-profits-from-coal-sales-to-utility-lobbying-group-members/.

[32] Philip Wegmann, *Joe Manchin May Be the Unfortunate Poster Child of Elizabeth Warren's Anti-Corruption Effort*, WASHINGTON EXAMINER (Aug. 21, 2018), https://www.washingtonexaminer.com/opin ion/joe-manchin-may-be-the-unfortunate-poster-child-of-elizabeth-warrens-anti-corruption-effort.

[33] Manuel Quinones & Elana Schor, *Sen. Manchin Maintains Lucrative Ties to Family-Owned Coal Company*, N.Y. TIMES (July 26, 2011), https://archive.nytimes.com/www.nytimes.com/gwire/2011/07/ 26/26greenwire-sen-manchin-maintains-lucrative-ties-to-family-64717.html?pagewanted=all.

recent financial disclosures show that he still holds stocks worth between $1 million and $5 million in Enersystems.[34]

Most of Manchin's income from Enersystems derives from a contract between Enersystems and American Bituminous Power Partners (AmBit), which operates a coal power plant located near Grant Town, West Virginia. The plant burns waste coal or refuse – also known as "gob"[35] – to generate electricity that is sold to Monongahela Power (Mon Power), a FirstEnergy subsidiary. The wastes burned at the plant are excavated from a gob pile on-site or procured by Enersystems from other mine refuse areas and trucked to Grant Town. The coal plant itself is described by one writer as "not much more than a flimsy steel warehouse with a smokestack" – in other words, "an old clunker in a world of Teslas" – and is easily the dirtiest coal plant in West Virginia.[36] It has also been the source of considerable wealth for Manchin since 1993, when the plant came on line – over $5 million during the past decade alone.

Over three decades, Manchin's influence wielded from his various political positions has protected the plant from laws, regulations, and economic forces that long ago would have forced the plant to close. Worse, its continued operation costs West Virginians tens of millions of dollars that FirstEnergy simply passes through to electric ratepayers blessed by the notoriously coal-friendly Public Service Commission (PSC).

Manchin has been notably prickly in responding to press inquiries in late 2021 and early 2022 regarding his relationship with Enersystems and the Grant Town power plant, admonishing reporters "[y]ou'd best change the subject now" or retorting "[y]ou got a problem?"[37] His hypersensitivity to the issue is somewhat understandable: it's a story of the sort of "good ol' boy politics" for which West Virginia has unfortunately come to be known, but that fails to survive the heightened scrutiny that accompanies an intense focus on "what Joe Manchin wants" in his newfound role as one of the most powerful politicians in shaping national energy policy.

The Grant Town power plant had a fairly unremarkable start; it was built in the early 1990s under an innovative law passed during the Carter administration, the Public Utility Regulatory Policies Act of 1978 (PURPA). Among other things, PURPA encouraged burning waste coal to generate electricity, as a way to clean up thousands of polluting waste coal piles throughout the United States. PURPA's

34 Sarah Kaplan & Dino Grandoni, *One Coal State Senator Holds the Key to Biden's Ambitious Climate Agenda. And It's Not McConnell*, Washington Post (Jan. 25, 2021), https://www.washingtonpost.com/climate-environment/2021/01/25/manchin-climate-congress/.
35 "Gob" is basically shale, clay, and coal waste that was separated from marketable coal decades ago when now-defunct mines were operating.
36 Jeff Goodell, *Manchin's Coal Corruption Is So Much Worse Than You Knew*, Rolling Stone (Jan. 10, 2022), https://www.rollingstone.com/politics/politics-features/joe-manchin-big-coal-west-virginia-1280922/.
37 Michael Kranish and Anna Phillips, *Manchin Cites a Blind Trust to Justify Climate Votes. But Much Income from His Family's Coal Company Isn't Covered*, Washington Post (Dec. 13, 2021), https://www.washingtonpost.com/politics/2021/12/13/manchin-blind-trust-enersystems-stock-climate-change/.

ratemaking provisions were designed to encourage power plant entrepreneurs other than utilities ("independent power producers") to enter the business of building power plants by allowing them to sell the electrical output of a plant at a price tied to the costs of the electric utility purchasing the plant's output – referred to as the utility's "avoided costs" – as opposed to the plant operator's actual costs of generating the electricity.[38] As turned out, however, Grant Town received special treatment by the PSC, which turned the concept of the utility's "avoided costs" on its head by approving a more generous contract for Grant Town – and one that was more costly for ratepayers – when the plant began to run into financial difficulties in 2006, while Manchin was Governor.

At that time, Manchin's chief of staff, Larry Puccio, is reported to have been dispatched to the PSC to convince the regulators, as well as FirstEnergy, that AmBit's contract with FirstEnergy needed to be sweetened in order to keep the Grant Town plant operating (which, of course, was necessary to keep payments to Enersystems flowing).[39] At the time, the PSC was chaired by a Manchin appointee (Jon C. McKinney, appointed by Manchin in 2005).[40] The result was the PSC's approval of a 25 percent increase in the "capacity" rate[41] for the plant's output – from $27.25 per megawatt to $34.25 – as well as an eight-year extension in the term of the agreement, to 2036. In recent years, the price paid by FirstEnergy for Grant Town's electrical output has far exceeded the value of the power in the energy markets – the plant lost $117 million between 2016 and 2021, and is projected to lose another $24 million in 2022.[42]

The West Virginia PSC simply flows through these losses to FirstEnergy ratepayers. In other words, "Manchin is effectively taking money right out of the pockets of West Virginians when they pay their electric bills."[43] Of course, much of the blame lies with the PSC; Jeff Goodell described it this way in a January 2022 *Rolling Stone* article:

> If the PSC were working in the best interests of West Virginians, it would have demanded that the money-losing Grant Town plant be shut down years ago. Instead, West Virginians have been paying millions of dollars each year in higher

---

[38] This had implications in both directions for the eligible power plant (referred to as a "qualifying facility" under PURPA): If the plant was particularly efficient, it had an opportunity to capture outsize profits. At the same time, however, if it was unable to earn a profit (or even cover its expenses) at price equal to the utility's avoided costs, the utility and its regulators had no obligation to "bail out" the plant with a more generous contract.

[39] Scott Waldman, *How Manchin Used Politics to Protect His Coal Company*, CLIMATEWIRE (Feb. 2, 2022), https://www.eenews.net/articles/how-manchin-used-politics-to-protect-his-coal-company/.

[40] *Id.*

[41] The power purchase agreement between AmBit and FirstEnergy contains a fairly common arrangement under which the payments for the electrical output of Grant Town are split between the "capacity" rate – which is based on the maximum output the plant can physically produce, in megawatts – and the "energy" rate – which is based on the amount of megawatt hours of electricity actually delivered to FirstEnergy.

[42] Scott Waldman, *A Coal Plant Fights to Stay Open. It Could Enrich Manchin*, CLIMATEWIRE (Nov. 17, 2021), https://www.eenews.net/articles/a-coal-plant-fights-to-stay-open-it-could-enrich-manchin/.

[43] Goodell, *supra* note 36.

electricity costs in order to keep running a dirty, inefficient power plant that is sickening and killing people with dirty air, but paying the Manchin family handsomely.[44]

The utter failure of the PSC to protect the interests of West Virginia's ratepayers is discussed further in Chapters 8 and 10.

Manchin's involvement on behalf of the Grant Town plant dates back to 1995. As a state senator, he backed a measure in the West Virginia legislature that gave tax breaks to West Virginia power plants that burned waste coal.[45] Later, as governor, he made sure that waste coal was designated an "alternative" fuel in a clean energy bill that ultimately produced the state's Alternative and Renewable Energy Portfolio Standard (discussed further in Chapter 9), thereby reclassifying one of the most carbon-intensive fuels in America as "something akin to solar, wind and hydropower."[46] In 2016, Manchin was able to derail a plan in the US Senate that would have given the Environmental Protection Agency (EPA) more authority to regulate coal ash – a byproduct of Grant Town also hauled by Enersystems – by securing passage of the Coal Combustion Residuals Regulatory Improvement Act, which allowed West Virginia to adopt coal ash disposal programs that were less restrictive than proposed by the EPA. A likely outcome? According to one industry observer, "lower costs for companies that handled coal ash, like Enersystems."[47] More recently, Manchin played an instrumental role in the insertion of $11.3 billion in the Bipartisan Infrastructure Bill to fund cleanup of unreclaimed coal mines abandoned years ago by bankrupt coal companies – monies that "could also be a boon for companies involved in the cleanup of waste coal from former mine sites, such as Enersystems."[48]

Apart from the decades Manchin has spent "pushing policies that benefit the [Grant Town] plant and the waste coal industry that helped make his family fortune,"[49] he has more generally consistently opposed efforts by the federal government to regulate carbon emissions, an initiative that would have serious implications for the coal industry (coal-fired power plants were the leading source of carbon emissions at the time). In his race for the US Senate in 2010, his Republican opponent, John Raese, launched an ad campaign claiming that Manchin would be a rubber stamp for President Obama. In response, then Governor Manchin filed suit against the Obama administration's supposed "attempts to destroy the coal mining industry" through a regulation known as the "stream protection rule." Shortly thereafter, Manchin ran his own television ad, infamously using a rifle to shoot at the cap-and-trade bill that would have regulated carbon emissions, which

[44] *Id.*
[45] Waldman, *supra* note 39.
[46] *Id.*
[47] *Id.*
[48] *Id.*
[49] Scott Waldman, *Joe Manchin-Connected Power Plant Hasn't Paid Rent in a Decade*, CLIMATEWIRE (Feb. 14, 2022), https://subscriber.politicopro.com/article/eenews/2022/02/14/joe-manchin-connected-power-plant-hasnt-paid-rent-in-a-decade-00008484.

passed the House of Representatives in June 2009. Manchin stated in the ad: "I sued the EPA, and I'll take dead aim at the cap-and-trade bill, because it's bad for West Virginia."[50]

Manchin was a strong opponent of President Obama's clean energy policies, and the EPA's Clean Power Plan in particular. In response to Obama's announcement in June 2013 regarding his administration's intentions to begin regulating greenhouse gas (GHG) emissions from coal-fired power plants, Manchin issued a statement that "[i]t's clear now that the president has declared a war on coal."[51] Following formal adoption of the Clean Power Plan in 2016, Manchin signed a letter opposing the measure – the only Democrat to join with the 33 Republican senators and 171 Republican members of the House who fought the plan.[52]

In the fall of 2013, Manchin played a lead role in derailing President Obama's appointment of Ron Binz as chairman of the Federal Energy Regulatory Commission (FERC); Binz had been labeled as "anti-coal" because of his actions as chairman of the Colorado Public Utility Commission from 2007 to 2011. In that role, Binz was known as an advocate for renewable energy and energy efficiency, and advised Colorado Governor Bill Ritter's office on a Colorado energy law that led to the closure of some coal-fired power plants. It was highly unusual for a confirmation fight over what was then thought to be a relatively "obscure position";[53] Matthew Wald of the *New York Times* observed that "the job at stake is at an agency most people cannot name."[54] When Manchin spoke near the end of Binz's committee hearing, he said that the Obama administration's energy policies were beating the "living crap" out of West Virginia and that he was "skeptical" of Binz but had not yet committed to a position on his nomination.[55] Within days, however, Manchin announced his decision to oppose Binz's nomination in a conference call with West Virginia reporters, thereby stripping the Democrats of their 12–10 vote advantage on the Senate Energy and Natural Resources Committee, whose approval was needed to send the Binz nomination to the Senate floor. Two weeks later, Binz withdrew his nomination, blaming the coal industry, utilities that use coal, and twelve groups with ties to the Koch brothers.[56]

[50] Nick Wing, *Joe Manchin Shoots Cap-and-Trade Bill with Rifle in New Ad*, HuffPost (Oct.11, 2010), https://www.huffpost.com/entry/joe-manchin-ad-dead-aim_n_758457.

[51] Juliet Eilperin, *Obama Unveils Ambitious Agenda to Combat Climate Change, Bypassing Congress*, Washington Post (June 25, 2013), https://www.washingtonpost.com/politics/obama-climate-strategy-represents-piecemeal-approach/2013/06/25/7bd9f20a-dd0a-11e2-bd83-e99e43c336ed_story.html?itid=lk_inline_manual_2.

[52] Bruggers, *supra* note 1.

[53] Darius Dixon, *Manchin Twist Hurts FERC Nominee*, Politico (Sept. 18, 2013), https://www.politico.com/story/2013/09/joe-manchin-ferc-097034.

[54] Matthew Wald, *An Unusual Public Battle over an Energy Nomination*, N.Y. Times (Sept. 15, 2013), https://www.nytimes.com/2013/09/16/business/energy-environment/a-federal-energy-nomination-sets-off-an-unusual-public-battle.html?searchResultPosition=1.

[55] *Id.*

[56] Hannah Northey, *Binz Blames "Right-Wing" Groups, Coal Industry for Sinking His FERC Bid*, Greenwire (Oct. 1, 2013), https://www.eenews.net/greenwire/stories/1059988441.

In June 2017, Manchin praised President Trump's decision to have the United States exit from the Paris Climate Agreement, claiming that such agreements need to strike a "balance between our environment and the economy" by "protect[ing] the American consumer as well as energy-producing states like West Virginia, while also incentivizing the development of advanced fossil energy technologies."[57]

JOE MANCHIN'S EVOLUTION ON CLIMATE CHANGE

In June 2014, on the heels of the Obama administration's release of its proposed Clean Power Plan to regulate carbon emissions from coal-fired power plants, Senator Manchin attracted some national attention when he reached out to Sheldon Whitehouse (Democrat, Rhode Island), one of the more progressive members of the US Senate, in an effort to find some "common ground" on climate change. They partnered in a joint appearance on the floor of the Senate, preceded by a joint interview with *Politico*, in which Manchin repeated his statement from earlier in 2014 that "7 billion people have had an impact on the climate" and accepted that climate change is "a problem that we're responsible for."[58] Whitehouse, for his part, acknowledged that coal and other fossil fuels are not going away anytime soon. According to the *Politico* interview, the two expressed the hope of creating a model for breaking the partisan logjam that has plagued the climate issue since the collapse of cap-and-trade in 2010 (highlighted, of course, by Manchin shooting a bullet through the cap-and-trade bill). Whitehouse said he would visit West Virginia to learn more about the coal industry if Manchin would come to Rhode Island for a firsthand look at how climate can impact the coast.

Manchin took up the offer, and visited Whitehouse in Rhode Island in October 2014, where Whitehouse's tour focused on the impacts of global warming on the state's coast, which has seen significant sea-level rise, as well as warming waters that, Whitehouse said, have decimated the biggest fishery in Narragansett Bay.[59] Whitehouse also showed Manchin a company that captures carbon dioxide (CO_2) from an ethanol plant and then uses it to grow algae that is used to feed livestock. In October 2014, Whitehouse reciprocated by visiting West Virginia, where the duo toured the National Energy Technology Laboratory in Morgantown and Longview Power, a coal-fired power plant just north of Morgantown.[60]

---

[57] Press Release, Joe Manchin, Manchin Statement on President's Decision to Leave the Paris Climate Agreement (June 1, 2017), https://www.manchin.senate.gov/newsroom/press-releases/manchin-state ment-on-presidents-decision-to-leave-the-paris-climate-agreement.

[58] Andrew Restuccia, *Middle Ground on Climate Change?*, POLITICO (June 24, 2014), https://www.politico .com/story/2014/06/joe-manchin-sheldon-whitehouse-climate-change-108253.

[59] Richard Salit, *Whitehouse Takes Coal State Senator on RI Climate Change Tour*, PROVIDENCE JOURNAL (Oct. 10, 2014), https://www.providencejournal.com/article/20141010/NEWS/310109922.

[60] David Gutman, *Manchin, Rhode Island's Whitehouse Tour W.Va. Energy Production, Look for Climate Solutions*, CHARLESTON GAZETTE-MAIL (Oct. 22, 2014), https://www.wvgazettemail.com/news/politics/ manchin-rhode-island-s-whitehouse-tour-w-va-energy-production-look-for-climate-solutions/arti cle_f7b96d8e-443e-5039-864b-a58404040425.html.

Following his tough reelection fight to retain his US Senate seat in 2018, Manchin was next in line to become ranking member – the top Democrat – on the Senate Energy and Natural Resources Committee. A senator can serve as a ranking member on only one committee; other Democratic senators on the committee with more seniority – Senators Maria Cantwell of Washington, Ron Wyden of Oregon, and Debbie Stabenow of Michigan – passed over the energy committee assignment in favor of taking on that role in other committees (Cantwell on Commerce, Wyden on Finance, and Stabenow on Agriculture). Senator Bernie Sanders of Vermont, an independent who caucuses with Democrats, also took a pass in favor of the party's top spot on the Budget Committee.[61]

Given's Manchin's pro-coal reputation and his perceived unconvincing position on climate change, he faced strong opposition from progressives and climate change activists in the Democratic party. The two Democratic candidates for president with the strongest platforms on climate change, Governor Jay Inslee of Washington and Tom Steyer, the billionaire philanthropist, both called on Senator Chuck Schumer of New York, the Democratic leader, to keep Manchin out of the ranking spot. According to an email sent by Governor Inslee to his supporters, Manchin "supports Donald Trump's dirty energy agenda" and "simply can't be trusted to make the bold, progressive decisions we need." Congresswoman-elect Alexandria Ocasio-Cortez, who was then the incoming House of Representatives' freshman from New York and later the chief architect of the "Green New Deal," also opposed Manchin's ascension to the ranking member position, citing the campaign contributions he had received from the coal industry during his 2018 Senate campaign. (Manchin was second on the list of the senators who received the most money from coal mining interests in 2018.)[62] Ocasio-Cortez argued, "I do not believe that we should be financed by the industries that we are supposed to be legislating and regulating and touching with our legislation."[63] The Sunrise Movement, an environmental advocacy group led by Ocasio-Cortez, protested outside Mr. Schumer's New York office to reinforce her point.

In response, Manchin did two things. First, he reversed his earlier position with respect to President Trump's nomination of Bernard McNamee to the FERC. McNamee was a very controversial appointment to the five-member commission; in his previous position as the executive director of the Office of Policy with the Department of Energy, McNamee was the architect of Energy Secretary Rick Perry's September 2017 proposal for a $34 billion bailout of the coal and nuclear industry that

[61] Sheryl Gay Stolberg, *Joe Manchin Faces Liberal Opposition in Bid to Be Energy Panel's Top Democrat*, N.Y. TIMES (Dec. 6, 2018), https://www.nytimes.com/2018/12/06/us/politics/joe-manchin-energy-committee.html.

[62] Coal Mining, OPENSECRETS, https://www.opensecrets.org/industries/recips.php?ind=E1210&recipdetail=S& sortorder=U&mem=Y&cycle=2018. Manchin received $40,550 in 2018, second only to Senator Luther Strange (Republican, Alabama).

[63] Aida Chavez, *Alexandria Ocasio-Cortez Leads Opposition to Coal Puppet Joe Manchin for Top Senate Energy Slot*, THE INTERCEPT (Nov. 30, 2018), https://theintercept.com/2018/11/30/alexandria-ocasio-cortez-leads-opposition-to-coal-puppet-joe-manchin-for-top-senate-energy-slot/.

FERC subsequently rejected in a unanimous 5–0 vote in January 2018.[64] McNamee subsequently went to work for the Koch Brothers-funded Texas Public Policy Foundation, where he gave a speech in February 2018 to Texas lawmakers that criticized renewable energy and environmental groups, called CO_2 "not a real pollutant," and described fossil fuels as "key to our way of life."[65] After being the lone Democrat on the Energy and Natural Resources Committee to vote to confirm McNamee, Manchin voted against the nomination on the Senate floor; he claims he did so after seeing video footage of Mr. McNamee's February 2018 speech. According to a statement issued by Manchin, "after viewing video footage, which I had not previously seen, where Bernard McNamee outright denies the impact that humans are having on our climate, I can no longer support his nomination to be a FERC commissioner."[66] Notwithstanding Manchin's opposition, McNamee was confirmed by the Senate in a 50–49 vote.

Second, Manchin used the occasion to issue a strong statement expressing his view on the role of human activity with respect to climate change: "Climate change is real, humans have made a significant impact, and we have the responsibility and capability to address it urgently."[67] (Manchin's acknowledgment of the role of human activity with regard to climate change was not new to those who followed him closely; as noted above, he said as much in his remarks at an energy conference at the WVU College of Law in February 2014.) But the affirmation seemed to satisfy his opponents, or at least soften their opposition in the eyes of Senator Schumer.

On December 10, 2018, Senate Democrats named Manchin as the ranking member on the Senate Energy and Natural Resources Committee. The following day, Manchin issued a statement acknowledging West Virginia's role as a leading energy producer and major contributor to advanced energy technologies, and expressed his intent "to ensure this progress is continued." His statement went on to say: "[T]he problems facing our country are serious, and I am committed to working with my colleagues on both sides of the aisle to find common sense solutions for long-term comprehensive energy policy that incorporates an all-of-the-above strategy and ensures our state and our nation are leaders in the energy future."[68]

[64]   Lorraine Chow, *"Conceivably the Worst": Groups, Lawmakers Blast Confirmation of Climate Denier to FERC*, DeSmog (Dec. 8, 2018), https://www.desmogblog.com/2018/12/08/conceivably-worst-bernard-mcnamee-confirmation-climate-denier-ferc.

[65]   Gavin Bade, *FERC Nominee McNamee Slams Renewables, Green Groups in Feb. Video*, Utility Dive (Nov. 20, 2018), https://www.utilitydive.com/news/ferc-nominee-mcnamee-slams-renewables-green-groups-in-feb-video/542702/.

[66]   Charles P. Pierce, *Meeting the Climate Challenge Requires Transforming Our Society. Are We Capable of That?*, Esquire (Dec. 6, 2018), https://www.esquire.com/news-politics/politics/a25425297/climate-change-trump-administration-green-new-deal/.

[67]   Sheryl Gay Stolberg, *Joe Manchin Faces Liberal Opposition in Bid to Be Energy Panel's Top Democrat*, N.Y. Times (Dec. 6, 2018), https://www.nytimes.com/2018/12/06/us/politics/joe-manchin-energy-committee.html.

[68]   Anthony Adragna, *Coal-Friendly Manchin Becomes Top Democrat on Senate Energy Committee*, Politico (Dec. 11, 2018), https://www.politico.com/story/2018/12/11/manchin-senate-energy-natural-resources-committee-1058526.

This was followed shortly thereafter by a March 2019 op-ed piece in *The Washington Post*, coauthored with Senator Lisa Murkowski (Republican, Alaska), who was then chairman of the Senate Energy and Natural Resources Committee. The senators joined in the statement that "[t]here is no question that climate change is real or that human activities are driving much of it," acknowledging that "[w]e are seeing the impacts in our home states."[69] Manchin cited the unprecedented flooding that occurred in West Virginia during the summer of 2016, which killed twenty-three residents and inflicted widespread damage across the state. According to the senators, "resource development and environmental stewardship must move in tandem," and they expressed their commitment "to putting forward bipartisan solutions to help address climate change."[70]

A few months later, in June 2019, Manchin joined Murkowski and three other senators on an international trip touring the Arctic – six countries in five days – that included an up-close look at the impact of climate change on Arctic communities. Accompanying Murkowski and Manchin on the trip were Sheldon Whitehouse (Democrat, Rhode Island), John Barasso (Republican, Wyoming) – who was chair of the Environment and Public Works Committee at the time – and Maria Cantwell (Democrat, Washington). In an appearance on *CBS's* Face the Nation the following weekend, Manchin acknowledged that "climate change is real – I saw it firsthand. I read about it before and heard and listened to all the scientists. So, we as humans have a responsibility to do something."[71] At the same time, Manchin said he could not support elimination of fossil fuel use "because that's not practical. You're not going to stop the rest of the sovereign countries of the world from using the energy in their backyard. But we can use it much cleaner."[72]

"ONE DEGREE OF SEPARATION" IN WEST VIRGINIA AND THE MISSING MBA DEGREE

In West Virginia, there is a proverb that says that everything is political except politics, and that is personal. It's a tiny state, with just two major universities, just one major law school and where many of us grow up in the same small towns or counties, so there ends up being just one degree of separation between people involved in business and politics and whatever else.

Conni Gratop Lewis, retired lobbyist for nonprofit groups[73]

[69] Lisa Murkowski & Joe Manchin, *It's Time to Act on Climate Change – Responsibly*, WASHINGTON POST (Mar. 8, 2019), https://www.washingtonpost.com/opinions/lisa-murkowski-and-joe-manchin-its-time-to-act-on-climate-change–responsibly/2019/03/08/2c4025f2-41d1-11e9-922c-64d6b7840b82_story.html.
[70] *Id.*
[71] Nick Sobczyk & Geof Koss, *Senators Get Heavy Dose of Climate on Trip North*, E&E DAILY (June 5, 2019), https://www.eenews.net/stories/1060483739.
[72] *Id.*
[73] Ian Urbina, *University Investigates Whether Governor's Daughter Earned Degree*, N.Y. TIMES (Jan. 22, 2008), https://www.nytimes.com/2008/01/22/us/22heather.html?searchResultPosition=12.

No story better illustrates this "proverb" than the case of Heather Bresch – the daughter of Senator Manchin – and the missing Executive MBA degree. On October 2, 2007, Ms. Bresch was promoted to chief operating officer of Mylan, a title that also carried with it a $500,000 annual salary.[74] Her chief responsibilities at the time? Leading the effort at Mylan to integrate German-based Merck KGaA following its acquisition by Mylan for $6.8 billion, transforming the latter into the world's third-largest generic drug company. At the time of the acquisition, Wall Street had raised concerns about whether Mylan had the management talent needed to make the acquisition successful. In announcing Bresch's promotion to chief operating officer – which happened the same day as the closing of the Merck acquisition – Mylan's press release (which was included in documents filed with the Securities and Exchange Commission) mentioned her MBA from WVU. That, in turn, prompted a routine inquiry on October 11 from the *Pittsburgh Post-Gazette* to confirm Bresch's academic credentials at WVU.

The first answer? WVU initially told the *Post-Gazette* that Bresch did not have an MBA. Eleven days later, however – after Bresch insisted that she was awarded the degree in December 1998 – WVU reversed its answer and, according to an October 22 letter from Dean R. Stephen Sears of the College of Business and Economics, she did complete all the course requirements for the Executive MBA. The letter from Sears instructed the admissions and records office to award Ms. Bresch the degree retroactively, by adding six classes to her record and awarding grades for two other classes for which she had received "incompletes," thereby giving her twenty-two additional credits to achieve the necessary forty-eight credits for the degree.

While this may have been the desired answer, it turned out to be the wrong one. Following a three-month long investigation, which produced a ninety-five-page report in April 2008, the scandal resulted in the stripping of the never-awarded MBA degree and the departure not only of Sears, but also Provost and Vice President for Academic Affairs Gerald E. Lang and WVU President Mike Garrison. The report concluded that "[a]n unnecessary rush to judgment, spurred in some measure by an understandable desire to protect a valued alumna and to respond to media pressure, produced a flawed and erroneous result."[75]

The scandal also produced a lot of unwanted national attention for the Mountain State that, according to the *New York Times*, cast a "shadow of cronyism" over the state's flagship university and illustrated the challenges of "untangling the mess" given "the tight web of personal ties between state political leaders and campus administrators and between the people involved in the controversy and those investigating it."[76]

74   Patricia Sabatini & Len Boselovic, *MBA Mystery in Morgantown*, Pittsburgh Post-Gazette (Dec. 21, 2007), https://www.post-gazette.com/business/businessnews/2007/12/21/MBA-mystery-in-Morgantown/stories/200712210224.

75   Ian Urbina, *Criticism for Degree to Governor's Daughter*, N.Y. Times (Apr. 25, 2008), https://www.nytimes.com/2008/04/25/education/25west.html?searchResultPosition=7.

76   *Id.*

By the time the dust settled and the investigative reports were digested, the "mess" included a tangle of personal ties that implicated numerous WVU and state leaders, including Joe Manchin, who was governor at the time the degree was supposedly earned. The notable strands of the web as the story developed are as follows:

- Mike Garrison – the WVU president whose office confirmed to the *Pittsburgh Post-Gazette* in October 2007 that Bresch indeed received her MBA ten years earlier – is frequently identified as a longtime friend of the Manchin family. He graduated from Fairmont West High School with Bresch in 1987 and they attended WVU at the same time. Garrison was a consultant and lobbyist for Mylan, and also served as chief of staff for West Virginia Governor Bob Wise. When Manchin was elected governor in 2008, Garrison served on the governor's transition team, along with Milan Puskar – the founder of Mylan and a leading donor to WVU – and other members of WVU's board of governors. At the time Garrison was being considered for WVU president in 2007, Puskar wrote a letter to the WVU search committee supporting his candidacy, citing the need for closer ties between Mylan and WVU.
- Heather Bresch's career at Mylan began shortly after Manchin, then a state senator, ran into Puskar at a WVU basketball game.[77] After getting her degree from WVU in 1991, Bresch started out at Mylan in 1992 as a data entry clerk.[78]
- Puskar, who passed away in 2011, made regular and generous contributions to WVU over the years, including $20 million in 2003, the largest gift to WVU at the time. The football stadium where the Mountaineers play is Milan Puskar Stadium. Puskar was also a major contributor to Manchin's campaigns for governor in 2004 and 2008. Coincidentally (or not), at the time Dean R. Stephen Sears of the College of Business and Economics wrote his instructions in 2007 to award Bresch her MBA degree, the position he occupied had been endowed by a $1.5 million gift from Puskar.[79]

One reporter referred to the circumstances as a "jaw-dropping symbiosis, taking cronyism almost to the nth degree, between the pharma giant Mylan, one of West Virginia's foremost political families, and its leading state university."[80] Then Governor Manchin issued the following statement in response to the WVU investigative report: "All I can hope for as a parent is that WVU's leaders will correct whatever problems that led to this situation so that no other student will have to go through this kind of ordeal in the future."[81]

Unfortunately, it would not be the last time that Manchin's daughter was featured in the national headlines. In 2016, Mylan came under fire for a "stratospheric" price

---

[77] Surin, *supra* note 5.
[78] Sabatini & Boselovic, *supra* note 74.
[79] *Id.*
[80] Kenneth Surin, *The Neoliberal Stranglehold on the American Public University*, COUNTERPUNCH (Jan. 16, 2017), https://www.counterpunch.org/2017/01/16/the-neoliberal-stranglehold-on-the-american-pub lic-university/.
[81] Urbina, *supra* note 73.

increase of its EpiPen, a handheld device – acquired by Mylan in 2007 through its acquisition of Merck – that treats life-threatening allergic reactions by automatically injecting a dose of epinephrine. Under Mylan, the wholesale price of an EpiPen increased from $56.64 in 2007 to $317.82 in 2015, a price hike of 461 percent.[82] (At the time, experts determined that the cost of producing an EpiPen was about $30.) In news stories about the controversy, the increase in the cost of an EpiPen was often compared with the rise in total compensation that Mylan paid to Bresch over the same period – an increase of 671 percent, from $2,453,456 in 2007 to $18,931,068 in 2015, according to reports from *NBC News*.[83] Bresch ended up testifying about the controversy regarding the price increase to the House of Representatives Oversight and Government Reform Committee in September 2016. Apart from the controversy regarding the price increase, Mylan later paid $465 million in settlement with the US Department of Justice in August 2017 to address allegations that it overcharged the US government by misclassifying the EpiPen as a generic rather than a branded product.[84]

In July 2019, Bresch announced her retirement from Mylan, on the heels of Mylan's merger with Upjohn, Pfizer Inc.'s off-patent branded and generic medicines business. As a result of the deal, she managed to walk away with nearly three times the $13.3 million in salary and bonuses that she received in 2018; her severance package included $18.6 million in cash (consisting of three times her $1.3 million base salary plus the highest bonus she had been paid) and vested benefits of $19 million, a total of $37.5 million.[85] As it turns out, a foreseeable outcome of the merger was the closure of the Mylan facility in Morgantown – it was "swiftly targeted" for closure a month after the November 2020 merger between Mylan and Upjohn by the resulting entity, Viatris – which resulted in the layoff of over 1,400 workers represented by the steelworkers union on July 31, 2021.[86] When Viatris announced plans to close the Morgantown plant, it told the staff it would move most manufacturing to India, and some to Australia, according to a plant employee.[87] In an interview with *Vanity Fair*, Mike Puskar's daughter, Johanna Puskar, said: "My father spent his whole life to make that company successful,

[82] Ben Popken, *Mylan CEO's Pay Rose over 600 Percent as EpiPen Price Rose 400 Percent*, NBC NEWS (Aug. 23, 2016), https://www.nbcnews.com/business/consumer/mylan-execs-gave-themselves-raises-they-hiked-epipen-prices-n636591.
[83] *Id.*
[84] *Mylan Finalizes $465 Million EpiPen Settlement with Justice Department*, CNBC (Aug. 17, 2017), https://www.cnbc.com/2017/08/17/mylan-finalizes-465-million-epipen-settlement-with-justice-department.html.
[85] Tim Grant, *Top Mylan Executives Could Share $93 Million Payout from Sale*, PITTSBURGH POST-GAZETTE (July 27, 2019), https://www.post-gazette.com/business/career-workplace/2019/07/29/Top-Mylan-executives-will-share-93-million-payout-from-sale/stories/201907290078.
[86] Katherine Eban, *"We Can't Reach Him": Joe Manchin Is Ghosting the West Virginia Union Workers Whose Jobs His Daughter Helped Outsource*, VANITY FAIR (July 23, 2021), https://www.vanityfair.com/news/2021/07/joe-manchin-is-ghosting-the-west-virginia-union-workers.
[87] *Id.*

and it took them less than 10 years to destroy it. They came and they robbed it blind till there was nothing left."[88]

AT THE END OF THE DAY, STILL A COAL GUY PUTTING THE COAL INDUSTRY FIRST

Manchin has certainly reveled in his newfound role as the point person on energy – as well as on broader spending issues in the shaping of a budget reconciliation package – in the early months of the Biden administration. And it's fair to say that the White House has been bending over backward to court Manchin to gain his support for President Biden's clean energy proposals. As an example, Manchin's wife, Gayle, was appointed by President Biden as cochair of the Appalachian Regional Commission (ARC), and becoming the first ARC federal cochair from West Virginia.[89] ARC is a federal–state partnership established by Congress in 1965 and, among other things, awards discretionary POWER (Partnerships for Opportunity and Workforce and Economic Revitalization) Grants throughout Appalachia for improvement of broadband and other critical infrastructure, entrepreneurial support, and training of displaced workers. During the four years preceding 2019, West Virginia received approximately $83 million in annual funding from ARC.

Another key appointment attributable to Manchin's influence at the White House is Dr. Brian Anderson, who was tapped by Biden in April 2021 to head up the Interagency Working Group (IWG) on Coal and Power Plant Communities and Economic Revitalization. As discussed further in Chapter 12, the IWG comprises several cabinet-level officials charged with coordinating the identification and delivery of federal resources to "revitalize the economies of coal, oil and gas, and power plant communities" and "assess opportunities to ensure benefits and protections for coal and power plant workers."[90] Five of the twenty-five geographic areas identified by the IWG as "hard-hit by past coal mine and plant closures and vulnerable to more closures" and designated as "Energy Communities" for investment and engagement are located in West Virginia.[91] Anderson is probably better known as Manchin's point person on federal research and development spending with a fossil fuel focus; as the former head of the National Energy Technology Laboratory (NETL) in Pittsburgh and Morgantown, he has been a consistent proponent of clean coal technology development of the Appalachian

---

[88] *Id.*

[89] Jeff Jenkins, *Biden Nominates Gayle Manchin to Run Appalachian Regional Commission*, METRONEWS (Mar. 26, 2021), https://wvmetronews.com/2021/03/26/biden-nominates-gayle-manchin-to-run-appalachian-regional-commission/.

[90] Exec. Order No. 14,008, *Tackling the Climate Crisis at Home and Abroad*, January 27, 2021, 86 FR 7619, https://www.federalregister.gov/documents/2021/02/01/2021-02177/tackling-the-climate-crisis-at-home-and-abroad.

[91] Interagency Working Group on Coal and Power Plant Communities and Economic Revitalization, *Initial Report to the President on Empowering Workers Through Revitalizing Energy Communities* (April 2021), https://netl.doe.gov/sites/default/files/2021-04/Initial%20Report%20on%20Energy%20Communities_Apr2021.pdf.

Storage and Trading Hub – "we need to build CO_2 pipelines" to support carbon capture and sequestration (CCS) (discussed in Chapter 2) – and converting coal into high-value materials like carbon fibers and graphene and creating "additional opportunities and additional industries with value added from coal."[92]

The White House courtship of Manchin has featured the dispatch of two cabinet secretaries to West Virginia: Secretary of Energy Jennifer Granholm in June 2021 and Labor Secretary Marty Walsh in August 2021. With Manchin as "tour director," an essential stop for each in their tour of the state was, of course, an underground coal mine. While Granholm may have been in West Virginia to "tout clean energy" and a future focused on renewable energy,[93] Manchin apparently wanted to redirect her attention to West Virginia's distant past. During Walsh's visit to a coal mine two months later, the Labor Secretary focused on whether all the safety protocols were in place, while Manchin took the occasion to proclaim that "the coal industry will be saved because it has to be."[94]

Manchin was part of the bipartisan group of ten senators that took the lead in crafting the $1.2 trillion bipartisan infrastructure package that passed the US Senate in May 2021.[95] West Virginia fared pretty well in some of the particular elements of the bill, such as the inclusion of $11.3 billion to reclaim abandoned mine lands (AML) as well as $4.5 billion to cap abandoned oil and gas wells. As discussed in Chapter 11, West Virginia is the number two state in the nation with respect to acres of unreclaimed mine land – 173,797 acres, or 20.4 percent of the total nationwide.[96] The costs of repairing the unreclaimed mine land in West Virginia is estimated to be slightly over $5 billion, or 24.4 percent of the national total.[97] And one third of the abandoned and unplugged wells in the nation are located within Appalachia, with West Virginia having the second highest number of such wells in the region. Given the disproportionate benefit that West Virginia would receive from a massive federal effort to reclaim AML and plug oil and gas wells, it is difficult to identify a program from the federal government that would be a better fit with West Virginia's infrastructure needs. The $1.2 trillion bipartisan infrastructure measure passed by the US Senate also includes $12 billion for Manchin's personal favorite – CCS – where

[92] James Marshall, *Q&A: Biden's Pick to Lead Coal Town Renewal on What's Next*, Greenwire (Aug. 5, 2021), https://www.eenews.net/articles/qa-bidens-pick-to-lead-coal-town-renewal-on-whats-next/.

[93] John Raby, *Granholm Joins Manchin in West Virginia to Tout Clean Energy*, AP (June 3, 2021), https://apnews.com/article/west-virginia-voting-rights-business-environment-and-nature-acd644d6d380baa87e9cff727fbf974f.

[94] Joselyn King, *U.S. Labor Secretary Marty Walsh Tours West Virginia Mine with Sen. Joe Manchin*, WV News (Aug. 22, 2021), https://www.wvnews.com/news/wvnews/u-s-labor-secretary-marty-walsh-tours-west-virginia-mine-with-sen-joe-manchin/article_88981564-01df-11ec-86c9-436efe4b776e.html.

[95] Kelsey Snell, *The Senate Approves the $1 Trillion Bipartisan Infrastructure Bill in a Historic Vote*, NPR (Aug. 10, 2021) https://www.npr.org/2021/08/10/1026081880/senate-passes-bipartisan-infrastructure-bill.

[96] Eric Dixon, Repairing the Damage: Cleaning Up the Land, Air, and Water Damaged by the Coal Industry Before 1977 11 (Apr. 2021), https://ohiorivervalleyinstitute.org/wp-content/uploads/2021/04/AML-Report-Dixon-ORVI-V1.1-4.pdf.

[97] *Id.*

Manchin continues to claim that "we can get there, we're close" to this game-changing technology that will produce a "valued use for the carbon, and make it into solid products to where we can use it for value-added ... that'd be great."[98]

Compounding the disproportionate benefit that West Virginia would receive from the $11.3 billion for AML reclamation is the personal benefit that Joe Manchin's family coal brokerage business, Enersystems, may derive from it, as noted earlier in this chapter. AML projects typically involve the removal of piles of "gob," and can be expected to produce a spike in Enersystems' business as AmBit and other companies take up new mine reclamation projects in West Virginia.[99]

Apart from the bipartisan infrastructure proposal, the White House proposed a $3.5 trillion spending plan – which evolved into the "Build Back Better" proposal – that would have been enacted through the budget reconciliation process. This measure contained the Biden administration's primary initiatives to address climate change and included, among other things, tax incentives for clean energy and electric vehicles, incentives for electric utilities to achieve carbon reductions in their generating portfolio – commonly referred to as a "clean electricity standard" – and funding for energy-efficient building weatherization and electrification projects. The Senate Energy and Natural Resources Committee was the primary architect of the "clean electricity" mechanism, which was passed by the House of Representatives Energy Committee as the Clean Electricity Performance Program, or CEPP. Manchin's statements regarding the Biden administration's Build Back Better proposal, and the CEPP in particular, have been particularly vexing for the White House and the more progressive members of the US Senate seeking to tackle climate change robustly.

Under the CEPP passed by the House Energy Committee, every utility would have been encouraged to supply an increasing amount of electricity each year from qualified low-carbon resources such as nuclear, hydropower, wind, solar, and geothermal, through a system of performance payments. The CEPP had a $150 billion price tag that would fund a $150 per MWh payment for utilities that increase their annual clean electricity by 4 percent year-over-year above 1.5 percent of the previous year's target. The CEPP would also include a $40 per MWh penalty for utilities that miss their annual target. Importantly for the coal-reliant utilities in West Virginia, every utility would start from where they currently are and would not need to meet the same overall level of clean electricity deployment. Rather than penalizing utilities that rely more heavily on fossil fuels, the goal of the CEPP was to have a national average of 80 percent clean electricity by 2031.

Manchin expressed early opposition to the CEPP, saying, "What's the urgency?" On *CNN's* State of the Union program on September 12, 2021, Manchin stated: "The

[98] Joe Manchin, *Face the Nation*, CBS NEWS (Aug. 1, 2021). https://www.cbsnews.com/news/transcript-senator-joe-manchin-face-the-nation-08-01-2021/.

[99] Donald Shaw, *Manchin Poised to Profit from Mine Reclamation Funding He Championed*, SLUDGE (Sept. 22, 2021), https://readsludge.com/2021/09/22/manchin-poised-to-profit-from-mine-reclamation-funding-he-championed/.

transition is happening. Now they're wanting to pay companies to do what they're already doing. Makes no sense to me at all for us to take billions of dollars and pay utilities for what they're going to do as the market transitions."[100] The problem, of course, is that the transition is not happening fast enough, particularly in West Virginia. So who has Manchin's ear on how fast the electric industry can move? The answer is Nick Akins, president and CEO of American Electric Power (AEP), with whom Manchin has a "long working relationship."[101] Akins is on the record as urging Manchin to slow the pace at which electric utilities are required to migrate from dirty to clean fuels. AEP, of course, relies on coal from West Virginia to fuel its coal-fired power plants, and its subsidiaries own three coal plants in West Virginia – the Mitchell plant, owned by Wheeling Power, and the Amos and Mountaineer plants, owned by Appalachian Power. As discussed in Chapter 10, in October 2021 AEP obtained approval from the West Virginia PSC to charge West Virginians nearly a half a billion dollars to keep these three coal plants open through 2040. Even though at the corporate level AEP has jumped on the "zero-carbon" bandwagon and committed to achieving an 80 percent reduction in emissions from 2000 levels by 2030, AEP remains on the coal-dependent path in West Virginia for the next two decades. And, as discussed in Chapter 4, AEP is failing miserably at reducing emissions at a pace consistent with its expressed corporate goal. With Akins at the helm, AEP is using its influence with Manchin to have the rest of the United States join West Virginia's refusal to embrace clean energy.

With respect to the broader Build Back Better proposal, Manchin stated that he's "very, very disturbed" by provisions he believes would eliminate fossil fuels.[102] This has been another of Manchin's consistent themes as he holds forth on energy policy from his newfound perch as point person on climate: We are going to address climate change through "innovation, not elimination." In a June 2021 interview with AEP's Nick Akins at the Edison Electric Institute's annual conference, Manchin took aim at "some of our environmental friends" and claimed that US coal-fired power plants were being unfairly singled out by environmentalists.[103] Rather than focusing on the elimination of forms of energy, said Manchin, we need to spend more money on CCS research and development. He repeated the "innovation, not elimination" theme in an appearance on *CBS News'* Face the Nation on August 1, 2021.

[100] Nick Sobczyk, Jeremy Dillon, & Hannah Northey, *6 Things to Watch as Panel Votes on Historic Environment Bill*, E&E DAILY (Sept.13, 2021), https://www.eenews.net/articles/6-things-to-watch-as-panel-votes-on-historic-environment-bill/.

[101] Coral Davenport, *This Powerful Democrat Linked to Fossil Fuels Will Craft the U.S. Climate Plan*, N. Y. TIMES (Sept. 19, 2021), https://www.nytimes.com/2021/09/19/climate/manchin-climate-biden.html.

[102] Manu Raju, *Joe Manchin Says He's "Very, Very" Disturbed About Reconciliation Proposals on Climate Change*, CNN (July 15, 2021), https://www.cnn.com/2021/07/14/politics/joe-manchin-reconciliation-climate-change/index.html.

[103] Scott Van Voorhis, *Manchin Defends Coal-Fired Plants, Expresses Concern over "Aggressive" Biden Climate Goals*, UTILITY DIVE (June 14, 2021), https://www.utilitydive.com/news/manchin-defends-coal-fired-plants-expresses-concern-over-aggressive-bide/601707/.

Manchin's "innovation, not elimination" narrative makes no sense, however. First, the elimination of coal as a major source of electricity generation in the United States had very little to do with the "environmentalists" that Manchin loves to attack. As discussed in Chapter 2, since the "shale gas revolution" began over a decade ago, cheap and plentiful natural gas has resulted in the closure of hundreds of coal-fired plants across the United States, as coal ceased to be a cost-effective fuel for the generation of electricity in competitive energy markets. More recently, electric utilities are finding that building new wind and solar facilities is a cheaper path than running existing coal plants (as described in Chapter 3). Manchin's blaming the demise of the coal industry on environmentalists is reminiscent of the tiresome and unproductive "war on coal" discussed in Chapter 5. A 2017 study from the Columbia Center on Global Energy Policy confirmed that environmental regulations played a very small part – about 3.5 percent – in contributing to the decline of the coal industry.[104]

Second, there is no breakthrough "clean coal" technology on the horizon that is going to make innovation the answer to achieving the necessary carbon emissions from coal plants. As simply stated by the Institute for Energy Economics and Financial Analysis in a piece published in 2019, "coal is dirty and any effort to make it 'clean' raises costs and reduces operational efficiency."[105] In other words, coal is already "out of the money" in US electricity markets – no electric utility or power plant developer would seriously consider building a new coal plant given the enormous price advantage of natural gas, wind, and solar – and making the additional investment in clean coal technology by capturing the carbon emissions, transporting them in pipelines, and sequestering them underground in suitable geologic formations does not improve the economics. Rather, it adds hundreds of millions of dollars of additional cost for each plant and diminishes the electrical output due to the parasitic nature of the additional carbon capturing equipment. Apart from the undisputed and compelling economic case against "clean coal," the technology simply does not exist today, and neither the United States nor any other nation is "very close" to deploying it commercially, notwithstanding Senator Manchin's fanciful claims to the contrary. The coal industry has been claiming since the beginning of the twenty-first century that clean coal technology is "just around the corner," but that corner never seems to come into view.

In the meantime, Manchin's opposition to the Build Back Better proposal and rejection of the CEPP successfully thwarted the delivery of what could have been a tremendous windfall to West Virginia in the form of federal spending that would

[104] Trevor Houser, Jason Bordoff, & Peter Marsters, *Can Coal Make a Comeback?* COLUMBIA/SIPA CENTER ON GLOBAL ENERGY POLICY (April 2017), https://energypolicy.columbia.edu/sites/default/files/Center%20on%20Global%20Energy%20Policy%20Can%20Coal%20Make%20a%20Comeback%20April%202017.pdf.

[105] Melissa Brown & Ghee Peh, IEEFA op ed, *China's "Clean" Coal Technology Dream Describes a Problem, Not a Solution*, INSTITUTE FOR ENERGY ECONOMICS AND FINANCIAL ANALYSIS (Nov. 12, 2019), https://ieefa.org/chinas-clean-coal-technology-dream-describes-a-problem-not-a-solution/.

have jump-started a clean energy industry and produced thousands of jobs for West Virginians. During Energy Secretary Granholm's September 2021 visit to the Mountain State, she claimed that West Virginia has the potential to be the "poster child" of the nation's transition toward cleaner, greener energy.[106] Citing a study carried out by the Center for Energy and Sustainable Development at the WVU College of Law,[107] Granholm claimed that getting to 80 percent of emission-free power in West Virginia would spur nearly $21 billion in new investment, put $172 million more every year into the pockets of West Virginians, and create tens of thousands of new jobs. The CEPP alone would have produced an estimated $18 billion of new clean energy investment in West Virginia by 2030, providing new tax revenue for local economic development that bolsters schools, property values, and local services.[108]

This is not a deal that Robert Bryd – in whose former seat Manchin sits – would walk away from. Yet Manchin was inexplicably determined to derail the measures that would likely confer more benefits on West Virginia than on any other state in the nation. Another casualty of the failure of the budget reconciliation package was an extension beyond 2021 for the expanded child tax credit (CTC) payments – originally enacted as part of the Biden administration's American Rescue Plan in March 2021 – which proved to be crucial for families in West Virginia. Almost two-thirds of CTC recipients in West Virginia used the money for food or clothing from July to October 2021, and nearly half used all or part of the money for housing.[109] In opposing inclusion of the measure in the budget reconciliation package, Manchin privately raised concerns in conversations with fellow Democratic senators that parents would use their CTC payments to buy drugs.[110]

Some, however, have observed that Manchin's motivations may not be so inexplicable. A September 2021 column by Maureen Dowd in the *New York Times* cited an article in the *Intercept* that concluded: "Manchin's claim that climate pollution would be worsened by the elimination of fossil fuels – or by the resolution's actual,

[106] Charles Young, *U.S. Energy Secretary Granholm: West Virginia Can Be "Poster Child" for Green Energy Transition*, WV STATE JOURNAL (Sept. 20, 2021), https://www.wvnews.com/statejournal/news/u-s-energy-secretary-granholm-west-virginia-can-be-posterchild-for-green-energy-transition/article_a5c1d6de-162a-11ec-80e5-2fbea9215bc5.html.

[107] *West Virginia's Energy Future: Built Back Better*, CENTER FOR ENERGY AND SUSTAINABLE DEVELOPMENT (August 2021), https://energy.law.wvu.edu/files/d/3ba79f26-3d25-4c5e-a016-b7966c092ff7/wvef-built-back-better-2021.pdf.

[108] James M. Van Nostrand, *Manchin Could Deliver Big Benefits for Working Families by Supporting This One Budget Provision*, WV STATE JOURNAL (Sept. 19, 2021), https://www.wvnews.com/statejournal/opinion/manchin-could-deliver-big-benefits-for-working-families-by-supporting-this-one-budget-provision/article_ceedf936-14f2-11ec-abb9-bba47e28f4f2.html.

[109] Christian Weller, *Child Tax Credit Is Crucial Lifeline for Families, Especially in West Virginia*, FORBES (Dec. 21, 2021), https://www.forbes.com/sites/christianweller/2021/12/21/child-tax-credit-is-crucial-lifeline-for-families-especially-in-west-virginia/?sh=56763af37832.

[110] Rebecca Shabad et al., *Manchin Privately Raised Concerns that Parents Would Use Child Tax Credit Checks on Drugs*, NBC NEWS (Dec. 20, 2021), https://www.nbcnews.com/politics/congress/manchin-privately-raised-concerns-parents-would-use-child-tax-credit-n1286321s.

more incremental climate provisions – is highly dubious, if not outright false."[111] According to the *Intercept*, "[w]hat would be unquestionably impacted ... is Manchin's personal wealth."[112] Dowd's column observed that Manchin "should be looking for ways to get West Virginia in touch with reality rather than living in the past."[113] Days later, in a column in the *New York Times* titled "Dear Joe Manchin: Coal Isn't Your State's Future," Paul Krugman, a Nobel laureate in economics, noted the tension between "a desire to do the right thing" and Manchin's "being influenced by lobbyists and his personal financial interests":

> What I do know, and you should, too, is that if Manchin torpedoes Biden – and the planet – on climate policy, it won't be because he's serving the interests of his constituents.
>
> [C]oal is West Virginia's past, not its present, and definitely not its future. .... [I]f Joe Manchin wants to actually serve the people of West Virginia, as opposed to pandering to their nostalgia, he'll support Biden's progressive agenda – including his climate agenda.
>
> [While] regions have every right to honor their history ... politicians should serve their constituents' real interests, not condescend to them by peddling impossible visions of restoring past glories.[114]

Apart from Manchin's potential negative influence over national climate policy, there is the lost opportunity to deliver much-needed assistance from the federal government to West Virginia. In an August 2021 column in the CHARLESTON GAZETTE-*Mail*, Lee Wolverton, Vice President of News and Executive Editor of HD Media (the owner of the *Gazette-Mail*), examined Youngstown, Ohio, and the failure of Jim Traficant, a congressman of seventeen years who represented Youngstown and Mahoning County, to do "a damn thing that truly mattered" during his years in Congress. Rather, according to Wolverton, "Traficant served himself first, foremost and always." Wolverton made the case that West Virginia desperately needs to avoid the same fate:

> Now, the jobs in the mines like the jobs in the mills are vanishing. A coal baron [Jim Justice] sits at the head of West Virginia government and others holding higher office here have their ties and their interests. Are those interests their own or West Virginia's? Whom do they serve?
>
> Don't be fooled by empty platitudes, bogus boasts or declarations from the bottom of someone's heart. The proof is in the damn jobs. The proof is in an economy lifted from the floor. The proof is in the full-time commitment to the hard

---

[111] Maureen Dowd, *Drowning Our Future in the Past*, N.Y. TIMES (Sept. 4, 2021), https://www.nytimes.com/2021/09/04/opinion/drowning-our-future-in-the-past.html.

[112] Daniel Boguslaw, *Joe Manchin's Dirty Empire*, THE INTERCEPT (Sept. 3, 2021), https://theintercept.com/2021/09/03/joe-manchin-coal-fossil-fuels-pollution/.

[113] Dowd, *supra* note 111.

[114] Paul Krugman, *Dear Joe Manchin: Coal Isn't Your State's Future*, N.Y. TIMES (Sept. 20, 2021), https://www.nytimes.com/2021/09/20/opinion/joe-manchin-coal-climate-biden.html.

work of breathing life into a battered state. The proof is in parlaying the role of Washington's primary power broker into putting West Virginians back to work.

If those who hold power now, those who've become so rich as the state has become so poor, can't provide that proof by the time polls open again, their names should be forgotten in favor of others committed to serving the state and her people first. West Virginia will find no better fate than Youngstown so long as her people allow the rot in the system to remain."[115]

Measured by the standard that Wolverton defines, it is very doubtful that Manchin will pass it. At the end of the day, he is still a coal guy who will put the interests of the coal industry – and perhaps his own financial interests – above serving West Virginians. And that's a real shame.

[115] Lee Wolverton, *Avoiding Youngstown's Fate*, CHARLESTON GAZETTE-MAIL (Aug. 13, 2021), https://www.wvgazettemail.com/opinion/columnists/lee-wolverton-avoiding-youngstowns-fate-opinion/article_db8b8879-8d6c-556a-a8e0-58188addddao.html?fbclid=IwAR1hMop4fAojrfc-dJqQBi6ZZI6S7-AsqGoVM_OiE5nYJZ_c756-guijXsQ#utm_campaign=blox&utm_source= facebook&utm_medium=social.

8

The Failure of the Public Service Commission to Serve the Public

Two energy policies in particular contributed to the disastrous results for ratepayers that became apparent at the end of "the lost decade." First, there was the failure of energy utilities during most of that period to engage in long-term planning known as "least cost planning" or "integrated resource planning." Integrated resource planning is a rigorous process that examines the full range of options – including both supply-side (generating resources) and demand-side (energy efficiency and conservation) – available to a utility to meet its resource needs at the lowest reasonable cost to its customers. Had integrated resource planning been in place prior to the "lost decade," the risk associated with nearly exclusive reliance on coal-fired generation would have been apparent, and the massive rate increases that followed when coal prices soared could have been avoided. Moreover, the opportunity to diversify into natural gas-fired generation as the shale gas revolution was unfolding could have been thoroughly explored.

Second, energy utilities failed to offer their customers much in the way of energy efficiency and other "demand-side" programs.[1] These programs, which reward customers for buying energy-efficient appliances or installing insulation, for example, not only provide them with the tools to enable them to control their energy costs; in most situations, energy efficiency is a lower-cost solution than additional investment by utilities in power plants. Before examining these policies in more detail, however, it is worth describing the role of one of the most powerful agencies in state government that almost no one has heard of: the West Virginia Public Service Commission (PSC).

THE WEST VIRGINIA PUBLIC SERVICE COMMISSION

The PSC is charged with regulating the rates and practices of all the investor-owned utilities in a state which, in addition to electricity and natural gas, include

[1] Energy efficiency is often referred to as a "demand-side" resource; rather than focusing on supplying additional electricity by building more generating plants (the "supply-side" solution) to meet the loads placed on the grid by utility customers, demand-side programs focus on reducing customers' energy usage.

telecommunications, water, and sewerage. The PSC in West Virginia is composed of three commissioners, appointed by the governor and subject to confirmation by the state senate. Commissioners serve six-year terms and, by statute, no more than two commissioners can be from the same political party. The West Virginia statute imposes an additional requirement that one of the commissioners must be a lawyer with not less than ten years' actual work experience in the legal profession as a member of a state bar.

The PSC is an independent agency, in that the commissioners have fixed terms, and can be removed before the end of their terms only for incompetency, neglect of duty, gross immorality, or malfeasance. The six-year terms are "staggered," such that every two years, one of the three commissioners' terms will expire. Thus, the ability of the governor to implement sweeping changes at the agency is very limited; he or she has the authority to appoint one of the three commissioners to serve as chairman, to serve at the governor's "will and pleasure," but can appoint new commissioners to the agency only upon expiration of an existing commissioner's term. The chairman serves as the chief administrative officer of the agency.

This structure – with three or five commissioners, staggered terms, and a limitation on the number of commissioners from the same party – is common across the utility regulatory commissions in the United States; many states adopted the same "suite" of laws in the early twentieth century to govern the regulation of retail utilities. The West Virginia PSC, for its part, was created by the legislature in 1913. The reason for creating state PSCs or public utility commissions (PUCs) as independent agencies is due largely to the large capital investment that is necessary to create and operate a utility, which in turn requires some stability and predictability in its regulation. If a governor could replace all of the commissioners upon election, for example, that would create a level of uncertainty that may make it difficult for utilities to raise the large amounts of capital necessary to provide safe, adequate, and reliable utility service. Use of staggered terms, with the ability to remove a commissioner only for "cause," creates the continuity and consistency in regulatory policies that helps allow utilities to raise capital to support their operations.

The West Virginia PSC is charged with setting "just and reasonable" rates, which is a very broad grant of authority. It gives the PSC considerable discretion in deciding what level of utility rates is "reasonable" and, in turn, empowers the PSC with considerable oversight authority over the utilities it regulates and the practices and policies followed by the utilities in providing utility service. As a practical matter, the power afforded to the PSC derives from the very deferential standard of review that would be applied by a reviewing court in the event a decision from the PSC were appealed: The process of setting rates is very complex and requires specialized expertise, and reviewing courts are reluctant to engage in second-guessing particular decisions made by a PSC in setting a utility's rates. So a utility that is unhappy with a particular PSC decision against the utility, or an intervenor group that is unhappy with a pro-utility decision by the PSC, is unlikely to be successful in seeking judicial review of the decision. Courts are simply unlikely to wade into the complexities of utility ratemaking.

The broad grant of authority to PSCs to set "just and reasonable" rates therefore gives the PSC oversight over a wide range of decisions by utility management. These decisions include the process for selecting the particular generating resources (e.g., coal, natural gas, or renewable resources) acquired by utilities to serve their customers, which involves integrated resource planning. The PSC's broad grant of authority also comes into play in whether utilities will be required to offer their customers a range of energy efficiency programs to help them manage their energy costs.

Leadership at the PSC during "the Lost Decade"

During most of "the lost decade," the chairman of the West Virginia PSC was Mike Albert, a former partner at the Charleston-based law firm Jackson Kelly, a firm that claims to "understand the coal industry from the inside."[2] Jackson Kelly describes itself as having "provided the highest quality legal resources and representation to coal clients nationwide" since the mid-1800s, and notes its distinction of being the first law firm in the United States to be named "Law Firm of the Year in Mining Law."[3] In a 2013 article by the Center for Public Integrity, Jackson Kelly was described as the "go-to law firm for the coal industry."[4]

Albert, for his part, had a thirty-five-year career at Jackson Kelly – including service as managing member of the firm's Business Law Practice and on the firm's executive committee – before "retiring" from the firm in 2007 upon his appointment to the PSC by then Governor Joe Manchin. Although Albert had spent a lot of his career at Jackson Kelly representing utility companies in PSC proceedings, when he was confirmed he promised senators that he would remain impartial as chairman of the PSC.[5] Albert was reappointed by Governor Earl Ray Tomblin in 2013 and continued as chairman under Governor Jim Justice; he served for a total of twelve years as chairman of the agency before he left the PSC in 2019 to return to Jackson Kelly as of Counsel.

No one has ever questioned Mike Albert's integrity or his qualifications to do the job as PSC chairman. With his prior experience representing utilities before his appointment to the PSC, and his longtime affiliation with a law firm whose reputation rests on its representation of the coal industry, it is, however, fair to inquire about the perspective that a utility regulator brings to the job. As noted above, the

[2] *Coal*, JACKSON KELLY PLLC, https://www.jacksonkelly.com/industries/coal.

[3] *Id.*

[4] Chris Hamby, *Coal Industry's Go-To Law Firm Withheld Evidence of Black Lung, at Expense of Sick Miners*, CENTER FOR PUBLIC INTEGRITY (Oct. 29, 2013), https://publicintegrity.org/environment/coal-industrys-go-to-law-firm-withheld-evidence-of-black-lung-at-expense-of-sick-miners/.

[5] Kate Mishkin, *Albert to Retire as Chairman of Public Service Commission*, CHARLESTON GAZETTE-MAIL (Feb. 7, 2019), https://www.wvgazettemail.com/business/albert-to-retire-as-chairman-of-public-service-commission/article_43cc6673-84dc-50f9-bd33-e919d65f15b2.html.

PSC has broad statutory authority in its oversight of utilities in West Virginia, and West Virginians depend heavily on the agency exercising that authority in a manner that both protects ratepayers and strikes a proper balance between the interests of utility shareholders and ratepayers. As explored in this chapter, and in Chapter 10, it is fair to say that the decisions made at the PSC while Mike Albert was chair were a good deal for the coal industry – no diversification whatsoever away from using coal to generate electricity, and frequent bailouts of coal-burning utilities by authorizing uneconomic coal plants to be placed on the backs of West Virginians during "the lost decade" – and a very bad deal for ratepayers.

It is not clear whether the prospects for protection of utility ratepayers by the PSC will improve following Albert's departure. His successor as chairman, appointed by Governor Jim Justice, is Charlotte Lane, who returned to the PSC for the third time in July 2019, having served as a commissioner from 1985 to 1989 and from 1997 to 2003, including serving as chairman from 1997 to 2001; she also had short stints in the West Virginia House of Delegates (1979–80, 1991–92, and 2017–18) interspersed among her terms on the PSC. Chairman Lane also served on the US International Trade Commission from 2003–11, having been appointed by President George W. Bush.

Upon her return from Washington, DC, in 2011, she ran unsuccessfully for Congress in the Second District, a seat that opened up when then Congresswoman Shelly Moore Capito decided to run for Senator Jay Rockefeller's seat when he announced his retirement in 2013. In announcing her candidacy, Lane claimed that creating jobs – her top priority – would happen by "reining in the EPA" and fighting against a national "war on coal."[6] Lane ended up coming in third in the Republican primary in May 2014; the seat was ultimately captured by Alex Mooney. She subsequently ran for the House of Delegates in 2016, winning election to represent District 35. (She came in fourth in the four-seat district, edging out the fifth-place candidate by only 250 votes; Senator Capito's son, Moore Capito, captured the most votes in the general election.) Lane lost in her bid for reelection in 2018, when she finished fifth out of the eight candidates on the general election ballot.[7] Eight months later, Justice appointed her for another tour of duty as chair of the PSC.

In the three races she has run for public office, Lane has raised a total of $522,319, with $71,975 of that coming from the energy and natural resources sector. Included among her donors are the utilities regulated by the PSC – American Electric Power (AEP) ($7,500), FirstEnergy ($5,000), and Dominion Energy (the parent company of Hope Dominion, a natural gas distribution company operating in West Virginia) ($5,000) – as well as Koch Industries ($5,000), Halliburton ($1,000), various gas and oil companies (Marathon [$5,500], Valero Energy [$2,500], EQT Corporation

6   Dave Boucher, *Charlotte Lane Officially Announces Campaign for Congress*, Charleston Gazette-Mail (Aug. 13, 2013), https://www.wvgazettemail.com/news/politics/charlotte-lane-officially-announces-campaign-for-congress/article_5d7e4572-ae44-5b8c-8228-1a7899b27cc2.html.
7   *Charlotte Lane*, Ballotpedia, https://ballotpedia.org/Charlotte_Lane.

[$1,500]), and coal operators (Murray Energy [$2,500], Patriot Coal [$2,500], Alpha Natural Resources [$2,500], and Consol Energy [$1,000]).[8]

This financial support from the fossil fuel industry drew national attention in connection with a bill Lane cosponsored during her term in the House of Delegates, HB 4268, which would have allowed fossil fuel companies to drill for oil and gas on private land without all of the landowners' consent. At a Judiciary Committee hearing on the bill in February 2018, Lane was one of the delegates called out by Lissa Lucas, a public witness testifying about the bill; Lucas was forcibly removed from the witness stand after devoting her testimony to listing the members of the committee who had received campaign contributions from the oil and gas industry. (The video of the hearing went viral; the incident is described in further detail in the section "Big Energy's Stranglehold on West Virginia Politics" in Chapter 9) A subsequent article in *Vice* identified Lane as the leading recipient of oil and gas donations of all the Republicans on the Judiciary Committee, with a total of $16,750.[9]

In addition to accepting campaign contributions from gas and electric utilities and coal, oil, and gas operators, Lane has lobbied legislators on behalf of many of them (Hope Dominion, FirstEnergy, and the West Virginia Oil and Natural Gas Association [WVONGA], among others).[10] In fact, as a lobbyist for WVONGA, Lane helped secure passage of a bill in 2015, SB 390, that has resulted in steady rate increases for natural gas company ratepayers over the past few years without the usual scrutiny of a PSC rate proceeding.[11] A *Mountain State Spotlight* article sums up the findings of its investigation as follows: "Charlotte Lane was a top lobbyist for utility companies. Now she regulates them. A little-known law she previously pushed has allowed them to charge West Virginians for expensive pipeline projects with little oversight and few consumer protections."[12] So, while the price paid by natural gas companies for their gas supply has gone down – due to the shale gas revolution discussed in Chapter 2 – those savings have been more than offset by amounts that gas companies have been able to recover through surcharges for "infrastructure" repairs to their natural gas distribution lines. For Hope Dominion customers, for example, the surcharge now amounts to nearly $100 a year for a typical customer, or about 14 percent of a typical Dominion customer's pretax gas bill. According to Tom

8   *Charlotte R. Lane*, FollowTheMoney.org, https://www.followthemoney.org/entity-details?eid=6680555&default=candidate.
9   Alex Kotch, *A Viral Video Revealed Big Energy's Stranglehold on West Virginia Politics*, Vice (Feb. 19, 2018), https://www.vice.com/en/article/d3wdn7/a-viral-video-revealed-big-energys-stranglehold-on-west-virginia-politics.
10 West Virginia Ethics Commission, Registered Lobbyists 47 (Oct. 5, 2016), https://ethics.wv.gov/SiteCollectionDocuments/Lobby/2016%20Lobbyist%20Stuff/Lobbyist%20Directory%20October%205%202016.pdf.
11 Lucas Mansfield & Ken Ward, Jr., *Natural Gas Is Getting Cheaper. Thousands Are Paying More to Heat Their Homes Anyway*, Mountain State Spotlight (Apr. 17, 2021), https://www.propublica.org/article/natural-gas-is-getting-cheaper-thousands-are-paying-more-to-heat-their-homes-anyway.
12 *Id.*

White, a lawyer at the Consumer Advocate Division, the rate recovery scheme that Lane lobbied for in 2015 lacks important consumer protections, leaving ratepayers vulnerable to escalating fees.[13]

Apart from the lack of consumer protections in the measure, there is the disturbing process by which the statute was enacted, which involved Lane's trading on a previous working relationship with David Ellis, a key official at the PSC – where she formerly served as his boss, as chairman of the agency – in crafting the measure. *Mountain State Spotlight* reviewed emails involving the legislation in which Lane served as the go-between for Dominion executive Jo Carol Farmer and Ellis, who served as Director of the Utilities Division when Lane was chairman. Ellis offered a few suggestions – one of which was to add additional time for the PSC to review the infrastructure project proposals – that were largely incorporated into the final bill. As noted by *Mountain State Spotlight*, Ellis appeared to sign off on the idea on behalf of the PSC, stating that the goal and intent of the legislation – "expedited cost recovery" – "appears to be reasonable."[14] After receiving Ellis's input, Lane wrote a summary of the legislation – titled the "Infrastructure Expansion, Development, Improvement and Job Creation Act" – and played up the "jobs, both locally and statewide" that would be produced by the measure, while only briefly mentioning in the final bullet point that "customers will expereince [sic] gradual rate adjustments."[15] The legislation passed unanimously in the Senate and with an overwhelming majority in the House of Delegates. Natural gas customers have been paying for Lane's success as a lobbyist ever since.

INTEGRATED RESOURCE PLANNING

Whether as a prudent utility practice or to comply with a statutory or regulatory requirement, most electric utilities in the United States engage in "integrated resource planning." Electric utilities have engaged in integrated resource planning since the late 1980s as the prudent means for utilities to develop long-term resource plans. A study carried out in 2011 by Synapse Energy Economics showed that thirty-nine of fifty states had a rule or requirement for long-term planning or procurement.[16] The requirement was also included as a matter of federal law, as part of the Energy Policy Act of 1992, which defined integrated resource planning as "a planning and selection process for new energy resources that evaluates the full range of alternatives ... in order to provide adequate and reliable service to [an electric

---

[13] *Id.*
[14] *Id.*
[15] *Id.*
[16] RACHEL WILSON & BRUCE BIEWALD, BEST PRACTICES IN ELECTRIC UTILITY INTEGRATED RESOURCE PLANNING (June 2013), https://www.synapse-energy.com/sites/default/files/SynapseReport.2013-06 .RAP_.Best-Practices-in-IRP.13-038.pdf.

utility's] customers at the lowest system cost."[7] Through sophisticated modeling techniques that take into account a range of scenarios (e.g., low, medium, or high coal prices, various assumptions about economic conditions and load growth), the risks of heavy, and virtually exclusive, dependence upon one fuel source for generating electricity (coal) would have been obvious. Rather, integrated resource planning is designed to produce a diversified portfolio of both supply- and demand-side resources that will result in the lowest reasonable costs for consumers over time.

Prior to the enactment of legislation in West Virginia in 2014 requiring integrated resource planning, utilities did not engage in any long-term planning that was subject to review by the public or regulators. Moreover, utilities failed to consider energy efficiency as a resource alongside traditional supply-side resources (e.g., coal plants); that is the "integrated" aspect of integrated resource planning – the cost-effectiveness of generating new resources is considered alongside the possibility that it may be cheaper to avoid the investment in a new power plant through promoting energy efficiency and conservation. The integration of supply- and demand-side resources results in all resource options being "stacked" from least costly to most costly, with the expectation that in developing its resource acquisition strategy, the utility will work its way up this "resource option" curve until supply achieves equilibrium with demand.

The reference to providing adequate and reliable service *at the lowest system cost* in the definition of integrated resource planning in the Energy Policy Act of 1992 reinforces the notion that the purpose of the exercise is to put the utility on the lowest cost path, for the benefit of its customers. (As discussed further in the section Energy Efficiency and Demand-Side Programs, utilities have a natural bias toward wanting to address any resource deficiency through building a power plant rather than eliminating the deficiency through energy efficiency or conservation.)

In disregarding the essential features of integrated resource planning, electric utilities in West Virginia failed to operate along the "least cost" path for their customers, the pursuit of which likely would have led to a diversified portfolio of resources, including natural gas, wind, solar, and energy efficiency programs. Rather, they followed an undiversified "coal path" – 88 percent of the state's electricity was generated from coal as of 2020 – that ultimately led to double-digit electric rate increases beginning around 2008.

The Incomplete Evolution of Integrated Resource Planning in West Virginia

With the passage of legislation in 2014 requiring electric utilities to engage in some form of integrated resource planning, the process has improved. It is still far short of what is necessary for a truly rigorous process that would result in lower rates for

---

[7] Energy Policy Act of 1992, Pub. L. No. 102–486, §111(d) (19), 106 Stat. 2796 (codified as amended in 16 U.S.C. § 2602(19) (2006)).

customers. A comparison of the "resource plans" submitted by FirstEnergy and the AEP subsidiaries operating in West Virginia (Appalachian Power and Wheeling Power) before and after the 2014 legislation illustrates the improvement in the planning process and, in the case of FirstEnergy, the continued deficiency.

The Pre-2014 Planning Documents

In the "Resource Plan" filed in August 2012 with the West Virginia PSC by FirstEnergy's subsidiaries operating in West Virginia – Monongahela Power (Mon Power) and The Potomac Edison Company – FirstEnergy stated that its objective in preparing the plan was "to identify the resources necessary to meet the companies' future energy and capacity obligations in a cost effective, prudent, and reliable manner," considering the options of both "supply and demand-side resources and market purchases."[18] While this statement would seem to suggest an equal consideration of supply- and demand-side options, the FirstEnergy Resource Plan later clarified that demand-side options were dismissed as "not a viable solution capable of meeting Mon Power's obligations" given the scale of the utilities' claimed resource need. In other words, the demand-side resources that make a resource plan "integrated" were not considered as a viable, long-term solution to Mon Power's significant energy and capacity needs.

After dismissing the demand-side options, the FirstEnergy Resource Plan went on to evaluate the various generation, or supply-side, alternatives. These alternatives included retrofitting Mon Power's existing generation to comply with the new air emissions standards promulgated by the Environmental Protection Agency (EPA) in its Mercury and Air Toxics Standard (MATS), which took effect in February 2012; building new baseload generation (coal, nuclear, or natural gas-fired combined-cycle combustion turbines); building or acquiring alternative energy resources (e.g., wind, solar, or hydro); and the acquisition of existing plants. The "preferred approach," according to the FirstEnergy Resource Plan, was to acquire existing generating plants from Mon Power's affiliate, Allegheny Energy Supply. The document claimed that "Mon Power is fortunate to have uncovered such an opportunity" to acquire an existing source of generation, given that such opportunities are "scarce since they require the intersection of a willing seller and an asset that meets the requirements of the prospective buyer." Under the transaction for which Mon Power later sought approval from the West Virginia PSC, Mon Power would acquire about 80 percent of the Harrison plant, a supercritical coal plant built in 1972 in Haywood, West Virginia with a generating capacity of 1,984 MWs, from Allegheny Energy Supply (this acquisition is discussed more fully in the Chapter 10).

In other words, in the face of dramatic increases in the price of coal over the preceding decade, and the likely additional cost increases associated with

---

[18]   FIRSTENERGY, 2012 RESOURCE PLAN: MONONGAHELA POWER COMPANY AND THE POTOMAC EDISON COMPANY (2012).

compliance with ever more stringent air emissions regulations by the EPA, FirstEnergy's solution for West Virginia was to propose to increase the state's reliance on coal, by purchasing an existing coal plant from an affiliate, without a thorough evaluation of alternatives that may indeed have been cheaper for West Virginians. Its Resource Plan was thus used simply as a vehicle to lay the foundation for its subsequent filing, in November 2012, to unload the uncompetitive Harrison power plant from FirstEnergy shareholders onto the backs of its West Virginia ratepayers.

Appalachian Power, for its part, did not submit any sort of long-term plan to West Virginia regulators prior to the passage of the 2014 legislation. It did, however, prepare an "integrated resource plan" (IRP) that it submitted to the Virginia State Corporation Commission in September 2011 pursuant to a Virginia statute requiring the preparation of such a document periodically. Although the Virginia statute contemplates an "integrated" resource plan, and Appalachian Power's filing appeared on its face to comply with the requirements of the statute, the resource plan was not, in fact, integrated. Specifically, there was nothing in the plan that evaluated demand- and supply-side resources on a "consistent and integrated basis"; in fact, the plan stated clearly that Appalachian Power would primarily, if not exclusively, be looking to supply-side resources to meet its energy and capacity needs.

Instead of comparing the cost of supply-side resources alongside demand-side solutions, the AEP Resource Plan simply assigned an arbitrary levelized cost figure ($40 per MWh) to demand-side resources, a "cost" figure that did not necessarily reflect the actual cost of those resources. Under the approach followed in the AEP Resource Plan, it was irrelevant that this $40/MWh levelized cost figure may have been substantially lower than the levelized cost of the supply-side options evaluated in the plan. Rather, the level of commitment to demand-side resources was determined by external factors – the extent of energy efficiency programs mandated by the PUCs in the various states in which AEP operates – and was merely "priced" by AEP for analysis purposes at $40/MWh. As it turned out, virtually all of the supply-side options at the time had a levelized cost per MWh far in excess of the $40/MWh figure assigned by AEP to demand-side resources.[19] Even AEP acknowledged in its Resource Plan that "[d]emand-side resources will likely play a significant role in satisfying capacity and energy requirements prospectively as they are the least-cost resource, even in significant amounts."[20] Notwithstanding this striking admission

---

[19] According to the Energy Information Administration's estimates of levelized cost of new generation resources, the cheapest supply-side resource, a natural gas-fired advanced combine-cycle combustion turbine, had a levelized cost of $63.10/MWh. The estimates for other generating resources climb steadily higher: $88.90/MWh for hydro, $96.00/MWh for wind, $97.70/MWh for a conventional coal-fired plant, $110.90/MWh for an "advanced" coal-fired plant, $111.40/MWh for a nuclear plant, $115.40/MWh for biomass, and $152.70/MWh for solar photovoltaic. *Levelized Cost of New Generation Resources in the Annual Energy Outlook 2012*, U.S. ENERGY INFORMATION ADMINISTRATION (2012), http://www.eia.gov/forecasts/aeo/pdf/electricity_generation.pdf.

[20] Virginia State Corp. Comm'n v. Appalachian Power Co., No. PUE-2011–00100 (Va. Sept. 1, 2011), Resource Plan, at 137–38.

that demand-side solutions were cheaper for customers than generating resources, Appalachian Power refused to allow demand-side resources to compete directly with supply-side measures, and proceeded with a resource plan that was almost exclusively devoted to more expensive supply-side resources.

The 2014 West Virginia Legislation

In March 2013, Delegate Tim Manchin (Democrat, Marion County) – a cousin of US Senator Joe Manchin – introduced a bill in the House of Delegates, cosponsored with six other delegates, that would have required electric utilities in West Virginia to engage in integrated resource planning. The bill as introduced, HB 2803, directed the West Virginia PSC to issue an order directing electric utilities to file their initial plans no later than September 1, 2015, and also to establish guidelines for the format and contents of the plans. The legislation further directed that the plans cover a planning period of no less than twenty years, and that utilities update their plans every two years. The legislation adopted the "integrated" aspect of the Energy Policy Act of 1992 by requiring that both supply-side and demand-side resources be addressed "on a consistent and integrated basis." The legislation further required the PSC to analyze and review the utilities' plans at a public hearing, and authorized the PSC to request further information from the utilities, as it deemed necessary.

In terms of the subsequent use of the plans, the legislation provided that the PSC "shall consider the information reported in the IRP when it evaluates the performance of the utility in rate and other proceedings." In other words, the plans could be taken into account in determining the prudence of the utilities' actions in subsequent rate proceedings. For example, if an IRP recommended a particular course of action – such as acquiring a natural gas plant as a new resource – a utility may be deemed to be "imprudent" if it chose to instead proceed with a different and more expensive resource. The legislation did not include the other essential feature of the Energy Policy Act's definition of integrated resource planning – that the goal of the process was to produce adequate and reliable utility service "at the lowest system cost." Instead, the legislation required the development of a "portfolio of resources that represents a *reasonable balance of cost and risk* for the utility and its customers."[21]

The legislation ultimately adopted by the West Virginia legislature in 2014 and codified at §24-2-19 of the West Virginia Code was materially different from the legislation initially introduced in March 2013. Rather than requiring plans every two years, the final legislation extended the requirement for plan updates to every five years, with the initial plans required to be filed no later than January 1, 2016. It should be noted that most states require IRPs to be updated every two to three years, to reflect changes in circumstances, including load forecasts, fuel prices, capital costs, conditions in the electricity markets, and environmental regulations. Of the twenty-

---

[21] H.B. 2803 (Reg. Sess.) (WV 2014).

seven states surveyed in the Synapse report, fourteen require IRP updates every two years, while eleven follow a three-year cycle.

The final legislation also abandoned the twenty-year planning period prescribed in HB 2803, and apparently left it up to the PSC to determine this issue. While the PSC is still required to "analyze and review" the IRPs, it is not required to hold any hearings with respect to the plans. And, most importantly, the "integrated" aspect was eliminated; rather than requiring supply-side and demand-side resources on a "consistent and integrated basis" – the language from HB 2803 – the final legislation stated that "[t]he Commission may consider both supply-side and demand-side resources when developing the requirements for the integrated resource plans." The final legislation also carried forward the "reasonable balance of cost and risk for the utility and its customers" from HB 2803 rather than adopt the requirement of "lowest system cost" from the Energy Policy Act of 1992.[22]

On March 19, 2015, the West Virginia PSC fulfilled its obligations under the statute by issuing its order providing guidance to the electric utilities on developing their IRPs. In that order, the PSC established the planning period as a "minimum ten-year forecast of the supply-side and demand-side resources expected to satisfy [the utility's] loads,"[23] thus departing from the twenty-year period used by most states. Of those states with IRP requirements surveyed in the Synapse report, one-half used twenty years as the planning horizon.

Neither the 2014 legislation nor the March 2015 PSC order included one of the elements commonly included in IRP requirements: stakeholder involvement. Many states require that participants in the utility ratemaking process be involved in the development of an IRP or, at a minimum, that the PUC provide some public process for the commissioners to receive comments on proposed IRPs. In defining the characteristics comprising a "full featured" IRP process, the authors of the Synapse report required that the process be "subject to public review." The rule in Washington, for example, provides that "public participation [is] essential to the development of an effective plan," and specifically requires the utility commission to "hear comment on the plan at a public hearing scheduled after the utility submits its plan for commission review."[24] The purpose of stakeholder involvement is to give interested parties an opportunity to help shape the utility's resource acquisition decisions early in the decision-making process.

Under typical utility ratemaking practices, the impact of utility resource acquisition decisions is felt only at the end of the process, when the plant is completed and the investment in the resource is added to the utility's rate base, usually resulting in a

[22] WV Code, Ch. 24, Public Service Commission, Art, 2, Powers and Duties of Public Service Commission, § 24-2-19, Integrated Resource Planning Required (2015), https://code.wvlegislature .gov/24-2-19/.

[23] West Virginia Public Service Commission, General Order No. 184.35, An Order Requiring Electric Utilities to File Integrated Resource Plans (Mar.19, 2015), http://www.psc.state.wv.us/scripts/ WebDocket/ViewDocument.cfm?CaseActivityID=420248.

[24] Washington Admin. Code § 480–100-238(5) (2013).

rate increase. It is too late at that point to encourage the utility to take a different path, and the recourse available to opposing stakeholders is to intervene in a rate proceeding and propose a disallowance reflecting the difference between the actual resource cost and the lower cost that the stakeholder's preferred path would have produced, based on a demonstration of imprudence. It is very difficult to carry the burden of proof to support such a disallowance, however, and the need to maintain a utility's financial integrity may constrain the PUC from imposing a disallowance, irrespective of the evidence.

The Post-2014 Integrated Resource Plans

FirstEnergy and AEP filed their first IRPs in West Virginia in late December 2015, just prior to the January 1, 2016 deadline established by the PSC order. FirstEnergy's was a combined plan for its two West Virginia operating subsidiaries, Mon Power and Potomac Edison, while the two AEP affiliates operating in West Virginia, Appalachian Power and Wheeling Power, filed separate IRPs. The FirstEnergy and AEP filings were markedly different in their direction and in the sophistication of their analyses; according to the comments of one industry expert cited in the *Charleston Gazette-Mail*, "[i]t's a tale of two utilities, in terms of one that gets it [Appalachian Power] and another [FirstEnergy] that is sticking its head in the sand."[25] FirstEnergy was described as a "Neanderthal utility" with respect to its posture toward renewable energy and the "primitive" nature of its analysis.

Appalachian Power's December 2015 IRP represented a vast improvement from the plan it filed with the Virginia State Corporation Commission (SCC) in 2012. For one thing, the plan was truly "integrated" in terms of treating demand-side and supply-side resources on a consistent and integrated basis, as required by the Energy Policy Act of 1992. Instead of attaching an arbitrary figure of $40 per MWh to energy efficiency and "siloing" the treatment of energy efficiency investments based on that figure (as opposed to posturing a head-to-head competition with supply-side resources, as Appalachian Power had done in its 2012 IRP filing in Virginia), the December 2015 IRP filing modeled energy efficiency as a resource alongside the supply-side resources under consideration by the utility, and committed to acquiring as much energy efficiency as its modeling suggested. In other words, the modeling scenarios used to identify the lowest-cost portfolio of resources for customers would determine the role to be played by energy efficiency programs, and Appalachian Power committed to seeking PSC approval of the energy efficiency programs necessary to achieve those levels of energy efficiency savings.

Second, with respect to the role of noncoal resources, the 2015 Appalachian Power IRP endorsed an aggressive effort to diversify its resource portfolio away from coal.

[25] Andrew Brown, *Appalachian Power Moves Toward Renewables, Mon Power Considering More Investments in Coal*, CHARLESTON GAZETTE-MAIL (Jan. 6, 2016), https://www.wvgazettemail.com/business/appalachian-power-moves-toward-renewables-mon-power-considering-more-investments-in-coal/article_572ea94e-57d4-58f3-9e2c-ca1b8dda58df.html.

The Appalachian Power "action plan" – the specific acquisitions that Appalachian Power identified to implement its IRP – included solar power (both utility-scale and distributed), wind power, demand response, and energy efficiency, along with conversion of one of its coal plants to burn natural gas. The Appalachian Power IRP used very sophisticated modeling to evaluate the various resource mix options under many scenarios, and concluded that its recommended resource mix would be in the best long-term interests of its customers in terms of achieving the lowest system cost.

The other AEP affiliate operating in West Virginia, Wheeling Power, had a much less impressive offering in its initial IRP. Because of Wheeling Power's acquisition of a 50 percent interest in the Mitchell Plant (discussed in Chapter 9), Wheeling Power had excess capacity that largely obviated consideration of any additional resources in the coming years, including energy efficiency. Thus the Wheeling Power IRP was very brief, inasmuch as there was little need to analyze resource options given the absence of any need for new resources.

FirstEnergy, the "Neanderthal utility" operating in West Virginia, earned its label with an IRP filing that continued to condemn renewable resources as too expensive and unreliable – referred to as "intermittent" resources in the IRP – and to downplay the role that energy efficiency could play in addressing a utility's resource needs, given the apparent massive need for capacity demonstrated in FirstEnergy's IRP. As in the case of its 2012 resource plan, which FirstEnergy used as the basis for justifying the acquisition of 80 percent of the Harrison coal plant (as discussed in Chapter 10), the utility used its 2015 IRP to lay the foundation for its proposed transfer of the Pleasants Station coal plant from its unregulated subsidiary, Allegheny Energy Supply, to its regulated subsidiaries in West Virginia, Mon Power and Potomac Edison. The FirstEnergy IRP exaggerated its load growth – an incredible 1.0 percent per year – to create a capacity shortfall of 1,300 MW, which coincidentally corresponded to the size of the Pleasants Station plant. And FirstEnergy completely mischaracterized the trends in natural gas quantities and price in order to create inflated wholesale market prices – thus suggesting that the Pleasants Station coal plant could generate revenues for West Virginia ratepayers through sales of excess energy in the wholesale power markets – when in fact the plant was uneconomic and a money-loser. (Were it not, FirstEnergy would not later seek to move the asset from its unregulated subsidiary – where the profits, if any, would inure to the benefit of its shareholders – to its regulated West Virginia subsidiaries, where ratepayers would bear the risks of the plant's ability [or inability] to compete in the competitive wholesale markets.)

The solution thus recommended in the December 2015 IRP submitted by FirstEnergy was to pursue the acquisition of the Pleasants Station coal plant as the preferred means of addressing the capacity shortfall suggested by its rigged analysis. As discussed in Chapter 9, this strategy would ultimately fail, but not due in any part to the rigors of the regulatory oversight provided by the West Virginia PSC. Rather, it was up to the Federal Energy Regulatory Commission (FERC) to expose the fraud, and thus do the job of protecting West Virginia ratepayers that the West Virginia PSC seems incapable of performing.

ENERGY EFFICIENCY AND DEMAND-SIDE PROGRAMS

Demand-side programs generally comprise three different approaches to reducing energy usage by utility retail customers: energy efficiency, conservation, and demand response. Energy efficiency is using technology that requires less energy to perform the same function, such as by using a light-emitting diode (LED) light bulb or a compact fluorescent light (CFL) bulb that requires less energy than an incandescent light bulb to produce the same amount of light. Another example is purchasing appliances certified by the EPA as "Energy Star" appliances which, although having a slightly higher purchase price, will use anywhere from 10 to 50 percent less energy each year than a non-energy efficient equivalent.

Energy conservation, on the other hand, involves using less energy by adjusting personal behavior or habits, such as by turning the lights off when leaving the room or by adjusting your thermostat to keep your house a little warmer in the summer or a little cooler in the winter. Energy conservation programs offered by utilities attempt to change their customers' behavior, such as through messaging grounded in behavioral science to produce simple, actionable cues that are relevant to customers and motivate them to save energy. Utilities can offer communications through multiple channels (e.g., the internet, mobile phones, mail) to help customers get engaged and focused on reducing energy consumption and saving money. An effective approach used by many utilities is to include information such as how the customer's energy use compares to that of similar homes in the same neighborhood, as well as personalized energy efficiency tips that provide customers with voluntary ways to save.

Energy efficiency and conservation programs funded by electric utility customers are offered in nearly every state in America. These programs target all market segments (residential, commercial, industrial, and agriculture) and include financial incentives – such as rebates for energy efficient appliances or heat pumps – technical assistance, education, and energy audits. Energy efficiency programs have been funded by electric utility customers for decades. They totaled about $5.8 billion in 2016, and are saving 0.75 percent of US electricity demand each year. Thanks to the effectiveness of these energy efficiency programs in nearly all states (along with appliance and equipment energy efficiency standards, tighter building codes, tax credits, and finance programs), electricity demand has been largely flat in the United States between 2010 and 2020.

Demand response – the third type of demand-side program – encourages customers to reduce or shift their electricity usage during peak periods in response to time-based rates or other forms of financial incentives. Methods of engaging customers in demand response efforts include offering time-based rates such as time-of-use pricing, which allow customers to see the difference in prices throughout a typical day and give them an economic incentive to shift their usage to lower-cost periods. By offering "peak" prices during the portion of the day when power prices are highest – between noon and 6 p.m., for example – and "off-peak" prices during the middle of the night when power prices are lowest, customers are compensated for shifting their usage to the extent possible, such as by operating their dishwasher, washing machines, and clothes dryers, or charging their electric vehicles, during "off-peak" periods. In addition, many utilities offer direct load control programs that enable them to cycle air conditioners and water heaters on and off during periods of peak demand in exchange for a financial incentive and lower electric bills.

On a larger scale, "curtailment service providers" (CSPs) can aggregate commercial customers within a region and offer the collective reduction in load as a product in the regional wholesale electricity market, for which participating customers are compensated. As an example, multiple Walmart locations within PJM Interconnection (the mid-Atlantic regional wholesale market in which West Virginia is located) could be aggregated by a CSP for purposes of reducing their electrical load during periods when the electrical demand in the region is highest (such as late afternoon during the summer, when air conditioning load reaches its peak), by remotely controlling the cycling of air conditioning units to achieve the promised load reduction. The control room at PJM – where the grid is managed to ensure that supply matches demand at all times to "keep the lights on" – thereby has the option of either dispatching a peaking power plant to increase the supply of electricity to meet the demand, or it can accept the offer from a CSP to reduce the demand for electricity, through the CSP's ability to manage energy use for a few hours at the participating Walmart stores in the region. The CSP (and the participating Walmart stores) are paid for the "product" they delivered – a reduction in electric load – in an amount roughly equal to what PJM would have paid to dispatch a power plant to operate to serve the load. In this manner, demand response programs can defer or eliminate the need to build new supply-side infrastructure, like peaking power plants and transmission and distribution assets. Utilities and grid operators can also rely on demand response programs as an economic resource that reduces the overall cost of power.

The utility must set prices for both energy efficiency and demand response programs that reflect the integration of the supply- and demand-side options, as required under integrated resource planning. In other words, just as the Walmart store participating in a demand response program should be compensated at the same level as PJM would have paid to dispatch a peaking power plant, a utility's energy efficiency program should offer financial incentives to participating customers that reflect the costs that the utility is able to avoid by not having to build or operate a supply-side resource (i.e., a generating plant). For example, utility customers could be offered rebates for purchasing Energy Star appliances that are set at a level that reflects the savings the utility would be able to achieve by not having to build or operate a power plant. The size of the rebate must correspond to that "avoided cost," to ensure that customers are receiving accurate price signals for the electricity savings they are producing. These rebates, in turn, would help customers cover the slightly higher costs of Energy Star appliances versus energy-inefficient alternatives. This reinforces the point from the discussion of integrated resource planning in the preceding section that demand- and supply-side options must be integrated; if they are not considered alongside each other on a consistent and integrated basis, demand-side options will be inadequately compensated, and the utility will likely pursue a supply-side option that is more expensive for customers in the long run.

The integration of demand- and supply-side resources has been the exception rather than the rule in West Virginia. Demand-side programs are rarely, if ever, evaluated as an option alongside the utilities' preferred approach of building more generating resources (usually coal plants). Much of the explanation for this dismal performance can be found in the preceding chapters: Promoting energy efficiency is inconsistent with the business of extracting and burning coal to generate electricity. The narrative goes like this: If utilities are successful in promoting energy efficiency, then utility customers will use less electricity, the coal plants will operate less often (or at a lower capacity), less coal will be mined, and coal miners will lose their jobs (and the state will lose the severance tax revenues that are produced by the extraction of coal). In other words, "that dog don't hunt" in West Virginia.

The problem, of course, is that this narrative is not viewed from the perspective of utility customers. Probably the greatest value of utility energy efficiency programs is that they give utility customers the tools that enable them to assert some control over their energy costs. Ratepayers have virtually no control over the *rates* charged by the investor-owned utilities in the state; these rates are regulated by the West Virginia PSC (which has done a truly dreadful job of protecting utility customers over "the lost decade"). But if energy efficiency programs were available to them, ratepayers would have some ability to control the size of the bills they pay. This is a key distinction that is often overlooked – the assumption is that with relatively low electricity *rates*, utility *bills* will be low as well. Low rates, however, do not lead to low energy costs. According to a study carried out by the American Council for an Energy Efficient Economy (ACEEE) – the leading national organization promoting energy efficiency – "residential customers in some of the bottom-ranking states [as measured by low electric rates] actually pay some of the highest electricity bills in the country."[26] This is certainly true in the case of West Virginia. Even though the average *rate* for residential electric customers in West Virginia in 2018 – 11.0 cents per kWh – was well below the national average (12.85 cents per kWh), the average

---

[26]   Michael Sciortino, Rachel Young, & Steven Nadel, Opportunity Knocks: Examining Low-Ranking States in the State Energy Efficiency Scorecard (May 2012), http://www.aceee.org/sites/default/files/publications/researchreports/e126.pdf.

monthly bill for residential customers in West Virginia ($126.70) was almost 8 percent higher than the national average monthly bill ($117.65). Expressed differently, only twelve states had lower residential electric *rates* than West Virginia, but only fourteen states had higher *bills*.

In addition to policymakers' pro-coal bias – and their corresponding indifference to consumers – two other factors contribute to West Virginia's dismal performance with respect to demand-side programs. First, utilities simply do not make as much money promoting energy efficiency as they do when they build power plants. Under the process for setting utility rates, utilities earn a profit, or return, on their investments in generating plants and other assets that are used to generate, transmit, and distribute electricity to retail customers. A $1 billion investment in a supercritical coal plant, for example, would increase annual profits by about $45 million (assuming the utility is allowed by the PSC to earn a 9 percent return on equity and the plant is financed equally with debt and equity). The math is pretty much the same for investments in transmission lines and the poles and wires that comprise the distribution network. In the case of demand-side programs, on the other hand, the utility is allowed only to recover the operating expenses associated with offering the program; there are no "assets" upon which the utility is allowed to earn a return. So there is an inherent bias by the utility in pursuing supply-side resources to the exclusion of demand-side options. This bias can be overcome only by a rigorous integrated resource planning process that tries to achieve the best outcome for customers – through a portfolio of both supply- and demand-side resources that produces the lowest cost over time – rather than accommodating the utility's interest in maximizing its profits for shareholders. (Frankly, the utility has a fiduciary obligation to its shareholders to try to maximize its profits, so this motivation is understandable. It is the regulator's obligation, however, to balance the interests of the utility in maximizing profits against the interests of consumers in obtaining electric service at reasonable rates.)

Second, promoting energy efficiency is contrary to an electric utility's economic interests, in the absence of an enlightened ratemaking policy by regulators. Policymakers have long recognized that a utility has a disincentive to promote conservation or to invest in energy efficiency programs given that, if successful, the utility will sell less of its product. Utility rates are typically set in a manner that assumes a particular level of sales during the period following the rate order. In order for the utility to have a reasonable opportunity to earn the rate of return awarded by the regulator, the utility generally needs to achieve the level of sales assumed when rates were set. If the utility promotes conservation by its customers or offers an array of energy efficiency programs, those programs, if successful, will likely result in a sales volume lower than the assumed level, and the utility will fail to earn its allowed rate of return.

In response to this dynamic, many utility commissions have adopted ratemaking mechanisms designed to hold the utility harmless from the profit impact of the lower volumes that are presumed to result from conservation and energy efficiency. The preferred approach is commonly referred to as "decoupling," which removes the link between sales volumes and profits. Decoupling is a ratemaking mechanism that tracks the "under-recovery" of profit margin attributable to the reduced volumes and allows the utility to increase its rates slightly in a subsequent rate case to keep it "whole" from those reduced volumes.

A second regulatory mechanism is a lost revenue adjustment, which is a prescriptive approach that typically considers the revenue reduction attributable to specific energy efficiency measures, and then adjusts rates to hold the utility harmless from the lost profit margin from those measures, based on the actual number of measures installed during a particular period. Unlike decoupling, lost revenue adjustment mechanisms do not eliminate the incentive of the utility to increase sales and, for that reason, are viewed only as a "short-term solution" by ACEEE. According to the 2020 *ACEEE State Scorecard* – the annual ranking of state energy efficiency programs issued by ACEEE – thirty-two states have addressed disincentives for investment in energy efficiency for electric utilities. Of these, fifteen have a lost revenue adjustment mechanism and seventeen have implemented decoupling.[27]

The West Virginia PSC has not acted to adopt as a matter of general policy any mechanism to address the disincentives faced by utilities for investing in energy efficiency programs. In the case of both of the AEP companies (Appalachian Power and Wheeling Power), however, the PSC has allowed the utility to make adjustments for lost revenues attributable to energy efficiency measures on a case-by-case basis when it evaluates AEP's energy efficiency programs. AEP has never sought to implement decoupling. FirstEnergy's demand-side programs are so negligible that it is wasted effort to try to gauge the impact on its profits from these programs.

The Benefits of Energy Efficiency

Apart from providing electric utility customers with the tools to help them control their energy costs, investing in energy efficiency programs produces other benefits. First, investing in demand-side resources generally leads to lower electricity rates, inasmuch as energy efficiency is a lower-cost resource than most supply-side (i.e., generation) options. This is one of the beneficial outcomes to integrated resource planning: It is considered to be one of four "major categories of lever" in developing and implementing demand-side resources. It is cheaper for utilities to fund energy efficiency measures than to devote additional resources to building new power plants and expanding the transmission and distribution (T&D) infrastructure. In addition to being less expensive than supply-side resources, energy efficiency

---

[27] WESTON BERG ET AL., THE 2020 STATE ENERGY EFFICIENCY SCORECARD 49 (Dec. 2020), https://www.aceee.org/sites/default/files/pdfs/u2011.pdf.

investments can save money. One of the most comprehensive studies of energy efficiency's savings potential, by McKinsey & Company in 2009, found that if it had invested $520 billion in energy efficiency, the United States could have reduced its annual energy consumption by 23 percent by 2020.[28] More importantly, this investment would have yielded present-value savings of roughly $1.2 trillion. In other words, the benefits from the savings achieved were more than twice as great as the costs.

How much cheaper is energy efficiency than supply-side resources? Americans spend over $400 billion per year on the production of electricity at a price of nine cents to over twenty cents per kWh, while utility spending on energy efficiency programs, amounting to approximately $8 billion per year, costs only about five cents per kWh. The Lawrence Berkeley National Laboratory (LBNL) prepared a comprehensive report that quantified the cost of saving electricity through energy efficiency programs, based on the cost performance of efficiency programs implemented between 2009 and 2015 that were funded by customers of 116 investor-owned utilities serving nearly 70 percent of US electricity needs.[29] The LBNL report showed that these programs delivered savings at a cost to the utility of 2.5 cents per kWh, with a total cost per kWh – including the amounts paid by utility customers for energy efficiency measures – of 5.0 cents per kWh.

Looking only at the utility cost, the figures ranged from 2.1 cents per kWh for programs in the residential sector, with a cost of 1.1 cents per kWh for residential lighting rebate programs and 2.9 cents per kWh for appliance and consumer electronics rebate programs. At the upper end of residential programs, the cost of whole-home retrofit programs was 6.9 cents per kWh, given that these projects are more comprehensive in scope, often including heating and air-conditioning system replacements. Of particular relevance to West Virginia, the LBNL report included the costs per kWh of residential energy efficiency programs administered by utilities in surrounding states, which ranged from 1.4 cents per kWh in Ohio to 3.1 cents per kWh in Maryland. Other states included in the LBNL report included Pennsylvania (1.8 cents per kWh), Kentucky (2.2 cents per kWh), and Indiana (1.7 cents per kWh).

For comparison purposes, the cost figure typically used for supply-side resources is the levelized cost of electricity (LCOE) which, as discussed in Chapter 2, allows the comparison of different technologies (e.g., wind, solar, natural gas) of unequal life spans, project size, different capital cost, risk, return, and capacities. In the US Energy Information Administration's *Annual Energy Outlook* for 2020, the LCOE for an ultra-supercritical coal plant was 7.6 cents per kWh, a natural gas-fired

[28] HANNAH CHOI GRANADE ET AL., UNLOCKING ENERGY EFFICIENCY IN THE U.S. ECONOMY (July 2009), https://www.mckinsey.com/~/media/mckinsey/dotcom/client_service/epng/pdfs/unlocking%20energy%20efficiency/us_energy_efficiency_exc_summary.ashx.

[29] IAN HOFFMAN ET AL., THE COST OF SAVING ELECTRICITY THROUGH ENERGY EFFICIENCY PROGRAMS FUNDED BY UTILITY CUSTOMERS: 2009–2015 (June 2018), https://eta-publications.lbl.gov/sites/default/files/cose_final_report_20200429.pdf.

combustion turbine was 6.7 cents per kWh, solar PV was 3.6 cents per kWh, and onshore wind was 4.0 cents per kWh.[30] Appalachian Power's 2016 IRP, on the other hand, included a LCOE estimate of a 150 MW wind facility coming online in 2017 at 6.3 cents per kWh. The bottom line is that utility investments in energy efficiency programs typically produce a lower cost path for customers than building supply-side resources.

Second, investments in energy efficiency produce other benefits to the electricity grid. Energy efficiency and demand response programs reduce the load placed on the grid – particularly during peak times – and thereby increase the reliability of the grid. Demand-side programs can also reduce or defer the need for utilities to invest in T&D infrastructure, because fewer electrons are moving over the wires. All other things being equal, vertically integrated utilities and other T&D firms can invest less in T&D capabilities if energy efficiency is effective and consumption decreases. This reduced investment ultimately should be reflected in lower utility rates over time.

Third, energy savings from demand-side resources produce environmental benefits because of the reduction in fossil-based resources in utilities' generation mixes. A study by Environment Northeast in 2009 calculated that expanded energy efficiency programs in the six New England states would result in avoided emissions from carbon dioxide (the primary greenhouse gas [GHG] pollutant from fossil fuel combustion) of about 18 million short tons, or a reduction of 8.3 percent below 2005 emission levels.[31] The exact amount and mix of reduced GHG emissions depend on when the energy savings occur, and on the nature of the carbon-emitting fuel used as a primary source in utilities' generation mixes. Because of the emissions benefits of energy efficiency, the EPA allows states to use energy efficiency to meet air quality regulations. In fact, states are able to receive direct credit for improvements in energy efficiency as part of their State Implementation Plans under the Clean Air Act. Thus, as federal air quality standards become more stringent, energy efficiency programs may be used by states to cost-effectively meet these new standards "by acting as a substitute for dirtier electricity sources."[32]

Finally, investments in demand-side resources can produce significant economic benefits through job creation. As of 2020, there were 2.3 million energy efficiency jobs in the United States, which comprises 40 percent of all energy jobs. Seventy

30   U.S. Energy Information Administration, Annual Energy Outlook for 2020 (Jan. 2020), https://www.eia.gov/outlooks/aeo/pdf/AEO2020%20Full%20Report.pdf. Pages 77–78 discuss the LCOEs, which are cited from the report.

31   Jamie Howland et al., Energy Efficiency: Engine of Economic Growth (Oct. 2009), https://acadiacenter.org/wp-content/uploads/2014/10/ENE_ExecSum_EnergyEfficiencyEngineof EconomicGrowth_FINAL.pdf.

32   Columbia Law School, Center for Climate Change Law, Public Utility Commissions and Energy Efficiency: A Handbook of Legal & Regulatory Tools for Commissioners and Advocates 7 (Aug. 2012), http://columbiaclimatelaw.com/files/2016/06/Welton-et-al.-2012-08-Public-Utility-Commissions-and-Energy-Efficiency.pdf.

percent of these workers were employed by small businesses.[33] Apart from the jobs provided by energy efficiency programs, broader economic benefits arise from: (1) direct spending by utilities (or, in some states, energy program administrators) on energy efficiency programs and staffing requirements; (2) indirect household and commercial spending on energy efficiency-related goods and services; and (3) increased economic activity as the energy bill savings are spent in the wider economy.

The Current Lack of Investment in Demand-Side Resources in West Virginia

By any account, West Virginia has a poor track record of investing in demand-side programs. A good measure of how West Virginia stacks up versus other states in the availability of energy efficiency programs is an annual survey, the *State Scorecard*, carried out by ACEEE. During "the lost decade," West Virginia consistently ranked in the bottom 5 percent of all US states – it was ranked number forty-nine in 2012 and 2018 and closed out the decade ranked in a three-way tie for number forty-eight in 2020, beating only Wyoming. Out of fifty possible points in the scoring methodology used in the 2020 *ACEEE State Scorecard*, West Virginia received only 5.5 points (one point less than its 2019 score of 6.5 points). In contrast, the number one state, California, received 43 points. It is also worth noting how much better the states surrounding West Virginia fared in the ACEEE rankings: Maryland was ranked sixth with 34.5 points, Pennsylvania nineteenth with 22 points, Virginia twenty-fifth with 18 points, Kentucky thirty-third with 13.5 points, and Ohio thirty-seventh with 11.5 points.

There are several reasons why West Virginia fares so poorly in the *ACEEE State Scorecard*. First, the state has no enunciated policy endorsing the importance of energy efficiency as a resource. Twenty-seven states have adopted an Energy Efficiency Resource Standard (EERS), which establishes an energy savings target that utilities must meet through energy efficiency programs. These standards set multiyear targets for electricity savings, such as 1 or 2 percent incremental savings per year or 20 percent cumulative savings by a stated deadline (e.g., 2025). They differ from state to state, but each is intended to establish a sustainable, long-term role for energy efficiency in the state's overall energy portfolio. According to the *ACEEE State Scorecard*, states that have an EERS policy in place have shown average energy efficiency spending and savings levels more than three times higher than those states without such a policy. In addition, savings from states with EERS policies accounted for approximately 80 percent of all utility savings reported across the United States in 2016 and 2017.[34]

---

[33] ACEEE, Alliance to Save Energy & Business Council for Sustainable Energy, Energy Efficiency Impact Report (2020), https://energyefficiencyimpact.org/wp-content/uploads/ExecSummary-EEReport-Printable-.pdf.

[34] Berg et al., *supra* note 27, at 44.

It is noteworthy that among the surrounding states, Maryland, Pennsylvania, and, most recently, Virginia, have all adopted an EERS. (Ohio had an EERS prior to July 2019, when the passage of HB 6 effectively terminated the state's EERS by 2020 by lowering utility savings targets from 22 to 17.5 percent, a level that most utilities were on the verge of meeting.)[35] In West Virginia, State House Delegates Barbara Evans Fleischauer and Mike Manypenny introduced legislation in 2012 that would have established an EERS requiring electric utilities to scale up their energy efficiency and conservation programs to achieve electricity sales reductions of 5 percent from 2009 levels by 2013, 10 percent by 2015, and 15 percent by 2017, and also to offer demand response programs that achieve the same savings targets.[36] The bill also included a proposed sharing mechanism that, among other things, would have addressed the lost revenue issue. The bill never made it out of committee. More recently, Delegate Evan Hansen (Democrat, Monongalia County) proposed a bill (HB 2588) during the 2021 legislative session that would have required electric utilities to ramp up their energy efficiency programs to achieve energy savings beginning at 0.5 percent in 2022 (below 2019 consumption levels) and steadily increasing to a 9 percent reduction by 2031. That bill died in committee as well.

Second, the biggest single driver in the *ACEEE State Scorecard* is the role of the utility sector which, according to ACEEE, delivers a substantial share of electricity and natural gas efficiency programs in the United States. Of the 50 points possible in the *ACEEE State Scorecard*, 20 points are allocated to this category. In the 2020 *ACEEE State Scorecard*, West Virginia had the distinction of being the *only state in the country with a negative score: minus 1.0.* (In contrast, the two states that performed best in this category, Massachusetts and Rhode Island, both scored 19.5 points, while the state ranked number one, California, had 16 points.) Out of 7 points possible in the scoring system for the size of annual electric energy efficiency program budgets – which reflects the level of customer-funded (either through utility rates or directly on customer bills through a surcharge) energy efficiency programs – West Virginia received only 0.5 points, based on energy efficiency program spending of only $7.6 million in 2019, or $4.24 per capita. (By comparison, the leader in per capita spending, Rhode Island, had $98.24 in 2019, while neighboring Maryland had the fourth highest per capita spending at $45.58; Pennsylvania's per capita spending was over three times that of West Virginia, at $15.43.) Similarly, West Virginia did not fare well in the ranking of net incremental electricity savings for 2019, saving only 52,221 MWh in 2019, which amounted to about 0.16 percent of

35 In 2019, Ohio passed House Bill 6 which, among other things, repealed the energy efficiency standards that were formerly in place under which Ohio utilities were required to reduce customers' energy use by 22 percent from 2008 levels by 2027. David Roberts, *Ohio Just Passed the Worst Energy Bill of the 21st Century*, Vox (July 27, 2019), https://www.vox.com/energy-and-environment/2019/7/27/8910804/ohio-gop-nuclear-coal-plants-renewables-efficiency-hb6.
36 West Virginia State Legislature, H.B. 2025 (2012).

2017 sales. (The leader in percentage sales reduction was Rhode Island [2.51 percent], with Maryland in third place at 2.14 percent).

The absence of effective energy efficiency polices such as an EERS (3 points possible) or decoupling (2 points possible) also hurt West Virginia in the rankings. Furthermore, West Virginia was penalized 1 point in the utility sector category due to the PSC's policy of allowing large customers to simply opt out of participating in utility energy efficiency programs, an option that had been exercised by twenty large customers. While these customers are obligated to document that they have achieved similar/equivalent savings irrespective of utility energy efficiency programs to retain their "opt-out" status, the PSC has never specified any methodology for evaluating the claims of energy and/or demand reduction that customers certify to the utilities. As noted in the *ACEEE State Scorecard*, this opt-out policy has negative consequences, including increasing the cost of energy savings for all customers and reducing the benefits; forcing remaining customers to indirectly subsidize the customers opting out inasmuch as they share some of the system benefits, while only the smaller customers are paying to support energy efficiency programs; and preventing utilities from capturing all highly cost-effective energy savings, which can contribute to higher overall system costs through the use of more expensive supply resources.

Third, West Virginia is particularly bad at addressing the needs of low-income customers, a segment of the population that should receive more, rather than less, attention in West Virginia, given its status as one of the poorest states in the country.[37] Low-income customers bear a disproportionate burden from energy costs; low-income households tend to live in less efficient housing and devote a greater proportion of their income to utility bills than higher-income households. As noted in the *ACEEE 2020 State Scorecard*, low-income customers would especially benefit from energy efficiency programs; low-income weatherization and energy efficiency retrofits can reduce a household's energy burden by 25 percent, on average, and this would not only put more money in ratepayers' pockets to cover other necessities beyond energy, but would also improve their comfort level and health. One of the metrics tracked in the *ACEEE State Scorecard* is strength of utility-led low-income programs and, not surprisingly, West Virginia fared poorly when evaluated alongside other states; it was one of only seven states to get a zero in the category. West Virginia utilities spent only $712,183 on low-income programs in 2019, or $1.14 per income-qualified resident. In contrast, Pennsylvania spent $27.78 per income-qualified resident, the eighth highest in the United States, with Maryland close behind at $21.09.

---

[37] Based on median household income, West Virginia ranked forty-ninth in the country in a 2019 survey by 24/7 WALL STREET, with a poverty rate of 16%. Samuel Stebbins, *America's Richest and Poorest States*, 24/7 WALL STREET (Oct. 1, 2019), https://247wallst.com/special-report/2019/10/01/americas-richest-and-poorest-states-8/.

Finally, the statistics cited in the *ACEEE State Scorecard* do not tell the full story. The energy efficiency programs offered by the investor-owned utilities operating in West Virginia are woefully deficient, but for different reasons. One utility, FirstEnergy, does not even try to offer energy efficiency programs in West Virginia, and is openly hostile to demand-side programs, based on statements in its IRPs and its public opposition to demand response programs. The other utility, AEP, actually integrates energy efficiency into its long-term planning and treats it as a resource alongside traditional supply-side resources, as discussed earlier in this chapter in the subsection The More Enlightened Policies of AEP. Its good intentions with respect to pursuing energy efficiency, however, are thwarted by opposition at the PSC itself. This "tale of two utilities" with respect to demand-side resources deserves a closer look.

The Neanderthal Policies of FirstEnergy

FirstEnergy's two subsidiaries operating in West Virginia, Mon Power and Potomac Edison, currently offer *no* energy efficiency programs for their customers. For seven years, from 2011 through 2018, FirstEnergy had two limited programs (a residential low-income program and a nonresidential lighting program) designed to produce savings of only 0.1 percent annually. Even those miniscule programs were offered under duress, as part of the settlement that led to PSC approval in October 2013 of the acquisition of the Harrison coal plant, as discussed in Chapter 10. As soon as the terms of the settlement agreement expired, so did the offering of energy efficiency programs. So what do FirstEnergy's long-term planning documents say about the potential role of energy efficiency in meeting resource needs? Both its 2012 "Resource Plan" and its 2015 IRP included the statement that "[b]ecause of the significant nature of Mon Power's capacity shortfall, *demand side resource options are not a viable solution* capable of meeting Mon Power's obligations" and thus "were *not considered* as a viable, long-term solution to Mon Power's significant capacity and energy needs."[38]

Given this conclusion in each report, neither contained an analysis of demand-side options on a consistent and integrated basis with supply-side options. Instead, the "preferred approach" recommended in both documents was for Mon Power and Potomac Edison to buy existing, uneconomical coal plants then owned by unregulated FirstEnergy subsidiaries, thereby shifting the cost burden of these plants from FirstEnergy shareholders to captive utility ratepayers in West Virginia. (In the 2012 Resource Plan, the "preferred resource" was the Harrison coal plant, acquired by Mon Power and Potomac Edison in 2013, as discussed in Chapter 10. In the 2015 IRP, the "preferred resource" was the Pleasants Station coal plant, which FirstEnergy unsuccessfully tried to sell to Mon Power and Potomac Edison in 2018.) As

---

[38] FIRSTENERGY, *supra* note 18, at 56; MONONGAHELA POWER COMPANY & THE POTOMAC EDISON COMPANY, 2015 INTEGRATED RESOURCE PLAN 56 (Dec. 30, 2015), http://www.psc.state.wv.us/scripts/WebDocket/ViewDocument.cfm?CaseActivityID=441858&NotType=WebDocket (emphases added).

FirstEnergy sees it, customers should pay more than 7 cents per kWh for electricity produced by old, inefficient coal plants instead of acquiring energy efficiency savings at a cost of about 2.5 cents per kWh. In fact, according to FirstEnergy, utilities should never pay to acquire energy efficiency resources; according to its 2012 Resource Plan, "[i]f an EE [energy efficiency] resource is cost-effective for the consumer, it stands to reason that the consumer, when faced with an economic decision of whether or not to install the EE resource, would eventually do so regardless of any out-of-market incentive or utility program."[39]

Such an approach, of course, is completely inconsistent with the concept of integrated resource planning, as it disregards the possible role of demand-side resources in favor of traditional supply-side solutions, which are higher cost but more profitable for FirstEnergy. The lack of rigorous analysis of energy efficiency as a resource option in the planning documents and in the applications for coal plant transfers was truly breathtaking, but it was sufficient to survive the unprincipled PSC review process, which led to PSC approval of both coal plant acquisitions as being in the "public interest," as discussed in Chapter 10.

FirstEnergy's hostility to energy efficiency and demand response programs is well known. In 2014, FirstEnergy's then CEO, Anthony Alexander, had an opportunity to describe his view of what, at that time, were current trends in the electric utility industry, in a speech before the US Chamber of Commerce:

> In the electricity utility industry, energy efficiency, renewable power, distributed generation, micro grids, roof-top solar and demand reduction are examples of what "sounds good" – and while they may all play some role in meeting the energy needs of customers, they are not substitutes for what has worked to sustain a reliable, affordable and environmentally responsible electric system.[40]

According to a report by the Institute for Energy and Economics Financial Analysis (IEEFA) in October 2014 regarding FirstEnergy's political and regulatory strategy, FirstEnergy's corporate policy included opposition to investments in energy efficiency given that energy efficiency represents "direct competition" to FirstEnergy's core business of selling electricity.[41] The report notes FirstEnergy's role as the "key player" in a successful legislative campaign in Ohio in 2014 to roll back a 2008 law that established basic standards for the use of energy efficiency and renewable energy by Ohio's utilities, as well as the $1.3 million fine that was levied by the Pennsylvania PUC in 2014 against

[39] FIRSTENERGY, *supra* note 18, at 40.
[40] *FirstEnergy CEO Takes National Stage; Says Regulatory Challenges and Mandates Make It Difficult for Electric Industry*, AKRON BEACON JOURNAL (Apr. 8, 2014), https://www.beaconjournal.com/story/news/2014/04/08/firstenergy-ceo-takes-national-stage/10656366007/.
[41] Tom Sanzillo & Cathy Kunkel, *FirstEnergy: A Major Utility Seeks a Subsidized Turnaround*, INSTITUTE FOR ENERGY AND ECONOMICS FINANCIAL ANALYSIS (Oct. 2014), https://ieefa.org/wp-content/uploads/2014/10/First-Energy_-A-Major-Utility-Seeks-a-Subsidized-Turnaround-OCT20141.pdf.

FirstEnergy subsidiary West Penn Power for its failure to meet its statutorily mandated energy efficiency target for 2011.

FirstEnergy has been a strident opponent of energy efficiency and demand response programs that participate in "capacity markets," which pay power plants (or other resources) for having their capacity available to meet peak demand. In addition to administering the wholesale energy markets discussed in Chapter 2, PJM also operates a capacity market. It conducts an annual auction to secure the amount of capacity that PJM expects will be needed to meet demand, plus a reserve margin, three years later. All resources – including energy efficiency and demand response, along with the more traditional supply-side options – bid into the auction, and all that clear the auction are awarded the market clearing price for their capacity. Excluding energy efficiency and demand response from participating in the capacity markets – as advocated by FirstEnergy – would result in higher capacity prices, because these low-cost resources would be prevented from bidding into the market. (It is cheaper to balance supply and demand in the capacity markets by reducing the demand side of the equation through energy efficiency and demand response than by providing additional supply through the construction of more generating plants.) The higher resulting capacity prices would, of course, benefit FirstEnergy by supporting its coal and nuclear generating plants.

FirstEnergy has also taken formal steps to exclude demand response from the capacity market. In 2014, the District of Columbia Circuit Court of Appeals over-turned a FERC order (Order No. 745) governing demand response programs,[42] which created some uncertainty about whether demand response would continue to be treated as a resource in wholesale capacity markets. FirstEnergy's response was to promptly file a complaint against PJM at FERC, seeking an exceptionally broad interpretation of the appeals court ruling by asking not only that demand response be removed from future auctions but that the results of the most recent auction be nullified and the auction redone without demand response. (This would have resulted in higher prices for capacity in PJM, benefitting FirstEnergy's power plants at the expense of electricity customers throughout the mid-Atlantic region.) Ultimately, FERC Order No. 745 was upheld by the US Supreme Court in 2019,[43] but FirstEnergy could not miss the opportunity to exploit the temporary uncertainty to pursue its objective of keeping demand response resources from participating in capacity markets.

The More Enlightened Policies of AEP
In the case of AEP's two operating companies in West Virginia, Appalachian Power and Wheeling Power, the PSC ordered Appalachian Power to submit an energy efficiency plan in 2009 with its 2010 rate case. The final order in 2010 directed the

---

[42]   Electric Power Supply Association v. FERC, 753 F.2d 216 (D.C. Cir. 2014).
[43]   FERC v. Electric Power Supply Association, 577 U.S. 260 (2016).

AEP companies to implement programs that included low-income weatherization, residential home audit, residential lighting, and commercial/industrial prescriptive incentives. According to the IRP filed by AEP with the Virginia SCC, these programs, which were approved in February 2011, were expected to result in 1.1 percent of installed saving in 2012. The actual results, however, fell far short; AEP achieved savings of only 0.4 percent in West Virginia in 2012.

Unlike FirstEnergy, however, AEP did not dismiss the role that energy efficiency could play in long-term planning. The AEP Resource Plan filed with the Virginia SCC contained several positive statements about the potential contributions of demand-side programs, and acknowledged that AEP companies had far more robust demand-side programs in states outside West Virginia. According to the AEP Resource Plan, "[d]emand-side resources will likely play a significant role in satisfying capacity and energy requirements prospectively as they are the least-cost resource, even in significant amounts." The AEP Resource Plan stated that "it is reasonable to assume that there is a fairly large well of latent cost-effective EE available."[44]

Even though the IRP statute passed in West Virginia in 2014 technically does not require the integration of demand- and supply-side resources, the IRP filed by Appalachian Power in December 2015 demonstrated how such integration is actually accomplished. Appalachian Power used a long-term optimization model, Plexos, to identify the optimal portfolio of future capacity and energy resources, including demand-side additions, which would produce the lowest and most stable customer rates over time, under fifteen different scenarios. For energy efficiency programs, the model considered up to eighteen unique "bundles" of residential and commercial measures taking into consideration cost and performance parameters. New energy efficiency resources were selected throughout the ten-year planning period. The programs providing the majority of the savings were commercial and residential lighting. By 2025, incremental energy efficiency programs were anticipated to reduce residential and commercial energy consumption by 3 percent. Overall energy efficiency savings were projected to provide a decrease in residential and commercial energy usage by 8 percent by 2025. The role of energy efficiency in meeting Appalachian Power's energy needs was proposed to increase from 0.2 percent to 2.7 percent over the ten-year planning period from 2016 to 2025.

Armed with the modeling results that recommended a greater role for energy efficiency in West Virginia, AEP filed an application with the West Virginia PSC in March 2017 for approval to scale up the demand-side programs at Appalachian Power and Wheeling Power. Among other things, AEP proposed adding four new energy efficiency programs[45] and substantially increasing its existing $10 million

---

[44] Integrated Resource Planning Report to the Commonwealth of Virginia State Corporation Commission, Case No. PUE-2011-00100, Sep. 1, 2011, at 60, https://www.scc.virginia.gov/DocketSearch#caseDocs/130183.

[45] "Bring-Your-Own Smart Thermostat," Small Business Direct Install, Multi-Family Direct Install, and Volt VAR Optimization expansion.

annual budget for demand-side programs to $11.5 million for July 2017–June 2018 and to $13.4 million for July 2018–June 2019, respectively. The proposed increase was not only flatly rejected by commission staff at the PSC, but staff's position was that AEP should entirely terminate its demand-side programs or, at a minimum, put them on a "hiatus." The staff witness testified that because neither of the AEP companies were in a position to need additional capacity, customers would be "worse off from an economic perspective" with the demand-side programs than without them. The case was ultimately resolved through a stipulation among the parties; the settlement required AEP to drop the proposed addition of the four new programs, and to slash its budget request for demand-side programs by $8.4 million over the two-year period.

Undaunted, AEP tried again in 2019 to expand its energy efficiency programs in West Virginia. It filed a proposal with the PSC in April 2019 to add one of the programs that had been rejected in 2017 (Small Business Direct Install) as well as a new program (Low Income Multifamily), and to increase spending for demand-side programs to $11.7 million annually for 2020 and 2021. Commission staff at the PSC took the same position as they did in the 2017 proceeding – the demand-side programs should be terminated in their entirety – and filed testimony that repeated largely the same analysis that it had offered in 2017. This time, however, staff were also able to cite as precedent the action by the Kentucky PSC in January 2018 to shut down the energy efficiency programs – then budgeted at $6 million annually – offered by AEP's affiliate, Kentucky Power. And staff pointed out that in Appalachian Power's most recent general rate case in West Virginia (filed in February 2019), over one-half of the proposed $111.4 million rate increase was attributable to declining loads (residential load had declined by 14 percent during the preceding four years). Given the AEP companies' lack of need for additional capacity, staff took the position that AEP customers who choose not to participate in energy efficiency programs would pay a total electric bill that would be higher than if the programs were discontinued.

As in the 2017 proceeding, the case was resolved through settlement, and AEP agreed to abandon its proposed expansion of energy efficiency programs. The $11.7 million annual budget that AEP had sought for demand-side programs was slashed by $3.1 million, to $8.6 million for each of the years 2020 and 2021.

The fatal flaw in commission staff's analysis, of course, was the failure to analyze the wisdom of energy efficiency programs from the perspective of the utility customer. Admittedly, the case for making investments in energy efficiency programs is more challenging for a utility with declining loads: If the utility already has excess capacity, why would it want to promote programs designed to reduce demand further? From the customer's perspective, however, the availability of energy efficiency programs provides some helpful tools to manage the ever-increasing electricity prices charged by West Virginia utilities. (According to the PSC's reporting, residential customers of Appalachian Power and Wheeling Power are paying more than double the price for electricity in 2021 than they did in 2008: $138.57 for a typical monthly bill in 2021 versus $62.46 in 2008.)[46] Yes, there are some costs associated with initiating and operating the programs that would be included in utility rates. But the economic analysis performed by AEP took those costs into account and still showed that the programs would be beneficial to customers.

Moreover, demand-side programs need to be considered as a resource, alongside the traditional supply-side solutions which, as mentioned in the section Integrated Resource Planning, is the "integrated" aspect of integrated resource planning. AEP's sophisticated modeling in connection with its 2015 IRP showed the level of energy efficiency investment that made sense as part of the overall portfolio of resources that would result in the lowest costs for customers over time. AEP was seeking simply to implement the level of energy efficiency programs prescribed by the rigorous modeling used in preparing its IRP, to complement its supply-side resources. As long as PSC staff and, more importantly, the PSC commissioners themselves, fail to consider energy efficiency (1) from the customer's perspective and (2) as a resource that warrants consideration on a "consistent and integrated basis" alongside supply-side options – as required by the Energy Policy Act of 1992 – customers in West Virginia will continue to live in drafty, uninsulated homes and pay higher electric bills than utility customers in the vast majority of US states.

Surrounding States and the Way Forward

The adjoining states of Virginia and Maryland can show the way for scaling up energy efficiency programs. Virginia was identified in ACEEE's *State Scorecard* as the leading state in the south – its ranking jumped four places from its 2019 ranking of twenty-ninth – and one of the top energy stories of 2020 was the enactment of the Virginia Clean Economy Act (VCEA).[47] Among other things, the VCEA established an Energy Efficiency Resource Standard (EERS) that sets multiyear electric savings targets for utilities through 2025; for subsequent years, the VCEA authorizes the Virginia SCC to adjust savings targets every three years thereafter. Virginia joins Arkansas as the only state in the south with an EERS.[48] Another provision in the VCEA requires utilities to prove they are achieving those targets before they are permitted to build new fossil fuel plants.[49] Finally, to support low-income customers, the Act includes measures to reduce energy burdens and cap monthly payments for low-income customers (6 percent of income for those with gas heating or 10 percent for those with electric heating).

---

[46] *Comparison of Growth in West Virginia Residential Utility Rate to Changes in the Consumer Price Index*, WEST VIRGINIA PUBLIC SERVICE COMMISSION (Feb. 26, 2021), http://www.psc.state.wv.us/Special_Reports/ratecomp_2021.pdf.

[47] BERG ET AL., *supra* note 27, at 15.

[48] *Id.*

[49] 2020 State Energy Efficiency Scorecard, Virginia Fact Sheet, ACEEE, https://www.aceee.org/sites/default/files/pdfs/ACEEE_ScrSht20_Virginia.pdf.

Maryland, ranked sixth in the 2020 *Energy Efficiency Scorecard*, has demonstrated steady improvement in energy efficiency programs since the enactment of the EmPOWER Maryland law, which was extended by the 2017 legislature to run through 2023.[50] The law originally called for utilities to reduce electricity usage by 2 percent annually by 2020. More recently, in 2020, Maryland enacted HB 662, which incorporates energy savings goals established in a 2019 Executive Order that called for 10 percent savings in respect of state-owned buildings by 2029.[51]

On this latter point, West Virginia is showing some modest movement in the right direction; in 2021, the West Virginia legislature passed HB 2667, which creates an energy efficiency cost saving program for state-owned buildings that would require energy usage to be benchmarked and energy savings to be reported using an EPA benchmarking tool.[52] (Energy benchmarking refers to measuring a building's energy use and comparing it to the energy use of similar buildings.) West Virginia spends approximately $88 to $100 million of taxpayer money on utilities each year in respect of 3,300–4,000 state-owned buildings.[53] HB 2667, which was originally drafted by Delegate Evan Hansen (Democrat, Monongalia County), aims to reduce energy usage by 25 percent compared to 2018 levels by the year 2030.[54]

[50] 2020 State Energy Efficiency Scorecard, Maryland Fact Sheet, ACEEE, https://www.aceee.org/sites/default/files/pdfs/ACEEE_ScrSht20_Maryland.pdf.

[51] *Id.*

[52] Mike Tony, *WV Senate Committee Approves Bill to Create Energy Efficiency Program for State Buildings*, CHARLESTON GAZETTE-MAIL (Apr. 6, 2021), https://www.wvgazettemail.com/news/energy_and_environment/wv-senate-committee-approves-bill-to-create-energy-efficiency-program-for-state-buildings/article_bd7a4859-2732-5a29-9a82-2383250f0ce2.html.

[53] *Id.*

[54] *Id.*

9

The Role of the Legislature in West Virginia's Failed Energy Policies

West Virginia's legislature has done more than its share in contributing to the failed energy policies during "the lost decade." This chapter explores several measures considered during this period that illustrate the collective mindset of lawmakers on energy issues. First, in 2009 West Virginia adopted a worthless "alternative and renewable energy portfolio standard" that deceptively suggested by its title that it was promoting renewable energy when, in fact, it did nothing to encourage renewable energy resources. Instead, it sanctioned many forms of fossil fuel-fired generation as "alternative energy" and therefore failed to produce any incentives to promote the development of renewable energy resources in the state. Second, in 2012 the legislature responded to a crisis of American Electric Power's (AEP) own making by passing a bill that allowed AEP to avoid a 30 to 40 percent rate increase – due entirely to its exclusive reliance on increasingly expensive coal to generate electricity – by authorizing AEP to issue long-term bonds to spread the rate increase to an entire new generation of ratepayers.

Finally, one thing at which the legislature excels is giving the coal industry whatever it wants in the interests of reducing costs and attempting – futilely – to keep coal competitive with other means of generating electricity in order to "save jobs." In the face of the overwhelming market forces that amassed against the coal industry during "the lost decade" – as discussed in Chapters 2 and 3 – the legislature was under constant pressure to take action to make it cheaper for coal operators to do business in West Virginia. The measures included repeated efforts to reduce safety protections for coal miners, a reduction in the coal severance tax from 5 to 3 percent in 2018, and, in an extraordinary action undertaken in a special session in 2019 that was convened solely for this specific measure, approving a $12.5 million tax bailout for an uneconomic coal plant.

Before looking at these particular legislative actions, however, it is worth briefly describing the role of campaign contributions in shaping the legislature's response to energy issues, a dynamic that one writer has referred to as "big energy's stranglehold on West Virginia politics."[1]

---

[1] Alex Kotch, *A Viral Video Revealed Big Energy's Stranglehold on West Virginia Politics*, VICE (Feb. 19, 2018), https://www.vice.com/en/article/d3wdn7/a-viral-video-revealed-big-energys-stranglehold-on-west-virginia-politics.

"BIG ENERGY'S STRANGLEHOLD ON WEST VIRGINIA POLITICS"

"Montani Semper Liberi!" This phrase, which is Latin for the state's motto "mountaineers are always free," were the parting words of Lissa Lucas, who was forcibly removed from a Judiciary Committee hearing of the West Virginia House of Delegates during her testimony in February 2018 on HB 4268, a "cotenancy" law that would have allowed fossil fuel companies to drill for oil and gas on private land without all of the landowners' consent. Rather than addressing her remarks to the substance of the bill, Lucas chose to use her allotted one minute and forty-five seconds to start listing the campaign donations to committee members from oil and gas companies. Chairman John Shott – who was identified by Lucas as having received $2,000 from FirstEnergy, $2,000 from Appalachian Power, $2,000 from the oil and gas law firm Steptoe & Johnson, $1,000 from Consol Energy, and $1,000 from EQT – had a problem with that, accusing Lucas of making "personal comments" as she read from her research of publicly available campaign finance data. When she nonetheless continued her listing of campaign donations to committee members, Shott had officers remove her from the hearing. The video of the incident went viral, and led to stories about Lucas in *The Washington Post, The Intercept,* and *The Rolling Stone.*

Lucas was a Democratic candidate for House District 7 at the time, and the national attention helped her generate $50,000 in campaign donations (as compared to the $4,000 she had raised prior to the incident). As noted in *The Intercept* article, Lucas's opponent, incumbent Jason Harshbarger, had been the beneficiary of a fundraising event the preceding December at the offices of the West Virginia Oil and Natural Gas Association, hosted by a "host committee" comprising many familiar names in the energy industry in West Virginia, including Sammy Gray of FirstEnergy, Bob Orndorff of Dominion Energy, Kevin Ellis of Antero Resources, Greg Hoyer of EQT, Pat McCune of Consol Energy, and Steve Stewart of Appalachian Power.

Harshbarger, a fourteen-year employee of Dominion Resources, defeated Lucas in the 2018 general election with 73 percent of the vote; he subsequently resigned from the seat in August 2019 to succeed Bob Orndorff as the new state policy director for Dominion Energy. According to Lucas,

> [t]his is exactly how our rigged political system works: bought politicians look out for their own personal financial interests, rather than represent the working families in their districts. So, his making the Dominion lobbying position official just means he's now being more straightforward about whom he's really working for. He did the job his donors told him to do – took away property rights, voted against educators and public employees, and so on – so now he gets that hinted-at reward.[2]

[2]   Brad McEhinny, *Delegate Jason Harshbarger Resigns the House Because of New Lobbying Job,* WV METRONEWS (Aug. 14, 2019), https://wvmetronews.com/2019/08/14/delegate-jason-harshbarger-resigns-the-house-because-of-new-job/.

ADOPTION OF AN ALTERNATIVE AND RENEWABLE ENERGY PORTFOLIO STANDARD

The Hijacking of a Renewable Energy Measure by the Coal Industry

In June 2009, West Virginia followed the lead of over thirty states in the United States and adopted a renewable portfolio standard (RPS), a measure requiring electric utilities to procure a minimum percentage of their electricity supply from renewable sources by a specified deadline (e.g., 15 percent of electricity from renewable sources by 2015). At the outset, the proposal for an RPS in West Virginia resembled similar measures that had been enacted by other states at the time. The "Renewable Portfolio Standards Sustainable Energy Act" was introduced in March 2009 by lead sponsor Delegate Barbara Evans Fleischauer of Monongalia County, and eight cosponsors, including a couple of big names from West Virginia's past, Staggers (Margaret, the daughter of a sixteen-term congressman from West Virginia, Harley Staggers), and Hatfield (Barbara "Bobbie" Hatfield from Kanawha County). The original bill, HB 2891, directed electric utilities in West Virginia to gradually increase their portfolio of renewable resources in their generation mix, from 5 percent in 2011–12 to 15 percent in 2021 and thereafter. The bill defined renewable energy resources to include the usual mix of renewables (solar, wind, biomass, geothermal, and low impact, small hydroelectric and micro hydro projects) and expressly excluded coal, natural gas, oil, propane, or any other fossil fuel or nuclear energy.

As it wound its way through the legislative process, however, the bill was hijacked by the coal industry. Delegate Harry Keith White (Democrat, Mingo County) claimed years later that he had worked with West Virginia Coal Association President Bill Raney in 2009 to come up with a workable final version of the bill.[3] Then Governor Joe Manchin conceded the prominent role of the coal industry in 2010 during his campaign for the US Senate in a special election to fill the seat of the late Robert Byrd. His Republican opponent, Morgantown businessman John Raese, began running an attack ad in September 2010 featuring the recently enacted Alternative and Renewable Energy Portfolio Act as "cap and trade, Manchin style." According to an interview with *RealClearPolitics* at the time, Raese asked: "Do the people of West Virginia trust a governor in the state of West Virginia who has already implemented cap and trade here in West Virginia?"[4] Manchin's response? He laughed off Raese's criticism of the law, saying "tell him he should read it first – the coal industry helped put it together." As observed by Ken Ward of

---

[3]   Phil Kabler, *New GOP Legislature Works to Repeal Alternative Energy Bill*, CHARLESTON GAZETTE-MAIL (Jan. 16, 2015), https://www.wvgazettemail.com/news/politics/new-gop-legislature-works-to-repeal-alternative-energy-bill/article_33919428-b5e6-5df4-99b1-2a2ef18fd24b.html.

[4]   Scott Conroy & Erin McPike, *Raese to Bank on Cap and Trade Against Manchin*, REALCLEARPOLITICS (Sept. 27, 2010), https://www.realclearpolitics.com/articles/2010/09/27/raese_to_bank_on_cap_and_trade_against_manchin_107317.html.

the *Charleston Gazette-Mail*, it should come as "no surprise" that Manchin has "carefully crafted (and named) his proposal so that it protects the coal industry."[5] At the time the bill passed, lobbyists for coal and electric utilities had signed onto it.

The Alternative and Renewable Energy Portfolio Standard (AREPS), enacted in 2009, required electric utilities to supply 25 percent of retail electric sales from eligible alternative and renewable energy sources by 2025 and provided for interim targets of 10 percent by 2015 and 15 percent by 2020. The energy sources classified as "renewable" for purposes of the AREPS were unremarkable; they included solar photovoltaic energy, solar thermal energy, wind power, run of river hydropower, geothermal energy, biomass, biologically derived fuel, fuel cell technology, recycled energy, and any other resource, method, project, or technology certified by the West Virginia Public Service Commission (PSC) as renewable. The two noteworthy aspects of the AREPS are: (1) its inclusion of "alternative energy" in addition to renewable energy, and (2) the ability to satisfy the *entire* procurement obligation through alternative, rather than renewable, energy sources.

First, "alternative energy resources" were defined to include "advanced coal technology" which, in turn, was defined as technology that is used in a new or existing energy-generating facility to reduce airborne carbon emissions associated with the combustion or use of coal. This includes carbon capture and sequestration (CCS) technology, supercritical technology, ultra-supercritical technology, pressurized fluidized bed technology, and any other resource, method, project, or technology certified by the PSC as advanced coal technology. Other "alternative energy resources" in the AREPS included coal bed methane, natural gas, fuel produced by a coal gasification or liquefaction facility, synthetic gas, integrated gasification combined-cycle technologies, waste coal, tire-derived fuel (yes, energy from burning tires!), and pumped storage hydroelectric projects. (Only two other states – Nevada and Rhode Island – included waste tires (or "tired-derived fuel") within their energy portfolio standards.) The inclusion of waste coal in the measure served then Governor Manchin's personal interests – his family coal brokerage business, Enersystems, purchases waste coal from mines and resells it to power plants as fuel, as discussed in Chapter 7.

Second, the AREPS, unlike the RPSs in effect in every other state, permitted the entire procurement obligation to be fulfilled by "alternative energy" sources, and thus was largely ineffective in stimulating the development of renewable energy resources. In fact, utilities were able to demonstrate compliance with the AREPS from its inception, through the use of alternative energy resources to the complete exclusion of those from renewable energy. The renewable energy portion of the bill functioned more like a "nonbinding goal" and was commonly classified as a "goal" rather than a "standard" in nationwide compilations of state energy policies at the time.

5   Ken Ward, Jr., *Early Thoughts on Manchin's Energy Plan*, COAL TATTOO (Feb. 11, 2009), http://blogs.wvgazettemail.com/coaltattoo/2009/02/11/early-thoughts-on-manchins-energy-plan/.

That the "goal" was satisfied even at the time the AREPS was enacted was confirmed in the PSC's 2012 report to the legislature. (Under the AREPS, the PSC was required to report to the legislature on the actions the utilities were taking to achieve compliance.) The PSC's report confirmed that, as of 2012, utilities in West Virginia were able to meet their compliance obligations under the AREPS entirely with "alternative" resources. Massive coal plants, because they use supercritical coal technology, qualified as "alternative energy resource facilities," and thus more than fulfilled the procurement obligation imposed by the AREPS. The supercritical coal plants in operation at the time included the John Amos Plant (2,900 MW, owned by AEP); the Harrison Power Station (1,984 MW, owned by FirstEnergy); the Mountaineer Plant (1,300 MW, owned by AEP); the Pleasants Power Station (1,300 MW, owned by FirstEnergy); and the Longview Power Plant (695 MW, a merchant plant). A large natural gas-fired plant, the Ceredo facility in Huntington (523 MW, owned by AEP) also qualified as an "alternative energy resource facility," as did two waste coal plants, Morgantown Energy Associates (68.9 MW) and Grant Town (80 MW), and the Willow Island facility (187 MW, owned by FirstEnergy), by virtue of 10 percent of its fuel supply being tire-derived.

Collectively, these fossil fuel-fired facilities represented 10,145 MW of generating capacity. Taking into account how much the coal plants were typically operating at the time (about 65 percent), this represented about 57,000,000 MWh of electricity generated annually, representing over 70 percent of total electricity production in West Virginia – 81,024,000 MWh in 2010. Thus, the obligation under the 2009 West Virginia AREPS to procure one quarter of the electricity supply from alternative or renewable resources by 2025 *could have been satisfied almost three times over by alternative sources using existing generating units, with twelve years to spare.* The AREPS did virtually nothing to stimulate development of renewable resources within West Virginia. Jeff Herholdt, Director of the West Virginia Division of Energy, confirmed this in a statement at the March 2013 West Virginia Coal Association 40th Annual Mining Symposium, stating that "[w]e're the only state that has an alternative portfolio standard that would be met with 100 percent coal."[6]

The Repeal of the Worthless Alternative and Renewable Energy Portfolio Standard

In one of the first actions of the 2015 West Virginia legislative session, the AREPS was repealed. In the November 2014 elections, Republicans took control of both the House of Delegates and the Senate chamber for the first time in the state's history; the Democratic Party had held control of the House of Delegates since the 1930s.

---

[6] Ken Ward, Jr., *Coal Lobby Wary, but Hopeful of Industry's Future*, CHARLESTON GAZETTE-MAIL (Mar 7, 2013), www.wvgazette.com/News/201303070070. Mr. Herholdt also said that the state's AREPS "is not bringing in the other energy sources," and "would have very little impact on coal production or use." According to Mr. Herholdt, "[w]e're not incentivizing renewables with this portfolio." *Id.*

Many of the Republicans were identified as "Tea Party" candidates, and some in particular ran on a platform of repealing the AREPS on the grounds that it was some sort of "cap-and-trade" legislation that should suffer the same fate as the Waxman–Markey bill that was famously (infamously?) used by US Senator Manchin as target practice during his 2010 race for the US Senate. According to one observer, more than forty Democratic delegates were targeted in campaign attack ads for supporting what Republicans called "West Virginia's cap-and-trade law." Other opponents of the AREPS claimed that it was threatening the West Virginia coal industry, inasmuch as it was forcing the electric utilities to displace coal-fired generation with renewable sources of electricity. Finally, some opponents claimed that the AREPS was causing utility rates to increase, given that renewable energy sources were more expensive than the thermal-based resources – primarily coal – upon which utilities would rely in the absence of a procurement obligation favoring renewable resources.

Of course, none of these arguments is true. There was nothing about the AREPS that created a "cap-and-trade" program. Although elements of the statute suggested the use of credits – "renewable" energy acquisitions were worth twice as much as credits from using "alternative" energy resources, and three credits were awarded for renewable energy generation located on a reclaimed surface mine – there was, in fact, no trading of such credits in the manner envisioned in a true cap-and-trade program. Why? A functioning cap-and-trade market requires scarcity of the commodity, which thereby encourages participants to engage in trading as a cost-effective means of achieving compliance. As noted in the preceding section, the AREPS was completely meaningless at its inception, given the ability of the utilities' procurement requirement to be satisfied *entirely* through "alternative" resources in the form of supercritical coal plants then operating in the state. In the absence of any scarcity of the credits necessary to achieve compliance with the AREPS, there was no trading, and thus no cap-and-trade.

Similarly, nothing about the AREPS resulted in any adverse impacts on the coal industry, nor on utility rates. As confirmed by the utilities' compliance filings with the PSC throughout the duration of the AREPS, *the electric utilities did absolutely nothing different in response to the enactment of AREPS than they would have done otherwise.* The procurement requirements imposed by the AREPS following its passage in 2009 were more than satisfied at the time of its enactment – hence the "worthlessness" of the AREPS – so it became impossible to argue that the measure had any adverse impact on the coal industry. The utilities were required to do *nothing* to alter their resource acquisition strategies in response to the measure. Correspondingly, the AREPS had no effect whatsoever in contributing to the massive rate increase that utility ratepayers were experiencing between the enactment of the measure in 2009 and its repeal in January 2015. Rather, it was the failure of the AREPS to require any meaningful diversification in the utilities' resource portfolio, and to avoid the perils of almost exclusive reliance on coal-fired generation during that period, that caused the massive rate increases to occur once coal prices began their dramatic rise in 2008.

Notwithstanding the utter lack of merit of any of the arguments advanced by the proponents of the repeal of AREPS, the measure passed nearly unanimously in both houses at the start of the 2015 legislative session – unanimously in the Senate, and 95–4 in the House. No "cap-and-trade" in West Virginia, by God! And thus West Virginia earned nationwide attention at the time for being the first state in the country to entirely repeal its RPS (which, of course, was not really a RPS at all, but the worthlessness of the measure in stimulating renewable energy production in West Virginia was not captured in national coverage of the event). Once again, West Virginia received national press attention, for all the wrong reasons. In national press coverage of the issue, attention was focused on West Virginia's enduring commitment to the coal industry. Delegate Gary Howell (Republican, Mineral County), for example, was quoted as saying that coal is a "diamond necklace hanging around the neck of West Virginia." Another legislator, Randy Smith (Republican, Preston County), who is also a coal miner, said he ran for public office specifically to repeal the AREPS.[7] Other national sources cited the development as "a clear win for right-wing activists, led by the corporate-backed American Legislative Exchange Council (ALEC)," which had been campaigning for years to roll back state-level renewable standards, mostly without success.[8]

SPREADING OUT THE PAIN OF COAL PRICE INCREASES OVER FIFTEEN YEARS

How Utilities Recover Their Power Costs

Utility rates are usually determined in a general rate case, which is a lengthy process – ten months in West Virginia – that starts when a utility submits a rate case filing with the PSC seeking a change in rates. That filing is usually very extensive, as the utility must demonstrate through the testimony of its officers and managers that it needs rate relief in order to earn a sufficient profit to attract the investment necessary "to keep the lights on." Over the course of the several months following the utility's rate request, the stakeholders in the process – parties to rate proceedings that represent various constituencies, such as industrial customers, environmental organizations, low-income groups, and residential ratepayers – conduct discovery, present opposing testimony, and participate in evidentiary hearings presided over by the PSC commissioners (or, in some states, administrative law judges). At the end of the process, the PSC issues an order granting all or a portion of the requested rate increase. The extensive length of

---

[7] John Light, *Score One for ALEC: West Virginia Is First State to Repeal a Renewable Energy Standard*, GRIST (Feb. 5, 2015), https://grist.org/climate-energy/score-one-for-alec-west-virginia-is-first-state-to-repeal-a-renewable-energy-standard/.
[8] *Id.*

time between the utility's request for higher rates and the effective date of the resulting rate relief is referred to as "regulatory lag," and provides an incentive for the utility to manage its costs.

In the case of an electric utility's power costs, however – the cost of the fuel used to generate electricity (coal, natural gas) or purchase electricity in the wholesale power markets – the process is different. Power costs are typically recovered through power cost adjustment mechanisms, which have been used for decades, at least as far back as 1973 when the first Arab oil embargo triggered a drastic increase in fuel oil prices that caused Con Edison to miss its quarterly dividend in April 1974, due to the mismatch between the fuel costs that it was paying and the level of cost recovery included in its electric rates. Utility stocks have traditionally been considered to be conservative, safe investments, and a reliable source of a stable dividend stream. So a utility missing its quarterly dividend caused regulators to reexamine the process through which utilities recover power costs.

Fuel costs comprise a very large portion of the utility's overall costs, and they can be unpredictable and largely outside the utility's control. As a result, most states provide an expedited rate process each year that takes weeks rather than months. This process typically involves two elements: (1) a projection of the power costs that the utility expects to incur over the subsequent twelve months, and (2) a true-up, or reconciliation, of the actual power costs the utility incurred during the preceding twelve months with the projections that it made in its filing during the previous year. In West Virginia, the power cost adjustment mechanism is referred to as the "expanded net energy cost," or ENEC, filing. (The term "expanded" acknowledges that the scope of the mechanism over the years has grown from examining the actual costs incurred by the utility to obtain fuel and fuel-related purchased power to include other cost components related to obtaining, generating, or transmitting power, such as purchased power and purchased transmission costs and costs associated with environmental compliance.)

ENEC filings became very controversial in the late 2000s, as coal prices in the United States doubled in response to worldwide demand for coal, driven largely by China's rapid economic development. Beginning in 2006, China surpassed the United States as the largest generator of coal-fired electricity, and it became a net importer of thermal coal in 2009. In response to this increase in global demand for thermal coal, domestic coal prices in the United States increased from $1.20 per million British Thermal Units (MMBtu) for delivered coal to the electric sector in 2000 to $2.64 per MMBtu in 2009 – a 220 percent increase – before declining to $2.39 per MMBtu in 2011. This more-than-doubling in coal prices – in addition to stimulating the coal industry acquisition frenzy discussed in Chapter 11 – drove massive rate requests by the AEP companies, Appalachian Power and Wheeling Power, in ENEC filings. In the 2009 ENEC proceeding, the AEP companies filed for the largest rate increase ever requested by a utility in West Virginia, based on fuel cost increases experienced in 2008 and 2009.

In response, the PSC ultimately authorized a $366.7 million rate increase, to be phased in over four years. The first-year rate increase of $106.6 million in and of itself represented a 10.5 percent increase in overall rates. The PSC anticipated that there would be subsequent rate increases in 2010, 2011, and 2012, with the "under-recovery" reduced to zero by June 30, 2013. The double-digit increase from 2009 was followed by a $96.2 million, or 8.2 percent, increase in the 2010 ENEC filing and a $95.2 million, or 7.5 percent, increase in the 2011 ENEC filing.[9]

In early 2012, however, the AEP companies were looking at the prospect of another 30 to 40 percent increase in power costs to be recovered in its annual ENEC filing. So on top of the fourth year of power costs deferred from the 2009 increase, AEP was planning to seek an increase in the range of $350 million. The cause of the increase? AEP cited a 70 percent increase in the price of coal from 2007 to 2011, increasing its annual coal costs from $720 million in 2007 to $1.2 billion by 2011. AEP's response? Go to the legislature for approval of a creative financing tool – "securitization" – that would allow the rate increase to be spread over enough years to make it nearly imperceptible to most ratepayers.

AEP's Legislative Fix for Its Mismanagement of Power Costs

AEP's "Valentine" for the ratepayers of Appalachian Power and Wheeling Power was the introduction, on February 14, 2012, of HB 4530, sponsored by Delegate Harry Keith White (Democrat, Mingo County), along with seven other sponsors. HB 4530 authorized the PSC to approve "consumer rate relief bonds" that would, among other things, spread out the anticipated $350 million ENEC rate increase for 2012 over several years. Notwithstanding the relatively late start for the legislative effort – five weeks into the sixty-day legislative session – the bill sailed through both houses in less than three weeks, passing the House of Delegates by a 95–0 margin on March 7, 2012. This is even more remarkable considering the complexity of the measure, which totaled thirty-five pages. It was approved by Governor Earl Ray Tomblin eight days later, on March 15, 2012.

How did AEP pull this off? The late Bill Howley in his blog, *The Power Line*, referred to the measure as AEP's "bubble bond bailout bill." The information sheet that AEP used in the legislature to sell its proposal included what Howley referred to as the "boldest misrepresentation": a big box at the top of page 1[10] (Figure 9.1).

What legislator could vote against that? A massive rate increase caused by a 70 percent increase in coal prices could just magically disappear due to this "regulatory tool" called securitization. The title of Howley's blog post? "When

---

[9] West Virginia PSC Case No. 12–0399-E-P, Appalachian Power Company and Wheeling Power Company, dba American Electric Power, Petition to Initiate the Annual Review and to Update the ENEC Rates Currently in Effect, *Commission Interim Order*, July 26, 2012, at 3.

[10] Appalachian Power, *Consumer Rate Relief Bonds. Securitization: A Regulatory Tool to Manage Customer Rates* (Feb. 14, 2012), http://www.stoppathwv.com/documents/Untitled001.pdf.

FIGURE 9.1 Fuel (ENEC) rate increases, 2012.

2012 Fuel (ENEC) Rate Increases	
Without securitization	With securitization
30–40%	0

Source: See *supra* note 10.

Half Truth = No Truth." Howley described it as "[l]ike the magician who pulls a rabbit out of his hat, APCo [Appalachian Power Company] appears to have performed a miracle. Voila! Ze rate increase disappears!"[11]

Securitization is an invention of Wall Street that allows a utility to issue bonds to cover a particular cost, with the repayment of those bonds secured by an ironclad dedication of a portion of the utility revenues solely for the purpose of repaying the bonds. It's like a first lien on a portion of the utility revenue that comes through the door – the money cannot be used for anything else, and the bonds will be repaid "come hell or high water," as they say in the business. This excerpt from AEP's prospectus to sell the bonds pretty much captures it:

> **Nonbypassability of consumer rate relief charges**: As long as consumer rate relief bonds issued under a final financing order are outstanding, the consumer rate relief charges authorized under the final financing order are nonbypassable and apply to all existing or future West Virginia retail customers of a qualifying utility or its successors and must be paid by any customer that receives electric delivery service from the utility or its successors.[12]

In other words, once the PSC signs off on the issuance of "consumer rate relief bonds," ratepayers are on the hook to repay the bonds, regardless of any changes in circumstances down the road. In fact, even if AEP stops delivering power, ratepayers will still have to pay. If a large industry tries to drop off the grid and self-generate, it will still have to pay. The boilerplate included in the thirty-five pages of the bill was so one-sided in favor of the utility (and its bondholders) and against ratepayers as to shock the conscience. A separate line item on each customer's bill – for repayment of the consumer rate relief bonds – confirmed that a portion of the utility's revenue stream was dedicated solely for repayment of the debt. Even the PSC's hands were tied once the bonds were issued: "A final financing order is irrevocable and the commission may not reduce, impair, postpone or terminate the consumer rate relief charges authorized in the final financing order or impair the property or the collection or recovery of

[11] Bill Howley, *When Half Truth = No Truth*, THE POWER LINE: THE VIEW FROM CALHOUN COUNTY (Feb. 17, 2012), https://calhounpowerline.wordpress.com/?s=half+truth.

[12] Prospectus Supplement (to Prospectus dated Nov. 1, 2013), $380,300,000 Appalachian Consumer Rate Relief Funding LLC Issuing Entity Senior Secured Consumer Rate Relief Bonds, at 27.

consumer rate relief costs."[13] Because the risk of nonpayment is so small – almost impossible, given the way HB 4530 was written – any bonds issued pursuant to its provisions would receive a very favorable credit rating, thereby allowing the utility to finance its costs at a much lower interest rate.

What's Wrong with This Picture? Using a Second Mortgage to Buy Groceries

While securitization is a legitimate tool that has been frequently used by utilities in specific circumstances, the tool does not fit with the circumstances created by AEP in 2012. Securitization should never be used to finance ongoing, routine operating expenses. But that is what AEP was proposing in 2012: its fuel costs (and revenues from wholesale sales) were out of whack with what it expected, and it needed to raise rates to cover the shortfall. It is a misuse of securitization, however, to finance normal operating expenses through issuance of bonds. It had never been done before, with good reason. It is financially irresponsible. It is like a homeowner using a second mortgage (or similar instrument with a ten- or fifteen-year term) to pay a normal, recurring expense, such as buying groceries.

Puget Sound Energy (PSE) was one of the first utilities in the country to use securitization, in 1992. PSE used securitization to spread out over time its investment in energy efficiency measures. These investments (insulation, windows, heating, ventilation, and air conditioning [HVAC], high-efficiency furnaces, etc.) have useful lives that extend many years. Securitization allowed the repayment of these investments to be refinanced at lower interest rates over a period that corresponded to the useful life of the underlying asset. While AEP referred to its fuel costs as "extraordinary" in the fact sheet it distributed to legislators, fuel costs are not extraordinary expenses. In AEP's case, they were extraordinarily high, due to AEP's power's mismanagement, but they are normal, routine operating expenses that need to be paid by current customers, not spread out over some future period. It is a violation of fundamental financial management principles to finance operating costs through long-term debt. Although AEP included examples of securitization in its information sheet, all of them involved the financing of long-term assets – transition and stranded costs associated with above-market generating assets, costs of environmental control equipment, and financing utility system infrastructure.[14] AEP could not come up with a single example where securitization was used to finance fuel costs.

Apart from the departure from sound financial practices, it is also a violation of fundamental ratemaking principles to force future ratepayers to bear costs that are being incurred by current customers. This is known as the "matching principle": Those who cause the costs, bear the costs. Or, stated differently, those who benefit from the power should pay for the power. Under AEP's misuse of securitization, 2012

---

[13] Consumer Rate Relief Bonds, § 24-2-4f(g)(3).
[14] Appalachian Power, *supra* note 10.

ratepayers would escape bearing the costs incurred by AEP to serve them. Rather, securitization would allow the costs to be shifted to future customers. There was a complete mismatch between costs incurred and revenue that would be received when the bonds are paid back in future years. Current ratepayers get subsidized; future ratepayers get burdened with costs not associated with the costs incurred by AEP to serve them at the time. It was great for AEP ratepayers in 2012, since they were able to dodge paying the actual costs of service. It was not so great for AEP ratepayers in subsequent years, who ended up paying utility rates completely unrelated to the costs incurred by the utility in serving them. It's a mismatch. It's not fair. And most utility commissioners abhor such practices in setting rates. Yet AEP's securitization of normal, recurring power costs embraced this mismatch, as it avoided the current pain of the $350 million under-recovery caused by its mismanagement.

In a blog post published at *Coalition for Reliable Power*, Keryn Newman described the situation as follows: "The issuance of consumer debt bonds will reward AEP by allowing them to recover their expenses, while their customers incur the liability of the company's poor planning over a longer period of time. Instead of fixing the problem, this merely shifts it onto the backs of our children and grandchildren."[15] So what is the long-term solution? Requiring utilities to engage in integrated resource planning, as discussed in the preceding chapter. At the same time that AEP was lobbying for passage of HB 4530, it was opposing another bill (SB 162), introduced by Senator Dan Foster, that would have required the utility to engage in an integrated resource planning process. Had AEP engaged in such a process a decade earlier – like virtually all other utilities in the country – it likely could have avoided the prospects of a $350 million rate increase, as it would have seen long ago the riskiness of continuing to rely so heavily on coal rather than diversifying its fuel supply. With proper planning – and the use of sophisticated modeling of various resource scenarios, using a variety of assumptions, in order to determine a portfolio of resources that results in the lowest cost, over time, to utility customers – a 70 percent increase in coal prices over four years should not have resulted in a 35–40 percent rate increase. A "high" coal price scenario, for example, would have shown natural gas-fired resources to be cost effective, and likely would have shown energy efficiency and conservation to be a more cost-effective means for AEP to meet its obligation to serve.

Unfortunately, the "band aid" strategy advocated by AEP became even more outrageous once HB 4530 was actually implemented by AEP and the PSC.

Exploiting the New Mechanism: How $311 Million Turned Into $380 Million

Although AEP consistently referred to an under-recovery "in excess of $350 million" when it lobbied the legislature for enactment of HB 4530, the actual

---

[15] Keryn Newman, *HB4530: We Need a Real Solution, Not a Band-Aid*, Coalition for Reliable Power, Feb. 16, 2012.

ENEC increase approved by the PSC in July 2012 was only $311.9 million.[16] Shortly after the PSC order was issued approving this ENEC increase, AEP filed its proposal seeking PSC approval to issue consumer rate relief bonds, in August 2012. How much would be financed? Rather than the $311.9 million authorized in July's ENEC order, or the $350 million that AEP mentioned in its lobbying effort, the filing requested authorization for the issuance of $422.3 *million* in consumer rate relief bonds. The requested amount was so far out of line with what anyone expected that in its order the PSC did not even provide a calculation of the total figure requested by AEP. The reader is left to add up the various elements of AEP's request – its "kitchen sink" of virtually every stray item on its books to dump into this creative financing scheme. So what was included in the request?: $26,022,676 of deferred *"bonus coal payments"* (really? "bonus payments" for coal on top of the 70 percent increase in coal prices between 2007 and 2011?); $25.5 million in revenue shortfalls due to "special rates" that the PSC approved for Century Aluminum (tied to the international price of aluminum, a bailout strategy that failed upon the shutdown of Century in February 2009); over $7 million in "upfront financing costs," to cover the fees of the lawyers and investment bankers who came up with this securitization scheme in the first place; and other stray deferred amounts on AEP's books totaling $78.3 million.[17]

After negotiations among the parties to the proceeding, the size of the bond issuance was reduced to $376 million. The upfront financing costs were reduced to $5.75 million, but the "bonus coal payments" and the Century bailout costs continued to be included at their requested amounts, along with the $311.9 million ENEC increase approved by the PSC in July 2012. When AEP ultimately issued the consumer rate relief bonds in November 2013, the amount was $380.3 million, comprising two separate issuances, or tranches, of bonds. Over what period would the bonds be repaid? Not five years. Not ten years. Not fifteen years. But *almost twenty years*. The first tranche, in the amount of $215.8 million, had a final maturity date of February 1, 2024, with a scheduled final payment date of February 1, 2023. The second tranche, in the amount of $164.5 million, had a final maturity date of August 1, 2031, with a scheduled final payment date of August 1, 2028. And, to top it off, the Prospectus reiterated the binding obligation of the PSC to ensure that the bonds would be repaid:

> The PSC guarantees that it will act pursuant to its financing order to ensure that expected [consumer rate relief] charges are sufficient to pay on a timely basis scheduled principal of and interest on the bonds and all other ongoing financial

[16] West Virginia PSC, *supra* note 9.
[17] West Virginia Public Service Commission, Case No. 12–1188-E-PC, Appalachian Power Company and Wheeling Power Company, both doing business as American Electric Power, Petition for Consent and Approval of Application to Securitize Uncollected Expanded Net Energy Costs Pursuant to W.Va. Code $ 24-2-4f and Affiliated Agreements Pursuant to W.Va. Code $ 24-2-12, *Financing Order*, Sept. 20, 2013.

costs. . . . The PSC's obligations relating to the bonds, including the specific actions that it has guaranteed to take, are direct, explicit, irrevocable and unconditional upon issuance of the bonds, and are legally enforceable against the PSC.[18]

The Collective Damage

So what is the bottom line of this adventure in utility financing? Here's a quick summary of all the ways in which this securitization gambit was wrong:

- A utility was able to avoid the consequences of its mismanagement of power costs, and simply pass on to ratepayers – albeit over nearly twenty years – costs that likely would not have been incurred had AEP taken any meaningful steps to assemble a diversified portfolio of resources (including demand-side programs).
- Ratepayers failed to receive any price signal regarding the costs of serving them, as rates changed imperceptibly notwithstanding a 70 percent increase in coal prices. When ratepayers get accurate price signals, they take actions in response. (It's basic economics, a concept called elasticity of demand).
- The transaction violated basic principles of finance, by using long-term debt to cover ordinary, recurring costs.
- The transaction violated the matching principle of ratemaking, by allowing the ratepayers who benefited from using the electricity generated in 2012 to avoid paying for it, and instead making ratepayers in years 2013 through 2028 pay for it.
- AEP, with the PSC's blessing, abused the securitization tool, by loading up what started out as a $311 million power cost under-recovery with a multitude of other questionable deferrals that happened to be on AEP's books at the time. It's free money! Let's take advantage of it!

Unfortunately, this is not an isolated example of the madness of utility regulation in West Virginia. Rather, it pretty much exemplifies everything that is wrong with the regulatory process. There is no accountability for utility imprudence, and no meaningful protection for the ratepayer. It gets worse, as we will explore in Chapter 10.

BAILING OUT A SINKING SHIP WITH TEASPOONS

Eliminating Safety Protection for Coal Miners

The first priority and concern of all in the mining industry must be the health and safety of our most precious resource, the miner.
Federal Mine Safety & Health Act of 1977[19]

---

[18] Prospectus Supplement, *supra* note 12, at 1.
[19] Federal Mine Safety & Health Act of 1977, Public Law 91–173, as amended by Public Law 95–164, section 2(a).

What better way to demonstrate how much the coal industry values its most precious resource than to ask the legislature to relax mine safety regulations to reduce costs. Several times during "the lost decade," the coal industry successfully passed bills in the West Virginia legislature to weaken mine safety standards in a futile effort to stay competitive in the face of overwhelming market forces by shaving a few pennies off the price of a ton of coal.

In 2012, for example, Governor Earl Ray Tomblin promised mine safety legislation as part of his State of the State address, on the heels of the Upper Big Branch mine disaster in April 2010 that killed twenty-nine miners due to a coal dust explosion. The governor had the benefit of recommendations from an independent team of investigators, the Governor's Independent Investigation Panel (GIIP), appointed by former West Virginia Governor Joe Manchin and led by Davitt McAteer, a former federal mine safety chief who had investigated other mine disasters in the state.

One of the strongest recommendations was to impose new criminal offenses for advance notice of government mine inspections and certain willful safety violations. According to Professor Pat McGinley of the West Virginia University College of Law, who was a member of the GIIP,

> For a century, from the Monongah disaster until today, thousands of coal miners have been maimed [or] killed in West Virginia's mines, while criminal prosecutions of responsible company officials has been virtually nonexistent. It is a cruel hoax to assert that criminal sanctions in West Virginia's mine safety law have any deterrent affect when criminal conduct by mine managers is not prosecuted.[20]

Rather than focusing on the recommendations from the GIIP, however, the governor's office introduced a bill that focused on drug and alcohol abuse in the mines, a problem all investigators agreed played no role at Upper Big Branch. McAteer said the governor's bill was a "distraction" from efforts to prevent another mine disaster, and urged consideration of safety measures that actually related to the cause of the Upper Big Branch disaster, such as new coal-dust meters and more advanced ventilation monitoring systems.

A separate House of Delegates bill was therefore necessary to address the GIIP's recommendation to impose criminal sanctions. As that legislation worked its way through the legislature, however, the language making it a crime to warn underground workers of an impending government inspection was weakened so that it applied only if it could be proven that the advance notice was done "with the intent of undermining" that inspection. And rather than charging a felony for anyone willfully violating any state mine safety standard, the criminal offense applies only to willful violations that cause the death of a miner.

---

[20] Ken Ward Jr., *Deal with Industry Weakened Mine Safety Bill*, CHARLESTON GAZETTE-MAIL (Feb. 27, 2012), https://www.wvgazettemail.com/news/special_reports/deal-with-industry-weakened-mine-safety-bill/article_4b0bb56a-e6f9-5f7a-bb2e-dce264abdde1.html.

In 2015, as the coal industry began to experience a round of bankruptcy filings, coal operators achieved the rollback of several standards that they claimed were "overly stringent" and made prices for West Virginia coal "less competitive."[21] The rollbacks were included in a bill (SB 357) titled the "Coal Jobs and Safety Act." Critics of the bill claimed that the measure "is putting profits ahead of the safety of miners." And Minority Leader Tim Miley (Democrat, Harrison County) said, "I'm really astounded that we're comparing safety, health and perhaps lives, with cost."[22] The legislation addressed several measures that were put into place after nine miners were killed in the Blacksville mine disaster in 1972 as a result of a fire in the mine. The Coal Jobs and Safety Act: (1) increased the distance that tracks need to be away from where miners are working from 500 feet to 1,500 feet; (2) abolished the Diesel Commission, which was charged with inspecting diesel equipment to ensure that it is safe before entering mines; and (3) revised regulations prohibiting miners from being in the vicinity of major equipment moves.[23] Cecil Roberts, President of the United Mine Workers of America, claimed that the "roll back [of] decades of critical safety and health improvements in the state's coal mines will put miners at greater risk of severe injury or worse. It is shocking that people who profess to be concerned about miners' safety can be so disingenuous about this legislation and the true potential it has for tragedy."[24]

The coal industry was back at it again in the 2016 session with HB 4726, which weakened two key provisions of the state's mine safety law that were passed in the wake of the January 2006 explosion that killed twelve miners at the Sago Mine, in Upshur County. Coal operators were allowed to cut back on mine rescue teams, by being able to rely on state agency rescue teams to serve as backups for their own specially trained teams in response to explosions and fires.[25] (Existing law required companies to provide at least two mine rescue teams to be available at all times when miners are underground.) Another provision in HB 4726 lowered the fines paid by coal operators for not reporting workplace accidents quickly.[26]

In 2017, the coal industry proposed yet another measure to eliminate mine safety enforcement, SB 582. Among other things, the legislation would have eliminated the ability of state mine safety office inspectors to issue notices of violation or levy fines

---

[21]   Phil Kabler, *Mine Safety Regulation Rollback up for House Vote*, CHARLESTON GAZETTE-MAIL (Feb. 26, 2015), https://www.wvgazettemail.com/news/politics/mine-safety-regulation-rollback-up-for-house-vote/article_9d540186-b47d-52f1-828a-d054460b9225.html.

[22]   *Id.*

[23]   *Id.*

[24]   Editorial Board, *Don't Sacrifice Coal Miner Safety for Profit*, EXPONENT TELEGRAM (Feb. 12, 2015), https://www.wvnews.com/theet/opinion/editorials/dont-sacrifice-coal-miner-safety-for-profit/article_f5e75218-6fbf-5d77-a1fc-5e3b7fced797.html.

[25]   Ken Ward Jr., *WV House Bill Weakens Mine Safety, but Is Touted as a Compromise*, CHARLESTON GAZETTE-MAIL (Mar. 1, 2016), https://www.wvgazettemail.com/business/wv-house-bill-weakens-mine-safety-but-is-touted-as-a-compromise/article_9cdb20cc-18fe-52a9-9f0f-1df16c9d716c.html.

[26]   *Id.*

on mine operators or coal companies for any safety hazards unless they can prove there is an "imminent danger" of death or serious physical harm. Ken Ward of the *Charleston Gazette-Mail* described the measure as follows:

> State safety inspectors wouldn't inspect West Virginia's coal mines anymore. They would conduct "compliance visits and education." Violations of health and safety standards wouldn't produce state citations and fines, either. Mine operators would receive "compliance assistance visit notices." And West Virginia regulators wouldn't have authority to write safety and health regulations. Instead, they could only "adopt policies … [for] improving compliance assistance" in the state's mines.[27]

The bill also required that the state rewrite all of its coal mine safety standards so that, instead of long-standing and separate state rules, mine operators would only be responsible for following US Mine Safety and Health Administration regulations. David McAteer, the mine safety expert who headed up the GIIP after the Upper Big Branch disaster, said the bill was "breathtaking in its scope." He was especially concerned about deferring state mine safety standards to the federal government: "It is shocking that, after all these years and the numbers of West Virginians who have died in the mines, for the state to even consider this. The state needs to be involved in making sure we are protecting our citizens. This should be one of the primary goals of the state government."[28]

The blowback from SB 582 was so great that it even attracted the attention of the *New York Times* editorial page, which described the measure as an example of "loose safety laws that endangered miners' lives and protected owners' profits" that was inspired by "President Trump's vow to bring back the coal industry's heyday." According to the editorial: "Political pandering is nothing new in Appalachia, where the coal industry has wooed and intimidated generations of state lawmakers to favor mine owners. But this latest bout, launched in tandem with Mr. Trump's fantasy job promises, can only leave remaining miners in greater danger on the job."[29] SB 582 was later withdrawn by its primary sponsor, Senator Randy Smith (Republican, Tucker County), who claimed he introduced legislation with that language "to get people's attention" and force various sides to the negotiating table on a mine safety bill.[30]

---

[27] Ken Ward, Jr., *WV Senate Bill Eliminates Mine Safety Enforcement*, Charleston Gazette-Mail (Mar. 14, 2017), https://www.wvgazettemail.com/news/politics/wv-senate-bill-eliminates-mine-safety-enforcement/article_9e9233c0-1f03-535c-9a70-c8b8ceebe097.html.

[28] *Id.*

[29] Editorial Board, *Compounding the Risk for Coal Miners*, N.Y. Times (Mar. 20, 2017), https://www.nytimes.com/2017/03/20/opinion/compounding-the-risk-for-coal-miners.html?_r=0

[30] Ken Ward Jr., *Senator Pulls WV Mine Safety Bill, Says Compromise Measure Coming*, Charleston Gazette-Mail (Mar. 21, 2017), https://www.wvgazettemail.com/news/politics/senator-pulls-wv-mine-safety-bill-says-compromise-measure-coming/article_71561bfc-fc55-55b2-93d9-96d981200208.html.

Giving up $60 Million in Severance Tax Revenues to Accomplish Nothing

Prior to 2019, the state of West Virginia imposed a severance tax of 5 percent on thermal and steam coal, which is used to generate electricity. The severance tax is based on the fair market value (rather than volume) of the extracted coal at the time the coal is sold, minus any federal energy tax. Of the 5 percent levy, 4.65 percent was allocated to state general revenues with the remaining 0.35 percent going to counties, three-quarters of which is allocated to coal-producing counties.

In the 2019 legislative session, however, the legislature passed a bill reducing the severance tax on coal from 5 percent to 3 percent, phased in over a three-year period. (The two percent reduction affects only the state's portion of the revenues.) The bill passed the House of Delegates by a vote of 88 to 11, resulting in a round of applause from coal miners affiliated with Murray Energy who were in the gallery. (In West Virginia, Murray Energy operates the Ohio County Mine near Benwood, the Marshall County Mine near Cameron, the Monongalia County Mine near Blacksville, the Harrison County Mine near Clarksburg, and the Marion County Mine near Mannington.)[31] The measure passed the Senate by a vote of 19 to 12. According to the fiscal note subsequently prepared by the Tax Department, the severance tax reduction would result in a loss to the state's general revenue of $58.6 million in the first year and $64.2 million in subsequent years.[32]

In signing the legislation, Governor Jim Justice cited an average coal price of $55 per ton, and said the cost savings would be $1.10 per ton for coal operators. According to Justice, "the state can afford to do without that $1.10, but the state can't afford to do without these jobs. Your multiplier effect on no tons is zero. You don't get severance tax on zero tons."[33] According to the West Virginia Center on Budget & Policy, the bill originated in committee just a few days prior to passage, and was supported by virtually no analysis. Just prior to a final vote on the bill, a fiscal note from the Senate Finance Committee was produced that showed that, at best, only 500 jobs would be created as a result of the tax reduction – and more likely only 100 jobs.[34]

Delegate Evan Hansen (Democrat, Monongalia County) spoke during the floor debate and questioned whether cutting the severance tax would be worth

---

[31]   Steven Allen Adams, *West Virginia House Votes to Lower Severance Tax on Steam Coal*, WHEELING INTELLIGENCER (Feb. 28, 2019), https://www.theintelligencer.net/news/top-headlines/2019/02/west-vir ginia-house-votes-to-lower-severance-tax-on-steam-coal.

[32]   Senate Committee on Finance, *HB 3142: Coal Severance Tax Cut*, Budget Bulletin (Sept. 20, 2019), http://www.wvlegislature.gov/legisdocs/committee/senate/finance/Budget-Bulletin-9-20-Final-(Coal-Severance).pdf.

[33]   *Justice Signs Bill Lowering Coal Severance Tax*, WV METRONEWS (Mar. 27, 2019) https://wvmetro news.com/2019/03/27/justice-signs-bill-lowering-coal-severance-tax/.

[34]   Sean O'Leary, *Will a Severance Tax Cut Put Coal Miners Back to Work? (Probably Not)*, WEST VIRGINIA CENTER ON BUDGET & POLICY (Mar. 1, 2019), https://wvpolicy.org/will-a-severance-tax-cut-put-coal-miners-back-to-work-probably-not/.

the jobs it might create. Hansen, the founder and principal of Downstream Strategies, an environmental consulting company in Morgantown, also questioned the ability of state policies to overcome the forces affecting the coal industry. "Our coal-fired plants can't compete because the price of wind and solar is going down considerably. Another reason why these plants are shutting down is because these companies across the country and across the world ... are committed to renewable energy."[35] Delegate Hansen also raised the question of how many jobs this would create and "the chairman of Finance said maybe 100. That's $600,000 per job, this one piece of legislation. Maybe it will create 500 jobs, that's $120,000 per job. That's still quite a lot," Hansen said, adding that dropping the price of steam coal by a few percentage points by slashing the severance tax does not change the overall economic picture for coal. "We've got coal-fired power plants shutting down across the country. We have coal-fired power plants shutting down in West Virginia and the reason is they can't compete ... because we have vast amounts of cheap natural gas that's cheaper than the coal we mine in West Virginia and it's not just one percent cheaper or two percent cheaper."[36]

While Governor Justice got the math right – a 2 percent reduction in severance tax on a ton of coal worth $55 would indeed produce savings of $1.10 – everything else he said was flat wrong. For the reasons given by Delegate Hansen, coal was "out of the money" in 2017 as a fuel for the generation of electricity, and lowering the price of coal mined in West Virginia by 2 percent was of no consequence whatsoever in the fight to save coal jobs. As discussed in Chapters 2 and 3, the market forces roiling the coal industry – in the form of cheap natural gas and cost-competitive renewables, as well as consumer demand for renewable energy, all cited by Delegate Hansen – are far too strong and overwhelming for a 2 percent reduction in costs to have any impact.

With respect to Governor Justice's point about whether the cost reduction would save jobs in West Virginia – he stated that "[i]f that $1.10 keeps this company and all of our thermal companies in West Virginia running then not only are we recouping the three percent, but we're recouping the benefits of all the jobs"[37] – the problem is that West Virginia coal, in particular, is uncompetitive compared to other regions in the United States. On this point, the West Virginia Center on Budget & Policy prepared the comparison shown in Table 9.1 based on data filed with the US Energy Information Administration.

---

[35]   Adams, *supra* note 31.
[36]   Brittany Patterson, *W.Va. House Passes Bill to Reduce Coal Severance Tax*, WV PUBLIC BROADCASTING (Feb. 28, 2019), https://www.wvpublic.org/news/2019-02-28/w-va-house-passes-bill-to-reduce-coal-severance-tax.
[37]   *Justice Signs Bill supra* note 33.

TABLE 9.1 *Average price of coal per ton shipped to electric power sector, by state, 2017*

State	Price ($)
West Virginia	53.84
Ohio	47.24
Kentucky	43.79
Pennsylvania	40.24
Illinois	31.44
Wyoming	28.72
Texas	27.17
National average	39.18

With a difference between $7 and $13 per ton between West Virginia coal and prices in the surrounding states, a $1.10 reduction does very little to close that gap, even assuming – probably incorrectly – that the coal operators flow all the tax reduction through to lower the price. More importantly, West Virginia's biggest competitor in the coal market is not its neighboring states but Wyoming which, although it has significantly higher taxes than West Virginia, benefits from greater productivity per miner (due to differences in extraction methods). Between 2001 and 2017, Wyoming's share of national coal production grew from 32.7 percent to 40.9 percent, while West Virginia's declined from 14.4 percent to 12.0 percent.

Thus the premise upon which the severance tax reduction was based, "[l]owering the tax rate will make West Virginia coal more competitive with mines in other states and countries" and "[o]ver time, loss in revenue due to a lower tax rate should be counteracted by an increase in overall mining activity," as stated in the Senate Committee on Finance's analysis,[38] is entirely false; the reduction does nothing but reduce state revenues by over $60 million at a time when it could have been used to provide the essential services of state government, such as fixing roads and support- ing schools and colleges. Senator Randy Smith (Republican, Tucker County), a coal mine safety employee, complained that the cut happened at the same time that Governor Justice was looking for every dollar possible to fix West Virginia's deterior- ating roads. "While he's looking for money for roads, he's having a dog and pony show to sign the coal severance tax bill," Smith said. Ted Boettner, then executive director of the West Virginia Center on Budget & Policy, observed that "handing over $60 million a year to mostly wealthy out-of-state corporations" is not going to help achieve the objective of attracting well-paying jobs and more investment in the communities of West Virginia. "In fact, it will do the opposite by taking millions of

---

[38]   Senate Committee on Finance, *supra* note 32.

dollars from our schools, roads and colleges while doing little to nothing to help coal-mining communities."[39]

The Tax Break for Pleasants Power Station

The Infamous History of Pleasants Power Station

The Pleasants Power Station (Pleasants) is a 1,300 MW coal-fired power plant located in Pleasants County, West Virginia, on Willow Island near Belmont. The cooling system for the plant, consisting of two huge towers 360 feet in diameter at their base and 400 feet high, draws water from the Ohio River, about 100 yards away. Tragically, one of these cooling towers stands as a stark reminder of one of the darkest days in West Virginia's history. On April 27, 1978, 51 construction workers fell 170 feet to their deaths when scaffolding inside the second cooling tower plant tore loose, an incident that then Governor Jay Rockefeller described as the worst nonmining industrial accident in the state's history. The scaffolding ringed the upper edge of the tower's inward-sloping walls and was designed to be moved upward as each succeeding layer of wall was poured. It was bolted to the twenty-eighth layer of concrete, which the crew had finished pouring the previous day. As the workers were beginning to hoist cement for the next layer, the layer of cement that had been placed only eighteen hours earlier began to peel away and the platform of workers fell to the ground below. Included among the victims were eleven members of the Steele family from nearby Shultz, West Virginia.[40]

Notably, this was not the first fatal accident at Pleasants; two men had previously died after falling from a smokestack, and another man was killed when a steel beam knocked him off the top of a boiler building. There had also been two fires at the site: a March 1977 fire that destroyed an office building, and a fire in a storage tank in early 1978.

Notwithstanding its sorrowful construction history, the plant was ultimately completed and commenced operation in 1980. The original cost of Pleasants, built by Allegheny Energy, was $677 million. Of the 3.5 million tons of coal burned at Pleasants annually when it operates at full capacity, about 80 percent comes from coal mines located in West Virginia. Following the acquisition of Allegheny Energy by FirstEnergy in 2011, Pleasants became a "merchant" power plant owned by FirstEnergy's unregulated subsidiary, Allegheny Energy Supply Company (AES).

As discussed more fully in Chapter 10, within a few years of FirstEnergy's acquisition of the plant, Pleasants began to be "out of the money" in PJM Interconnection; in other words, the price AES was bidding into the PJM energy markets, based on the cost of producing power at Pleasants, was above the market clearing price established through the competitive auction process. FirstEnergy therefore began to pursue a different strategy: transfer the plant from its unregulated subsidiary AES to its regulated subsidiaries in West Virginia, Mon Power and Potomac Edison, thereby shifting

[39] *Justice Signs Bill, supra* note 33.
[40] Iver Peterson, *51 Killed in Collapse of Scaffold at Power Plant in West Virginia*, N.Y. Times (Apr. 28, 1978), https://nyti.ms/1kP8R6k.

the risks of the unprofitable plant from its shareholders to the captive ratepayers in West Virginia, where the PSC would presumably allow full cost recovery of the plant's operation in retail rates. FirstEnergy filed an application with the West Virginia PSC in March 2017 to do so, ultimately receiving approval from the PSC in January 2018. Due to an adverse ruling from the Federal Energy Regulatory Commission (FERC), however, FirstEnergy decided not to proceed with the transaction (as discussed further in Chapter 10). Without a path to cost recovery for Pleasants, FirstEnergy announced in February 2018 that the plant would cease operations on January 1, 2019.

The demise of FirstEnergy's unregulated operations ultimately led its other merchant subsidiary, FirstEnergy Solutions, to file for Chapter 11 bankruptcy in March 2018. As part of an asset purchase agreement submitted to the bankruptcy court in February 2019, Pleasants was transferred to FirstEnergy Solutions. Under an October 2018 settlement agreement, FirstEnergy (as the parent of both AES and FirstEnergy Solutions) committed to continue to operate Pleasants through May 2022 "in order to fulfill existing capacity requirements." AES had previously submitted formal notification to PJM in February 2018 that it intended to close down the plant as of June 1, 2022. These "existing capacity requirements" refer to the capacity market operated by PJM. Merchant power plants, such as Pleasants, have two sources of revenue, the energy market and the capacity market, both operated by PJM (the operation of PJM's energy market was described in Chapter 2). As noted above, Pleasants was largely "out of the money" in the energy market, and the plant was thus frequently not called into service by the operators in the PJM control room.

In the case of PJM's capacity market, power plant operators participate in an annual auction conducted by PJM for the right to offer capacity about three years out, as described in Chapter 8. (The notion is that this process results in a price signal for power plant operators to ensure that sufficient generation will exist to meet future demand.) In the capacity auction conducted by PJM in August 2018, for example, successful bidders would be obligated to be ready, willing, and able to dispatch their power plants to produce power – as called upon by PJM – for the calendar year beginning June 1, 2021 through May 31, 2022. As in the energy market, the process is a competitive one, with winning bidders selected on the basis of the offers for capacity they submitted, until the necessary amount of capacity is secured by PJM. As in the energy market, capacity offers can be "out of the money" by being above the market clearing price, in which case the power plant operator loses this potential source of revenue. Merchant power plants like Pleasants rely heavily on capacity revenue and typically cannot operate without this source of revenue.

The Sudden, Urgent Need for a Bailout
So the situation as of July 1, 2019 was that Pleasants would operate only as necessary to fulfill "existing capacity requirements" through May 31, 2022, and then close down, in accordance with the notification AES had provided to PJM in February 2018. In mid-July, however, FirstEnergy, working closely with Governor Jim Justice's office,

developed a bailout proposal for Pleasants that purportedly would allow the plant to continue operating after May 2022. According to the "Fact Sheet" prepared by FirstEnergy Solutions, if Pleasants could avoid paying its business and occupation (B&O) tax of $12.5 million to the state, that cost reduction would allow Pleasants to compete in the then upcoming capacity auction at PJM, scheduled for August 2019, for capacity to be delivered between June 1, 2022 and May 31, 2023. As FirstEnergy Solutions described the situation in its Fact Sheet, *"[w]ithout B&O Tax relief, Pleasants cannot compete economically, cannot participate in the upcoming capacity auction and will be forced into a premature retirement."*[41] Never mind, of course, that FirstEnergy had already admitted that Pleasants was uneconomic when it put the plant up for sale in 2016, or when it made the decision in 2017 to try to transfer the plant from AES – where its shareholders had to bear the losses – to its regulated ratepayers in West Virginia. Or that FirstEnergy had already announced in February 2018 that Pleasants would cease operations on January 1, 2019. Or that AES had formally notified PJM in February 2018 that Pleasants would cease operating on June 1, 2022.

Based on the strategy hatched in the governor's office on Monday, July 15, 2019, Governor Jim Justice announced in a special proclamation at 6 p.m. on Friday, July 19 that a bill to provide $12.5 million in tax relief for Pleasants would be added to the agenda of a special session of the legislature otherwise dedicated to education funding. According to the proclamation issued by the governor's office, Pleasants "has faced financial strain over the past several years because, due to its status as a Merchant Power Plant, it faces taxes that other plants do not have to bear. Pleasants Power Station is the only power plant in West Virginia subject to this hindrance which makes its power rates uncompetitive in the market."[42]

House Bill 207 (HB 207) was quickly drafted and circulated to legislators on Sunday evening, July 21. The one-page measure was introduced in the House of Delegates on Monday, July 22, followed by a hearing before the House Finance Committee, where FirstEnergy Solutions CEO John Judge told the Committee that as FirstEnergy Solutions works to emerge from bankruptcy, a $12.5 million tax break could "make or break it" for the Pleasants plant. According to Judge's testimony, "[g]iven the revenue and cost situation of this plant, it is very much on the edge and even $12.5 million, in this case, makes a difference."[43] Judge testified that FirstEnergy Solutions spent about $400 million a year on the plant.

In order to take immediate action, the House had to vote to suspend West Virginia constitutional rules to avoid having to read the bill three consecutive times,

[41]　FirstEnergy Solutions, *Elimination of the B&O Tax for Pleasants Power Station*, Fact Sheet (emphasis in original).

[42]　Press release, Office of the Governor, Gov. Justice Amends Special Session Call; Adds Bill to Save Pleasants Power Station (July 19, 2019), https://governor.wv.gov/News/press-releases/2019/Pages/Gov .-Justice-amends-special-session-call;-adds-bill-to-save-Pleasants-Power-Station.aspx.

[43]　Emily Allen & Brittany Patterson, *Pleasants Power Station Slated to Receive $12 Million in Tax Relief*, WV PUBLIC BROADCASTING (July 23, 2019), https://www.wvpublic.org/news/2019-07-23/pleasants- power-station-slated-to-receive-12-million-in-tax-relief.

a process that would have allowed more time for scrutiny. The following day (Tuesday, July 23), the measure passed the House by a vote of 77 to 5. The compressed timeline for debate of the bill drew criticism from Democrats. "We got this bill on Sunday and people wanted us to suspend the rules on Monday," said Delegate Barbara Evans Fleischauer (Democrat, Monongalia County). She continued: "And with all these questions – normally when we give a tax break, we look at it compared with the rest of our budget."[44] "It feels like log-rolling," said Delegate Larry Rowe (Democrat, Kanawha County).[45] It passed the Senate unanimously the same day, and was sent to Governor Justice for his signature on July 24. The only change to the bill was to adopt an amendment that accelerated the effective date of the tax cut from July 1, 2020 to January 1, 2020. Erin Beck of the *Register Herald* summed up the process nicely: "In two days' time, and with no input from any expert outside observers on the potential impact of the bill, West Virginia lawmakers have rushed through a bill that cuts $12.5 million in annual state revenue to bail out a bankrupt company in hopes of keeping an uncompetitive coal-fired power plant running."[46]

Several Democrats expressed skepticism that the bill would have any impact in keeping the plant open. "If I believed that three years from now these jobs will be here, I'd vote for this bill in a heartbeat," said Delegate John Doyle (Democrat, Jefferson County). "It is simply the economy and the market. If I am right, then House Bill 207 is not a job saving bill, it becomes just another corporate giveaway."[47] Delegate Rowe tried unsuccessfully to amend the bill to limit the tax exemption to five years, allowing the legislature to study the economic implications of the bill during the regular session. (The bill is silent as to how long the exemption will last.) Delegate Evan Hansen (Democrat, Monongalia County) cited the ongoing energy transition away from coal as context for what was happening at Pleasants. He remarked, "I think, we as a Legislature, have a responsibility to [do] what we can to manage that transition, so we have a 'just' transition. So that we're not just putting a band-aid on each crisis that comes our way, and not just giving tax break after tax break when they ask for it."[48]

Meanwhile, the governor's campaign issued a press release touting the governor's role in passing the bill to "save" Pleasants. According to the press release:

> West Virginia's coal industry, which was on life support during Barack Obama and the Democrats' War on Coal, is seeing a revival under Jim Justice's leadership. The

---

[44] *Id.*

[45] Erin Beck, *With Little Scrutiny, Lawmakers Bail Out Struggling Coal Plant*, REGISTER-HERALD (July 23, 2019), https://www.register-herald.com/with-little-scrutiny-lawmakers-bail-out-struggling-coal-plant/article_7303ba72-adb4-11e9-9b62-4f3ef30738c6.html.

[46] *Id.*

[47] Kate Mishkin, *WV Legislature Approves $12.5M Tax Break for Pleasants Power Station*, CHARLESTON GAZETTE-MAIL (July 23, 2019), https://www.wvgazettemail.com/news/politics/wv-legislature-approves-12-5m-tax-break-for-pleasants-powerstation/article_4ade6d97-2fb1-53d0-9dc7-29ee3370f955.html.

[48] *Id.*

governor led the fight to reduce the coal severance tax, and just this week helped pass a bill to save the Pleasants Power Station. The results speak for themselves – under Jim Justice's administration, West Virginia's economy is booming.⁴⁹

Of course, as noted by Phil Kabler of the *Charleston Gazette-Mail,* "if the War on Coal is over, why the necessity to give a $60 million annual tax break to the 'booming' coal industry, and a $12.5 million annual tax cut to keep open an aging coal-fired power plant?"⁵⁰

Disclosure of the FirstEnergy–Justice Entanglements

The same day that the tax break legislation was forwarded to the governor's office for signature, the *Parkersburg News and Sentinel* ran a story revealing that a coal company owned by Governor Justice, Bluestone Energy Sales Corporation, was being sued by the operator of Pleasants, FirstEnergy Solutions, as part of the latter's bankruptcy proceeding in the US Bankruptcy Court of the Northern District of Ohio.⁵¹ According to FirstEnergy's complaint filed in December 2018, Bluestone owed $3.1 million to FirstEnergy for the value of excess coal stockpiles that Bluestone allegedly agreed, in 2016, to buy back from FirstEnergy Solutions. Attorneys for FirstEnergy asked the court to turn over the final payment due by Bluestone and declare Bluestone in breach of contract. In a pleading filed with the bankruptcy court in late January 2019, Bluestone admitted that it had an agreement to pay for the remaining stockpiled coal, but claimed that it had never agreed to an amount of money. Brian Abraham, general counsel for Governor Justice, said the office was unaware of the legal action between FirstEnergy and Bluestone, and it never came up during discussions about saving Pleasants.⁵²

Following disclosure of the pending litigation, several legislators expressed concern that the matter had not been disclosed prior to legislative action on the Pleasants tax break. "Absolutely. Should have been disclosed. Should have been information made available to us," Senate President Mitch Carmichael (Republican, Jackson County) said.⁵³ Senate Finance Chairman Craig Blair

---

⁴⁹ Phil Kabler, *Statehouse Beat: If Coal Is Booming, Why Does It Need This Much Help?,* CHARLESTON GAZETTE-MAIL (July 27, 2019), https://www.wvgazettemail.com/news/columnists/phil_kabler/state house-beat-if-coal-is-booming-why-does-it-need-this-much-help/article_78c76c69-34cf-538f-88fb-ef5a12c0c72b.html.

⁵⁰ *Id.*

⁵¹ Bluestone is one of 116 companies owned by Justice and listed on his 2019 financial disclosure with the state Ethics Commission and, notably, was never placed in a blind trust (instruments commonly used by elected officials to give control of personal assets to outside parties to avoid any conflict of interest); only Justice's Glade Springs Resort in Raleigh County and Wintergreen Resort in Virginia are held in blind trusts.

⁵² Steven Allen Adams, *FirstEnergy Solutions in Court Battle with Justice-Owned Company,* PARKERSBURG NEWS & SENTINEL (July 24, 2019), https://www.newsandsentinel.com/news/local-news/2019/07/firstenergy-solutions-in-court-battle-with-justice-owned-company/.

⁵³ Brad McElhinny, *Lawmakers Wish Lawsuit Had Been Disclosed Prior to Votes on Power Plant Bill,* WV METRONEWS (July 27, 2019), https://wvmetronews.com/2019/07/27/lawmakers-wish-lawsuit-had-been-disclosed-prior-to-votes-on-power-plant-bill/.

(Republican, Berkeley County) said he wished he had known about the case but said the bill would still have passed because he felt it was the right thing to do: "The governor should have told us what was going on. I have no idea behind the scenes whether that had a bearing. I don't believe it did." Blair added, "I don't like being out in the dark and dealing with questions like this now because the governor wasn't transparent."[54] House Minority Leader Tim Miley (Democrat, Harrison County), who also voted for the bill, said

> [w]hen you are in public office you bend over backwards to make sure your actions are beyond scrutiny and that your motives are never questioned. I think the governor should have avoided this scrutiny by disclosing the litigation between his company and FirstEnergy Solutions. When you don't disclose that information, people are left to wonder whether there was some ulterior motive behind the governor pushing this legislation so hard.[55]

According to Delegate Mick Bates (Democrat, Raleigh County), the ranking Democrat on the Finance Committee,

> [t]he whole thing smells ripe. It is a sad day when you have to start your questioning of anyone that comes before the West Virginia Legislature with a bill or issue, 'Have you any ongoing financial disputes or legal actions pending with our governor or one of his mismanaged businesses?' I would hope that we would have a full and complete explanation from the company and Governor Justice before he signs the legislation.[56]

Survival of the "Magic Kingdom"

That full and complete investigation never happened. Six days later, and only fifteen days after the inaugural meeting in the governor's office, the bill was signed in an elaborate ceremony in the shadows of the plant itself – described by enthusiastic West Virginia Coal Association Vice President Chris Hamilton as a "magic kingdom in my eyes."[57] The attendees at the ceremony included House Speaker Roger Hanshaw (Republican, Clay County), PSC Chair (and native of Pleasants County) Charlotte Lane, Mon Power President Holly C. Kauffman, and Department of Environmental Protection Secretary Austin Caperton. Following remarks by Hamilton, Pleasants County Commissioner Jay Powell, and FirstEnergy Solutions CEO John Judge, Dave Hardy, the Secretary of Revenue and "master of ceremonies" for the event, turned the microphone over to Governor Justice.

---

54 *Id.*
55 *Id.*
56 *Id.*
57 Press Release, Office of the Governor, Gov. Justice Signs Bill Saving Pleasants Power Station from Closure (July 30, 2019), https://governor.wv.gov/News/press-releases/2019/Pages/Gov.-Justice-signs-bill-saving-Pleasants-Power-Station-from-closure.aspx.

The governor immediately took the opportunity to address the allegation that "some level of impropriety" was involved and that it was "the driver in all the effort to push this thing through and get this thing done." He stated:

> I want to tell you, it's an incredible insult to me. It's an incredible insult to my honor, but it's also an insult to FirstEnergy. Now, I want to tell you with every fiber in me, I am a Christian through and through, and I would tell you that not only never, beyond never, I'll never, ever do anything for me over the goodness of our state and especially you. Now, it's just absolutely nothing but the very thing that I think continues to destroy West Virginia and destroyed West Virginia for decades and decades and decades. There's not one cell in me that knew anything, anything about a lawsuit that existed with my companies – maybe I should have known – but not one cell.
>
> These people, these FirstEnergy people are great people. You, as miners that are working for Bob Murray, great people. .... Now let me just tell you just this: Nobody, nobody is going to support you more than I, nobody's going to go to bat for you more than I, nobody believes in coal more than I. And I mean it when I tell you that the coal industry in our state is unbelievably important, and we've got to preserve it, in every way.[58]

Those "Great People" from FirstEnergy

There's more to the story, of course. First, following the bailout of Pleasants, campaign contributions flowed in a big way from FirstEnergy to Governor Justice. On June 20, 2019 – less than a month before the meeting with FirstEnergy Solutions – Justice received a $2,800 donation from FirstEnergy's political action committee (PAC). Although the Justice campaign returned the donation on August 5, 2019 – six days after signing HB 207 – FirstEnergy's PAC sent Justice a new $2,800 check on October 24, 2019, at a political fundraiser in Clarksburg. All in all, after pushing the tax break through, Justice received $21,050 in campaign donations in 2019 for his primary and general election races from FirstEnergy's PAC and associates of FirstEnergy, including:

- $6,800 from Anthony Alexander, the former CEO of FirstEnergy Corporation ($2,800 for the primary election and $1,200 for the general election on October 17, 2019, followed by another check for $2,800 on October 24, 2019 [$1,200 to the primary and $1,600 to the general election]);
- $2,800 from Kimberly Jones, wife of current FirstEnergy Corporation CEO Charles Jones;
- $2,800 from Cynthia Boich, wife of Wayne Boich of Boich Cos. (which owned a stake in a coal mine in Montana with FirstEnergy Corporation);
- $2,800 from Larry Puccio, a lobbyist for FirstEnergy Corporation;
- $2,800 from Angel Moore, another lobbyist for FirstEnergy Corporation.

[58] *Id.*

FirstEnergy-associated donations made up 3 percent of the $700,625 raised by Justice in campaign donations as of July 2020.[59]

When asked about the extent of campaign contributions from FirstEnergy and allegations about any connection with the Pleasants bailout, Governor Justice responded:

> From the standpoint of hinting that I would take a campaign donation and everything and do it inappropriately is just ridiculous. It's off the chart. There's no chance in all the world I would do such a thing. I self-fund an incredible amount of my campaign. If anybody doesn't think we fully vet with all the lawyers every single donation that comes in, you're just absolutely whistling through the whatever.[60]

Second, as it turns out, about the same time that FirstEnergy Solutions was putting on a full-court press in West Virginia for a $12.5 million bailout of Pleasants, its parent company was doling out over $60 million in bribes in Ohio to secure the passage of HB 6, which provided for a $1.3 billion bailout of FirstEnergy's two nuclear power plants. On July 21, 2020, Republican Ohio House Speaker Larry Householder, four associates, and a nonprofit (Generation Now) through which funds were allegedly funneled by FirstEnergy, were charged with participating in a racketeering enterprise that financially benefited Householder and his associates. According to the criminal complaint filed in the US District Court for the Southern District of Ohio, FirstEnergy Corporation – identified in the indictment as Company A – spent more than $60 million between 2018 and 2020 to ensure the passage of HB 6. The law, passed on July 17, 2019 – about the same time as the initial meeting in Governor Justice's office that led to the Pleasants bailout – imposes an 85-cent fee per month on most residential ratepayers in Ohio, starting in 2021, to generate $170 million per year, $150 million of which would go to FirstEnergy Solutions (now Energy Harbor) to keep its Davis-Besse and Perry nuclear plants operating.

Following the release of the indictments in Ohio involving FirstEnergy's alleged racketeering activities, Kanawha County Commissioner Ben Salango, the Democratic nominee for governor, called for an investigation into the circumstances that led to Justice's decision to add a bill to the 2019 first special session to grant the B&O tax break to Pleasants. "I think the U.S. Attorney's Office or the ethics commission needs to get involved and start taking a look at this," Salango said. "If they're not already."[61] Governor Justice dismissed the allegations as the actions of "a desperate candidate who is so far behind in the polls that we're about to lap him."

---

[59] Steven Allen Adams, *FirstEnergy Associates Donate Thousands to Justice Campaign After Power Plant Tax Break*, Parkersburg News and Sentinel (July 23, 2020), https://www.newsandsentinel.com/news/business/2020/07/firstenergy-associates-donate-thousands-to-justice-campaign-after-power-plant-tax-break/.

[60] *Id.*

[61] Paul Giannamore, *Salango Challenges Justice on his FirstEnergy Dealings*, WTOV (July 22, 2020), https://wtov9.com/news/local/salango-challenges-justice-on-his-first-energy-dealings.

According to Justice, "you've got desperate political tactics and everything from liberal people who love to cast stones. We don't have time for it."[62]

The Sham of the Pleasants Bailout

The $12.5 million tax break for Pleasants was a sham in so many ways.

First, there was no "emergency" that warranted extraordinary treatment in a special session of the legislature. FirstEnergy Solutions had known about Pleasants' financial challenges for months prior to the mid-July 2019 meeting in the governor's office, and was well aware of the timing of the PJM capacity auction in August 2019, the outcome of which purportedly would "make or break" the continued operation of Pleasants. Yet no proposals were offered during the regular legislative session; rather, HB 207 was jammed through a special session in a single day before the public could mount campaigns either in support or opposition. As stated in *The Herald Dispatch*, "[t]hat's no way to run a legislature unless you want to guarantee that the fix is in."[63] Add to that: (1) the governor's lack of transparency about the litigation between one of his coal companies and FirstEnergy Solutions; (2) the apparent pay-to-play campaign contributions that Justice garnered in the months following the bailout; and (3) the outrageous conduct of those "great people from FirstEnergy" in Ohio at about the same time as the plot to pass HB 207 was hatched. Thus we have a story that is ignominious even by the high bar (or low bar, depending upon your point of view) of politics-as-usual in West Virginia.

Second, the claim in FirstEnergy Solutions' "Fact Sheet" that the B&O tax represents an "unfair tax burden" on Pleasants, as well as the statement in the governor's July 19 proclamation that Pleasants "faces taxes that other plants do not have to bear" and that it "is the only power plant in West Virginia subject to this hindrance," are simply false. *Every single coal plant in the state of West Virginia* pays a B&O tax or its equivalent. The six regulated plants operated by AEP and FirstEnergy recover the B&O tax from ratepayers through utility rates. Simply because the regulated plants are able to recover their B&O taxes in rates does not change the analysis – it is still a cost of operating a coal plant that needs to be considered in evaluating whether the plant should continue operating. The only other merchant plant operating in the state, Longview Power LLC, entered into a Payment in Lieu of Taxes (PILOT) agreement with Mon County that replaced the B&O tax with another form of equivalent payment. FirstEnergy Solutions never explained why Pleasants should be treated differently than any other coal plant in the state. In fact, as a result of the tax break, Pleasants now benefits from a competitive advantage over other coal plants that will likely result in adverse effects for regulated utility customers, as the other plants that continue to pay the B&O tax are

[62] Adams, *supra* note 59.
[63] *Editorial: Legislature Acted Too Quickly on Pleasants Bailout*, WILLIAMSON DAILY NEWS (July 26, 2019), https://www.williamsondailynews.com/opinion/editorial-legislature-acted-too-quickly-on-pleasants-bailout/article_a7754908-8b23-57cd-883b-4e26ffc53b68.html.

in a relatively worse position to the extent that they compete with Pleasants in the PJM energy markets to sell excess energy (i.e., energy not needed to serve retail customers).

Third, Pleasants has no basis for avoiding payment of its B&O tax any earlier than June 2022. If the premise of this sham has any validity at all – and it doesn't – any relief from the B&O tax should be applicable only for purposes of its August 2019 bid into the PJM capacity market, which is based on Pleasants' costs for generating power to be delivered beginning in *June 2022*. Yet HB 207, as amended, relieves Pleasants of its B&O tax obligation as of *January 1, 2020*, over two years earlier than is relevant to the capacity-related costs for its PJM bid. At best, FirstEnergy Solutions made a case for a $12.5 million tax break effective as of June 1, 2022, and walked away with an extra $30.2 million[64] due to the premature effective date, all to the detriment of taxpayers in West Virginia.

Fourth, FirstEnergy Solutions failed to demonstrate how relief from the B&O tax would make any meaningful difference in the ability of Pleasants to compete in the PJM capacity auction. Plant operators seeking to offer capacity to PJM submit a bid based on the economics of the plant, taking into account a forecast of the payments the plant would receive from sales into the separate energy market. Based on the testimony of FirstEnergy CEO John Judge to the House of Delegates Finance Committee that the plant's annual operating costs were $400 million, the elimination of the $12.5 million in B&O tax liability would reduce expenses by only about 3 percent annually. Legislators were properly skeptical that such a miniscule reduction in expenses, in the face of massive market forces roiling the coal industry, would make any difference. As explained in the FirstEnergy Solutions "Fact Sheet," the plant needs to receive payments from sales into the energy market, in addition to being paid for successfully competing in the capacity market.[65] Pleasants is generally "out of the money" in the energy market due to its relatively high marginal costs of operation, which are the basis for bids into the energy market, as compared to nuclear, natural gas, wind, and solar facilities. That analysis gets worse, rather than better, for the 2022–23 capacity year which the B&O tax relief is directed toward. As noted by Delegate John Doyle (Democrat, Jefferson County), HB 207 is likely "not a job saving bill [but] just another corporate giveaway."[66]

Fifth, the figure of 3.5 million tons of coal referred to in the "Fact Sheet" – not all of which comes from West Virginia – is overstated.[67] FirstEnergy Solutions failed to mention the then current capacity factor for Pleasants (i.e., how much the plant was operating, given that it had to compete with lower-cost suppliers to sell its energy into

---

[64] $12.5 million for 2020, $12.5 million for 2021, and $5.2 million for January through May 2022.

[65] FirstEnergy Solutions, *supra* note 41.

[66] Jake Jarvis, *House, Senate Pass Bill to Give Pleasants Power Station a Tax Break*, WV News (July 23, 2019), https://www.wvnews.com/news/wvnews/house-senate-pass-bill-to-give-pleasants-power-station-a-tax-break/article_f6991e80-6f57-5b7a-a552-d8779f34f0de.html.

[67] FirstEnergy Solutions, *supra* note 41.

the PJM energy markets). As noted above, the plant operated far less than 100 percent of the time given its uncompetitive cost profile, which is why being sold to the regulated utility customers in West Virginia was proposed. For 2018, the capacity factor for the plant was only 62 percent,[68] and those figures nationwide dropped precipitously in subsequent years. The average capacity factor nationally for coal plants in 2018, for example, was 53.6 percent, and that figure dropped to 47.5 percent for 2019 and to 33 percent for the first four months of 2020. The economic benefits of the continued operation of Pleasants, including the burning of West Virginia coal, were vastly overstated in the FirstEnergy Solutions "Fact" Sheet.

But, of course, no one in the legislature (or hardly anyone) asked any tough questions of FirstEnergy before approving the bailout. If a coal plant claims it needs tax relief to stay open, then the legislature is going to eliminate the tax. This is not much different from coal operators claiming that a reduction in the coal severance tax is necessary for them to remain competitive – the state can just figure out a way of meeting the essential needs of the public with $60 million less in revenue. And it is not much different from coal operators claiming that burdensome safety regulations are costing too much and rendering their operations uncompetitive – maybe the miners just need to be more careful. At the same time, maybe the receptiveness of the legislative to coal industry demands should not be surprising: For nearly twenty years, Friends of Coal has been driving home the point that "no state and industry are as closely identified with one another as West Virginia and coal."

---

[68] 7,021,328 MWh in actual generation compared to 11,251,968 MWh at full capacity (1,288 megawatts x 8,760 hours).

10

Bailing Out the Coal Industry on the Backs of West Virginia's Electric Ratepayers

In 2008, West Virginia had the lowest electricity prices in the country. By 2020, eleven other states had lower prices. In fact, over this period, electricity prices in West Virginia increased faster than in any other state in the nation. For the reasons described in Chapter 8, the blame for this development can be laid almost entirely at the failure of the West Virginia Public Service Commission (PSC) to adopt policies that protected the interests of electric utility ratepayers.

But apart from the systemic failure, four decisions of the PSC during "the lost decade" stand out as being particularly irresponsible and costly for ratepayers: approval for West Virginia electric utilities to acquire four aging, inefficient coal plants that formerly were owned by their affiliated unregulated subsidiaries. These four coal plants – the Harrison and Pleasants Station plants owned by FirstEnergy and the Mitchell and Amos coal plants owned by American Electric Power (AEP) – were losing money in the competitive wholesale electric markets, with the losses borne by shareholders. The response of utility management? to adopt a devious strategy to transfer the units from the unregulated side of the house – the "merchant" operations discussed in Chapter 2 – to the regulated side (FirstEnergy's operating companies of Mon Power and Potomac Edison and AEP's operating companies of Appalachian Power and Wheeling Power, respectively), thereby shifting the burden of these money-losing assets to West Virginia electric ratepayers.

A helpful analogy is to think about the Life cereal commercial that ran during the 1970s and early 1980s featuring three brothers at the breakfast table and the undesired bowl of Life cereal sitting in front of two of them:

KID #1:   What's this stuff?
KID #2:   Some cereal. Supposed to be good for you.
KID #1:   Did you try it?
KID #2:   I'm not gonna try it. You try it.
KID #1:   I'm not gonna try it.
KID #2:   Let's get Mikey!

KID #1:   Yeah!

[Kid #2 slides the bowl toward Mikey, seated at the other end of the table]

KID #2:   He won't eat it. He hates everything.

[Mikey starts eating the cereal]

KID #2:   He likes it! Hey, Mikey!

How are the coal plant deals like the Life cereal commercial? FirstEnergy and AEP were stuck with four uneconomic coal plants they no longer wanted. The utility shareholders certainly didn't want the losses from the plants to depress their earnings. No other utility or power producer wanted them – they were clearly losing money, and had little if any value. The solution? Bring them to West Virginia! West Virginians like coal! West Virginia will take them! And, just like Mikey surprising his two brothers by eating the dreaded Life cereal, the West Virginia PSC took the deal. Rather than protecting consumers from the obvious strategy of a corporate bailout, the West Virginia PSC approved each of the acquisitions, resulting in double-digit rate increases as the aging coal plants simply could not compete with lower-cost resources (primarily natural gas, but increasingly wind and solar as well) in the wholesale markets. (As discussed in the section FirstEnergy's Attempted Reprise with Pleasants Station, the Pleasants Station deal, while approved by the West Virginia PSC, was ultimately not consummated due to the refusal of the Federal Energy Regulatory Commission [FERC] to approve it.)

This chapter examines each of these coal plant acquisitions, as well as the conditions in the energy markets that created the circumstances leading to them.

THE DECLINING VALUE OF COAL-FIRED GENERATION

Chapters 1 and 2 described the transformation that was underway in the electric generation markets in the early 2010s due to the impact of environmental regulations and the emergence of cheap and plentiful natural gas as a formidable competitor to coal-fired generation.

As discussed in Chapter 1, the Environmental Protection Agency (EPA) issued its Mercury and Air Toxics Standard (MATS) rule in December 2011. The MATS rule required electric utilities to invest in additional emissions control measures (primarily scrubbers) for their coal plants to enable them to achieve compliance with the more stringent regulatory requirements applicable to mercury and other hazardous air pollutants under the Clean Air Act. Utilities were faced with the question of whether such investments were worthwhile, given the age of their coal plants and their relative efficiency – that is, how efficiently the plant converts coal into electricity, usually measured according to the "heat rate" of the plant, with a lower heat rate being more efficient. In many cases, utilities determined that the investments were not cost-effective, and could not be justified to the rate regulators. In those situations, the coal plants were simply retired rather than committing the additional funds to achieve compliance with MATS.

In February 2012, for example, FirstEnergy announced that Mon Power would be retiring three older coal-fired power plants located in West Virginia (Albright Power Station, Willow Island Power Station, and Rivesville Power Station) by September 1, 2012, citing the impact of the MATS rule.[1] The total capacity of these regulated plants was 660 megawatts (MW), or about 3 percent of FirstEnergy's total generation portfolio. It should be noted that for the three preceding years, these plants served mostly as peaking facilities, generating, on average, less than 1 percent of the electricity produced by FirstEnergy. Mon Power had completed a yearlong study of its older, unscrubbed, regulated coal-fired units to evaluate the potential impact of significant changes in environmental regulations, and determined that additional investments to implement MATS and other environmental rules would make these plants even less likely to be dispatched. As a result, the decision was made to retire these West Virginia plants rather than continue operations. FirstEnergy made a similar announcement in January 2012 that its unregulated generation subsidiaries would retire six older, coal-fired power plants located in Ohio, Pennsylvania, and Maryland by September 1, 2012.[2]

Some explanation is in order regarding "unregulated generation subsidiaries," as both FirstEnergy and AEP have such subsidiaries. In fact, it was this type of subsidiary that owned the coal plants that FirstEnergy and AEP were proposing to transfer to their respective regulated subsidiaries operating in West Virginia, subject to the approval of the West Virginia PSC. Many utilities throughout the country have both regulated subsidiaries and unregulated (or competitive) subsidiaries, each of which own generating plants. In the case of regulated subsidiaries, their rates and profits are closely regulated by state public utility commissions (PUCs), and the costs of operating their generating units are recovered through the rates paid by retail utility customers. In a sense, ratepayers are the "captive" buyers of the electrical output from such plants. So long as the plants are "used and useful" in providing electric service, the utility is permitted to recover their costs of operation from the utility's retail ratepayers.

The role of the PUCs is to ensure that the rates charged by the utilities they regulate are "just and reasonable" or, in other words, that the utility is not trying to impose excessive costs on consumers. When Mon Power made the decision in February 2012 to close down its three regulated coal plants in West Virginia, it was presumably based on the analysis it performed demonstrating that further investment in the plants to achieve compliance with the MATS rule was imprudent, and likely would not have been recoverable in rates inasmuch as the investment could

---

[1] Barry Cassell, *FirstEnergy to Shut Three More Coal Plants This Year*, TRANSMISSION HUB (Feb. 8, 2012), https://www.transmissionhub.com/articles/2012/02/firstenergy-to-shut-three-more-coal-plants-this-year.html.

[2] *FirstEnergy, Citing Impact of Environmental Regulations, Will Retire Six Coal-Fired Power Plants*, PR NEWSWIRE (Jan. 26, 2012), https://www.prnewswire.com/news-releases/firstenergy-citing-impact-of-environmental-regulations-will-retire-six-coal-fired-power-plants-138115263.html.

not be justified to the West Virginia PSC. (Recall that although the plants comprised about 3 percent of FirstEnergy's total generation portfolio, they generated on average less than 1 percent of the electricity produced by FirstEnergy; in other words, they operated fairly infrequently. The economic analysis does not improve by sinking additional millions of dollars to install scrubber to reduce hazardous emissions.)

In the case of generating plants owned by unregulated subsidiaries, however, the analysis is far different. As discussed in Chapter 2, these plants are commonly referred to as "merchant" plants, as opposed to regulated plants. They have no captive ratepayers to bear the costs of their operation. Rather, the output of a merchant plant is typically sold into the competitive wholesale markets. As is the case for many products, electricity is bought, sold, and traded in both wholesale and retail markets. The purchase and sale of electricity to end-use customers is done in the retail market, where state PUCs regulate the rates that the utility is able to charge for the electricity it delivers. The purchase and sale of electricity to resellers (entities that purchase goods or services with the intention to resell them to someone else) is done in the wholesale market. In these markets, the owners of the merchant plant bear the risk that the plants will be economic (i.e., profitable) through their ability to sell power into the wholesale markets at a price that is greater than the costs incurred in generating the power. If the plants are profitable, the merchant plant owners (i.e., the utility shareholders) keep the profits, and the level of such profits is not limited by rate regulation. If the plants are not profitable, then these shareholders bear the losses, as the utility has no ability to recover them from retail customers.

As described in Chapter 2, the "market clearing price" is determined in the PJM Interconnection energy market through a competitive auction process. Whether or not a merchant generating plant makes money depends on whether the bid that it submits to PJM – which in turn is based on the costs it incurs to generate the power – "clears the market." Merchant plants that are "in the money" will receive the market clearing price for the electricity that they deliver to the market, regardless of the level of their submitted bid. Merchant plants that submit a bid in excess of the market clearing price are simply not dispatched at the time, and will fail to capture any revenue to cover their costs. If this situation persists, the plants will ultimately close, as they are uneconomic and cannot compete with other power suppliers that are able to generate power more cheaply.

The proposals from FirstEnergy and AEP to transfer their merchant coal plants to their West Virginia regulated subsidiaries came at a time when coal plants were faring poorly in the competitive wholesale markets, due primarily to the impact of the shale gas revolution (as discussed in Chapter 2). In 2012, low natural gas prices drove coal-fired generation on the PJM electricity market to a record low; the load-weighted average energy price across PJM was $35/MWh, a ten-year low.[3] While

[3] Monitoring Analytics LLC, 2012 State of the Market Report for PJM 51 (2012), https://www.monitor inganalytics.com/reports/PJM_State_of_the_Market/2012/2012-som-pjm-volume2-sec2.pdf.

coal-fired generation fell, generation from natural gas units increased 39 percent in 2012.[4] Future prices at the time suggested that market energy prices would remain around $40/MWh through 2019 (which turned out to be a fairly good projection).[5] In addition to the impact of market forces, future environmental regulations, particularly those on climate change, were expected to impose significant costs on coal-fired generating units. At the same time, the depletion of less costly coal deposits (which increases mining production costs) and international coal market volatility were causing uncertainty in future domestic coal prices.

As a result of these circumstances, many utilities in the United States that owned coal plants began to sell them at "fire sale" prices. A September 2013 report by Fitch Ratings estimated that FirstEnergy's merchant coal-fired power plants lost 63 percent of their value between 2008 and 2013 as a result of these unfavorable market conditions.[6] Similarly, a report by UBS Investment Research put a "zero equity value" on FirstEnergy's other merchant subsidiary, FirstEnergy Solutions.[7] Testimony filed in the PSC proceeding involving Mon Power's proposed acquisition of the Harrison plant reported the following transactions at about the same time period:[8]

- In March 2013, Ameren announced its was selling 4,561 MW of supercritical coal capacity to Dynegy for $825 million, or at a cost per kW of $180.88.
- In March 2013, Dominion Energy announced it was selling 2,868 MW of supercritical coal capacity and 1,424 MW of natural gas-fired capacity to Energy Capital Partners for $650 million, or at a cost per kW of $130.
- In August 2012, Exelon announced it was selling 2,265 MW of supercritical coal capacity to Riverstone Holdings for $400 million, or at a cost per kW of $176.60.

For comparison purposes, FirstEnergy sought a price of $1.163 billion in the proposed Harrison transfer, or a cost per kW of $785.91, which was almost five times higher than the average per kW price from what were then recent transactions. Utilities in other states may have been forced to sell their coal plants at distressed prices, but why should that apply in West Virginia? The West Virginia PSC loves coal! As it turned out, FirstEnergy was right – it got most of what it wanted in the Harrison deal.

[4] *Id.*
[5] PJM Interconnection, Coal Capacity at Risk for Retirement in PJM: Potential Impacts of the Finalized EPA Cross State Air Pollution Rule and Proposed National Emissions Standards for Hazardous Air Pollutants 28 (Aug. 26, 2011).
[6] Cathy Kunkel, Re-Regulating Coal Plants in West Virginia: A Boon to FirstEnergy, a Burden to Ratepayers 2 (Sept. 2016) (citing Fitch Ratings, *The Erosion in Power Plant Valuations*, Sept. 5, 2013), https://ieefa.org/wp-content/uploads/2016/09/Re-regulating-Coal-Plants-in-West-Virginia_September-2016.pdf.
[7] *Id.* (citing UBS Investment Research, "FirstEnergy Corp: Competitive Dis-Synergies," July 30, 2014).
[8] James M. Van Nostrand, Harrison Plant Proposal a "Bad Deal," Charleston Gazette-Mail (May 15, 2013), http://blogs.wvgazettemail.com/coaltattoo/2013/05/15/guest-post-harrison-plant-proposal-a-bad-deal/.

FIRSTENERGY'S BLUEPRINT FOR A BAILOUT: THE HARRISON PLANT TRANSFER

FirstEnergy's Application to the West Virginia PSC

As described in Chapter 8, FirstEnergy used its August 2012 Resource Plan to lay the foundation for its regulated subsidiaries in West Virginia, Mon Power and Potomac Edison, to acquire the remaining portion of the Harrison coal plant, which is a huge, 1,984 MW facility built in the early 1970s in Haywood, West Virginia. The Harrison plant was already partly owned by Mon Power (20 percent), while the rest was owned by FirstEnergy's unregulated subsidiary, Allegheny Energy Supply. The 80 percent of the plant owned by Allegheny Energy Supply operated as a merchant plant that was consistently "out of the money" at PJM, and thus losing money for the FirstEnergy shareholders.

The deal proposed by FirstEnergy to sell Allegheny Energy Supply's 80 percent share of Harrison was great for its shareholders, but bad for the Mon Power and Potomac Edison ratepayers. The deal was contrary to the public interest in the following respects:[9]

- The proposed transaction would have given Mon Power more capacity than it needed, thereby precluding it from pursuing other, cheaper options, such as energy efficiency, natural gas-fired generation, and purchases from the wholesale market.
- The Resource Plan underlying the proposed transaction completely ignored energy efficiency as an alternative, even for a portion of the needed capacity. As noted in Chapter 8, FirstEnergy's 2012 Resource Plan stated that "demand side resource options are not a viable solution capable of meeting Mon Power's obligations ... [as they] do not address energy shortfalls as significant as the shortfall faced by Mon Power." This was particularly problematic given that the proposed acquisition price for the Harrison plant was 7.4 cents/kWh, which was substantially greater than the cost of energy efficiency measures.
- The price for the Harrison plant acquisition was inflated far above what utility regulators ever would allow under "generally accepted ratemaking principles," which rely on the net book value of the plant, or its original cost less accumulated depreciation, as the value of the plant for ratemaking purposes. The net book value of the portion of the Harrison plant proposed to be transferred was $574 million ($1.24 billion less $667.3 million in accumulated depreciation). FirstEnergy was proposing to include an "acquisition adjustment" of $589.6 million that would have more than doubled the acquisition cost of the plant for West Virginia ratepayers, to $1.163 billion. This "acquisition adjustment" was purportedly based upon "a purchase accounting fair value measurement

[9] *Id.*

component … related to the completion of the FirstEnergy/Allegheny merger in February 2011," according to FirstEnergy testimony.[10] Such "fair value adjustments," also known as "goodwill" adjustments, are rarely allowed to be recovered from utility ratepayers under generally accepted ratemaking practices.

- The proposed price for the Harrison plant acquisition was substantially over-stated and did not reflect the current value of the plant, based on the then recent coal plant deals summarized above in the section *The Declining Value of Coal-Fired Generation*.
- The Resource Plan relied on by FirstEnergy in its filing failed to consider and properly evaluate the various alternatives. Market purchases, or relying on power purchases from the wholesale market, was the primary alternative iden-tified in the Resource Plan. But the wholesale price projections used in the Resource Plan, and upon which FirstEnergy rejected market purchases as an alternative, were based upon outdated, inaccurately high – about 30 percent too high – projections of Henry Hub natural gas market prices. As a result, the analysis substantially overstated the cost of the "alternative," which made the Harrison plant transaction look relatively cheaper by comparison. The analysis in the Resource Plan also completely failed to evaluate the risks associated with exclusive reliance on coal-fired generation.
- It was clear that the transaction was an integral part of FirstEnergy's financial restructuring to exit from its money-losing competitive generating business, which should not be subsidized by West Virginia ratepayers.
- The application at the PSC created the false impression that rejection of the transaction would have resulted in closure of the plant and laying off coal miners. In reality, the proposal was nothing but a financial bailout for FirstEnergy's shareholders; the plant would not have ceased operating if Mon Power were not authorized to do this deal. Rather, FirstEnergy would have been subjected to the wholesale power marketplace, and would have been forced to sell the output at competitively determined prices rather than the inflated price, 7.4 cents/kWh, FirstEnergy was proposing in the transaction, with any shortfall borne by FirstEnergy shareholders.

West Virginia PSC Approval of the Transfer

Following two rounds of evidentiary hearings before the West Virginia PSC, several parties to the proceeding entered into a Stipulation setting forth the proposed terms upon which the PSC should approve the transaction. Among other things, the

---

[10] *Id.* (citing the Direct Testimony of Kevin G. Wise, West Virginia Public Service Commission, Case No. 12-1571-E-PC, Monongahela Power Company and the Potomac Edison Company, Petition for Approval of Generation Resource Transaction and Related Relief, at 7).

Stipulation provided for a substantial reduction in the sales price for the Harrison plant than proposed in the application, from $1.2 billion to $868 million, which represented a reduction from $776 per kW to $565 per kW. Other elements of the Stipulation were "concessions" agreed upon by FirstEnergy, including:

(1) a commitment to increase employment in West Virginia by fifty employees, mostly in the distribution sector;

(2) a $100,000 retirement of renewable energy credits to spur the development of renewable energy resources;

(3) three separate $500,000 contributions over a five-year period for the purposes of low-income energy assistance, home weatherization assistance, and to spur energy efficiency initiatives in public schools in the Mon Power and Potomac Edison service territories;

(4) increased energy efficiency targets (maintaining existing programs at the negligible savings level of 0.1 percent per year); and

(5) a commitment to develop a competitive request for proposals (RFP) for any capacity resource additions in the future.

In an order issued on October 7, 2013,[11] the West Virginia PSC approved the transfer, accepting most of the terms of the Stipulation among the parties. The PSC noted that even after reflecting the reduced purchase price recommended in the Stipulation, the seller, Allegheny Energy Supply, would still receive an amount that was $257 million greater than the net book value of the plant. The PSC therefore conditioned recovery of this $257 million from ratepayers on the operation of a sharing mechanism that would reflect the extent to which sales of excess power from the plant into the wholesale market provided sufficient margins to fund such recovery. In other words, the Stipulated purchase price of $868 million could be included in the West Virginia rate base only if sales into the wholesale market from the plant – in excess of the power required by retail customers – provided sufficient profits to justify inclusion of the $257 million over and above net book value in the regulated rate base.[12]

Commissioner Ryan Palmer filed a spirited and compelling dissent, pointing out that any recovery of amounts in excess of the net book value of the plant – whether or not conditioned on operation of the sharing mechanism adopted by the PSC – would violate a previous PSC order inasmuch as FirstEnergy agreed not to seek to recover such "goodwill" or acquisition adjustments in rates when it acquired Allegheny Energy in 2010. According to his dissent: "At its best, the Companies' attempt to burden ratepayers with the entire $1.2 billion purchase price for the Harrison plant, including the Acquisition Adjustment, is another example of

---

[11] West Virginia PSC, Case No. 12–1571-E-PC, Monongahela Power Company and the Potomac Edison Company, Petition for Approval of Generation Resource Transaction and Related Relief, Commission Order, issued Oct. 7, 2013.

[12] *Id.* at 35.

'corporate enthusiasm.' At its worst, the originally proposed transaction is a textbook write-up of which JP Morgan and Samuel Insull would be proud."[13]

Commissioner Palmer also criticized the "results-driven assumptions in Mon Power's models," including:

(1) overstated projected company specific load growth (1.4 percent);
(2) overstated projections of market wholesale prices and off-system sales;
(3) an assumed low-capacity factor (25 percent) for natural gas plants;
(4) an assumed high-capacity factor (75 percent) for operation of the Harrison plant;
(5) failure to account for known and lower than forecasted PJM capacity prices;
(6) failure to account for potential increased costs from new EPA effluent limitations under the Clean Water Act;
(7) failure to consider the possibility of purchasing part or all of an existing natural gas-fired power plant;
(8) failure to account for the "war on coal" and a potential carbon tax or costs due to other related regulation;
(9) failure to consider demand-side options such as energy efficiency and demand response; and
(10) failure to account for the lack of a coal supply contract for Harrison after 2013.

Commissioner Palmer further expressed concerns about continued heavy reliance on one fuel source – coal – in Mon Power's generating portfolio, noting that "this overreliance on one fuel source, and the imposition on ratepayers of a large, long-term fixed cost for twenty-five years regardless of whether the Harrison acquisition proves cost-effective, will expose ratepayers to an unreasonable level of risk."[14] He questioned the wisdom of "going 'all in' on coal, at a time when the coal industry is under attack and the general school of thought is to diversify."[15]

Not surprisingly, Commissioner Palmer left the PSC shortly thereafter, taking a position with the Federal Communications Commission. He was clearly not part of the Mike Albert "support the coal industry at all costs" team at the PSC.

Post-Transaction Analysis of the Harrison Plant Transfer

In September 2016, the Institute for Energy Economics and Financial Analysis (IEEFA) released a report analyzing whether West Virginia ratepayers had benefited from the transfer of the 80 percent share of the Harrison coal plant from Allegheny Energy Supply to Mon Power and Potomac Edison.[16] The report concluded that the acquisition of the Harrison power plant by FirstEnergy's regulated affiliates failed to

---

[13]   *Id.* (Dissenting Opinion of Commissioner Palmer, issued Oct. 7, 2013, at 5).
[14]   *Id.* at 7.
[15]   *Id.*
[16]   KUNKEL, *supra* note 6.

produce any financial benefit to Mon Power and Potomac Edison customers. To the contrary, IEEFA estimated the deal had cost customers more than $160 million relative to what they would otherwise have paid for electricity, while at the same time shielding FirstEnergy from suffering a comparable loss had the plant continued to be owned by Allegheny Energy Supply. According to IEEFA's calculations, the acquisition imposed a cost, on average, of about $130 on every Mon Power and Potomac Edison residential customer, and about $600 on commercial customers. The primary cause? FirstEnergy had assumed high wholesale market prices in its analysis, which made the Harrison output appear relatively more cost-competitive and also exaggerated the ability of Mon Power to sell the excess power (recall that the capacity acquired by Mon Power was far in excess of its needs, and FirstEnergy assumed that the excess energy would be sold into the competitive wholesale markets). In fact, low wholesale energy prices continued into the future – which had been predicted by opponents to the transaction in their testimony submitted to the PSC and which Commissioner Palmer largely incorporated into his analysis – thereby leaving a huge gap in revenue recovery for the plant that had to be picked up by ratepayers.[17]

Frankly, the analysis is not all that complicated, and the PSC could have easily found a basis for rejecting the transaction had it taken a properly skeptical view of it. It was patently obvious to anyone following the electric utility industry at the time that cheap and plentiful natural gas, caused by the shale gas revolution discussed in Chapter 2, and resulting low wholesale power prices, were squeezing coal plants and forcing merchant generators – such as FirstEnergy's Allegheny Energy Supply – to figure out an exit strategy. The bottom line was this: If wholesale prices really stayed as high as FirstEnergy was predicting in its application, why would Allegheny Energy Supply be selling the plant? It would have been a moneymaker for shareholders. The same market dynamics that forced FirstEnergy to pursue a bailout continued into the future, except now the ratepayers were bearing the costs instead of FirstEnergy shareholders. Commissioner Palmer, looking at the evidentiary record in the case, figured it out, and exposed the sham. Chairman Mike Albert and Commissioner Jon McKinney chose not to apply the same rigorous scrutiny; consequently, Mon Power and Potomac Edison ratepayers will be paying the consequences for that lapse for the foreseeable future.

AEP FOLLOWS SUIT WITH AMOS AND MITCHELL

AEP followed FirstEnergy's lead by proposing, in December 2012, to have its West Virginia and Virginia subsidiary, Appalachian Power, purchase an 867 MW share of Unit 3 of the John Amos power plant and 50 percent (780 MW) of the Mitchell power plant – a total of 1,647 MW – from its unregulated competitive subsidiary, AEP Generation Resources. Both power plants are located in West Virginia; Amos Unit 3 was placed in service in 1973 and Mitchell in 1971. The proposed purchase

---

[17]   *Id.* at 6.

price, the net book value of the plants, was $702/kW. The remaining 50 percent of the Mitchell plant would be sold to AEP's regulated subsidiary, Kentucky Power.

The Virginia State Corporation Commission Rejects Appalachian Power's Proposal

A complicating factor for Appalachian Power, however, is that it operates in both Virginia and West Virginia, thus requiring approval of both the West Virginia PSC and the Virginia State Corporation Commission (Virginia SCC) for its proposed acquisition of portions of the Amos and Mitchell coal plants. While the Virginia SCC approved the acquisition by Appalachian Power of the share of the Amos coal plant, it rejected the acquisition of the 50 percent share of the Mitchell plant, finding that the combination of the acquisitions would have resulted in Appalachian Power being far too reliant on one generating fuel (coal). AEP was thus left with an urgent need to develop a creative strategy that would allow it to transfer the Mitchell plant from its unregulated subsidiary to West Virginia's ratepayers.

Undaunted, AEP essentially "unwound" a previous merger of sorts between its two subsidiaries operating in West Virginia (Appalachian Power and Wheeling Power). The two subsidiaries are separate corporations within the AEP system, and together serve over 478,000 customers in West Virginia. In 2006, the PSC consolidated the West Virginia rates of the two utilities, and their retail customers thereafter paid the same tariff rates, even though they maintained their historically separate and distinct corporate identities and power supply arrangements. In 2009, however, the two utilities proposed to merge, and to operate as a single public service utility. Once merged, Wheeling Power customers would be supplied with power from the existing legal and contractual power supply resources of Appalachian Power. Under a joint stipulation filed with the West Virginia PSC in November 2009, the merger would not take place before January 1, 2012.

To achieve the desired unloading of both the Amos and Mitchell coal plants from its unregulated subsidiary to the regulated ratepayers of West Virginia, AEP pulled the plug on the proposed merger of Wheeling Power and Appalachian Power. As noted above, the Virginia SCC had approved the acquisition of the Amos plant by Appalachian Power, but not the proposed transfer of the Mitchell coal plant. So what was the creative solution crafted by AEP? Have Wheeling Power acquire the interest in the Mitchell plant, since the West Virginia PSC would surely not balk at approving another transfer of an uneconomic coal plant from an unregulated subsidiary to the regulated rate base in West Virginia, where the captive customers of Wheeling Power would bear the risks and costs. Appalachian Power in West Virginia would simultaneously proceed with its own application to the West Virginia PSC for approval of the transfer of the portion of the Amos plant that had been approved by the Virginia SCC.

AEP's Applications to the West Virginia PSC

Similar to FirstEnergy's proposed Harrison plant transfer, AEP's proposal to the West Virginia PSC was very much about what was in the best interest of the AEP system – and the AEP shareholders – rather than about meeting the electricity needs of Appalachian Power's or Wheeling Power's customers at the lowest cost. According to an analysis prepared in July 2013 by two energy experts,[18] the respective applications at the West Virginia PSC for the transfers relating to the Amos and Mitchell plants were flawed for the following reasons:

- AEP followed FirstEnergy's playbook and assumed unrealistically high wholesale market prices through 2040 which, when coupled with an unrealistically high gas price forecast, made the coal plant transfers look economically competitive. The energy market price forecast used by AEP was about 30 percent higher than actual market prices in 2012. For 2013–19, its energy market price forecast averaged nearly 40 percent higher than energy market futures at the time. AEP's gas price forecast was also more than 10 percent higher than current futures at that time.[19]

- AEP's analysis included a relatively low price on carbon (less than $20 per ton) through 2030. By comparison, the Obama administration was using a carbon price of $38 per ton at the time.[20] (Putting a price on carbon is commonly used to capture the estimated cost of anticipated regulation of GHG emissions.)

- The units that Appalachian Power and Wheeling Power were proposing to acquire (Amos 3 and Mitchell) have restricted scrubbing capability – they can only handle coal with sulfur content below 4.5 pound per million British Thermal Units (MMBtus) – thereby exposing ratepayers to the higher price and increased volatility of low-sulfur coal.[21]

- AEP made no attempt to "test the market" to determine the fair market value of its assets – which would have been a valuable exercise given the distressed sales of coal plants that were occurring at the time – nor did it issue a competitive RFP to see if there were better options in the market to meet the needs of Appalachian Power and Wheeling Power ratepayers.[22]

- AEP failed to adopt policies that might have encouraged third-party generation within its service territories, which might have helped meet a portion of the claimed capacity needs.[23]

- Similar to the deficiency in the Resource Plan relied upon by FirstEnergy in its Harrison application, AEP did not assume any meaningful role for

[18] DAVID SCHLISSEL & CATHY KUNKEL, MOUNTAIN STATE MANEUVER: AEP AND FIRSTENERGY TRY TO STICK RATEPAYERS WITH RISKY COAL PLANTS (July 20, 2013), https://ieefa.org/report-mountain-state-maneuver-aep-and-firstenergy-try-to-stick-ratepayers-with-risky-coal-plant/.
[19] *Id.* at 7.
[20] *Id.* at 8.
[21] *Id.* at 8–9.
[22] *Id.* at 9.
[23] *Id.*

energy efficiency, which also could have helped to meet its long-term capacity needs.[24]

- AEP foreclosed its participation in the PJM capacity markets, which could have been relied upon to meet a portion of its capacity shortfall. (Recall that in addition to energy markets, PJM operates capacity markets through which utilities may buy or offer to sell capacity – the ability to deliver power – at a future date.) AEP's strategy to decline participation may, to some extent, have forced the PSC's hand to approve the transaction, by removing an available option.[25]

West Virginia PSC Approval of the Amos Plant Transfer

In an order issued on December 13, 2013, the West Virginia PSC approved Appalachian Power's proposed acquisition of two-thirds of the Amos 3 coal plant, finding that:

(1) Appalachian Power required significant additions to its capacity resources in the immediate future to offset a projected capacity shortfall;

(2) there was not sufficient, reasonably priced capacity available from demand-side resources equivalent to the capacity from the two-thirds of Amos 3 that Appalachian Power proposed to purchase;

(3) the acquisition of two-thirds of Amos 3 would allow Appalachian Power to cover its projected 2015 capacity shortfall and leave a margin to cover future growth in capacity requirements;

(4) acquiring capacity through the purchase of two-thirds of Amos 3 was the least-cost alternative for Appalachian Power ratepayers when compared to market purchases for an extended period of time or to market purchases for a limited period of time and then acquisition of optimum amounts of natural gas-fired generation.[26]

West Virginia PSC Approval of the Mitchell Plant Transfer

On December 30, 2014, the West Virginia PSC issued its order approving Wheeling Power's acquisition of 50 percent of the Mitchell coal plant from AEP's unregulated subsidiary, AEP Generation Resources, Inc. The order approved the terms of a Stipulation agreed upon by the parties to the proceeding which, among other things,

[24] *Id.*
[25] *Id.*
[26] West Virginia Public Service Commission, Case No. 12-1655-E-PC, *Petition for Consent and Approval of Appalachian Power Company Consummating an Arrangement for the Transfer to It of 1647 MW of Generating Capacity Presently Owned by Ohio Power Company, an Affiliate, Pursuant to W.Va. Code 524-2-12, and Associated Agreements*, Commission Order, issued Dec. 13, 2013.

provided for a "phasing in" of the cost of Mitchell into rates over time, given that the plant's generating capacity was far greater than the needs of Wheeling Power's customers. Specifically, the Stipulation provided that only 82.5 percent of the portion of the Mitchell plant acquired by Wheeling Power would be included in rates immediately, with the remaining 17.5 percent being added to rates no later than January 1, 2020. The PSC concluded in its order that the Mitchell Plant, like the Amos Plant, was a high-quality, environmentally compliant, base-load coal plant that had performed well for the AEP system for decades. The PSC further observed that the Mitchell Plant had ample coal supply options because of its location on the Ohio River and its close proximity to the Appalachian coal fields; substantially complied with current EPA standards with relatively minor upgrades; and was expected to continue to provide competitive generation well into the future.[27]

FIRSTENERGY'S ATTEMPTED REPRISE WITH PLEASANTS STATION

Following the playbook of the successful transfer, in 2013, of its uneconomic Harrison plant from Allegheny Energy Supply to Mon Power and Potomac Edison, FirstEnergy announced in 2016 that it planned to seek approval from the West Virginia PSC to sell all or a portion of its 1,300 MW Pleasants Power Station to FirstEnergy's West Virginia-regulated subsidiary, Mon Power. As in the case of the Harrison plant, the owner of the Pleasants Power Station was FirstEnergy's competitive subsidiary, Allegheny Energy Supply. As noted in Chapter 8, FirstEnergy used its December 2015 integrated resource plan (IRP), filed with the West Virginia PSC, to lay the foundation for the proposed acquisition. Its IRP concluded that the best option for supplying Mon Power's future capacity needs would be to purchase an existing coal plant to meet a projected 850 MW capacity shortfall. On FirstEnergy's first quarter 2016 earnings call, CEO Chuck Jones made it clear which coal plant FirstEnergy was talking about: "We filed our integrated resource plan with West Virginia. I think later this year, they'll start taking a look at it seriously, and it's up to the West Virginia Commission to decide would Pleasants be the appropriate solution. Obviously, we have a model in place already with Harrison ... ."[28]

To create the impression that it was actually testing the market to determine whether Pleasants Station was the best resource to meet Mon Power's needs, Mon Power determined that it would pursue the acquisition of capacity resources via a RFP administered by a third-party, Charles River Associates (Charles River). Mon Power issued the RFP on December 16, 2016, seeking to acquire: (1) one or more generating facilities (existing, new, or sufficiently in-development) amounting to approximately 1,300 MW of unforced capacity; and (2) up to 100 MW of demand response resources. In each case, the RFP stated that resource(s) should be located within

[27] West Virginia Public Service Commission, Case No. 14-0546-E-PC, *Petition for Acquisition of Mitchell Plant by Wheeling Power Company*, Commission Order, issued Dec. 30, 2014.
[28] KUNKEL, *supra* note 6, at 2.

a particular geographic area of PJM – the Allegheny Power Systems (APS) zone – which coincidentally(?) happened to be the zone in which Pleasants Station was located. On February 27, 2017, Charles River provided Mon Power an Opinion Letter recommending the acquisition of Pleasants Station as the winning bidder, and Mon Power selected AE Supply as the winning bidder and subsequently entered into an asset purchase agreement to acquire Pleasants Station.

FirstEnergy's strategy failed miserably. As a transaction between affiliated entities, the proposed transfer required the approval of FERC. In an order issued on January 12, 2018, FERC rejected the proposed transfer, finding that FirstEnergy had failed to demonstrate that the transaction was in the public interest, as required by FERC's Merger Policy Statement.[29] FERC cited two reasons for its decision. First, it expressed doubts – with good reason – that the West Virginia PSC would do an adequate job of protecting West Virginian retail ratepayers from inappropriate cross-subsidization of unregulated affiliates by regulated retail utilities (in other words, that the PSC would not protect Mon Power ratepayers from having to bear costs that were properly allocated to FirstEnergy's unregulated operations). According to FERC, FirstEnergy failed to demonstrate that West Virginia had "adopt[ed] or has in place ring-fencing measures to protect customers against inappropriate cross-subsidization or the encumbrance of utility assets for the benefit of the 'unregulated' affiliates, and failed to provide any evidence that any ratepayer protections regarding cross subsidies are proposed in the proceeding before the West Virginia PSC."[30] This observation is a fairly damning statement of a federal regulatory agency regarding West Virginia PSC's miserable track record in protecting retail ratepayers.

Second, FERC found that the RFP conducted by Mon Power in December 2016 was essentially a sham in that it failed to satisfy FERC's requirements for transparency. Specifically, FERC found that the "product" sought by Mon Power in its RFP was overly narrow "because the stated objective could have been achieved if the RFP considered [power purchase agreements] and resources that were outside of the APS zone."[31] FERC dismissed the application without prejudice, urging Mon Power to address its capacity shortfall "in a way that provides non-affiliate competing suppliers with the same opportunity as an affiliate to meet the utility's needs"[32] – in other words, a real RFP that actually tests the market rather than a contrived solicitation designed to produce the answer that FirstEnergy wanted.

Undaunted, the West Virginia PSC nonetheless approved the proposed transaction, subject to conditions that FirstEnergy and Mon Power would have to accept. In its order issued on January 26, 2018, the PSC took note of FERC's rejection of the

[29] Federal Energy Regulatory Commission, Docket Nos. EC17-88–000 and ES18-4–000, *Order Rejecting Disposition and Acquisition of Generation Facilities and Dismissing Assumption of Liabilities*, issued Jan. 12, 2018.

[30] *Id.* at 12.

[31] *Id.* at 31.

[32] *Id.* at 35.

transaction, but noted that, at the time of its decision, the time for seeking reconsideration at FERC had not yet expired.[33] The PSC therefore proceeded with its action on the transaction. To its credit, the PSC expressed some skepticism at the projections offered by FirstEnergy in its application, finding that:

> [T]he uncertainties of achieving [the net benefits claimed by FirstEnergy], at the level projected by the Companies, are high. PJM market prices have been low in recent years. It appears that there is a high likelihood of an extended period of low PJM market prices and continuing evolution of PJM Market rules may not be tilting in a direction that will allow benefits to the extent projected by the Companies.[34]

The PSC therefore found the approval to be contrary to the public interest unless the applicants agreed "to shoulder the responsibility of the excess cost of Pleasants, vis-a-vis the market, if their projections are significantly in error." The PSC's solution was to impose a requirement that applicants "guarantee that the Companies will compensate customers during any year that market prices produce capacity and energy revenues from Pleasants that are below the full revenue requirements imposed on customers due to Pleasants."[35]

FirstEnergy subsidiaries Mon Power and Potomac Edison ultimately rejected the conditions that the West Virginia PSC imposed for the transfer of Pleasants Station, and also decided not to seek a rehearing of the FERC order that rejected the transfer for not being consistent with the public interest. The swindle having been exposed to such an extent that even the West Virginia PSC had to balk, FirstEnergy was stuck with Pleasants Station for the time being. However, as discussed in Chapter 9, FirstEnergy went back to the well the following year with its scheme to convince the legislature to bail out Pleasants Station with a $12.5 million reprieve from the B&O tax.

THE "GIFT" TO UTILITY SHAREHOLDERS THAT KEEPS ON TAKING: THE DECADES-LONG BURDEN OF COAL PLANT OWNERSHIP

As it turned out in the Life cereal commercial, Mikey liked the product, as did his two brothers. The commercial ends as follows:

NARRATOR: When you bring Life home, don't tell the kids that it's one of those nutritional cereals you've been trying to get them to eat. You're the only one who has to know.

Unlike the cereal commercial – which has a happy ending – the electric ratepayers in West Virginia do not have a happy ending; they face a very

[33] West Virginia Public Service Commission, Case No. 17–0296-E-PC, *Monongahela Power Company and The Potomac Edison Company, Petition for Approval of a Generation Resource Transaction and Related Relief*, Commission Order, issued Jan. 26, 2018.
[34] *Id.* at 54.
[35] *Id.*

expensive and option-constrained future. And pretty much everyone looking at the evidence in the cases – except, apparently, the PSC commissioners (excluding Ryan Palmer, of course) – had to know that the outcome was not going to be a happy ending for ratepayers. It's just not that complicated. Beginning in 2012, coal ceased to be a cost-effective means of generating electricity, and the owners of merchant coal plants – in this case, Allegheny Energy Supply and AEP Generation Resources – needed an exit strategy out of the competitive generation business, a Mikey of sorts who would take the unwanted Life cereal off their hands. If the coal plants are a bad deal for their owners when they are operating as merchant generating assets, why would they suddenly become a good deal for new owners – the ratepayers – simply by virtue of accounting entries that move the asset from one subsidiary to another? They don't. As Ryan Palmer noted in his dissent, this scheme is a transaction about which JP Morgan and Samuel Insull would be proud.

Unfortunately, the consequences of the ill-advised decisions of the PSC to approve the transfers of the Harrison, Amos, and Mitchell coal plants will be borne by West Virginia ratepayers for the next two decades. FirstEnergy indicated in its 2015 IRP that it intends to keep Harrison operating at least through 2035. AEP's filing at the PSC for recovery of the costs related to compliance with the EPA's effluent limitation guidelines (ELG) (discussed in Chapter 8) makes it clear that AEP intends to continue operating the Mitchell and Amos plants (along with its other coal-fired plant, Mountaineer) until 2040.[36] And the PSC continues to double down on the state's continued uneconomic commitment to coal-fired generation, regardless of the adverse impacts on ratepayers. In a decision issued in August 2021, the PSC approved AEP's request to make the necessary investment of $383.5 million at the Mitchell, Amos, and Mountaineer plants to comply with the ELG regulations and enable the plants to remain open beyond 2028.[37] The result is yet another rate increase for AEP customers, who will bear a surcharge of 38 cents per month to cover the additional investment. The decision is particularly remarkable for the Mitchell plant, given that AEP's own analysis in the case showed that ratepayers would save about $27 million per year by closing Mitchell in 2028 and replacing it with other AEP-owned generation. In other words, the utility conceded that it did not make economic sense for ratepayers to pay for this additional investment, given the availability of cheaper resources. But AEP chose to leave it up to the PSC to make

---

[36]   West Virginia Public Service Commission, Case No. 20–1040-E-CN, *Appalachian Power Company and Wheeling Power Company, Application for a Certificate of Public Convenience and Necessity for the Internal Modifications at Coal Fired Generating Plants Necessary to Comply with Federal Environmental Regulations and Surcharge*, Commission Order, issued Aug. 4, 2021, http://www.psc.state.wv.us/scripts/WebDocket/ViewDocument.cfm?CaseActivityID=569959.

[37]   Mike Tony, *WV Public Service Commission Approves Keeping Mitchell Plant Operational Through 2040, Electric Rate Hike*, CHARLESTON GAZETTE-MAIL (Aug. 4, 2021), https://www.wvgazettemail.com/news/energy_and_environment/wv-public-service-commission-approves-keeping-mitchell-plant-operational-through-2040-electric-rate-hike/article_14da3378-33f0-5fe8-82a5-52a7230d32f6.html.

the decision, irrespective of the adverse impacts on ratepayers, knowing that the PSC would make the pro-coal decision and approve the investment.

In explaining the decision, PSC Chairman Charlotte Lane said the commission was "very concerned" about what she contended would be a likely shortage of electricity caused by shutting down the Mitchell plant prematurely. "We recognize that in the future, for new power supply resources, we may have to rely more on intermittent resources such as wind and solar," Lane said. "It is premature, however, to begin abandoning our traditional base load power supply resources, which can be upgraded to meet environmental requirements."[38] Shortage of electricity from prematurely closing down Mitchell and replacing it with wind and solar? Such a statement suggests complete ignorance – or worse still, intentional obliviousness – of the interconnectedness of the regional wholesale market and the obligation of the regional wholesale market operator, PJM, to ensure the adequacy of generating resources to "keep the lights on." The lights won't go out from the shuttering of Mitchell in 2028, and Chairman Lane presumably knows better.

As early as 2016, PJM issued a report concluding that the PJM system would not have any significant reliability issues operating with up to 30 percent of its energy (as distinct from capacity) provided by wind and solar generation.[39] In other words, the "intermittency" of renewable energy resources cited by Chairman Lane can be addressed through the operation of regional wholesale markets and the availability of other resources to "firm up" variable wind and solar generation. PJM bears the primary obligation for "keeping the lights on" and avoiding the "shortage of electricity" cited by Chairman Lane. The PSC once again made a decision in the interests of the coal industry and contrary to the interests of the ratepayers it is statutorily charged with protecting, and it did so on the basis of a flimsy explanation that completely disregards the critical role played by the operator of the regional wholesale power market under the Federal Power Act and applicable FERC orders.

Other state commissions, not surprisingly, reached different conclusions than the West Virginia PSC regarding the economic case for keeping the Mitchell, Amos, and Mountaineer plants open after 2028. The regulatory agencies in both Kentucky and Virginia acted to protect ratepayers by rejecting AEP's request for rate recovery of the ELG compliance costs. The Mitchell plant is 50 percent owned by Kentucky Power, and the Kentucky PSC rejected AEP's request for recovery of the ELG costs, finding that Kentucky Power failed to prove that the investment was cost-effective.[40]

---

[38] *Id.*

[39] *Renewable Integration Study Reports*, PJM (Mar, 31, 2014), https://www.pjm.com/committees-and-groups/closed-groups/irs/pris.aspx.

[40] Mike Tony, *Uncertainty over Mitchell Plant's Future Persists After WV, KY Regulators' Differing Rulings*, Charleston Gazette-Mail (Aug. 5, 2021), https://www.wvgazettemail.com/news/energy_an d_environment/uncertainty-over-mitchell-plants-future-persists-after-wv-ky-regulators-differing-rul ings/article_120324d6-4c5c-5c07-b0a2-7b3e190f57ef.html?fbclid=IwAR1SgDB_CMJMi0Q4g ATJj1LM3kt3YgPGFrIvPPy9Fky3MIYMY_s9Ce5JiuE#utm_campaign=blox&utm_source=faceboo k&utm_medium=social.

The Amos and Mountaineer plants are owned by Appalachian Power, which is regulated by both the West Virginia PSC and the Virginia SCC; these plants are considered to be a "shared" resource between Virginia and West Virginia for cost-allocation purposes. The Virginia SCC rejected AEP's request for recovery of the additional investment to keep Amos and Mountaineer open beyond 2028.[41]

Also not surprisingly, the story gets worse for West Virginia ratepayers. In the face of Virginia and Kentucky regulators just saying "no" to their state's ratepayers bearing a share of the ELG costs at Amos and Mitchell, AEP decided simply to reopen its case at the West Virginia PSC and ask West Virginians to pick up the slack. According to AEP's September 2021 filing, the price tag would increase from the $383.5 million approved by the PSC in its August 2021 order to $448.3 million, as a result of reallocating the shares not borne by Virginia and Kentucky ratepayers to West Virginia ratepayers. What's another $65 million when the PSC has already approved wasteful expenditures of nearly $400 million? And obviously the commissioners on the West Virginia PSC are much more discerning than the regulators in Virginia and Kentucky who failed to appreciate the value of spending hundreds of millions of dollars to keep uneconomic coal plants open for another twelve years. And there's one more thing that AEP had going for it when it refiled its case in September 2021 to stick West Virginia ratepayers with the costs that Virginia and Kentucky would not accept: Bill Raney – the retired head of the West Virginia Coal Association and the primary architect of the Friends of Coal campaign (discussed in Chapter 5) – had taken his seat as the newest member of the West Virginia PSC, having been appointed by Governor Jim Justice in early August 2021 to fill the seat of retired Commissioner Brooks McCabe. Following a hastily arranged one-day hearing that was convened less than three weeks after AEP's refiling, the PSC issued an order in mid-October approving the revised request.[42]

And just to make it perfectly clear that the PSC wants these plants to keep operating through 2040 – regardless of whether cheaper sources of energy may become available – the order further directs AEP to "proceed with construction and take all necessary steps to operate the Plants beyond 2028 and extend their operations to at least 2040."[43] It is apparently irrelevant that AEP never formally requested approvals for any expenditures after 2028. Nor does the PSC apparently care about the magnitude of any costs associated with such "necessary steps" which, of course, will simply be flowed through to ratepayers. The continued investments in these uneconomic coal plants will lead to massive rate increases for AEP ratepayers in the future, given the growing inability of coal plants to compete in the wholesale

[41]   *Id.*
[42]   West Virginia PSC, Case No. 20–1040-E-CN, *Appalachian Power Company and Wheeling Power Company, Application for a Certificate of Public Convenience and Necessity for the Internal Modifications at Coal Fired Generating Plants Necessary to Comply with Federal Environmental Regulations and Surcharge*, Commission Order, issued Oct. 12, 2021.
[43]   *Id.* at 15.

energy markets. Apparently all that matters to the PSC is that these coal plants continue operating through 2040, which represents a substantial windfall for AEP and its shareholders. And it helps explain why Nick Akins, AEP's president and chief executive officer, lobbied Senator Manchin to oppose the Clean Electricity Performance Program, as discussed in the section At the End of the Day, Still a Coal Guy Putting the Coal Industry First (Chapter 7). With continued operation of three large coal-fired power plants in West Virginia through 2040, AEP likely would not have fared well under a program promoting decarbonization.

So now the electric ratepayers of West Virginia get to subsidize the ratepayers in Virginia and Kentucky by bearing nearly $65 million in additional costs to keep Mitchell and Amos open past 2028. These plants were uneconomic at the time they were unloaded by AEP's unregulated subsidiary in 2013 and 2014 – after all, that's why shareholders were dumping them – and the economics have not improved in the last several years. In fact, given the dramatic decline in the costs of renewable energy during "the lost decade" (as discussed in Chapter 3), they could be replaced *now* with wind and solar at a cost saving for ratepayers, as confirmed in a study by the Center for Energy and Sustainable Development, *West Virginia's Energy Future*, which is discussed in Chapter 12.[44] It's a gift to utility shareholders, courtesy of the PSC, that will just keep costing West Virginia ratepayers.

[44] WVU COLLEGE OF LAW CENTER FOR ENERGY AND SUSTAINABLE DEVELOPMENT, WEST VIRGINIA'S ENERGY FUTURE (Dec. 2020), https://energy.law.wvu.edu/files/d/b1ff11183-e9ae-4ad0-93bf-aa3afa1da785/wv-s-energy-future-wvu-col-cesd-final.pdf.

11

Coal Operators Get Rich and West Virginia Gets to Clean Up the Mess

When coal prices rose in 2009–10 due to increased demand for coal exports – primarily as a result of the industrialization of developing nations (China and India in particular) – the response in the coal industry was a series of consolidations and acquisitions by coal companies at staggering prices. These transactions were highly leveraged (i.e., largely funded through heavy use of debt), which put the coal companies in a precarious position financially once coal prices resumed their inevitable decline as US electric utilities reduced their use of coal, and exports decreased as the world began to consider the climate change impacts of continuing to burn coal. As a result, several large coal companies went bankrupt and, since 2012, more than sixty mine operators have filed for bankruptcy.

The first liabilities the coal operators manage to shed during bankruptcy are the employee benefits (pension and health care) promised to miners, followed by environmental obligations (promises to reclaim mine sites and clean up polluted streams). In both circumstances, taxpayers generally provide the "backstop" to ensure some funding for miners' pension and health benefits and environmental remediation of abandoned mine lands. Meanwhile, members of the senior management teams at these same coal companies walk off with substantial "retention bonuses" to ensure that managers with such coveted business acumen would not abandon their posts. A prime example is Alpha Natural Resources' bankruptcy filing in 2016, which requested $11 million in bonuses for its executives while requesting relief from the "legacy liabilities" commonly faced by coal producers: over $680 million in reclamation obligations, $160 million in water treatment costs, more than $158 million in black lung benefits, and $600 million of debt to the United Mine Workers' pension plan.

This chapter examines the consolidation of the coal industry, and the impact of the subsequent bankruptcies on coverage for environmental liabilities in West Virginia, given the failure of state regulators to force mine operators to post bonds or otherwise obtain insurance that would cover the full cost of land reclamation or water treatment at their mines. Instead, operators in West Virginia were allowed to post bonds in smaller amounts, or to contribute inadequate amounts to an alternative bonding system that will fall woefully short of the amount necessary to perform the required reclamation. This failure to require the coal industry in West Virginia to "clean up its mess" has existed – and has been well-documented – since the 1980s. As a consequence of this gross neglect of duty by state environmental regulators, West Virginians face two equally unacceptable courses of action: pay higher taxes to cover billions of dollars in cleanup costs or continue to bear the widespread and lingering environmental degradation from the legacy of coal operations. Left untreated, closed mines raise a range of environmental and community health risks, from sinkholes to acid contamination of water courses.[1]

A FEDERAL PROGRAM WITH GOOD INTENTIONS, BUT BAD IMPLEMENTATION

Throughout the twentieth century, thousands of bankrupt coal operators were able to abandon mines without reclaiming them. In response, Congress enacted the Surface Mining Control and Reclamation Act of 1977 (SMCRA), which was designed to ensure that funds would be available to address the impacts of surface mining. The statute's preamble does a good job of describing the impacts of failing to act:

> [M]any surface mining operations result in disturbances of surface areas that burden and adversely affect commerce and the public welfare by destroying or diminishing the utility of land for commercial, industrial, residential, recreational, agricultural, and forestry purposes, by causing erosion and landslides, by contributing to floods, by polluting the water, by destroying fish and wildlife habitats, by impairing natural beauty, by damaging the property of citizens, by creating hazards dangerous to life and property by degrading the quality of life in local communities, and by counteracting governmental programs and efforts to conserve soil, water, and other natural resources.[2]

Many of these abandoned sites that were created prior to SMCRA's enactment remain untreated today; according to the US Geological Survey, reclaiming mining lands abandoned in West Virginia before SMCRA would cost at least an estimated $1.3 billion.[3]

SMCRA was designed to prevent bankrupt coal companies from shifting to government (and, ultimately, to taxpayers) the costs of restoring thousands of acres of mined land and treating millions of gallons of polluted mine water. Instead

---

[1] Mark Olalde, *US Coal Hasn't Set Aside Enough Money to Clean Up Its Mines*, Climate Change News (Mar. 14, 2018), https://www.climatechangenews.com/2018/03/14/us-coal-hasnt-set-aside-enough-money-clean-mines/.

[2] 30 U.S.C. § 1201(c).

[3] Patrick McGinley, *Will Taxpayers Foot the Cleanup Bill for Bankrupt Coal Companies?* The Conversation (May 9, 2016), https://theconversation.com/will-taxpayers-foot-the-cleanup-bill-for-bankrupt-coal-companies-56415.

SMCRA, if properly implemented, would force coal operators to address and incorporate the cost of reclamation in their business planning by requiring them to bear the costs, at the time they secure mining permits, of bonds or other financial guarantees to ensure that if they fail to fully reclaim mines, there will be money available to do the job. SMCRA requires the cost of reclamation to be calculated before any mining can begin. These calculations, in turn, must consider each mine site's topography, geology, water resources, and revegetation potential, thereby ensuring that sufficient funds will be available to fully reclaim the abandoned mine land, even if the coal operator fails to perform. "Fully reclaiming" the land means that it must be restored to "a condition capable of supporting the uses which it was capable of supporting prior to any mining."[4] This restoration may include replacing the topsoil,[5] restoring the "approximate original contour,"[6] disposing mine wastes,[7] protecting the local hydrology,[8] and reinvigorating the surrounding area.[9]

SMCRA allows coal operators to post three kinds of bonds to satisfy this requirement: (1) a surety bond, which is a third-party guarantee that would pay out to the government in the event that the operator fails to reclaim the land;[10] (2) a collateral bond, under which the operator posts assets as collateral that can be seized by the government and used to fund the reclamation;[11] or (3) a self-bond, which allows a coal operator to act as guarantor of its own reclamation obligation.[12] A coal operator is permitted to use self-bonds only when it can establish that it is in good financial health.[13]

For a variety of reasons, coal operators began to use self-bonds far more frequently than surety or collateral bonds in the early years of "the lost decade." Assuming the coal company is capable of adequately demonstrating its financial strength, self-bonding is an attractive option for qualifying coal operators because it frees up cash or other assets that would otherwise be necessary to collateralize a company's reclamation obligations. In 2014, for example, Cloud Peak Energy received approval from the Wyoming Department of Environmental Quality to replace $200 million in surety bonds with self-bonds, which Cloud Peak estimated would save approximately $2 million in annual premiums.[14] By the middle of the decade, the total amount of self-bonded reclamation obligations was sizable, totaling nearly $2.8

---

4   30 U.S.C. § 1265(b)(2).
5   *Id.* at § 1265(b)(5)–(6).
6   *Id.* at § 1265(b)(3).
7   *Id.* at § 1265(b)(10)–(11).
8   *Id.* at § 1265(b)(10).
9   *Id.* at § 1265(b)(19)–(20).
10   10 C.F.R. § 800.20.
11   *Id.* at § 800.21.
12   *Id.* at § 800.50.
13   *Id.* at § 800.23.
14   Jayni Foley Hein et al., Self-Bonding in an Era of Coal Bankruptcy 5 (Aug. 2016), https://policyintegrity.org/files/publications/Coal_Self-Bonding_Report.pdf.

TABLE 11.1 *Reclamation bond totals for top four US coal companies (millions of dollars)*

Company	Surety bonds	Collateral bonds	Self-bonds
Peabody Energy	293	299	1,431
Arch Coal	155	11	486
Cloud Peak Energy	434	0	200
Alpha Natural Resources	399	212	676

billion across the four largest coal operators (Peabody, Alpha Natural Resources, Arch Coal, and Cloud Peak Energy).[15] Peabody had guaranteed about 71 percent of its total reclamation obligations – $1.43 billion out of $2.023 billion – through self-bonds, even though its net worth at the time was only $918 million.[16] Table 11.1 shows the reclamation bond totals for the largest coal companies in the United States.

According to a report prepared by New York University's Institute for Policy Integrity,[17] self-bonding makes little sense in an era of coal company bankruptcies. For one thing, existing regulations fail to account for parent–subsidiary corporate structures, under which a subsidiary mining company might meet the financial health requirements for self-bonding, even though its assets may be required to satisfy the parent company's debts if the parent files for bankruptcy. Another problem is that regulators often fail to keep tabs on the financial health of self-bonded companies and, once the financial distress becomes apparent, it is too late to do anything: If a company fails to qualify for self-bonding, requiring it to post alternative bonds or collateral may drive it into bankruptcy, further jeopardizing the company's ability to meet reclamation obligations. The executive director of the Interstate Mining Compact Commission describes this decision as a Catch-22: "[I]f the state chooses to insist on alternative financial assurances or collateral as a result of the company's diminished financial situation, the threat to the company's financial solvency would only increase."[18]

Self-bonding creates a particular issue in bankruptcy inasmuch as self-bonds are not secured by any assets. In the event a coal operator enters bankruptcy, the government may not be able to recover the full value of a company's reclamation obligation because a self-bond is treated by the company like unsecured debt, which falls to the end of the collection line.[19] As part of the bankruptcy process, state

[15] *Id.* at 5.
[16] Joshua Macey & Jackson Salovaara, *Bankruptcy as Bailout: Coal Company Insolvency and the Erosion of Federal Law*, 71 STAN. L. REV. 879, 896 (2019).
[17] FOLEY HEIN ET AL., *supra* note 14, at 5.
[18] GREGORY E. CONRAD, MINE RECLAMATION BONDING – FROM DILEMMA TO CRISIS TO REINVENTION: WHAT'S A STATE REGULATOR TO DO? 9 (Feb. 11, 2014), http://imcc.isa.us/uploads/1/1/9/1/119191866/emlf_bonding_presentation_final.pdf.
[19] FOLEY HEIN ET AL., *supra* note 14, at 6.

environmental regulators often agree to "write down" the self-bonding obligation, given the absence of an asset backing the obligation. In the face of the growing use of self-bonding for reclamation obligations, in 2014 federal regulators began, in the Interior Department's words, "exploring concerns related to the efficacy of self-bonding practices and procedure" used by states, but took no immediate action. This failure to act would prove to be costly given the financial collapse of the coal industry that began to occur during the middle of the decade.

A HISTORY OF PROGRAM MISMANAGEMENT IN WEST VIRGINIA

While SMCRA's framework would seem by design to provide adequate measures to achieve environmental protection, it has not worked out that way in West Virginia, primarily for two reasons. First, similar to other environmental laws such as the Clean Air Act and the Clean Water Act, administration of SMCRA is largely delegated to the states. While SMCRA is a federal law overseen by the Office of Surface Mining Reclamation and Enforcement (OSMRE) within the Department of the Interior, once OSMRE approves a state program, the state administers SMCRA independently and maintains "exclusive jurisdiction" over the enforcement of SMCRA minimum permitting standards. OSMRE retains some oversight authority to ensure that the state program complies with SMCRA. In the case of West Virginia, the agency charged with enforcing SMCRA – the Department of Environmental Protection (DEP) – has never been up to the task, even from the outset, in 1981, when the federal government approved West Virginia's SMCRA program.[20] The concept of "cooperative federalism" – delegating to states the authority to administer and enforce federal pollution laws – works only when the state actually has the capability and the political will to do the job. DEP had neither.

Second, SMCRA grants states the flexibility – a foolish delegation of authority in the case of West Virginia – to set up an "alternate" to a bonding system that is designed to achieve the objectives and purposes of a bonding program. This alternative bonding system has been described by a court as a "collective risk-spreading system that ... allows a State to discount the amount of the required site-specific bond to ... less than the full cost needed to complete reclamation of the site in the event of forfeiture."[21] Such a system is allowed only so long as it ensures both that: (1) there is an economic incentive for the permittee to complete reclamation; and (2) "the regulatory authority will have available sufficient money to complete the reclamation plan for any areas which may be in default at any time."[22] These funding systems do not, of course, provide the same certainty as the use of surety bonds and collateral bonds. Moreover, they will, by design, fail to produce adequate funding. Rather, according to Joe Pizarchik, a lawyer from Pennsylvania who

[20]   30 C.F.R. § 948.10.
[21]   *Pennsylvania Federation of Sportsmen's Clubs, Inc. v. Kempthorne*, 497 F.3d 337, 341 (3rd Cir. 2007).
[22]   10. C.F.R. § 800.11(e).

directed OSMRE during the Obama administration, allowing the use of bond pools was simply a "political decision to subsidize the industry."[23]

Not surprisingly, West Virginia elected to implement an alternative bonding system, accomplished through a "Special Reclamation Fund." Under the West Virginia system, an operator posts a site-specific penal bond, not exceeding $5,000 per acre.[24] In the event a permittee fails to complete reclamation, and if the reclamation costs at the mine exceed the penal bond amount, DEP then draws funds from the Special Reclamation Fund to complete the reclamation plan.[25] The site-specific bond and Special Reclamation Fund are thus meant to operate together to ensure that DEP will have sufficient money to "complete the reclamation plan for any areas which may be in default at any time," as required by SMCRA. This alternative bonding system was approved by OSMRE in 1983.[26]

DEP never required site-specific calculations of what reclamation would actually cost, however. Instead, it imposed a reclamation fee based on the number of tons of coal mined. DEP thus failed from the outset to ensure that coal operators set aside enough funds to cover the reclamation obligation. And federal regulators did not do their jobs, either; as early as 1991, OSMRE was aware that the West Virginia reclamation bonding program failed to satisfy the federal statutory requirement for adequate funding. It acknowledged in 1995 that, since 1989, its annual reviews had shown that West Virginia's alternate bonding system's liabilities exceeded assets and, by 1994, the deficit was $22.2 million.[27]

In 2001, a federal district court found that West Virginia's federally approved state alternate bonding fund was hugely underfunded and could not guarantee reclamation of mines abandoned by bankrupt coal companies as required by SMCRA. The court held that state and federal regulators' decade-long failure to institute a fully funded bonding system had created a "climate of lawlessness." According to Federal District Court Judge Charles Haden:

> [T]he direct consequences of the agency's decade-long delay [include] thousands of acres of un-reclaimed strip-mined land, untreated polluted water, and millions (potentially billions) of dollars of State liabilities. The indirect results, however, may be more damaging: a climate of lawlessness, which creates a pervasive impression that continued disregard for federal law and statutory requirements goes unpunished, or possibly unnoticed. Agency warnings have no more effect than a wink and a nod, a deadline is just an arbitrary date on the calendar and, once passed, not to be mentioned again. Financial benefits accrue to the owners and operators who were not required to incur the statutory burden and costs attendant to surface

---

[23] James Bruggers, *Blackjewel's Bankruptcy Is a Harbinger of Trouble Ahead for the Plummeting Coal Industry*, INSIDE CLIMATE NEWS (Mar. 3, 2021), https://www.courier-journal.com/story/news/2021/03/03/blackjewel-bankruptcy-illustrates-problem-zombie-mines/6898076002/.

[24] W.Va. Code § 22–3–11.

[25] *Id.* at § 22–3–11(g).

[26] Fed. Reg. at 37610.

[27] *West Virginia Highlands Conservancy v. Norton*, 161 F. Supp. 2d 676, 679 (S.D.W.Va. 2001).

mining; political benefits accrue to the state executive and legislators who escape accountability while the mining industry gets a free pass.[28]

THE RISKY CONSOLIDATION OF OPERATORS IN THE COAL INDUSTRY: SETTING THE STAGE FOR COLLAPSE

At the start of "the lost decade," coal companies went on a buying spree, merging with or acquiring other coal operators at sky-high prices. What drove the frenzy? Back in 2009, everyone believed the world was running out of metallurgical coal, or "met coal," the type that goes into making steel. Prices spiked above $340 a ton as demand from fast-growing China was off the charts. The future also seemed secure for thermal or steam coal, which is used to generate electricity; although the shale gas revolution was getting under way, coal was still responsible for producing 44.5 percent of US electricity supply in 2009, compared to a 23.3 percent share for natural gas.

The coal company acquisitions announced between 2008 and 2013 included the following:

- Patriot Coal Corporation acquired Magnum Coal Company for $709 million (April 2008);
- Cleveland-Cliffs offered to buy Alpha Natural Resources for $10 billion (July 2008 – the deal later collapsed);
- Rio Tinto Energy America (RTEA) transferred its western US coal business, which included the Spring Creek coal mine, the Antelope coal mine, Cordero Mining, and 50 percent of the Decker coal mine to Cloud Peak Energy (December 2008);
- Alpha Natural Resources acquired Foundation Coal Holdings for $1.5 billion (May 2009);
- Arch Coal acquired the Jacobs Ranch coal mine from Rio Tinto for $761 million (September 2009);
- Massey Energy acquired Cumberland Resources Corporation for $960 million (March 2010);
- Rio Tinto sold its remaining shares in Cloud Peak Energy for $573.3 million (December 2010);
- Alpha Natural Resources acquired Massey Energy for $7.1 billion, a 21 percent premium over Massey's stock price at the time (January 2011);
- James River Coal Company acquired International Resource Partners and Logan & Kanawha Coal for $475 million (March 2011);
- Arch Coal acquired International Coal Corp. for $3.4 billion (May 2011);
- Murray Energy acquired five of Consol Energy's longwall coal mines in West Virginia for $3.5 billion (December 2013).

[28] *Id.* at 683–84.

According to David Gagliano of BMO Capital Markets, these companies issued debt to buy other companies at "absolutely the peak of the market." Within five years, met coal prices dropped below $100 a ton as China's explosive economic growth cooled, along with its demand for steel or coal. The bottom dropped out of the market for thermal coal as well, as the shale gas revolution took off and natural gas surpassed coal as the leading fuel for generating electricity for the first time, in April 2015. When prices for met and steam coal collapsed, "these companies literally imploded," according to Gagliano. Stock in Alpha Natural Resources was selling for 4 cents per share in August 2015, as compared with the $128 per share that Cleveland-Cliffs had offered to pay in 2008. Between the beginning of 2009 and the end of 2015, the shares of many coal companies had plummeted more than 90 percent, and several had declared bankruptcy. Consol Energy, however, saw its shares decline only 60 percent over the same period, largely as a result of the sale of coal assets to Murray Energy and its transformation "from being a pure coal company to being a coal and natural gas company," according to Gagliano. Murray Energy continued its spending spree by acquiring mines in West Virginia and Illinois, which helped saddle the company with about $2.7 billion in funded debt, as well about $8 billion in actual or potential obligations to fund pension and benefit plans.[29]

THE FINANCIAL COLLAPSE OF THE COAL INDUSTRY, AND THE SHEDDING OF LIABILITIES

Unable to pay the loan interest and principal from their highly leveraged acquisitions, the largest coal producers in the United States began to seek bankruptcy protection in the middle of the decade to restructure about $30 billion in debt. The bankrupt companies included James River Coal (April 2014), Patriot Coal (May 2015), Walter Energy (July 2015), Alpha Natural Resources (August 2015), and Arch Coal (January 2016). When Peabody Energy Corporation, the world's biggest private-sector coal producer at the time, filed for bankruptcy in April 2016, it sought to restructure $8.4 billion in debt. Its capitalization had fallen from $20 billion in 2011 to $38 million at the time of bankruptcy. Before the carnage ended, the top four coal producers from 2011 – Peabody Energy, Arch Coal, Alpha Natural Resources, and Cloud Peak Energy – which collectively accounted for more than half of US coal production at the time, all declared bankruptcy.[30] A second wave of bankruptcies occurred during 2019. When Murray Energy filed for bankruptcy in October 2019, it was the largest privately owned coal firm in the United States and

---

[29] Taylor Telford & Dino Grandoni, *Murray Energy Files for Bankruptcy as Coal's Role in U.S. Power Dwindles*, WASHINGTON POST (Oct. 29, 2019), https://www.washingtonpost.com/business/2019/10/29/coal-giant-murray-energy-files-bankruptcy-coals-role-us-power-dwindles/.

[30] U.S. Energy Information, *Top Four U.S. Coal Companies Supplied More Than Half of U.S. Coal Production in 2011* (Oct. 2, 2013), https://www.eia.gov/todayinenergy/detail.php?id=13211.

became the eighth US coal producer to file for bankruptcy in the space of twelve months as the price of the coal fell by 38 percent from a year earlier.

As the coal operators began to emerge from bankruptcy proceedings, it became clear how effective they had been at using the restructuring process to flout federal environmental laws – and SMCRA in particular – that were meant to ensure that lands degraded by their extractive activities would be restored.[31] According to the EPA and the Department of Interior, the restructuring agreements secured through bankruptcy were "obviously a carefully constructed scheme to evade environmental liabilities through discriminatory classifications and treatment of environmental general unsecured creditors as opposed to other general unsecured creditors."[32] Four of the largest coal producers (Peabody, Arch Coal, Alpha Natural Resources, and Cloud Peak Energy) used Chapter 11 bankruptcy proceedings to discharge or otherwise avoid approximately $5.1 billion in regulatory debts: $1.9 billion in environmental liabilities under SMCRA and $3.2 billion in retiree benefits (e.g., pension and health care obligations).[33] These regulatory obligations together accounted for 22 percent of the total debt discharged in the bankruptcies.[34]

And the real environmental liabilities owed by the coal operators are likely to be substantially greater. An OSMRE report found that the bonds forfeited by bankrupt coal companies in Kentucky, for example, covered only 52.8 percent of the true cost of reclaiming the degraded land.[35] Moreover, the EPA estimates that it will cost $50 billion to manage the environmental hazards created by the more than 250,000 abandoned and inactive coal mines that have yet to be reclaimed (this includes not only coal mines but mines that were used to extract metals and other minerals).[36]

Two bankruptcies in particular – Patriot Coal (which was formed from mines spun off from Peabody Energy and Arch Coal) and Alpha Natural Resources – rocked West Virginia, and illustrated how effectively the coal operators could manipulate the federal bankruptcy laws to shed environmental and employee obligations. Their agility at shedding environmental liabilities was, of course, aided by the utter failure of the West Virginia DEP to administer SMCRA in a manner that would ensure reclamation of mine lands in West Virginia.

---

[31]   Macey and Salovaara, *supra* note 16 at 882.
[32]   United States', States', and Tribes' Objection to Debtors' Second Amended Joint Plan of Reorganization at 1, *In Re Peabody Energy Corp.*, No. 16–42529–399 (Bankr. E.D. Mo. Mar. 9, 2017), ECF No. 2648.
[33]   Macey and Salovaara, *supra* note 16 at 883 and table 2 at 933.
[34]   *Id.*
[35]   Kentucky Department for Natural Resources & Lexington Field Office, OSMRE, *Annual Evaluation Report* (2017), https://perma.cc/8WWU-V2F4.
[36]   Scott Streater, *Polluted Mines as Economic Engines? Obama Administration Says "Yes,"* N.Y. TIMES (Feb. 26, 2009), https://archive.nytimes.com/www.nytimes.com/gwire/2009/02/26/26greenwire-pol luted-mines-as-economic-engines-obama-admin–9896.html?pagewanted=all.

Patriot Coal: Doomed to Fail from the Beginning

Patriot was used by Peabody Energy and Arch Coal as a tool for shedding their environmental and pension obligations. In the case of Peabody, Patriot acquired only 13 percent of Peabody's coal reserves when it was spun off, but it managed to assume 40 percent of Peabody's health care liabilities ($557 million) and $233 million of environmental liabilities.[37] In the case of Arch Coal, it was able to spin off its Magnum Coal Company – with several Appalachian coal mines – to Patriot; Arch gave up 12.3 percent of its assets, but was able to stick Patriot with 96.7 percent of its retiree health care liabilities.[38] Within two years, Patriot had accumulated over $2 billion in environmental and retiree obligations formerly held by Peabody or Arch, prompting the United Mine Workers of America to allege that Patriot was a "company created to fail"[39] – and it did. Patriot filed for its first bankruptcy in August 2012, with assets of $3.6 billion versus liabilities of $3.4 billion, including $700 million of environmental liabilities.[40] Of the $1.8 billion in liabilities Patriot was able to discharge in the bankruptcy, $1.1 billion represented health care and pension liabilities owed to retired coal miners who had spent their careers at Peabody or Alpha.[41] Patriot was also able to delay compliance with environmental obligations relating to selenium water discharge.[42]

The reorganized Patriot survived only eighteen months, and filed for bankruptcy again in May 2015, which resulted in a sale of all its assets. Blackhawk Mining was able to purchase Patriot's most desirable mines, and assumed responsibility for reclaiming only the mines that it purchased. The remaining assets – which included Patriot's Federal No. 2 mine near Fairview, West Virginia and Hobet 21 mountaintop removal complex along the Boone–Lincoln County line, and their associated hundreds of millions of dollars in reclamation obligations – were picked up by the Virginia Conservation Legacy Fund (VCLF), a nonprofit headed up by Tom Clarke. He was a former nursing home operator with a track record, as it would turn out, of "drain[ing] substantial funds from his projects into a web of related companies – through which he can then use funds for his own benefit – all while denying payment or entirely defaulting on legitimate debts owed to creditors."[43]

---

[37] Macey & Salovaara, *supra* note 16, at 912.
[38] *Id.*
[39] *Id.* (citing Ken Ward, Jr., *Patriot Bankruptcy Case Heating Up*, CHARLESTON GAZETTE-MAIL (Aug. 25, 2012), https://www.wvgazettemail.com/news/special_reports/patriot-bankruptcy-case-heating-up/article_0ca4d57b-09cd-5153-8d9b-5a0126a011d4.html (quoting the United Mine Workers Journal)).
[40] *Id.* at 914.
[41] *Id.*
[42] *Id.* at 915.
[43] *Id.* at 918 (citing the Official Committee of Unsecured Creditors' Motion for an Order Pursuant to Bankruptcy Rule 2004 Authorizing the Examination & Production of Documents by Thomas M. Clarke exhibit C at 10, *In re Mission Coal Co.*, No. 18–04177 (TOM) (Bankr. N.D. Ala. Nov. 12, 2018), ECF No. 245).

VCLF's creative but sketchy business plan was to fulfill Patriot's environmental obligations by planting trees as carbon offsets that would be bundled with the purchase of coal from the Patriot mines. In other words, the purchase of a ton of coal would be coupled with the commitment by VCLF to plant enough trees to offset the carbon emissions that would be generated by combusting the coal. Among the stakeholders who bought into the scheme was the miners' union at the Federal mine, which invested $10 million in the operation. The coal market was already tanking, however, and there was no interest by electric utilities in purchasing the higher-cost coal that resulted from tacking on the cost of the carbon offset.[44] The venture failed miserably and ERP Environmental Fund (ERP), the company that was created by Clarke to manage and operate his mines, ultimately laid off all of its employees and completely abandoned its mining operations in early 2020. As discussed in the section *Patriot Part IV: The Demise of ERP*, in March 2020 this abandonment forced the West Virginia DEP to acknowledge – at least temporarily – the inadequacy of its Special Reclamation Fund, and to seek emergency relief in the courts.

Alpha Natural Resources: Using "Accounting Gimmickry" to Stick It to West Virginia

When Alpha Natural Resources filed for bankruptcy in August 2015, it was the fourth largest coal producer in the country and had a substantial presence in Central Appalachia in addition to its western coal mines in Wyoming's Powder River Basin. Alpha used the Chapter 11 bankruptcy proceeding to split into two companies: Contura, which would inherit the "crown-jewel" mining assets in the Powder River Basin, and a reorganized Alpha ("Alpha II"), which would be stuck with the unprofitable Appalachian mines (along with much of Alpha's environmental and retiree liabilities).[45] To create the false impression in the bankruptcy proceedings that Alpha II would be financially viable, Alpha omitted significant capital expenditures from Alpha II's books and, as a result, Alpha II had insufficient cash flow to meet its obligations almost immediately after emerging from bankruptcy.

　　The West Virginia DEP claimed at the time that Alpha's senior management "knew about but did not disclose these impending 'unaccounted-for' expenditures to ensure consummation of [the] Contura sale and chapter 11 plan for their own benefit and to secure the releases of environmental liability."[46] These releases included

---

44　Michael Corkery & Michael Wines, *A Curious Plan to Fight Climate Change: Buy Mines, Sell Coal*, N.Y. TIMES (Oct. 1, 2016), https://www.nytimes.com/2016/10/02/business/energy-environment/a-curious-plan-to-fight-climate-change-buy-mines-sell-coal.html.

45　Macey & Salovaara, *supra* note 16, at 921–22.

46　*Id.* at 923 (citing Response of the West Virginia Department of Environmental Protection to the Reorganized Debtors' Motion to Approve Settlements with Contura Energy, Inc. & the First-Lien Lenders at 4, In re Alpha Nat. Res., Inc., No. 15-33896 (KRH) (Bankr. E.D. Va. Nov. 15, 2016), ECF No. 3543).

Alpha reducing its $244 million reclamation obligation in West Virginia to a $24 million superiority claim and a $15 million letter of credit.[47] This "deal" in West Virginia, along with a similar arrangement with regulators in Wyoming, gave Alpha a legal right to abandon over $500 million in cleanup costs that it would have had to pay had it been forced to liquidate. Alpha was thus allowed to continue mining, even though it could not meet the self-bonding requirements (a company in bankruptcy is almost by definition not financially strong enough to meet self-bonding requirements) and could not afford to post alternative bonds, thereby violating SMCRA's permitting and bonding provisions.[48]

Alpha II then proceeded to shed its own reclamation obligations by selling mines affiliated with those obligations to other companies. Lexington Coal, operated by Jeff Hoops, took over many of Alpha II's idle mines, along with $192 million of self-bonds associated with those mines, while Alpha II kept twenty active mining operations. Contura sold several mines to a small company called Blackjewel, also operated by Jeff Hoops, and was able to "unload hefty reclamation obligations from [its] books."[49] After shedding their respective environmental liabilities, Alpha II and Contura merged again in April 2018 to rejoin the two pieces of the original Alpha Natural Resources: "Each company had separately shed its high-liability mines, and the two were now able to recombine with only their profitable assets."[50] Alpha managed to use the bankruptcy proceedings to reduce reclamation liabilities by about $200 million, and to eliminate another $355 million in obligations through subsequent divestitures to Lexington and Blackjewel. Through the series of reorganizations, Alpha successfully sheltered its profitable mines from over half a billion dollars' worth of environmental liabilities. Blackjewel would later gain national attention when its miners in Harlan County, Kentucky – whose final paychecks had bounced when Blackjewel declared bankruptcy in 2019 – blocked a loaded coal train for weeks in protest.[51]

Patriot Part IV: The Demise of ERP

In March 2020, ERP (the Tom Clarke-related entity charged with managing the mines in West Virginia that the VCLF picked up in Patriot's second bankruptcy), ceased operations. West Virginia DEP described the situation as follows:

> After years of operating on a shoe-string budget with a challenging organizational and management structure and accruing, in the process, hundreds of violations of the surface mining and water pollution laws, [ERP] has reached the end of the line. [ERP] is woefully insolvent, has no cash, has no operating cash flow, has laid off all

---

[47] *Id.* at 919.
[48] *Id.*
[49] *Id.* at 925.
[50] *Id.*
[51] Bruggers, *supra* note 23.

its management and employees, and, but for DEP and [ERP's] surety bond issuer stepping in and providing limited emergency funding over the past few weeks, would not have been able to carry on even the very limited operations it has maintained up to now. Meanwhile, the violations and unabated enforcement orders have continued to mount and indeed accelerate. Just in the last month, DEP issued roughly forty orders to show cause relating to unabated cessation orders relating to dozens of outstanding and unabated violations of their permits and surface mining and water pollution control laws. And even more problematically [ERP's] cessation of operations has left [its] many mining sites unmanned, unsecured, unmaintained, and in various stages of land and water disturbance and incomplete reclamation that, without immediate and decisive action, will begin to threaten imminent and identifiable harm to the public's health and safety on many of its mine sites.[52]

Faced with these circumstances and the existential threat to West Virginia's SMCRA bonding program, on March 26, 2020 West Virginia DEP filed an Emergency Motion in the Circuit Court for Kanawha County, West Virginia, requesting that ERP be placed in a receivership and that a special receiver be appointed to take immediate control of ERP's assets and operations. The Motion was accompanied by the affidavit of Harold Ward, director of the Division of Mining and Reclamation and deputy secretary of DEP. It contained the following statements about ERP:

- ERP holds more than 100 permits issued by DEP.[53]
- Since 2015, DEP has issued 160 notices of violation against ERP, 118 failure to abate cessation orders, and 41 orders to show cause why relevant ERP permits should not be revoked.[54]
- ERP has acknowledged to DEP that it is in material default of its permit and reclamation obligations but has no sources of cash or other assets available for reclamation and water treatment.[55]
- As of March 19, 2020, ERP laid off all its employees and ceased operations.[56]
- By late 2019 or early 2020 ERP had not only run out of funds but encumbered most of its valuable assets.[57]
- ERP continues to accrue violations, which were expected to worsen during the spring as precipitation increases.[58]

---

[52]   Circuit Court of Kanawha County, West Virginia, Civil Action No. 20-C-282, Plaintiff's Motion for Temporary Restraining Order and Preliminary Injunction and Temporary and Preliminary Appointment of a Special Receiver, Mar. 26, 2020, at 1, https://www.baileyglasser.com/assets/htmldo cuments/Motion%20for%20TRO%20et%20al.pdf.

[53]   *Ohio Valley Environmental Coalition v. Caperton*, U.S. District Court, Southern District West Virginia, Civil Action No. 3:20-cv-470, Ward Affidavit, ¶ 9.

[54]   *Id.* ¶¶ 5–7.

[55]   *Id.* ¶ 9.

[56]   *Id.* ¶ 10.

[57]   *Id.* ¶ 58.

[58]   *Id.* ¶ 12.

The affidavit also addressed the inability of DEP to remedy ERP's reclamation operations through the alternative bonding system approved by OSMRE:

- At the time ERP acquired its permits, DEP estimated reclamation costs to be "in excess of $230 million" with potentially "hundreds of millions" more in water treatment liabilities.[59]
- DEP is unsure that the surety bond provider can pay out the full $115 million in bonds that should be available for reclaiming ERP's permits.[60]
- Reclaiming permits through the Special Reclamation Fund "would overwhelm the fund both financially and administratively," and therefore reclamation may not be completed as required by SMCRA.[61]

Due to the obvious inadequacy of West Virginia's alternate bonding system to address ERP's violations and reclaim its mines, DEP requested a receivership. As stated in its Emergency Motion:

DEP stands poised at the precipice of having to revoke [ERP's] permits, forfeiting the associated surety bonds, and transferring responsibility for cleaning up [ERP's] mess to the State's Special Reclamation Fund, potentially bankrupting [ERP's] principal surety and administratively and financially overwhelming the Special Reclamation Fund, the State's principal backstop for all revoked and forfeited mine sites in West Virginia.[62]

The court granted the Motion, and appointed a receiver along with an operating budget of $1 million.

Notwithstanding this description of the dire situation regarding the viability of its alternate bonding mechanism, DEP did not think that the ERP-related developments required it to notify OSMRE that its SMCRA program was imperiled. Rules adopted by OSMRE to implement SMCRA require that the state "shall promptly notify [OSMRE], in writing, of any significant events or proposed changes which affect the implementation, administration or enforcement of the approved State program."[63] The rule further defines "significant events" as including "[s]ignificant changes in funding or budgeting relative to the approved program."[64] Given that West Virginia's Special Reclamation Fund had a balance of $174 million as of December 31, 2019, only 10 percent of which DEP was authorized to spend in a year, and default on the ERP permits would trigger reclamation costs in excess of $230 million and require additional hundreds of millions of dollars to treat the polluted water at ERP's mine sites, it would seem that DEP had an obligation to inform OSMRE of the significant event regarding ERP's insolvency. After all, DEP

[59] *Id.* ¶¶ 25–26.
[60] *Id.* ¶ 63.
[61] *Id.* ¶ 64.
[62] Circuit Court of Kanawha County, *supra* note 52, at 3.
[63] 30 C.F.R. § 732.17.
[64] *Id.* at § 732.17(b)(6).

admitted in its Emergency Motion that ERP's insolvency alone threatened to "overwhelm" the Special Reclamation Fund, and acknowledged that the insurer would likely be unable to perform on the full $115 million of surety bonds.

But it required a lawsuit by citizen groups in West Virginia – the Ohio Valley Environmental Coalition, West Virginia Highlands Conservancy, and Sierra Club – to force DEP to issue the required notification to OSMRE. In denying DEP's motion to dismiss the citizen groups' lawsuit, the US District Court for the Southern District of West Virginia found, as a matter of law, that the groups' "allegations present a plausible claim because the alternative bonding system is an important source of funding for the state's SMCRA program and may be significantly impacted when a major permit holder becomes insolvent."[65] Six weeks later, DEP finally sent OSMRE a letter notifying the agency and its director of significant events affecting the SMCRA program and potentially necessitating a program amendment.

Consistent with its refusal to raise the issue with OSMRE without being forced in litigation to do so, DEP remains in denial about the obvious inadequacy of its alternative bonding system under SMCRA. Incredibly, the Annual Report sent by the Special Reclamation Fund Advisory Council to the legislature on January 26, 2021 concluded that existing fund levels were adequate and that there was no need to increase the fees imposed on coal operators to provide funding for the Special Reclamation Fund. (The current rate is 27.9 cents per ton of clean coal mined in West Virginia, 15 cents per ton of which is paid into the Special Reclamation Water Trust Fund [SRWTF] with the remaining 12.9 cents per ton being paid into the Special Reclamation Fund.) This intentional obliviousness should not be surprising. As the citizen groups commented in their court pleadings, "the makeup of the Special Reclamation Fund Advisory Council has been designed to favor the coal industry"; and they noted that the representative of the "general public," Christopher Pence, is a coal industry attorney.[66] Bill Raney, then president of the West Virginia Coal Association, also served on the Advisory Board at the time. As discussed in the next section, this glaring neglect of duty will likely result in West Virginians bearing billions of dollars in unfunded reclamation costs or, worse still, continuing to bear the vast environmental degradation associated with years of surface mining.

DEP AND ITS "HOUSE OF CARDS"

The impending collapse of the funding structure for coal reclamation in West Virginia has been known for years, and is well-documented. In 2015, for example, a preliminary OSMRE analysis found that roughly 41 percent of the outstanding mining permits from the West Virginia DEP were held by companies whose parent

---

[65] *Ohio Valley Environmental Coalition v. Caperton, supra* note 53, at 10.
[66] Letter from Mike Becher, Appalachian Mountain Advocates to Glenda Owens, Acting Director OSMRE (Mar. 12, 2021) at 5, n.5 (on file with author).

corporations were in bankruptcy.[67] In April 2015, local OSMRE Field Office Director Roger Calhoun urged DEP to take a closer look at the coal industry downturn and its impact on the reclamation program, especially given increased attention focused on previously ignored water pollution problems, such as discharges of toxic selenium. Lewis Halstead, then deputy director of DEP's Division of Mining and Reclamation, was quoted as saying "I've been here 36 years, and there has never been 41 percent of the permits in bankruptcy."[68] A subsequent report in 2017 by OSMRE in West Virginia noted that 59 percent of all active and inactive mining permits were owned by a company that had been in some stage of bankruptcy in the previous two years. The report warned that "[t]he state will face potential reclamation liability as a result of those bankruptcies well into the future."[69]

The crisis is driven by several factors, none of which DEP chooses to acknowledge. First, the fundamental premise of an alternative bonding system fails when the coal industry is in a rapid state of decline. It is beyond dispute that there will be inadequate revenues being deposited into the Special Reclamation Fund going forward; projections of the funding stream into the future simply cannot assume that historical levels of coal production will continue. It is equally beyond dispute that the projected level of claims upon the fund, which are based on historical levels of mine closures, are vastly understated. But the actuarial study relied upon by the Special Reclamation Fund Advisory Council in West Virginia does just that, by relying on outdated projections of forfeiture rates from decades past. Maintaining an assessment of 27.9 cents per ton on mined coal makes sense only if there is a sufficient volume to generate additions to the fund that would come close to covering the liabilities. And historical permit forfeiture rates provide no guidance whatsoever on the number of claims against the fund that will follow from the collapse that is currently occurring in the coal industry.

On this point, John Morgan, a Kentucky mining engineer who serves on an advisory council that monitors that state's special reclamation fund, recognized in 2015 that a different approach is necessary to ensure that reclamation funds have adequate money: "Current studies, using historic bankruptcy and permit-bond forfeiture rates, might no longer accurately project what's going to happen in the coal industry, now or in the future."[70] Bond pools are a vestige of "a different industry," explained Matt Hepler, a scientist with Appalachian Voices, a nonprofit advocacy group based in coal country. "They were designed when coal was

---

[67] Ken Ward, *Concerns Grow About Coal Industry Pensions, Reclamation*, Charleston Gazette-Mail (Aug. 9, 2015), https://www.wvgazettemail.com/news/special_reports/concerns-grow-about-coal-industry-pensionsreclamation/article_8e862b31-9efc-529c-bdd1-17aa8e57da43.html.

[68] *Id.*

[69] Olalde, *supra* note 1.

[70] Ward, *supra* note 67.

booming. They were not designed to handle an industry-wide collapse."[71] Yet this sort of historical-based approach continues to be used by the Special Reclamation Fund Advisory Council in West Virginia. Peter Morgan of the Sierra Club points out that, by their very nature, alternative bonding mechanisms are based on an expectation that mine abandonments "would be rare and not tied to any industry-wide issues."[72]

Historic permit bond forfeiture rates, for instance, do not capture the presence of thousands of "zombie mines" – mines that for all practical purposes have ceased operations and have fallen into disrepair, but have not formally closed – that litter the landscape of Central Appalachia. West Virginia Governor Jim Justice and his family, for example, own companies that hold thirty-nine coal mine permits in Virginia, most of which are sitting idle on the ridges along the border with Kentucky. According to Virginia's Department of Mines, Minerals, and Energy, these mines have accumulated about 800 violations since 2012 for regulatory noncompliance ranging from water pollution to insufficient monitoring. The cost of cleaning up the mines belonging to just one of the Justice family's companies is $134 million, thereby overwhelming Virginia's bond pool of about $10 million, which is intended to back cleanup at more than 43,000 acres of disturbed land.[73]

Second, even if the revenue levels and claims were trending at historical levels and the actuarial studies were valid, the amounts collected in the fund were never going to be sufficient to accomplish the necessary reclamation and address water contamination issues. The amount in the Special Reclamation Fund, combined with all other individual reclamation bonds held for each mine, works out at less than $3,200 an acre. A 2017 actuarial report commissioned by the Special Reclamation Fund Advisory Council estimated, however, that cleanup costs in West Virginia ranged from $7,840 per acre for surface mines to $28,460 per acre for underground mines. "It is one of the bigger public failures that has gone under the radar," said West Virginia University Law Professor Patrick McGinley, who has forty years' experience in the industry. According to McGinley, the level of bonding in general is too low and, in Appalachian states in particular, is "preposterous, absolutely ridiculous."[74] And, according to Sierra Club's Peter Morgan, "[o]ne thing that is particularly clear in Appalachia is that these bonds are not being designed to capture the costs of water treatment." A presentation regarding the bonding program at an OSMRE conference in 2013 noted that with respect to water treatment costs, the trust funds are "underfunded" inasmuch as new standards

---

[71]   Mark Olalde, *Exposed: West Virginia and Other States Relying on "House of Cards" to Pay for Coal Mine Cleanup*, DeSmog (June 25, 2020), https://www.desmogblog.com/2020/06/25/coal-surety-bond-pools-liabilities-mine-cleanup/.

[72]   Bruggers, *supra* note 23.

[73]   Olalde, *supra* note 71.

[74]   Olalde, *supra* note 1.

regarding selenium, and total dissolved solids (TDS) were not considered in many of the trust funds or in bond calculations.[75]

An example of these water treatment costs is the Martinka mine in Marion County, which is one of the properties taken over by ERP following Patriot's second bankruptcy filing. The Martinka mine has been closed for years, but both surface and groundwater flow into the mine void. When the level of water in the mine void gets too high, it can be discharged through "unauthorized point sources." To avoid this issue, water from the mine void is pumped and treated for contaminants before being discharged into tributaries of the Tygart River. The costs associated with the pumping and treatment is approximately $900,000 per year. When ERP suspended operations in March 2020, the level of water within the mine came within 4–6 feet of what DEP determined to be a critical pool elevation, potentially resulting in the discharge of contaminated water into the receiving stream that supplies drinking water for thousands of West Virginians. West Virginia DEP was therefore forced to step in and start providing funds to repair and replace the pumps to keep water continuously pumped and treated.[76]

Third, the Special Reclamation Fund is, for all practical purposes, already exhausted, based on what has already occurred with the March 2020 abandonment by ERP of its operations in West Virginia and the impact of other near-certain defaults. While the insolvency of ERP alone has been enough to "overwhelm" the Special Reclamation Fund – by DEP's own admission, according to its Emergency Motion – ERP is not the only mine operator in West Virginia holding permits that may soon require reclamation through the state's alternative bonding system. The recent bankruptcy of Blackjewel LLC, including its affiliate Revelation Energy and other subsidiaries, resulted in bond forfeiture at three mines in Kanawha County, West Virginia. West Virginia DEP had been in ongoing litigation with the company for years as a result of ongoing water quality problems at those mines and Revelation's failure to meet its reclamation obligations. Separately, Lexington Coal Company, which holds more than 150 mining permits in West Virginia and is operated by Blackjewel's former CEO Jeff Hoops, is embroiled in litigation brought by Blackjewel, which claims that Hoops inappropriately stripped assets from Blackjewel in favor of Lexington. Other companies such as Southeastern Land LLC, are not currently in bankruptcy, but are subject to ongoing litigation by DEP for permit violations across dozens of permits. Consequently, the financial threat to West Virginia's alternative bonding system is not limited to one company alone, but includes the threatened insolvencies of at least several other mining companies with significant reclamation and water treatment liabilities.

Fourth, the Special Reclamation Fund will be quickly overwhelmed by the impact of the meltdown on the horizon due to the imminent failure of the insurers

[75]   *Id.* (citing OSM Bonding Program, at 6, http://imcc.isa.us/uploads/1/1/9/1/119191866/erv_barchenger_bonding_presentation.pdf).

[76]   Ward Affidavit, *supra* note 53 ¶¶ 14–21.

that issued the surety bonds on which West Virginia DEP is relying to fund the reclamation costs. The surety bonds issued by insurance companies essentially guarantee that a third party will fill pits, seal shafts, and mitigate water and air pollution. According to a 2018 report by the Government Accountability Office, about 76 percent of the more than $10 billion in coal cleanup bonds are held as sureties.[77] The problem is that the large insurance companies that once wrote surety policies, such as Zurich Insurance Group and Travelers Casualty and Surety Company of America, have bailed from the coal surety market, leaving fewer than a half-dozen insurers that have assumed much more liability than they can handle. As described by Bob Mooney, who spent two decades as a coal regulator with both OSMRE and the state of Ohio, "The bonds are sort of immaterial because a lot of the surety companies will go under. So, even though there's a bond, there's not."[78] According to one broker in the surety business, the insurers win business based on how much collateral they require (or don't require), thereby creating a "race to the bottom," with smaller insurance firms capturing large amounts of coal business. Insurance providers make "quick money" on premiums but, faced with their coal customers going under, they may quickly fail in a manner similar to the failure of the subprime mortgage bundles that helped kick off the 2008 recession.[79]

The Indemnity National Insurance Company – which holds $125 million in surety bonds backing up the obligations of ERP in West Virginia – is described as the "poster child" for the risks currently posed by the surety companies. West Virginia DEP acknowledged in its Emergency Motion to Kanawha County Circuit Court that if it tried to rely on Indemnity National to cover ERP's cleanup costs, the move could end up "potentially bankrupting [ERP's] principal surety."[80] Indemnity National acknowledged its precarious financial position in the Blackjewel bankruptcy proceedings in West Virginia, where it argued against allowing Blackjewel to abandon its permits in a January 11, 2021 filing. Indemnity National said it had issued $170 million in reclamation bonds on behalf of Blackjewel, covering nearly 200 mining permits across West Virginia, Tennessee, Virginia, and Kentucky, and has another $230 million backing up Jeff Hoops-affiliated companies in the region. All in all, Indemnity National guarantees more than $900 million in coal surety bonds for thirty-eight companies across West Virginia, Kentucky, and Virginia. "The bonding companies were never making an assessment of what their risk was," Professor McGinley said, "[s]o, they were backing bonds far beyond their ability to pay if there was a bankruptcy."[81] According to one analysis, the worst-case scenario of Indemnity National's failure "would push the coal

[77] *Coal Mine Reclamation: Federal and State Agencies Face Challenges in Managing Billions in Financial Assurances*, U.S. GOVERNMENT ACCOUNTABILITY OFFICE (Mar. 6, 2018), https://www.gao.gov/products/GAO-18-305.

[78] Olalde, *supra* note 71.

[79] *Id.*

[80] Ward Affidavit, *supra* note 53¶ 63.

[81] Olalde, *supra* note 71.

industry into unprecedented territory and would leave hundreds of millions of dollars in cleanup liability unprotected."[82]

Of course, the demise of the surety industry is not a surprise to regulators, as they have been aware of the risks for more than twenty years. As far back as 2000, OSMRE and regulators throughout Appalachia had to scramble to find replacement surety coverage when an insurance provider (Frontier Insurance Company) lost its listing with the US Treasury.[83] Ten years later, Travelers – a large surety provider before it exited the market – wrote to OSMRE, telling the agency that severely insufficient bonds were problematic not only for surety providers and states, but also posed risks to state alternative bonding programs "with the possibility of draining or even bankrupting state bond pools in the event of default."[84] Staff at OSMRE seemed to be well aware of the risks, according to a presentation at a mining conference in 2013 that warned there was already a "lack of diversity in the surety industry: too few companies holding all the bonds."[85] While regulators have the legal authority to demand that coal companies provide additional collateral and that insurance companies only accept risk they can handle, the practical problem is that further stressing the last vestiges of the coal industry could push more companies into bankruptcy, making it even less likely that the necessary reclamation and water treatment will occur.

The current situation was captured in a "Legislative Audit Report" regarding the Special Reclamation Funds issued in June 2021 by the Post Audit Division of the Joint Committee on Government and Finance and the West Virginia Office of the Legislative Auditor.[86] Among other things, the report found that:

- The West Virginia DEP has failed to comply with state and federal law in its oversight of the reclamation program.
- The bonds in place currently cover only 10 percent of the estimated reclamation costs.
- Five insurers hold 90.7 percent of the state's coal mining reclamation bonds, with Indemnity National holding 66.9 percent of the total.
- In the case of permits listed as inactive, DEP has consistently failed to require coal companies to maintain bonds equal to the reclamation cost, as required by state and federal law. According to the report, failure of the fifty-six currently

---

[82] *Id.*

[83] WV Department of Environmental Protection, *Rule 38 CSR 2 Section 11.3.a.3 Mining Reclamation Surety Bond Requirements*, Legislative Audit Report (Sep. 24, 2019), http://www.wvlegislature.gov/legisdocs/reports/agency/PA/PA_2019_692.pdf.

[84] Olalde, *supra* note 71.

[85] *Id.* (citing OSM Bonding Program, at 6, http://imcc.isa.us/uploads/1/1/9/1/119191866/erv_barchenger_bonding_presentation.pdf).

[86] Post Audit Division, Joint Committee on Government and Finance and the West Virginia Office of the Legislative Auditor, Special Reclamation Funds Report (June 7, 2021), http://www.wvlegislature.gov/legisdocs/reports/agency/PA/PA_2021_722.pdf.

inactive sites lacking full cost bonding would impose reclamation costs of $279 million on the fund.

- DEP has no process in place even to ensure that funds collected for forfeited bonds are actually used to cover the reclamation costs of properties for which they were posted.

Summing all this up, Professor McGinley laments: "Who pays? The damaged environment? The communities that are blighted by unreclaimed mine sites? It's the end of the road, so where's the money coming from? This was all foreseeable."[87] And, of course, it's much worse than that – we are well beyond speculation as to what previously may have been foreseeable. Given the developments over the past few years, the impact on West Virginians – whether in the form of billions of taxpayer dollars for reclamation and water treatment, or simply allowing the blight on communities to continue – is known with virtual certainty, through West Virginia DEP's own admission in the ERP-related court pleadings in March 2020. And sadly, the neglect of duty continues, as confirmed by the June 2021 Legislative Audit Report.

---

[87] Olalde, *supra* note 71.

12

What the Future Could Hold if Leaders Choose to Lead

West Virginia faces a challenging future. Given the resource acquisition decisions that have been made during "the lost decade" by the two utilities operating in the state – and with the approval (unwisely) of the Public Service Commission (PSC) – the state's electricity supply is still 88 percent coal-fired as of 2020, and electricity rates will likely continue to increase because of the failure to diversify into cleaner, more economical ways of generating electricity. The job creators – large employers thinking about locating or expanding their operations – are not attracted to a state where access to renewable energy is difficult and the prospect of continuing price increases is certain. Energy supplies that are both high-cost and carbon-intensive put the state at an extreme competitive disadvantage compared to surrounding states that have adopted progressive energy polices and fully embraced the benefits of low-cost renewables.

And it's not just the large corporations that are bearing the impact of these backward energy policies. West Virginians are paying ever-increasing electricity rates and do not have access to the tools that would help them manage their energy costs – in the form of utility energy efficiency programs – because the PSC has utterly failed to adopt policies that put ratepayers first, such as by requiring FirstEnergy and American Electric Power (AEP) affiliates in West Virginia to offer the same energy efficiency programs that they offer their customers in the surrounding states.

West Virginia also bears the legacy impacts of decades of irresponsible and opportunistic coal operators that have fully exploited lax regulatory and environmental policies to leave the Mountain State badly scarred from decades of strip mining and mountaintop removal without paying the costs – either through surety bonds or payments to the Special Reclamation Fund – necessary to ensure that land reclamation will occur. Those costs will now fall on West Virginia taxpayers or, worse still, the land will never be reclaimed, leaving coal communities throughout the state with the scars and environmental carnage of an industry that was never required to clean up after itself (contrary to the purpose and design of the Surface Mining Control and Reclamation Act [SMCRA]).

West Virginia continues to suffer from a declining population – the 2020 census showed the Mountain State had the largest population drop of any state in the country with a 3.2 percent decrease – and nation-leading statistics in all the wrong categories: a poverty rate of 16 percent (the sixth highest among the fifty states),[1] the second lowest median household income in the country,[2] nation-leading rates of obesity, heart attacks, and diabetes, and a number two ranking in the prevalence of general health of adults as either fair or poor, as of 2018.[3] The state is desperate to attract and keep its rising young talent, as evidenced by a program announced by Governor Jim Justice in April 2021 that would pay $12,000 for remote workers to relocate to the state.[4]

At the same time, West Virginia is failing to capitalize on its feature attractions – a strategic location that provides easy access for nearby large population centers, beautiful scenery, recreational opportunities, and a reasonable cost of living – because of a lack of infrastructure and the necessary investment in things that are important to the sort of young professionals that the state is trying to attract, such as good roads, good schools, and access to good broadband service. Faced with these challenges, the state legislature does little to address them, and earned national attention in 2021 for passing bills against participation by transgender girls in sports, severely restricting needle exchanges, and preventing the enforcement of federal gun laws and "red flag" provisions within West Virginia. Meanwhile, the legislature voted down a bill that would have established a program to revitalize and economically diversify struggling coalfield communities because, according to one veteran political observer, "legislators find even making the merest concession to the fact that coal isn't coming back to be heresy."[5]

This concluding chapter is devoted to identifying some of the policies that should be given serious consideration as the state moves forward in the third decade of the twenty-first century. But the indispensable elements of this strategy are leadership and political will, and the courage to tell West Virginians what they need to hear rather than what they want to hear. What West Virginians need to hear is that the energy industry has undergone, and is continuing to undergo, a fundamental

[1] Press Release, West Virginia Center on Budget and Policy, Data Released Today Shows West Virginia Had 6th Highest Poverty Rate in the Country Even Before COVID Hardship, More Relief Needed (Sept. 17, 2020), https://wvpolicy.org/data-released-today-shows-west-virginia-had-6th-highest-poverty-rate-in-the-country-even-before-covid-hardship-more-relief-needed/.

[2] Id.

[3] *Fast Facts, Statistics About the Population of West Virginia*, WEST VIRGINIA DEPARTMENT OF HEALTH AND HUMAN RESOURCES (2018), https://dhhr.wv.gov/hpcd/data_reports/pages/fast-facts.aspx.

[4] Rachel Trent, *Remote Workers Can Get Paid $12,000 to Move to West Virginia*, CNN (Apr. 18, 2021), https://www.cnn.com/2021/04/18/us/west-virginia-move-incentive-remote-workers-trnd/index.html.

[5] Phil Kabler, *Statehouse Beat: D-Word Best Describes Past Session*, CHARLESTON GAZETTE-MAIL (Apr. 17, 2021), https://www.wvgazettemail.com/news/statehouse-beat-d-word-best-describes-past-session/article_924ab9cc-3df0-5c2b-837d-6934849ab063.html.

transition, and the source of energy upon which West Virginia built its culture and reputation ceases to be economically viable. "Clean coal technology" and identifying new products that can be manufactured with coal are not the answer. Coal is already "out of the money" as a fuel for the generation of electricity, and adding hundreds of millions of dollars of additional investment to implement "clean coal technology" does not improve the economic analysis. It is this coal-centered mindset that led to West Virginia leading the nation with respect to increases in electricity prices during "the lost decade." It is time to embrace the technologies of the twenty-first century, and those are the clean energy solutions of renewable energy, energy storage, and energy efficiency. West Virginia has missed out completely on the clean energy revolution that has been underway since the beginning of "the lost decade." But it is not too late to position the Mountain State to catch up. Let's start with leadership.

WHAT REAL LEADERSHIP LOOKS LIKE: PITTSBURGH AND SOAR

Pittsburgh to the north and eastern Kentucky to the south offer good examples of what real leadership looks like: leadership that recognizes a fundamental transition is underway, and embraces the obligation of leaders to help manage that transition. What West Virginia had throughout "the lost decade" was leadership that either failed to recognize the inevitable transition in the energy industry that was occurring – which is doubtful, as Joe Manchin and Shelley Moore Capito are too smart for that – or, worse, recognized it and abandoned their obligations as leaders to help the state navigate that transition in favor of the easier path of declaring that a "war on coal" was underway and blaming an Obama-led Environmental Protection Agency (EPA) that, in fact, really had very little to do with the demise of the coal industry. The end result for West Virginians was a "cop out": rather than acknowledging that a clean energy revolution driven by innovation and market forces was clearly underway and, instead, blaming "outside forces" as the cause of the coal industry's decline – in the form of Obama and his climate "activists" at the EPA – there was an abdication of responsibility by West Virginia's leaders to provide leadership to their citizens in managing the transition.

Pittsburgh faced a similar transition in the 1980s, as the steel and coal industries were in a steep decline with an equally dismal future. But in contrast to West Virginia's experience, municipal leaders in Pittsburgh stepped up to the challenge and charted a new future for the Steel City, featuring higher education, healthcare, and high tech. At the start of "the lost decade" eastern Kentucky was seeing the same signs of the demise of the coal industry as was equally obvious in West Virginia, and political leaders in the Bluegrass State – on a bipartisan basis – chose not to blame Obama and his "job-killing" EPA, but to start serious discussions about the future of eastern Kentucky through Shaping Our Appalachian Region (SOAR).

Pittsburgh: From a Coal and Steel Town to a Center of "Eds and Meds"

We're not a coal town. We were, and we were great at it. But we're not anymore.
Michael Huber, Uber driver in Pittsburgh[6]

Prior to the late 1970s, the economy in the Pittsburgh region was grounded in the steel industry. The region was still employing close to 300,000 in manufacturing trades. Chris Briem, a University of Pittsburgh economist and expert on the region's demographics, claims that for decades the region did not need to diversify into other industries: "Pittsburgh didn't do a lot of other things because we were so good at making steel for so long. Everything was geared toward steel: the work force, the supply network, the entire economy."[7] And, as noted by Pittsburgh historian Joel Tarr, a professor at Carnegie Mellon University, these were relatively high-paying jobs: "We created a blue-collar middle class in the steel industry. Wages were quite high and unions had sweetheart contracts."[8]

Then the steel industry underwent a dramatic transformation. Between 1979 and 1987, the Pittsburgh region lost 133,000 manufacturing jobs.[9] As Briem stated, "the volume of jobs lost coupled with the speed with which they disappeared was virtually unprecedented."[10] The job loss was attributable to improved productivity within the industry due to new technologies as well as the shifting of jobs abroad and into nonunion mini-mills. By November 1982, the region's unemployment rate hit 15 percent, in what the *Pittsburgh Post-Gazette* referred to as "nearing the bottom of a slow, post-war whirlpool."[11] The bottom would occur a few months later, in January 1983, when the region's unemployment rate peaked at 18.2 percent, with 212,400 people out of work.[12] Beaver County lost at least five major steelmaking plants, and unemployment surged to 28 percent – higher than for many states during the Great Depression.[13] And it was not just the loss of jobs; it was also the loss of population, as people moved away to find employment elsewhere. Between 1970 and 1990, the city lost a full 30 percent of its population, leaving behind an elderly demographic.[14] For

---

6   Kim Lyons, Emily Badger, & Alan Blinder, *A Revitalized Pittsburgh Says the President Used a Rusty Metaphor*, N.Y. TIMES (June 2, 2017), https://www.nytimes.com/2017/06/02/upshot/a-revitalized-pittsburgh-suggests-the-president-used-a-rusty-metaphor.html?searchResultPosition=15.

7   Patricia Sabatini, *For Pittsburgh, This Recession Is Nothing in Comparison to '80s*, PITTSBURGH POST-GAZETTE (Mar. 17, 2009), https://www.post-gazette.com/business/top50/2009/03/17/For-Pittsburgh-this-recession-is-nothing-in-comparison-to-80s/stories/200903170338.

8   *Id.*

9   Bill Toland, *In Desperate 1983, There Was Nowhere for Pittsburgh's Economy to Go But Up*, PITTSBURGH POST-GAZETTE (Dec. 23, 2012), https://www.post-gazette.com/business/businessnews/2012/12/23/In-desperate-1983-there-was-nowhere-for-Pittsburgh-s-economy-to-go-but-up/stories/201212230258.

10 Sabatini, *supra* note 7.

11 Toland, *supra* note 9.

12 Sabatini, *supra* note 7.

13 Toland, *supra* note 9.

14 *Id.*

decades, Pittsburgh's population was one of the oldest in the country. In the 1990s, for example, Allegheny County (in which Pittsburgh is located) had the second-oldest population of large counties in the United States, behind only a geriatric zone in Florida.[15]

This economic devastation, and its causes, mirrors the demise of the coal industry in West Virginia over the past thirty years: well-paying jobs in an undiversified economy that disappeared due to technological advances (mechanization in the case of coal) and broader shifts due to market forces (the shift away from using coal to generate electricity). And younger workers leave due to the lack of opportunities, leaving an older population behind. That is where the similarities end, however; although deindustrialization in the Steel City was a "protracted and painful experience,"[16] Pittsburgh successfully reinvented itself through a "new growth model" that embodied "quiet leadership from across the public, private, and civic sectors, by people who understood the need to move away from a sole reliance on heavy industry."[17] According to *The New Localism*, "focusing on developing technological strengths has put Pittsburgh among the thirty or so global cities that are positioned as leaders in next-generation technologies."[18] How did it happen?

It is worth noting that this was not Pittsburgh's first experience with a successful public–private partnership. In what was known as Pittsburgh's first "Renaissance" – an effort in the 1940s and 1950s to clean up the city's air and water and spur redevelopment – Mayor David L. Lawrence used an inaugural address to declare that he was "convinced that our people want clean air."[19] An air quality ordinance was approved in 1949, and a "cooperative civic culture" developed between Mayor (and later Pennsylvania Governor) Lawrence and industrialist Richard King Mellon.[20] This "Lawrence model" was later described as "very much in [the] DNA" of Pittsburgh,[21] and the model would be replicated in the 1990s under Mayor Thomas J. Murphy, Jr.

Murphy – whose father was employed at US Steel's South Side Works – was sworn into the first of five terms in the Pennsylvania state House of Representatives representing Pittsburgh's North Side in January 1983.[22] Ten years later, in 1993, Murphy became the fifty-seventh Mayor of Pittsburgh, and served for twelve years. To Murphy, it was quite apparent in the 1980s that in contrast to earlier "boom and

---

[15]   Steven Kurutz, *Pittsburgh Gets a Tech Makeover*, N.Y. Times (July 20, 2017), https://www.nytimes .com/2017/07/22/style/pittsburgh-tech-makeover.html.

[16]   David Streitfeld, *For Pittsburgh, There's Life After Steel*, N.Y. Times (Jan. 7, 2009), https://www .nytimes.com/2009/01/08/business/economy/08collapse.html.

[17]   Bruce Katz, *Why the Future Looks Like Pittsburgh*, The New Localism (Sept. 26, 2017), https://www .thenewlocalism.com/research/why-the-future-looks-like-pittsburgh/.

[18]   *Id.*

[19]   Lyons, Badger, & Blinder, *supra* note 6.

[20]   Jim O'Toole, *The Political Makeover of a Rust Belt City*, Politico (Feb. 4, 2014), https://www.politico .com/magazine/story/2014/02/pittsburgh-political-makeover-of-a-rust-belt-city-103040/.

[21]   *Id.*

[22]   Toland, *supra* note 9.

bust" cycles in Pittsburgh's economy, "this was permanent. It was done. We needed to move on with our lives."[23] Several factors came into play to make the transformation possible. The local universities – Carnegie Mellon, the University of Pittsburgh, and Duquesne University – were used to pour state funds into technology research, with Murphy playing a critical role in steering state pension funds to seed high-tech investments in the region.[24] At the federal level, Senator Arlen Specter and Congressman John Murtha (from nearby Johnstown) were able to use earmarks and their powerful positions on the Senate and House Appropriations Committees to direct millions of federal dollars to the city's various research efforts.[25]

Murphy also gives a lot of credit to Dr. Richard Cyert, who was president of Carnegie Mellon University from 1972 to 1990. According to Murphy, Cyert was the one "driving this conversation. He was the first person I heard who said the universities could be the economic drivers for the region."[26] In a 2014 article in the *Pittsburgh Post-Gazette*, two-term mayor Bill Peduto compared Carnegie Mellon, along with the University of Pittsburgh, to the iron ore factories that made Pittsburgh an industrial power in the nineteenth century – the local resource "churning out that talent" from which the city is fueled.[27] Murphy, for his part, is credited with attracting investment for the "urban amenities" – the new ballparks on the North Side, riverfront rehabilitation, and miles of bike trails along the three rivers.[28]

Today, Pittsburgh features a diverse economy that encompasses health care, education, finance, and technology. And its residents are now younger and well-educated. In contrast to the 1990s, when Pittsburgh was a place twentysomethings fled or avoided,[29] the proportion of the city's population aged sixty-five or older is currently *lower* than for the nation as a whole.[30] And in an economy driven by educational and medical institutions, the younger workers in the city's economy are among the most educated in the country. According to the 2010 Census, for the younger portion of Pittsburgh's workforce – those aged 25–34 – Pittsburgh was tied with Washington DC, and ahead of Boston and New York, in the proportion of its workforce holding graduate professional degrees.[31]

Given Pittsburgh's transformation from a steel town to a center for "eds and meds," it landed with a thud when then President Trump cited Pittsburgh when explaining his reasoning for pulling the United States out of the Paris (climate) Agreement in June 2017. Trump said at the time that, "I was elected to represent the

---

[23]   *Id.*
[24]   Streitfeld, *supra* note 16.
[25]   O'Toole, *supra* note 20.
[26]   *Id.*
[27]   Kurutz, *supra* note 15.
[28]   O'Toole, *supra* note 20.
[29]   Kurutz, *supra* note 15.
[30]   O'Toole, *supra* note 20.
[31]   *Id.*

citizens of Pittsburgh, not Paris."[32] Then Mayor Bill Peduto was "livid" when he heard Trump's remarks, noting that Pittsburgh, like many other US cities, has committed to reducing its emissions regardless of US participation in the international climate agreement. Peduto tweeted that, "As the Mayor of Pittsburgh, I can assure you that we will follow the guidelines of the Paris Agreement for our people, our economy & future."[33] The *New York Times* observed that the reference to Pittsburgh was a "rusty metaphor" for the occasion given that "[t]he former steel hub has spent the last 30 years trying to remake its economy in precisely the mold that climate advocates envision."[34]

Kentucky's Shaping Our Appalachian Region (SOAR)

During the fall of 2013, while the "war on coal" was raging in West Virginia, two political leaders in Kentucky – one a Republican and the other a Democrat – decided to move beyond the rhetoric and start a process for managing the transition of the economy in eastern Kentucky away from coal. (Beginning in 2008, eastern Kentucky lost 11,787 or 79 percent of its coal mining jobs over the subsequent eleven years.)[35] Democratic Governor Steve Beshear and Republican Congressman Hal Rogers – then chair of the powerful Appropriations Committee in the US House of Representatives – challenged a diverse group of citizens to design, develop, and execute a regional dialogue. That resulted in an organization known as Shaping Our Appalachian Region (SOAR), which held its first of what has now been nine annual conferences in December 2013 in Pikevlle, Kentucky. Over 1,500 people attended the first conference; it was opened by Beshear who said that coal's role as the "kingpin employer" of the region was in a steep decline and "to ignore that is to blindfold ourselves and stick our heads in the sand."[36] According to one media account of the day's proceedings, both Beshear and Rogers "gave a frank assessment of the reality that those coal jobs lost are not likely to come back anytime soon – no matter what the EPA does – and how leaders and citizens must work to find new ways to breathe life into the region if it is to have any hope for the future."[37]

SOAR produced its first Regional Blueprint for a twenty-first-century Appalachia in 2016. It now describes its mandate as "fill[ing] the economic gaps left by the decline of the coal industry," and its goal as "to spur economic development to

[32] Lyons, Badger, & Blinder, *supra* note 6.
[33] Abigail Abrams, *Pittsburgh Mayor Bill Peduto Hits Back at President Trump: "We Will Follow the Guidelines of the Paris Agreement,"* TIME (June 1, 2017), https://time.com/4802340/paris-agreement-pittsburgh-mayor-bill-peduto-donald-trump/.
[34] Lyons, Badger, & Blinder, *supra* note 6.
[35] SOAR, BLUEPRINT. A PLAN FOR OUR FUTURE 6 (2021), http://www.soar-ky.org/wp-content/uploads/2021/05/2021-SOAR-Blueprint.pdf.
[36] Joe Sonka, *A SOARing Start: Political Leaders Look to Transition Eastern Kentucky's Economy as Coal Declines*, LEO WEEKLY (Dec. 13, 2013), https://www.leoweekly.com/2013/12/a-soaring-start/.
[37] *Id.*

replace not only the jobs lost related to the coal industry, but [to embrace] the digital economy to create opportunities across all employment sectors."[38] SOAR has proven effective at using partnerships to leverage federal investments in the region: In 2019, partnerships and opportunities facilitated by SOAR leveraged nearly $52 million in federal investments in the area. For 2020, the Appalachian Regional Commission (ARC) made its largest investment in a single state during a fiscal year in decades – $36.5 million in investments in Kentucky. ARC describes its support for the SOAR initiative as demonstrating "the power of leveraging ARC's resources with forward-thinking leadership, financial support from other regional and public partners, and the energy and innovation of local residents."[39]

Both Congressman Rogers and Governor Beshear (now Andy Beshear, Steve's son and the current Kentucky governor) remain active in the organization. During the 2020 SOAR Summit, for example, they announced two new projects in Pike and Boyd counties ($4.27 million to expand and equip the Pikeville Medical Center's Leonard Lawson Cancer Center and $4 million to purchase health care equipment at the King's Daughters Health System) that were selected for funding through the abandoned mine lands (AML) pilot grant program, which was designed to revitalize the coalfields in Kentucky's Appalachian region through economic development.[40]

Leadership West Virginia Style

Nothing like the bipartisan leadership demonstrated in Kentucky occurred in West Virginia throughout "the lost decade." The only thing bipartisan in West Virginia was the consistent, unanimous rhetoric across party lines attacking the EPA and blaming the "war on coal." West Virginia officials clung to the disingenuous narrative that if only the EPA would leave the coal industry alone, the coal jobs would come back. Democratic Governors Joe Manchin and Earl Ray Tomblin (and, for seven months, Jim Justice); Republican Governor Jim Justice; Democratic Senators Byrd, Rockefeller, and Manchin; Republican Senator Capito; Democratic Congressmen Nick Rahall and Alan Mollohan; and Republican Congressmen David McKinley, Shelley Moore Capito, Evan Jenkins, and Alex Mooney all, in one form or another, blamed the EPA and the Obama administration for the decline in the fortunes of the coal industry during "the lost decade," and most sponsored or supported legislation to interfere with the EPA's regulation of greenhouse gas (GHG) emissions. In the case of Senators Byrd and Rockefeller, both had a change of heart with respect to the coal industry and started saying the things that needed to

[38] SOAR, https://www.soar-ky.org/.
[39] *Shaping Our Appalachian Region (SOAR)*, Appalachian Regional Commission, https://www.arc.gov/investment/shaping-our-appalachian-region-soar/.
[40] Press Release, Congressman Hal Rogers, Gov. Beshear, Rep. Rogers Announce More Than $8 Million for Eastern Kentucky at SOAR Summit (Oct. 29, 2020), https://halrogers.house.gov/press-releases?ID=6201AF36-AB6F-4DE4-A2DF-4277D01F6E03..

be said (Byrd's written declarations in the last year of his life and Rockefeller's June 2012 speech on the floor of the Senate), but both knew at the time of their new-found courage that they would likely never face the voters again. Such one-shot revelations do not really have any durable impact on the electorate, and their remarks were quickly forgotten in favor of the populist "war on coal" rhetoric of Senators Manchin and Capito and the entire West Virginia Congressional delegation.

Unlike in Kentucky, where a Democratic governor and a powerful Republican Congressman began speaking as early as 2013 about an inevitable transition that was coming to the coalfields of eastern Kentucky, no suggestion was ever made in West Virginia during "the lost decade" that the coal jobs would not be coming back. What was the motto of Jim Justice's campaign for reelection in 2020? "Jim Justice: He Never Gave Up on Coal." Is that leadership? It seems ridiculous in light of what everyone could see was happening in the coal industry. What is worse is the role that Justice apparently played in derailing about $2.1 billion of investments in modern natural gas-fired generating plants that could have brought jobs, economic activity, and energy diversity to the state, all in furtherance of his own personal interests in the coal industry and to demonstrate that "he never gave up on coal."

West Virginia desperately needs its leaders to start providing leadership through the energy transition that is well underway or, if not, to step aside and make way for a new generation of politicians that is not afraid to say what needs to be said, and that will consider taking the sort of bold actions discussed in the remainder of this chapter.

WEST VIRGINIA-STYLE INFRASTRUCTURE? RECLAIMING MINE LANDS AND PLUGGING OIL AND GAS WELLS

For the past five years, the White House, whether occupied by Donald Trump or Joe Biden, has been talking about a massive federal infrastructure package to rebuild the nation's transportation system (highways, roads, bridges, public transit, and other essential public works), with some disagreement among politicians about how broadly to define "infrastructure." For example, does it include access to high-speed broadband? Does it include charging structure for electric vehicles (EVs)? Does it include modernizing water systems around the country? Does it include retrofitting existing housing and building stock?

One category of expenditure that should be of particular interest to West Virginia is spending a few billion dollars to repair the environmental degradation left behind by decades of extracting fossil fuels: reclaiming coal mine lands and plugging abandoned oil and gas wells. President Biden has consistently defined "infrastructure" in his various proposals, to include funding to address these issues. His original

$2 trillion American Jobs Plan proposal, for example, would include $4.7 billion for plugging old wells and $11.3 billion for cleaning up abandoned mines.[41]

Why would it be good for West Virginia if "infrastructure" were defined to include plugging wells and cleaning up abandoned mine lands? First, it is going to be very expensive to clean up the mess that has been left behind by the fossil fuel industry in West Virginia, and without substantial assistance from the federal government, the cleanup is simply not going to happen, leaving West Virginians burdened with the degradation and continuing environmental impacts. Second, spending billions of dollars to reclaim abandoned mines and plug old oil and gas wells would create thousands of good-paying jobs. And these jobs would be a pretty good match with the skillset of the former coal miners and oil and gas workers who have lost their jobs as a result of the energy transition that is underway. On this point, President Biden stated in March 2021 that he wants to put pipefitters and miners to work capping the wells "at the same price that they would charge to dig those wells."[42] Moreover, the jobs would be located in the communities that have suffered the greatest economic and environmental impacts as a result of irresponsible extraction practices by the fossil fuel industry. Third, this infrastructure spending would produce considerable climate benefits, in the form of reducing the GHG emissions that are currently leaking from unplugged wells and unreclaimed mine lands.

Looking at the issue of oil and gas wells, a recent report by the Ohio River Valley Institute (ORVI) estimates that there are 538,000 unplugged abandoned oil and wells in the four states that comprise the mid and upper Ohio River Valley region, and it would cost between $25 billion and $34 billion to plug these abandoned wells.[43] Of the unplugged abandoned wells, 75,821 are located in West Virginia, along with another currently abandoned 335,000 oil and gas wells.[44] The costs for plugging abandoned wells in West Virginia ranges from $54,011 to $115,949 per well.[45] Taking the midpoint of the cost estimate suggests a figure of about $6.5 billion to plug the 75,000+ wells in West Virginia.

A federal program to carry out this work could create about 15,000 jobs per year over twenty years or 303,000 job years at a total cost of $25 billion.[46] As noted in the ORVI report, these job figures are nearly equivalent to the decline in upstream oil and gas jobs in the region between 2014 and 2019. As far as climate benefits are

[41] Juliana Kaplan, *Here's Exactly How Biden's $2 Trillion of Infrastructure Spending Breaks Down*, INSIDER (Mar. 31, 2021), https://www.businessinsider.com/what-is-in-bidens-infrastructure-bill-package-american-jobs-plan-2021-3.

[42] Matthew Daly, *Biden Infrastructure Plan Would Spend $16 Billion to Clean Up Old Mines, Oil Wells*, PBS NEWS HOUR (Apr. 1, 2021), https://www.pbs.org/newshour/nation/biden-infrastructure-plan-would-spend-16-billion-to-clean-up-old-mines-oil-wells.

[43] TED BOETTNER, REPAIRING THE DAMAGE FROM HAZARDOUS ABANDONED OIL & GAS WELLS: A FEDERAL PLAN TO GROW JOBS IN THE OHIO RIVER VALLEY AND BEYOND (Apr. 2021), https://ohiorivervalleyinstitute.org/wp-content/uploads/2021/04/Repairing-the-Damage-from-Hazardous-AOG-Wells-Report.pdf.

[44] *Id.* at 13.

[45] *Id.* at 26.

[46] *Id.* at 8.

concerned, eliminating the methane emissions from these unplugged abandoned oil and gas wells would achieve reductions of 71,000 metric tons of methane or 1.8 million metric tons of carbon dioxide equivalent (CO_{2e}), or about the same as 2 million pounds of coal burned in one year.[47] The adverse impacts of unplugged wells are not limited to methane emissions, of course; they also create health and safety risks through leaching other pollutants into the air such as volatile organic compounds (VOCs) that damage local air quality. Leaks from abandoned wells, such as oil, brine, and drilling byproducts, have also been linked to the contamination of groundwater supplies and soil, which can undermine drinking water, agriculture activity, and property values. Gas or methane leaking from wells can also cause dangerous explosions.[48]

Turning to abandoned mine lands, the damage from unreclaimed land from coal mining includes clogged streams, water pollution, mine fires, landslides, and deforested land. Coal AMLs include not only abandoned mines themselves, but damage from coal extraction and processing, such as polluted streams, coal loading facilities, and methane leaking from abandoned mines. As discussed in Chapter 11, in 1977 Congress passed the SMCRA to handle the reclamation of mines from that point forward. With respect to existing abandoned mine lands, Congress enacted the AML program. Since 1977, 978,000 acres and $7.9 billion worth of damage – only about 27 percent of the total – has been cleaned up under the AML program.[49] Given the rapid decline of the coal industry and the severe underfunding of the AML program relative to the massive backlog of unreclaimed damage, AML fees will be inadequate to repair the remaining damage. Another recent report by ORVI estimates that more than 850,000 acres of damage have yet to be repaired – 84 percent of which is concentrated in the seven Appalachian states of Pennsylvania, West Virginia, Ohio, Kentucky, Alabama, Virginia, and Tennessee.[50] The estimated cost of repairing the damage is between $18.3 and $24.4 billion, which is significantly higher than the $11 billion in unreclaimed construction costs in the federal AML inventory. According to the ORVI report, these unreclaimed costs will likely grow to between $21 and $33.6 billion by 2050.[51]

According to the report, 5.5 million people in Appalachia live within one mile of an AML site, including one in three West Virginians.[52] West Virginia is the number two state in the nation with respect to acres of unreclaimed mine land, at 173,797 acres or 20.4 percent of the national total.[53] The costs of repairing the unreclaimed

[47]   *Id.*
[48]   *Id.* at 6.
[49]   Eric Dixon, Repairing the Damage: Cleaning Up the Land, Air, and Water Damaged by the Coal Industry Before 1977 (Apr. 2021), https://ohiorivervalleyinstitute.org/wp-content/uploads/2021/04/AML-Report-Dixon-ORVI-V1.1-4.pdf.
[50]   *Id.* at 4.
[51]   *Id.*
[52]   *Id.*
[53]   *Id.* at 11.

mine land in West Virginia is estimated to be slightly over $5 billion, or 24.4 percent of the national total.[54]

The climate benefits of reclaiming AML are significant. Methane emissions from abandoned coal mines are the eleventh largest source of such emissions in the United States.[55] There is also a carbon sequestration benefit of planting trees on the unreclaimed AML acreage. Reforesting only one-quarter of unreclaimed AML acreage could potentially sequester 232,000 metric tons of CO_2 annually – about as much as is emitted from powering 40,000 homes for a year.[56]

Apart from the climate benefits, reclaiming AML would minimize the existing environmental impacts, such as the runoff and sediment from surface-mined AMLs that clogs waterways and increases flooding. According to the ORVI report, AMLs continue to clog 5,500 miles of streams, a situation that will result in more flooding as peak rainfall increases in some areas due to extreme weather events caused by climate change.[57] In addition, AMLs discharge at least 320,000 gallons of water pollution per minute.[58]

Of particular interest to West Virginia is the disproportionate impact of AML damage on impoverished areas in the United States. Abandoned coal mines are located predominantly in rural communities that are the frontline for a confluence of economic, social, public health, and environmental crises. Many rural communities in coal regions – particularly in Appalachia – have experienced persistent economic distress and poverty for decades. The poverty rate in counties with AML damage is higher than the national average, especially in Appalachia where it is 15 percent higher.[59] Within AML counties, poverty among people of color, women, young people, and those without a college degree is higher than average.[60]

The ORVI report recommends that Congress appropriate $13 billion in AML reclamation over the next ten years (or $1.3 billion annually) which would support 6,909 direct jobs comprising 3,178 construction jobs with a $30 assumed hourly gross pay; 3,317 design jobs with state/tribal agencies; and 484 federal administration jobs.[61] In addition to direct jobs, 10,384 induced and indirect jobs would be supported, resulting in 17,293 total jobs.[62] The ORVI report further recommends appropriating more funding in subsequent years to complete nearly all the remaining AML cleanup by 2050. The $26.3 billion in total AML reclamation costs would support an estimated 138,024 direct job-years and 344,403 total job-years.[63]

[54] *Id.*
[55] *Id.* at 4.
[56] *Id.*
[57] *Id.*
[58] *Id.*
[59] *Id.* at 7.
[60] *Id.*
[61] *Id.* at 44.
[62] *Id.*
[63] *Id.*

Given the disproportionate benefit that West Virginia would receive from a massive federal effort to plug oil and gas wells (one third of the abandoned and unplugged wells are within Appalachia, and West Virginia has the second highest number of such wells in Appalachia) and to reclaim AML – given West Virginia's status as the number two state in the country in AML acres with over 20 percent of the total – it is difficult to identify a program from the federal government that would better fit West Virginia's infrastructure needs. As it turned out, the $1.2 trillion bipartisan infrastructure package was too good a deal to pass up; in addition to gaining Joe Manchin's support, both Senator Capito and Congressman McKinley crossed the aisle to vote for the measure, thus capturing a share of the $16 billion for reclaiming AMLs and plugging wells for West Virginia. This is good news, as the environmental impacts of failing to act are only going to get worse with the passage of time. West Virginia has already experienced deadly flooding from extreme weather events, and it is essential that streams be relieved of the sediment from AML that contributes to flooding. It is also significant that the environmental impacts are falling disproportionately on impoverished rural communities in West Virginia that are ill-prepared to cope with them. In the absence of a massive infusion of federal dollars to help with the cleanup effort, West Virginia will continue to bear the ruinous scars associated with decades of irresponsible fossil fuel extraction.

REGULATORY REFORM AT THE PSC, AND REAL PROTECTION FOR CONSUMERS

Close behind the failure of elected policymakers to act in the interests of West Virginians during "the lost decade" is the dismal failure of appointed officials, specifically the PSC, to adopt regulatory policies and issue decisions that protect energy ratepayers from the imprudent decisions of the electric utilities serving the state. As discussed in Chapter 8, the PSC is a very powerful agency that is granted broad authority under West Virginia law to provide close oversight over energy utilities and set "just and reasonable" rates. The primary mission of the PSC is to protect ratepayers from exploitation by monopolies – utilities that have been granted the exclusive franchise to serve communities throughout West Virginia – and to balance customers' interests in being charged reasonable rates against the utilities' interests in earning a fair profit, attracting capital on reasonable terms, and maintaining their financial integrity (the constitutional standard for "just and reasonable" rates). How that balance is struck by public utility commissions throughout the country is very much up to the regulators, given the broad grant of statutory authority and the reluctance of reviewing courts to wade into the complex technicalities of utility ratemaking.

In West Virginia, that balance has been struck firmly on the side of the utilities, with little regard to protecting customers from the massive rate increases that occurred throughout "the lost decade." As described in Chapter 3, no state in

America had faster electricity price increases during "the lost decade" than West Virginia; prices grew at five times the national average between 2008 and 2020. This outcome was due to numerous unwise decisions by the PSC (described in Chapters 8 and 10), including approval of the transfer of three aging, inefficient coal plants from the shareholder side of the ledger to the ratepayers' side, as well as the failure to require utilities to offer energy efficiency programs and to follow a rigorous long-term planning process. The narrative of "what's good for the coal industry is good for West Virginia" certainly guided the PSC's decisions throughout "the lost decade" and, probably more than any other example, the results proved the cruel falsehood of the guiding principle. Allowing the utilities to continue to be nearly 100 percent dependent on one fuel source without diversifying into cheaper, cleaner sources of electricity might have been good for the coal industry, but it is clear that, notwithstanding the PSC's shameful efforts to do so, the coal industry cannot and should not be bailed out on the backs of West Virginia's electric ratepayers. They simply cannot afford it, and never have been able to do so.

The starting point for regulatory reform at the PSC is at the commissioner level. Three commissioners are appointed by the governor, subject to senate approval, and are charged with making sure that the balance between ratepayer and shareholder interests is struck fairly. The governor also designates one of the three commissioners to be the chairman, who serves as the chief administrative officer of the agency and largely sets the agenda (for better or worse). Ratepayer interests have really not had a seat at the table given the composition of PSC commissioners throughout "the lost decade."

As discussed in Chapter 8, for most of that period the PSC was led by Mike Albert, a former partner at the well-known coal industry law firm Jackson Kelly and who previously represented utilities in rate proceedings before the PSC. He presided over the approval of all three of the senseless coal plant transfers that occurred during "the lost decade," and voted to approve a fourth. Since his retirement in 2019, the agency has been headed by Charlotte Lane, a former lobbyist for FirstEnergy and oil and gas interests who was heavily supported by campaign contributions from the energy industry while she served in the West Virginia legislature and when she ran unsuccessfully for Congress. She also infamously secured the passage of pro-gas company legislation that has resulted in steady rate increases for natural gas service even as the cost of gas has declined. Consumers do not have a chance at the agency with such leadership, and the results speak for themselves in the form of the massive increase in rates experienced during "the lost decade" as well as the continuing burden on ratepayers saddled with aging, inefficient coal plants.

Ensuring appointment of commissioners who are mindful of their obligations to consumers is the responsibility of the governor in selecting individuals with the requisite background and expertise. How has Governor Jim Justice fulfilled that responsibility? Miserably. In addition to the appointment of Charlotte Lane as chairman, in August 2021 Justice appointed Bill Raney, the former head of the West Virginia Coal Association, to an open seat on the Commission following the expiration of Brooks McCabe's term, as discussed in Chapter 8.[64] Raney retired from the Coal Association in January 2021 at the age of seventy-three, and was described at the time as the "original Friend of Coal." (As discussed in Chapter 5, "Friends of Coal" was initiated under Raney's watch in 2002, and he presided over its evolution to the "war on coal" during the Obama years.) While Raney headed the Coal Association, the organization "wielded tremendous legislative influence, helping shape state laws favorable to the coal industry."[65]

Chairman Lane expressed excitement at the addition of Raney to the regulatory panel, noting that she had worked with Raney for forty years. In fact, Raney was her client when she represented the Coal Association in the PSC proceeding involving the transfer of the Harrison coal plant, one of the three foolish coal plant acquisitions discussed in Chapter 10.[66] No individual in West Virginia is more closely identified with the coal industry than Bill Raney, and he will now be on the PSC through 2027 making decisions, along with Lane, on utility filings seeking rate relief and approval of resource acquisitions. There is little hope for stringent regulatory oversight to reign in utility rate increases, or the adoption of policies promoting energy efficiency and renewable energy, with Lane and Raney calling the shots. West Virginians will continue to bear the consequences of unending rate increases and resource acquisition decisions that favor coal to the exclusion of cleaner, lower-cost resources.

The PSC's decision in October 2021 to approve AEP's proposal to spend $448.3 million on environmental compliance costs to keep its three West Virginia coal plants (Mitchell, Amos, and Mountaineer) open through 2040 is a prime example of the continued dismal failure of the PSC to protect ratepayers. As a result of the decision, West Virginia ratepayers will be picking up an additional $65 million in costs that should have been paid by AEP customers in Virginia and Kentucky, as described in Chapter 8. When regulators in those states wisely rejected AEP's proposal to spend additional money keeping uneconomic coal plants open beyond 2028, AEP simply refiled its case to dump the costs on West Virginia customers, knowing that the PSC would approve it. And AEP was right; it was the first major decision in Raney's term of service on the Commission, and once again he delivered for the coal industry, to the detriment of West Virginia ratepayers.

In the absence of any hope that the appointment authority will be exercised in a responsible manner by the governor, the statute governing the qualifications for commissioners should be amended to require that, at a minimum, one commissioner must have a track record of representing consumer interests, so that at least that voice has a chance of being heard in the decision-making process. (The statute

[64] Mike Tony, *Gov. Justice Appoints Former WV Coal Association Head to Public Service Commission*, CHARLESTON GAZETTE-MAIL (Aug. 5, 2021), https://www.wvgazettemail.com/news/energy_and_envir onment/gov-justice-appoints-former-wv-coal-association-head-to-public-service-commission/arti cle_0af77f08-4fd8-5389-915b-365d6142020b.html.

[65] *Id.*

[66] *Id.*

already requires that one of the commissioners must be a lawyer with at least ten years of practice experience, so why not also explicitly require a commissioner to have background and experience in consumer protection issues?)[67] Alternatively, the statute could be amended to require a Consumer Advisory Council that would represent the public in advising PSC commissioners on matters relating to the protection of consumer interests, as is the case in Pennsylvania.[68]

Apart from changes at the decision-making level, regulatory reform would include devoting more resources to protecting the public interest in cases that are litigated at the PSC. When a utility seeks a general rate increase, it submits a massive filing to the PSC consisting of over a dozen pieces of prepared testimony by utility witnesses – usually officers, but sometimes outside expert witnesses as well – accompanied by stacks of supporting workpapers and a cost-of-service study. In West Virginia, the process takes ten months from start to finish (the statutory suspension period), including time for discovery, the filing of opposing testimony by intervenors, and a trial-type hearing in front of the three commissioners. In most states, staff at the utility regulatory agency present a complete case in response to the utility's filing, addressing each of the various elements included in the utility's rate request. For every financial expert, economist, accounting witness, engineer, or power supply witness presented by the utility, the "advocacy staff" at the agency offer an opposing witness, to give the commissioners a complete evidentiary record upon which to base its decision. As an example, if the utility claims that a reasonable salary for its CEO is $5 million annually, a staff witness might propose an adjustment to reduce that expense item to, say, $2.5 million, based on a survey of CEO salaries paid at comparably sized utilities.

However, this process pretty much does not exist at the West Virginia PSC. Very few witnesses testify on behalf of the PSC staff in a typical utility rate filing. Most issues in a utility rate filing go unchallenged; the agency simply lacks the resources to present an "opposing case" in response to the utility's filing, unlike the process in virtually every other state in the country. Rather, the "consumer" perspective is represented solely by the Consumer Advocate Division (CAD), which was created by the West Virginia legislature in 1981 to represent the interests of residential customers in PSC proceedings. Although CAD is a division of the PSC, it is independent from it and has a separate budget and staff – a *very small* budget and staff. As Jackie Roberts, CAD director before leaving in December 2020 to take a job at the PSC, stated: "I have three attorneys, two analysts and a woman who runs everything in the office. We are completely outgunned, number-wise, but we work hard to know what the important issues are and to litigate those."[69]

[67] West Virginia Code § 24-1-3.
[68] *About the PUC, Consumer Advisory Council*, PA PUC, https://www.puc.pa.gov/about-the-puc/consumer-advisory-council.
[69] Mike Tony, *West Virginia's Consumer Advocate Stepping Down*, CHARLESTON GAZETTE-MAIL (Dec. 29, 2020), https://www.wvgazettemail.com/news/energy_and_environment/west-virginias-consumer-advocate-stepping-down/article_7cd75849-37e6-570b-929c-9df736873dda.html.

CAD does do a decent job, given its limited resources. But it is impossible to cover all the routine filings made just by the electric utilities (not to mention the gas, water, and telephone companies) which consist of annual power cost adjustment filings, frequent general rate increase requests, and the occasional nonroutine case involving a major resource acquisition (such as the coal plant transfers discussed in Chapter 10) or a proposal for rate recovery of additional investments in existing coal plants – such as the AEP proceeding for approval to spend a few hundred million dollars to keep its West Virginia coal plants operating until 2040. Utility rate proceedings involve very complex accounting, engineering, and financial issues, and the PSC's decision must be based on an evidentiary record that fully explores not only the utility perspective, but whether there might be a lower cost alternative that would result in lower rates for customers. While CAD might be doing an adequate job given its limited resources – a budget of around $1 million annually – it is a cruel hoax to suggest that consumers are really represented at the PSC. CAD's existence allows policymakers in West Virginia to "check the box" that consumers are represented in PSC proceedings, but neither CAD nor PSC staff are provided with anything approaching the resources necessary to truly protect the public interest. The consequence of these inadequate resources? We only need to look at the massive rate increases and foolish coal plant transfers that were approved by the PSC during "the lost decade." The utilities pretty much got everything they wanted, and West Virginians have paid the price: rate increases at five times the national average during "the lost decade" as well as the ongoing burden of paying for uneconomic coal plants in their rates for the foreseeable future.

CLEAN ELECTRICITY STANDARD

West Virginia should adopt a clean electricity standard (CES). As demonstrated by the CESs adopted in other states, this can be accomplished either through legislation or through administrative action at the PSC. (Legislation would be far preferable, as it would be more durable and would send a stronger signal to the energy markets about West Virginia's commitment to a clean energy future.) An example of a CES is the 100 percent by 2035 zero-carbon standard proposed by President Biden, which faces an uncertain future in Washington, DC due to, among other things, the lack of support from Senator Manchin. (In the budget reconciliation process, the CES has evolved into the Clean Electricity Payment Program [CEPP], which would provide $150 billion in incentives for electric utilities to decarbonize their electricity supply or, alternatively, impose penalties for failure to do so. Because of the fiscal impact of the measure, it is eligible for inclusion in the budget reconciliation process, which requires only fifty-one votes for passage rather than the sixty-vote filibuster-proof margin.)

In the absence of a national CES, West Virginia could enact its own CES, as several states have already done. The target established in a CES would, of course, reflect that West Virginia is starting off with a 90 percent coal-fired electricity supply, and would incorporate a more realistic goal – maybe 60 percent carbon free by 2035 – that still means significant movement but is attainable. The case for a CES for West Virginia is compelling. First, it would establish what has long been espoused by Joe Manchin as the centerpiece of his energy policy – an "all-of-the-above" approach. A CES would favor zero-carbon resources to the exclusion of carbon-emitting resources, and strong economic incentives would follow. (Because utilities would be obliged to procure a growing percentage of zero-carbon resources, a premium would be paid for those resources versus carbon-emitting resources.) Zero carbon would include renewables (wind, solar, and hydro) and nuclear, as well as fossil fuel-fired resources (coal and natural gas) that employ carbon capture and sequestration (CCS) technology to capture the GHG emissions from the plants before they reach the atmosphere. A CES would thus stimulate the sort of investment in CCS technology that has long been championed by Senator Manchin. Because the approach would be market-based, however – in other words, it would be technology neutral, and zero-carbon resources would compete against each other based on how cheaply they can produce electricity – CCS would have to be demonstrated to be cost-effective versus renewables in order to compete as a resource option for electric utilities.

A second major advantage of a CES is that it would send a strong message to the energy marketplace that West Virginia is "open for business" for clean energy developers. In the absence of institutional support for clean energy, developers will be reluctant to devote any significant resources to pursuing projects in West Virginia. Utilities conducting requests for proposals (RFPs) for clean energy projects currently do not attract robust responses because of skepticism by developers – justified, given the PSC's actions in rejecting AEP's previous efforts to obtain approvals for renewable projects in West Virginia – about whether the deals will be completed and the projects built. Enactment of a CES would address these concerns, as developers would see a strong, binding commitment by West Virginia that it is truly interested in participating in the fast-growing clean energy markets.

PROMOTING ENERGY EFFICIENCY THROUGH A STATE ENERGY SAVINGS TARGET

West Virginia should also adopt an energy efficiency resource standard (EERS), which would establish electricity savings targets – such as a 2 percent annual reduction, for example – that electric utilities must be required to achieve by prescribed deadlines. Utilities would meet these targets through ramping up their energy efficiency programs and offering their customers additional opportunities for energy savings. To illustrate the concept, the *West Virginia's Energy Future* study by the Center for Energy and Sustainable Development assumed each utility would implement energy efficiency programs sufficient to capture savings of 0.25 percent of total electric load in 2021, increasing by 0.15 percent increments annually until achieving savings equal to 2 percent of total electric load in 2030.[70] Another example is the bill (HB 2588) sponsored by Delegate Evan Hansen (Democrat, Monongalia County) during the 2021 legislative session, which would have required electric utilities to ramp up their energy efficiency programs to achieve energy savings beginning at 0.5 percent in 2022 (below 2019 consumption levels) and steadily increasing to a 9 percent reduction by 2031.

In the absence of legislative action – which is the preferred route inasmuch as the standard would be durable – an EERS can be established administratively through action at a reconstituted PSC. The case for an EERS is an easy one. First, as discussed in Chapter 8, the electric utilities operating in West Virginia (FirstEnergy and AEP) offer extensive energy efficiency programs in the surrounding states in which they operate, so it would be a fairly easy lift for them to offer the same programs to West Virginians. Second, it would position West Virginia to participate in the job growth in energy efficiency service providers, which produces the most jobs in the clean energy sector. Most of the clean energy jobs are in energy efficiency (as discussed in Chapter 8) and West Virginia is completely missing out on these opportunities because the PSC does not require West Virginia utilities to offer these services. It's that simple.

Third, it would give West Virginians the tools they need to help manage their energy costs. While electricity *rates* are still below the national average, electric *bills* in West Virginia are above the national average, because the building stock in West Virginia has not benefited from the investment in energy efficiency measures – insulation, thermal windows and doors, high efficiency furnaces, and water heaters – that improve the comfort level in homes as well as reducing energy bills. Fourth, energy efficiency programs will result in lower electric rates over time. At a cost of about 2.5 cents per kWh, it is much cheaper to invest in demand-side resources (energy efficiency programs) than supply-side resources (generating plants). A rigorous integrated resource planning process, discussed in the next section, would show that scaled-up energy efficiency programs could play a significant part in a utility's resource portfolio. The legislation establishing an EERS should also require the PSC to implement some sort of decoupling mechanism (as discussed in Chapter 8) to ensure that utilities are not financially penalized for helping their customers to lower their energy costs.

REQUIRE A RIGOROUS INTEGRATED RESOURCE PLANNING PROCESS

As described in Chapter 8, West Virginia adopted a statute in 2014 requiring utilities to periodically prepare and submit to the PSC an integrated resource plan (IRP).

---

[70] WVU College of Law Center for Energy and Sustainable Development, West Virginia's Energy Future 20, 22 (Dec. 2020), https://energy.law.wvu.edu/files/d/b1ff1183-e9ae-4ad0-93bf-aa3a fa1da785/wv-s-energy-future-wvu-col-cesd-final.pdf.

The requirements in the statute are incomplete, however. The statute does not require the two most fundamental elements of an IRP: (1) that the goal is the portfolio of resources that results in the lowest costs to customers over time, and (2) that supply- and demand-side resources should be *integrated*, so that utilities are required to consider cheaper demand-side options (energy efficiency and conservation programs) alongside supply-side options (additional generating resources). As a result of these deficiencies, both of the IRPs submitted by FirstEnergy (in 2015 and 2020) failed to integrate energy efficiency into the planning process, and thus the utility does not include energy efficiency programs as part of its resource portfolio, to the detriment of its customers. Irrespective of the requirements of the statute, the PSC could require the integration of supply- and demand-side resources, and a reconstituted PSC could be expected to do just that. In the absence of such action at the PSC, the statute should be amended to include the "integrated" aspect which is so essential to making the process work for customers.

Another deficiency in the statute is that it does not require any particular review process to be followed by the PSC once the IRPs are filed with the agency. In the case of both the 2015 and 2020 IRPs, the PSC accepted comments from the parties, but took no action on the comments and made no decision with respect to the adequacy of the IRPs other than to acknowledge their filing. The PSC should be required to evaluate the adequacy of the IRPs to determine compliance with the statute, and to ensure that the essential purposes of the IRP process are satisfied. As discussed in Chapter 8, FirstEnergy used its 2015 IRP to make the case for its foolish and ultimately unsuccessful effort to transfer the Pleasants Station plant from its merchant subsidiary to the regulated rate base in West Virginia. A rigorous IRP process would have resulted in that IRP being rejected by the PSC, as it failed to critically analyze the resource options available to FirstEnergy in favor of the contrived path – ultimately rejected by the Federal Energy Regulatory Commission – that served the interests of FirstEnergy shareholders to the detriment of FirstEnergy ratepayers. Irrespective of what is required by statute, of course, the PSC could adopt a process that allowed comments by interested parties, followed by whatever formal procedures are necessary to facilitate the close scrutiny that an IRP requires (if the process is to be truly effective in protecting ratepayers). A reconstituted PSC could be expected to adopt such a process, obviating a statutory revision to address this issue. In the absence of regulatory reform at the PSC, the statute should be amended to provide for a stakeholder review process at the PSC following by a PSC decision either accepting or rejecting a utility's IRP.

MAKING CLEAN ENERGY A MAJOR PART OF WEST VIRGINIA'S ENERGY FUTURE

Electric utilities in West Virginia need to move robustly to integrate clean energy resources – renewables (wind and solar) and energy efficiency – into their portfolios.

Large customers are demanding it (as discussed in Chapter 4). The numbers – the economics of wind and solar versus fossil fuels – compel it (as described in Chapter 3). And West Virginia needs it to be able to compete in the growing regional renewable energy economy.

The two major electric utilities operating in West Virginia – AEP and FirstEnergy – each completed their second IRPs in December 2020. As discussed in Chapter 8, both utilities continue to rely heavily on coal-fired generation, with very little movement over the ten-year planning horizon to integrate renewables or energy efficiency into their business model. West Virginia needs to do better. In December 2020, the Center for Energy and Sustainable Development at West Virginia University College of Law, working with power modelers and economic consultants at Synapse, GridLab, and Downstream Strategies, released its own version of what AEP and FirstEnergy could accomplish if they went down a path – referred to as "Ramped Up Renewables" – that moved more robustly toward a clean energy future. The report, entitled *West Virginia's Energy Future*, compared this "Ramped Up Renewables" path with a "Continued Coal Dependence" scenario that largely reflected the strategy that AEP and FirstEnergy adopted in their 2020 IRPs.

The numbers were quite striking, and very encouraging for the future of West Virginia if the state can simply turn the corner and start capturing the benefits of the clean energy revolution that is occurring all around it. The FirstEnergy companies – Mon Power and Potomac Edison – are currently 99 percent coal-fired, while AEP's Appalachian Power is about 72 percent coal-fired, with the rest of its power coming from natural gas (19 percent), renewable energy (5 percent), and hydro (4 percent). AEP's Wheeling Power subsidiary is currently 100 percent coal-fired, with its exclusive reliance on the Mitchell coal plant (see Figure 12.1).

Under the "Ramped Up Renewables" scenario modeled in *West Virginia's Energy Future*, the utilities would robustly scale up their investments in wind, solar, and energy efficiency, and reduce their dependence on coal and natural gas. By 2035, the generation portfolio for each utility, under both the "Ramped Up Renewables" and "Continued Coal Dependence" scenarios, are shown in Figures 12.2, 12.3, and 12.4.[71]

Because of the cost competitiveness of wind and solar – recall the 90 percent decline in the cost of solar energy and the 71 percent decline in the cost of wind energy during "the lost decade," as described in Chapter 3 – and dramatic improvements in battery storage technology, the transformation of both AEP's and FirstEnergy's generating portfolios depicted in the "Ramped Up Renewables" scenario can be achieved by 2035 at pretty much the same cost for ratepayers (the difference is less than 5 percent) as continuing down the coal-dependent path charted by the utilities in their 2020 IRPs.[72] And if there is a "price on carbon" as a

[71] *Id.* at 19–20.
[72] *Id.* at 23.

CURRENT ENERGY GENERATION BY WEST VIRGINIA'S ELECTRIC UTILITIES

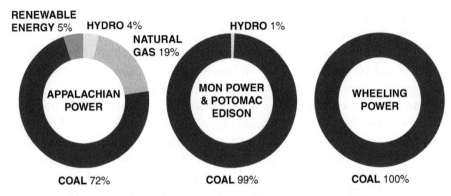

FIGURE 12.1 Current energy generation by West Virginia's electric utilities. *Source*: See *supra* note 70.

APPALACHIAN POWER: GENERATION IN 2035

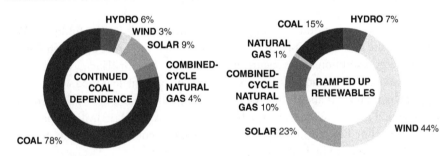

FIGURE 12.2 Appalachian Power: Generation in 2035. *Source*: See *supra* note 70.

WHEELING POWER: GENERATION IN 2035

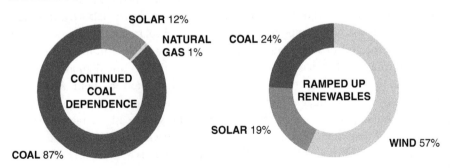

FIGURE 12.3 Wheeling Power: Generation in 2035. *Source*: See *supra* note 70.

MON POWER (INCLUDING POTOMAC EDISON): GENERATION IN 2035

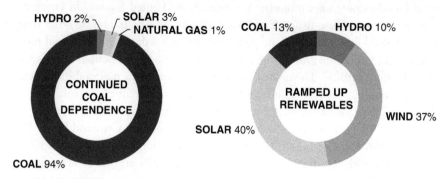

FIGURE 12.4 Mon Power (including Potomac Edison): Generation in 2035. *Source:* See *supra* note 70.

result of legislation at the regional or federal level, the "Ramped Up Renewables" scenario would actually produce savings for customers.[73] Apart from the impact on utility rates, the clean energy path would produce benefits for West Virginia in the form of job creation – the solar project and energy efficiency installations in the "Ramped Up Renewables" scenario alone would create the equivalent of almost 3,000 full-time jobs[74] – as well as billions of dollars in health benefits by avoiding illnesses and health-care costs that are attributable to continued emissions from coal plants.[75]

There are other impacts associated with the early retirement of coal plants under this clean energy path, such as the disproportionate burden on the communities in which the coal plants, and the coal mines supplying them, are located. And in some cases, there may be some remaining investment in the prematurely retired coal plants that need to be recovered. As discussed in the next section, as well as in the section Securitization to Address Coal Plant Retirements, there are existing and developing measures available to address these issues.

ADDRESSING THE TRANSITIONAL NEEDS OF WEST VIRGINIA'S COAL COMMUNITIES

Large coal-fired power plants provide many benefits to the communities in which they are located, including hundreds of high-paying jobs (and the indirect jobs they support) as well as considerable property tax revenues to support local schools and municipal operations. The closing of a coal plant therefore creates repercussions that fall disproportionately on these communities. President Biden has recognized

[73] *Id.*
[74] *Id.* at 24.
[75] *Id.* at 28.

the impact that the clean energy revolution is having on the economic health of fossil fuel-dependent communities throughout the United States. On January 27, 2021, the White House issued Executive Order 14008 which, among other things, acknowledged that "[m]ining and power plant workers drove the industrial revolution and the economic growth that followed, and have been essential to the growth of the United States."[76] The order went on to state that "as the nation shifts to a clean energy economy," it is essential that the federal government play a role in "foster [ing] economic revitalization of and investment in these communities."[77] The Executive Order creates an Interagency Working Group on Coal and Power Plant Communities and Economic Revitalization, comprising several cabinet-level officials charged with coordinating the identification and delivery of federal resources to "revitalize the economies of coal, oil and gas, and power plant communities" and "assess opportunities to ensure benefits and protections for coal and power plant workers."[78]

In its Initial Report issued in April 2021,[79] the Interagency Working Group identified twenty-five geographical areas "hard-hit by past coal mine and plant closures and vulnerable to more closures" that are priorities for investment and engagement as "Energy Communities."[80] Notably, this list of "Areas with high concentrations of direct coal sector jobs" (see Table 12.1), includes five areas in West Virginia (defined according to Bureau of Labor Statistics [BLS] Area), including the number one and number three ranked communities.[81]

According to the Initial Report, these communities "include workers directly employed in coal mining and power generation, and also the workers in related jobs in logistics and services, residents who are dependent on coal-related tax revenue to fund schools, fire houses, police stations, and infrastructure – as well as fenceline communities and other communities impacted by environmental and health effects of fossil energy generation."[82]

The Initial Report also identified existing federal programs that could provide funding of $37.9 billion for immediate investments in these Energy Communities, including:

---

[76] Executive Order No. 14008, *Tackling the Climate Crisis at Home and Abroad*, 86 FR 7619 (Jan. 27, 2021), https://www.federalregister.gov/documents/2021/02/01/2021-02177/tackling-the-climate-crisis-at-home-and-abroad.

[77] *Id.* § 217.

[78] *Id.* § 218.

[79] Interagency Working Group on Coal and Power Plant Communities and Economic Revitalization, Initial Report to the President on Empowering Workers Through Revitalizing Energy Communities (Apr. 2021), https://netl.doe.gov/sites/default/files/2021-04/Initial %20Report%20on%20Energy%20Communities_Apr2021.pdf.

[80] *Id.* at 3.

[81] *Id.* at 22–24.

[82] *Id.* at 1.

TABLE 12.1 *Areas with high concentrations of direct coal sector jobs*

Rank	BLS area	Counties
1	Southern West Virginia nonmetropolitan area	Greenbrier, Logan, McDowell, Mercer, Mingo, Monroe, Nicholas, Pocahontas, Summers, Webster, Wyoming
3	Wheeling, West Virginia – Ohio	Belmont, Marshall, Ohio
11	Northern West Virginia nonmetropolitan area	Barbour, Braxton, Calhoun, Doddridge, Gilmer, Grant, Hardy, Harrison, Jackson, Lewis, Marion, Mason, Morgan, Pendleton, Pleasants, Randolph, Ritchie, Roane, Taylor, Tucker, Tyler, Upshur, Wetzel
23	Beckley, West Virginia	Fayette, Raleigh
24	Charleston, West Virginia	Boone, Clay, Kanawha

(1) grant funding for infrastructure projects;
(2) resources to deploy innovative low-carbon technologies on power plants and industrial facilities;
(3) financing and grant funding programs to remediate AMLs, orphaned oil and gas wells, mine-impacted water, and brownfields;
(4) funding for small businesses, community development financial institutions, local nonprofit organizations, and economic innovation hubs;
(5) grant funding for workforce development by regional economic development organizations.[83]

Apart from resources provided by the federal government, there is precedent for powerplant owners to provide transition funding upon closure of a coal plant. In 2011, TransAlta Corporation, the owner of the Centralia plant, a 1,466 MW coal-fired generating plant in western Washington, had to decide whether to invest in retrofits to the plant in order to maintain regulatory compliance or instead adopt a plan to retire the plant, which was built in 1971.[84] TransAlta chose to retire the plant as of December 2025. In connection with that decision, it entered into an agreement with Washington's governor to fund an economic and energy transition plan. Under the plan, TransAlta is providing $55 million in funding through annual payments of $4.583 million between 2012 and 2023. The contributions are allocated among three different funds: a weatherization fund ($10 million) to support residential energy efficiency and weatherization measures for low-income and moderate-income residents; an economic and community

---

[83] *Id.* at 2.
[84] West Virginia PSC Case No. 20–1040-E-CN, *Appalachian Power Company and Wheeling Power Company Application for a Certificate of Public Convenience and Necessity for Internal Modifications at Coal-Fired Generating Plants Necessary to Comply with Federal Environmental Regulations*, Direct Testimony of Sean O'Leary, 7 (May 6, 2021), http://www.psc.state.wv.us/scripts/WebDocket/ViewDocument.cfm?CaseActivityID=564945&NotType=%27WebDocket%27.

development fund ($20 million) for "education, retraining and economic development specifically targeting the needs of workers displaced from the [Centralia plant]"; and an energy technology fund ($25 million) for "energy technologies with the potential to create considerable energy, air quality, haze or other environmental benefits located in or otherwise to the benefit of the State of Washington."[85]

As of April 2021, forty-two grants totaling $17.5 million have been issued from the funds, with an additional $8 million set aside to compensate workers who will be laid off from the Centralia plant when it closes as well as $1 million to fund training and education for workers and their families.[86] In addition to these coal transition grants, which are funded by TransAlta's shareholders rather than recovered from utility ratepayers, TransAlta is proposing to build a 180 MW utility-scale solar array near Centralia on the site of the closed coal mine.[87] TransAlta has also become a minority owner of a 136 MW wind farm in the county.[88]

The utility owners of the coal-fired power plants in West Virginia facing retirement should be expected to fund comparable energy and economic transition plans to provide assistance to the communities that will be adversely affected by plant retirements. And, just as in the case of TransAlta's coal transition plan for closure of the Centralia plant, these funds should come from shareholder dollars, rather than being recovered from utility ratepayers. In fact, such a proposal was presented to the West Virginia PSC in the proceeding involving AEP's filing to recover nearly $98 million in ratepayer money to bring the Mitchell Plant, jointly owned by AEP subsidiaries Wheeling Power and Kentucky Power, into compliance with the federal effluent limitation guidelines (ELGs) to allow the plant to continue operating through 2040. In testimony filed on behalf of West Virginia Citizen Action Group, Solar United Neighbors, and Energy Efficient West Virginia, Sean O'Leary, a senior researcher with ORVI, recommended that Wheeling Power should not spend the money to keep Mitchell open beyond 2028. His testimony proposed instead that AEP spend the $49 million (one half of the $98 million expenditure, corresponding to Wheeling Power's ownership share in Mitchell) on an economic and energy transition plan similar to the one adopted by TransAlta for the Centralia plant, with an Energy Efficiency/Weatherization Fund, an Economic and Community Development Fund, and an Energy Technology Fund.[89] Not surprisingly, that proposal was summarily rejected by the PSC in its rush to commit ratepayers to spend whatever was necessary to keep Mitchell open through 2040.

AEP's shareholders have fared very well from Wheeling Power's ownership of the Mitchell plant, given the circumstances of the transfer of the plant from AEP's merchant subsidiary to Wheeling Power in 2014. As discussed in Chapter 10, all three

---

[85]   *Id.* at 8.
[86]   *Id.* at 8-9.
[87]   *Id.* at 10.
[88]   *Id.*
[89]   *Id.* at 21.

of the coal plants transferred from the competitive subsidiaries of AEP and FirstEnergy were terrible deals for ratepayers, and should never have been approved by the West Virginia PSC. When the plants became uneconomic in the early 2010s as a result of cheap and plentiful natural gas from the Marcellus Shale and falling wholesale power prices, they should have been closed; this would have resulted in the remaining investment in the plants being entirely borne by shareholders. Instead, the West Virginia PSC allowed them to be included in the regulated rate base in West Virginia, with the costs borne by ratepayers. Given these circumstances, it is altogether proper for the shareholders of AEP and FirstEnergy to make some effort to atone for this regulatory giveaway by fully funding, at shareholder expense, comprehensive coal transition plans as each of their uneconomic coal plants finally cease operating.

SECURITIZATION: EASING THE PAIN OF EARLY RETIREMENT OF COAL PLANTS

As discussed above, the Center for Energy and Sustainable Development's report *West Virginia's Energy Future* confirms that it is cheaper for ratepayers if utilities install new wind and solar projects rather than continuing to operate existing coal plants. This is primarily due to the "zero" fuel costs associated with wind and solar facilities versus fuel costs – the supply of natural gas and coal – to operate traditional thermal plants. Ceasing to operate the coal plants to capture these savings, however, may result in coal plants being retired before their capital cost is fully recovered in rates (or, in other words, before the plants are fully depreciated to zero). When transitioning from coal-fired power plants to new renewable energy facilities, other states have benefited from a tool commonly referred to as "securitization"[90] – a refinancing tool discussed in Chapter 9 in the context of the debt that was issued by Appalachian Power in 2012 to cover the excess fuel costs that the utility incurred as coal prices rose sharply in 2010.

The key ingredient in this process is paying off the remaining cost of a retiring power plant with low-cost debt, which allows the utility to reduce the amount that customers are paying for the old power plant. Simultaneously, the utility then no longer has fuel, operations, and maintenance costs for the old power plant because it has been retired. Using the savings from low-cost debt and eliminated operations costs, the utility is then able to finance and build new renewable energy projects. The capital balance for the old power plant is replaced with a similar or larger capital balance for new renewable energy projects. Figure 12.5[91] demonstrates the basic concepts of this refinancing tool.

As described in Chapter 9, electric utilities in West Virginia are already authorized to undertake securitization transactions, and the PSC has experience with this refinancing process. Some minor revision to the statute will be necessary to expand the scope of the authorization to accommodate the circumstances created by the early retirement of

---

[90] WVU COLLEGE OF LAW CENTER FOR ENERGY AND SUSTAINABLE DEVELOPMENT, *supra* note 69, at 31.
[91] *Id.* at 32.

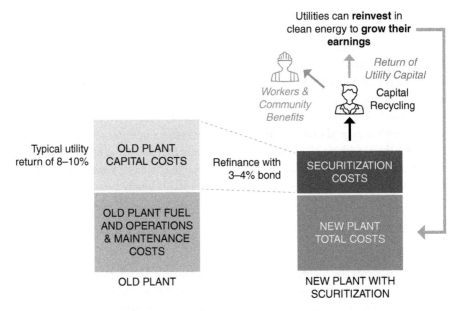

Utilities can **reinvest** in clean energy to **grow their earnings**

Return of Utility Capital

Workers & Community Benefits

Capital Recycling

Typical utility return of 8–10%

OLD PLANT CAPITAL COSTS

Refinance with 3–4% bond

SECURITIZATION COSTS

OLD PLANT FUEL AND OPERATIONS & MAINTENANCE COSTS

NEW PLANT TOTAL COSTS

OLD PLANT

NEW PLANT WITH SCURITIZATION

FIGURE 12.5 Use of securitization to reduce costs. *Source*: See *supra* note 70 and Rocky Mountain Institute, *How to Retire Early* 29 (June 2020), https://rmi.org/wp-content/uploads/2020/06/How-to-retire-early-June-2020.pdf.

generating units. Because the securitization process makes such financial sense for utilities and their customers, this legislative fix should be uncontroversial. It will be an important element in positioning West Virginia's electric utilities to provide the clean energy resources demanded by the markets of the twenty-first century.

ARMED WITH THE NECESSARY RESILIENCE TO OVERCOME

The failure of leadership throughout "the lost decade" has not served West Virginians well. At the same time, the state's greatest resource – its people – are capable of tackling these challenges. West Virginians are incredibly resilient, probably because they have had to strengthen their resiliency in the face of unnecessary hardships that have been imposed on them as a result of failed political leadership. Maybe it is time to stop testing their resilience. West Virginians need to be inspired and led by enlightened, engaged leadership, and with a roadmap – a game plan – that boldly addresses the issues and puts the state on a path where it is positioned to compete in the twenty-first century. The recommendations in this concluding chapter are intended to provide that roadmap. But the first step is sending the signal that West Virginia's best days are ahead of it, by looking forward rather than backward, and demanding that West Virginia's political leaders show some leadership for a change.

Acknowledgments

When I arrived in West Virginia in July 2011, I had a few years' experience as a clean energy advocate from my work in New York at the Pace Energy and Climate Center in White Plains. And I had decades of experience working on energy issues which had allowed me to develop a deep understanding of energy markets and how electric utilities are regulated. But being an energy lawyer in Seattle and Portland is a far cry from dealing with the dynamics of the coal industry and electric utilities in Appalachia. Similarly, during my brief stint in New York before moving to West Virginia, mine was one of many voices on clean energy issues, so I was accustomed to having plenty of company in my work on regulatory and policy issues. I really didn't know what to expect to find "on the ground" in West Virginia in terms of fellow warriors in the battle to address climate change in a state that represents "ground zero" with respect to both the adverse economic impacts of the clean energy transformation and the mindset that we need to understand if we are going to be successful in addressing climate change.

I quickly learned that there are many good people who have been advocating on these issues for decades in West Virginia, in the face of very intimidating and fierce opposition by the coal industry, the politicians who have come to represent and defend the coal industry, and the utilities that generate electricity using coal. The biggest source of inspiration for me over the past ten years has been my colleague at the West Virginia University (WVU) College of Law, Pat McGinley. He litigated the first mountaintop removal case – and won. His endowed professorship at WVU is named after the courageous judge in that case, Judge Charles Haden. McGinley is a nationally recognized expert on the Surface Mining Control and Reclamation Act (SMCRA), a complex environmental statute that I have tried to cover – probably not to Pat's satisfaction – in Chapter 11. He is the leading expert on the Freedom of Information Act (FOIA) in West Virginia. Eric Eyre, the Pulitzer Award-winning journalist formerly with the *Charleston Gazette-Mail* and now with *Mountain State Spotlight*, credits Pat and his wife Suzanne Weise with their mastery of FOIA, which produced the information that enabled Eric to expose the origins of the opioid epidemic in West Virginia. As Eric states in his novel *Death in Mud Lick*:

> It's a safe bet that the distributors' shocking painkiller numbers would never have been made public without the tireless efforts of lawyers Pat McGinley and Suzanne Weise. They spent thousands of hours of their time researching case law, preparing and filing legal briefs, and arguing cases in court ... prov[ing] that the sharpest legal minds don't always hang their hats at white-shoe law firms in New York and Washington.[1]

Pat also served on the governor's independent investigative team for both the Sago Mine disaster and the Upper Big Branch (UBB) coal mine disaster, in which a total of forty-one miners lost their lives due to cavalier practices of the mine operators and failures of government to enforce mine safety laws. During the UBB investigation, he asked tough questions. At one point, during a break in the interviews, a government investigative team member initially commented, "Who does he think he is, Clarence Darrow?" Before long, however, the federal investigators were so impressed with the wealth of information that Pat was obtaining from witnesses that they adopted his questioning style, and dug out the truth. For more than four decades, Pat's work as a legal scholar, teacher, and public interest environmental litigator has been committed to the rule of law, speaking truth to power, mentoring law students and lawyers, and empowering families and communities marginalized by discrimination based on race, wealth, or ethnicity.

The role of courageous journalists in West Virginia deserves special mention. In my research to compile the facts presented in this book, no source is cited more frequently than the *Charleston Gazette-Mail*, referred to by the *Washington Post* as the "feisty" newspaper that has played an important role in keeping the coal industry in check in West Virginia.[2] For decades, the maxim under which the *Gazette-Mail* has operated is "sustained outrage," a term coined by W. E. "Ned" Chilton III, the maverick publisher who led the *Gazette* from 1961 until his death in 1987. The "sustained" part reflects Chilton's view that it wasn't enough to do a story or two about an injustice – it took in-depth coverage to fix a wrong. During "the lost decade,"[3] the outrage about the issues covered in this book was sustained primarily by Ken Ward, Jr., a staff writer for the *Gazette-Mail* for over twenty-eight years who also authored a blog, *Coal Tattoo*, that closely covered the coal industry. He was named a MacArthur Fellow, often referred to as the "genius" grant, in 2018. When the *Gazette-Mail* declared bankruptcy in 2018,

[1] Eric Eyre, Death at Mud Lick: A Coal Country Fight Against the Drug Companies That Delivered the Opioid Epidemic 258 (2020).

[2] Steven Mufson, *A West Virginia Newspaper Is in Bankruptcy. The Powerful Coal Industry Celebrates*, Wash. Post (Feb. 16, 2018), www.washingtonpost.com/business/economy/a-west-virginia-newspaper-is-in-bankruptcy-the-powerful-coal-industry-celebrates/2018/02/16/f0e3d4e4-085c-11e8-8777-2a059f168dd2_story.html.

[3] Throughout the book I refer to the ten years from 2009 to 2019 as "the lost decade." It was a period of fundamental and inevitable transition in the energy industry during which political leaders in West Virginia utterly failed to provide any leadership and instead created and relied upon the fiction of a "war on coal."

the prospect of "hard hitting coal correspondent" Ken Ward receiving a pink slip was enthusiastically celebrated by hundreds of coal industry representatives at a coal mining association meeting.[4] After leaving the *Gazette-Mail* in 2020, he joined ProPublica as a reporter and cofounded *Mountain State Spotlight*, along with his former *Gazette-Mail* colleagues Eric Eyre and Greg Moore, to continue Ned Chilton's mission of "sustained outrage" in West Virginia.

The fearless in-depth reporting of Ken Ward, Eric Eyre, Paul Nyden (another star reporter for the *Gazette-Mail* who took on the coal industry over safety problems in the mines and environmental degradation from lax regulation until his death in January 2018),[5] and Phil Kabler (longtime author of the "Statehouse Beat" column in the *Gazette-Mail*) made this book possible. Coincidentally, the Nobel Peace Prize in 2021 was awarded to two journalists, Maria Ressa and Dmitri A. Muratov, for "their courageous fight for freedom of expression in the Philippines and Russia."[6] While taking on Big Coal in West Virginia does not equal taking on Rodrigo Duterte in the Philippines or Vladimir Putin in Russia, the Nobel Prize winners were selected as "representatives of all journalists who stand up for this ideal in a world in which democracy and freedom of the press face increasingly adverse conditions," and that certainly applies to the journalists in West Virginia who have carried on Ned Chilton's legacy of "sustained outrage."

In writing this book, I have had the benefit of some excellent students who served as my research assistants, including Jordan Maddy and Amanda Demmerle – both of whom accepted clerkships at the Fourth Circuit Court of Appeals upon their graduation from WVU – and Maddie Hinkle, who has been a tremendous help over the past couple of years with her research and organization skills. I also appreciate the institutional support of the WVU College of Law and the financial support of the Hodges/Bloom Research Fund.

Finally, and certainly not least of all, a deep thanks to my wife Elizabeth Van Nostrand, who has not only provided patient support for my writing endeavors over the past two years but, more importantly, tolerated my ranting about the issues and experiences in West Virginia that compelled me to write this book. She has been a consistent sounding board as I developed many of the themes in telling the narrative in this book, and has read more than a few pages of the manuscript as I drafted it. Elizabeth is an expert in public health law, and I am indeed fortunate to have a partner who is equally compassionate about addressing complex, controversial issues and trying to make a difference in people's lives.

---

4 Mufson, *supra* note 2.
5 Ken Ward, Jr., *Nyden Remembered as Crusading Reporter, Loyal Friend and Mentor, Great Storyteller*, CHARLESTON GAZETTE-MAIL (Jan. 6, 2018), www.wvgazettemail.com/news/nyden-remembered-as-crusading-reporter-loyal-friend-and-mentor-great-storyteller/article_141953f8-53cc-5b91-bb78-c925e829f8a5.html.
6 THE NOBEL PEACE PRIZE 2021, www.nobelprize.org/prizes/peace/2021/summary/.

Index

installed capacity, 63–74
lower-cost resource, 227
offshore wind, 81
onshore, 184

small installations, 85
technology, 69, 183
WVU Mountaineers, 102–3
Wyoming, the state of, 5, 8

Lightning Source UK Ltd.
Milton Keynes UK
UKHW020948130722
405777UK00015B/573